D0966292

CONSTITUTIONAL SENTIMENTS

Constitutional Sentiments

András Sajó

Yale UNIVERSITY PRESS
New Haven & London

Yale University Press books may be purchased in quantity for educational, business, or promotional use. For information, please e-mail sales.press@yale.edu (U.S. office) or sales@yaleup.co.uk (U.K. office).

Set in Galliard old Style and Copperplate 33 types by
IDS Infotech Ltd., Chandigarh, India.
Printed in the United States of America.

Library of Congress Cataloging-in-Publication Data
Sajó, András.
Constitutional sentiments / András Sajó.
p. cm.
Includes bibliographical references and index.
ISBN 978-0-300-13926-6 (cloth : alk. paper) 1. Constitutional law.
2. Civil rights. I. Title.
K3165.S235 2011
342—dc22

2010027465

A catalogue record for this book is available from the British Library.

This paper meets the requirements of ANSI/NISO Z39.48-1992 (Permanence of Paper).

10 9 8 7 6 5 4 3 2 1

CONTENTS

FOREWORD

Theoretical and historical reflection about the reality and the concept of law suffers from no shortage of unsolved problems. One of the most intriguing questions concerns the foundations of the modern edifice of constitutionalism and human rights, a core part of what strives to be a new civilized architecture of right. A classical answer to this question asserts that the base of constitutionalized legal orders can only be carved out of the enduring material of rational thought: The book of constitutionalism and human rights is written by the swift hand of reason as modernity overcomes the obscure and irrational emotionalism of the past. The historical genesis of constitutionalism based on human rights is in consequence an element of the epochal process of the rationalization of modernity.

Constitutional Sentiments challenges this view and tells in captivating scientific prose a quite different, gripping, and disquieting story. Its leading hypothesis is that constitutions and human rights are not the offspring of reason and rationality, but the products of individual and, most important, social emotions. Feelings, not reason—it argues—play a pivotal role in the making, maintenance, and development of constitutional systems. Of particular importance is fear. The dread of cruelty and oppression generates the idea of the necessary neutrality of the legal order underlying modern constitutionalism, the central tool for creating a society without destructive emotions respecting the rights of others.

The argument is based on an analytical approach but has certainly a normative point of not only marginal concern. It buttresses liberalism through a reinterpretation of the very foundations of the constitutional project that started with the revolutions of the eighteenth century. The aim of the argument is not to debase reason-based modernity but, to the contrary, to continue the projects of the Enlightenment, which were not to oppress emotion but to prevent the enslavement of human beings by unrestricted passions: "The enemy of reason is not passion, it is fanaticism" (3). The preconditions for this new fortification of liberal constitutionalism are a deepened understanding of the unacknowledged springs of law and a thorough lack of naïveté: "We are not passion's slaves, but we have to apply cunning for reason's success" (13).

The argument combines systematic and historical perspectives. It develops a social-constructivist model of constitutional sentiments embedded in contemporary findings of neuroscience and psychology about the emotional underpinnings of moral reasoning that have stirred much debate. It outlines the role of human rights and how "specific emotional inclinations support privileged claims of action that are then recognized as human rights" (31). It develops a skeptical descriptive account of the underpinnings of a universalistic account of human rights (though taking it as logically superior to relativism) and tries to illuminate the irritating power of anticonstitutional sentiments.

The two classical cornerstones of modern constitutionalism are discussed in rich historical detail and with a refreshing new look at the primary sources documenting the birth of constitutional orders. First, the making of the French Declaration of the Rights of Man and Citizen and its emotional underpinnings are reconstructed. Second, the crucial role of fear of oppression and its normative consequences are traced to account for the genesis of decisive characteristics of the Constitution of the United States.

In addition, particular important problems of modern constitutionalism are addressed, including slavery, freedom of expression and assembly, the regulation of religions, and popular sovereignty. The role of shame in constitutional sentiments is the object of final reflections, drawing from examples including South Africa and Germany and endorsing a possible positive function of shame through reconciliation: "After all, shame may generate recognition of responsibility" (299).

The study addresses abstract and foundational questions without neglecting quite concrete problems. It draws on an impressive range of materials, mastering contemporary human rights law and constitutional law through a richly textured comparative perspective; legal and social history; and social and individual psychology. The book is not eclectic and stays focused on the central questions pursued. But as these questions are of such a nature that they drive reflection necessarily beyond the boundaries of positive law, there is no alternative but to tackle the problems head on with different theoretical tools, which is done with admirable erudition.

In recent years there has been increasing interest in the role of emotions in various quarters of intellectual enquiry. The well-defined stance of *Constitutional Sentiments* breaks new ground for serious thought in this area in more than one way. One may not or may only partly agree with its main thesis and its concrete theoretical findings and search for other or at least additional foundations of liberal constitutionalism. One may think that the findings of some parts of contemporary cognitive science (a very heterogeneous field) referred to are more doubtful than they appear, or that the social constructivist model of emotion-building is not the last theoretical word about the role of emotions in social life and the underlying relationship of individual and community. Or one may ask questions about the concrete content of the sentimentalism of human rights, and specifically wonder whether there are not normative principles in the background of the description and argument that fit uneasily in the outlined theoretical framework. Everybody reflecting on these issues, however, would be ill advised not to spend much and careful thought on the arguments advanced, which so eloquently test traditionally held beliefs.

The study has the great merit of putting an important and classical problem which has certainly been too much neglected back on the table of legal, social, and—not least—historical scholarship. There is plenty to be learned from this magisterial work about the complexities of legal institutions and the hidden genealogies of their making. And it formulates a clear and convincing lesson—concise, passionate, and with the courage to challenge dominant ideas: Without consciousness of the emotional preconditions of constitutionalism and human rights, these fragile human creations with their powerful, civilizing but destructible impact on individuals in history and today's life will certainly not be understood and—most important—maintained, given the old and new, culture-sowing, havoc-breeding tides and torrents of human sentiment.

Matthias Mahlmann

ACKNOWLEDGMENTS

In modern days, very little has been written on constitutional sentiments, a classic topic in the days of Montesquieu and Blackstone ("Law is the embodiment of the moral sentiment of the people"). I started this project many years ago in response to the challenge behavioral economics posed to constitutional economics, and in view of the recurrence of passion and irrationality in democratic politics. When I first claimed that lawyers apply emotionally shaped social constructs, I ran into bewilderment; this is the well-deserved pittance of the harmless eccentric. In a moment of intellectual isolation and resulting self-doubt, one is particularly grateful for (unexpected) support given to his work that exists mostly in nebulous outlines; understandably I am in particular debt to the Center for Advanced Study in the Behavioral Sciences, Palo Alto, for ten fruitful months on their premises, and to Central European University, Budapest, for all the support I received there throughout many years. Last but not least, the Institute of Law of the Hungarian Academy of Sciences is also to be mentioned for, among its other virtues, the freedom granted and intellectual support and stimulus received there all my academic life, and especially the encouragement and example coming from my late masters, Gyula Eörsi and Vilmos Peschka. I am grateful to Michel Troper for his comments on the chapter dealing with the French Revolution, and to Martin Krygier, Stephen Holmes, Matthias Mahlmann, András Gerő, and Mrs. A. M. for reading and commenting on various drafts. For editorial support I have to thank Zsuzsa Kovács, Vera Major, Júlia Mink, Jim Tucker, Lorri Bentch, Mónika Ganczer, and Katherine Scheuer.

ABBREVIATIONS

AP = Jérôme Mavidal and Emile Laurent, eds., *Archives parlementaires de 1787 à 1860: Recueil complet des débats législatifs et politiques des Chambres françaises, imprimé par ordre du Corps législatif. 1e série, 1787–1799* (Paris: P. Dupont, 1875–1889).

ECtHR = European Court of Human Rights

ECHR = ECtHR judgment

U.S. = United States Supreme Court decision

INTRODUCTION

> The control of individual feelings by reason, a vital necessity for every courtier. . . .
>
> —Norbert Elias

> Not to wear his heart on his sleeve. . . .
>
> —Chief Justice Burger advising Justice Blackmun

"Reason, cold, calculating, unimpassioned reason, must furnish all the materials for our future support and defence." Reason is detached, perhaps cold and unemotional. It is believed that thanks to these features reason is uniquely capable of finding truth and right. The calculating coldness enables reason to know our world and to navigate in it successfully. Emotions might be nice and warm, but they are detrimental to reason exactly for these reasons. Modernity believes that it has to stand up for "the wisdom of reason against the treachery and temptations of the passions."[1] Therefore, emotions were relegated to second-class citizenship in the realm of human psyche.

Modernity's wisdom outwitted itself. Societies may pretend that they follow reason's dictates, but as far as individuals are concerned, "emotions can flood consciousness . . . because the wiring of the brain at this point in our evolutionary history is such that connections from the emotional systems to the cognitive systems are stronger than connections from the cognitive systems to the emotional systems."[2] Social institutions may have mechanisms to counter the emotionality of the people who operate the institutions, but they operate with bounded rationality at best. We are not passion's slaves, but we have to apply cunning for reason's success.

Constitutionalism and the administration of justice are often presented as institutions that improve efficiency in human affairs by promising the eradication of emotion from the constitutional public sphere. Constitutional law tends to disregard emotions. Why is that so? A historical path dependence operates here. The American Bill of Rights and the 1789 French Declaration of the Rights of Man and Citizen provided to the modern world the paradigm of fundamental rights.[3] The French Declaration offered a rationalistic frame, and this is what became prevalent in constitutional thought. However, it would be wrong to consider the Declaration to be a pure negation of sentiments and an example of the modernist plot of enlightened reason. The French Revolution was a sentimental revolution. At least, this is how the Marquis de Lafayette argued at the National Assembly in favor of the Declaration: "Let me call to mind the *sentiments* which Nature has engraved in the heart of every citizen, and which take a new force when they are solemnly recognized by all: For a nation to love liberty, it is sufficient that she knows it; and to be free, it is sufficient that she wills it."[4]

In this approach, liberty exists in natural sentiments and reason is there only to remind us of our sentiments. However, positivist science and legal positivism succeeded in pushing moral sentiments into oblivion. I do not intend to challenge the appropriateness of the normative assumptions of human rationality that characterize the concept of law, although I will show how exceptional pure rationality is in view of what we know about human cognition. Most of the time human reason and the social institutions that embody (bounded) rationality are capable of steering emotions in a sociable way, at least to a certain extent. But in order to understand the actual processes shaping constitutional law and the legal order, one has to take into consideration the contribution of emotions. Constitutional institutions operate in interactions between more rational and more emotional elements of human thought and social cooperation. A descriptive model that renders the emotions their due might help to develop more efficient regulatory models.

The reason-emotion opposition that lies at the heart of the prevailing legal regulatory model is scientifically unsustainable; even to assume that this is the paradigm that guides law disregards a whole body of law that in fact handles emotions without repressing or neglecting them. In certain instances, law provides selective protection to emotions, as the case of freedom of religion clearly demonstrates. Reason systematically errs because of the intervention of emotions in decision-making;[5] in many instances human decisions are emotion-driven. Law intends to create a sterile mental environment for its own application because it considers the dictates of emotions misleading and impermissible. Legal decisions are designed to be purely cognitive—above all, deductive and subject to cognitive control. Where this seems impossible, intuitive decisions are separated from the rational as is the case with the jury system. Even the jury is pushed toward rationality: prosecutors may emphasize that jurors should not sympathize and should be cold-blooded.[6]

Of course, modern law is an attempt at anti-passionate rationalization, and not an unsuccessful one, especially compared to legal systems based on trial by ordeal. I disagree with people who take pride in debasing reason-based modernity. At a time when reason is under suspicion, constitutions join the usual suspects in the academic roundup. However, the reason-passion opposition remains a gross simplification: the goal of the Enlightenment was not the oppression of sentiments; it was all about self-control that enables propriety in the display of sentiments. The Enlightenment intended to liberate man from superstition. The enemy of reason is not passion, it is fanaticism. This message of Voltaire needs to be remembered in our age of new fanaticism.

Legal scholarship and policy-makers have to prepare themselves for new and perhaps shocking knowledge about human decision-making: "neuroscience will probably have a transformative effect on the law, despite the fact that existing legal doctrine can, in principle, accommodate whatever neuroscience will tell us. New neuroscience will change the law, not by undermining its current assumptions, but by transforming people's moral intuitions about free will and responsibility."[7] There is a growing body of scholarship in economics, social science, and certain areas of law that intends to "rehabilitate" emotion and review human behavior relying on models of cognition where emotions are at least equal partners in human judgment.

The research agenda is heavy with policy implications. The consequence of the new paradigm is that "it is not only impossible but *undesirable* to factor emotion out of the reasoning process."[8]

We should not allow the bad reputation of passions to guide us in passing judgment on emotions. Passions may blind us, but we need blindness to act at all in too many situations.

In this book I intend to consider the role of emotions in constitutional law, accepting that one cannot understand human behavior and law as a purely rational venture. Without an interdisciplinary approach to the formation of constitutional law and constitutional institutions, we will only embellish an impoverished conception of the constitution as a set of pompous words.

My research hypothesis is that emotions, through complicated mechanisms, do have an actual impact on constitutional design and law. At the same time, constitutional design is a half-conscious venture of emotion management, and constitutional law and politics have unintended consequences in the emotional culture. By improving our knowledge regarding emotions, we can improve constitutional design. I hope that in the long run a closer relationship between sentiments, which serve as social-normative shorthand in constitutional and political reasoning, and emotions, understood here in a scientific sense (for example, neuroscience), can be developed.

Such research has to consider many interrelated matters: first, it is about the impact of sentiments and assumptions regarding emotions on constitutional law; secondly, it is about the effort of constitutional law to handle and shape public sentiments; thirdly, the public reactions, including emotional reactions to constitutional arrangements, are to be considered; and finally, it is about the actual impact of constitutional and other legal designs on the social construction and use of sentiments. Having regard to these matters will enable the discussion of policy issues on how to deal with emotions.

I am not offering any definition of emotions in the constitutional context. Instead, I use the eighteenth-century term "sentiment" to indicate that in constitutional design what matters is the assumption about social emotions. Sentiments refer to prevailing language usage regarding the social interpretation of behavior and related expectations. While in the

Middle Ages behavior was taken to be shaped by certain passions, this was gradually replaced by conceptions of interest as the proper source of guidance for, and basis and explanation of, social behavior. It should be added that the eighteenth-century cult of sentiments originated in, among other sources, a successful attempt to submit them to social control under Louis XIV. The technique, based partly in court manners, faded away in favor of scientific positivism, but it seems to me that it is back in the culture of narcissism. Indeed, in a culture of narcissism, rational arguments are replaced by narratives of suffering that are amplified in the hope of manufacturing indignation and compassion. Emotions are once again legitimately displayed publicly and serve as the basis of claims, even for rights, as is the case with victims' rights and the public's rights to be free from fear, ending with collective anger that demands stoning or capital punishment as a right. Intensity of feelings is a sign of honesty and commitment, and in a hedonistic world that is short of enthusiastic commitments, such public sentiments carry weight. In democratic politics, the majority is what counts, but this mechanical opinion offers limited genuine support and commitment; it is the intensity of feelings of committed groups (be they animal rights activists, minority defenders, or religious zealots) that counts.

The term "constitution" is used here in a broad sense. It goes beyond constitutional texts and includes various judicial and other legally and socially relevant meanings, constitutional conventions, practices, and customs that emerge in the use of public power. On the other hand, at least for the time being, I limit myself to constitutional settings that emerge under the paradigm of constitutionalism. Here, constitutionalism entails a combination of freedom-enhancing rights (exemplified in nineteenth-century liberalism) and democracy. Such constitutionalism constitutes a crucial part of the reason-based modernity project, something that became quite problematic recently because, among other things, of the neglect and mistreatment of emotions in favor of a distorted reason. This does not mean that passions should rule, but a constitutional strategy that is unable to answer them will become suboptimal, blamed for being blind and unresponsive and, as the case of illiberal democracies indicates, it will end up in the junkyard of the irrelevant.

This book intends to be descriptive: it offers an up-to-date account of the way emotions did and could shape constitutional institutions. I do not claim that moral sentiments and related moral principles should govern law, but I take into consideration for law how the human brain operates in matters of morality, or how people disregard what the assumed moral emotions would dictate. Even if what influential sociobiologists like Wilson claim, that there are hardwired "moral facts" (for example, the prohibition on incest), were true, this does not determine the specific moral choices and resulting legal choices to a full extent. To some extent, the choices depend on how the problem is framed in the culture and influenced by situational circumstances in emotionally determined cognition.

I will describe mental and historical processes where constitutional sentiments are formed by and shape constitutional institutions. Paying what is due to sentiments in the analysis of social institutions and values makes us aware of the fallibility of cognitive approaches that claim to be reasonable. I do not intend to celebrate emotions and produce an analysis that would argue in favor of following the dictates of the heart in constitutional matters. There is too much evidence about the inconveniences intuitions have generated in public policy. Moral indignation mobilizes against injustice, but the same gut feelings block critical analysis and reevaluation. The moral police that "encroaches on the most unquestionably legitimate liberty of the individual" recruits its staff from emotions and moral intuitions. Anyway, we are not interested here in the "aberrations of existing moral feeling."[9] What matters is the cunning of institutions that mobilize intuitions and bias against aberrations.

Given the interdisciplinary complexity of law and emotions studies, it is imperative to be specific about what is related to what and why, even if I end up in a "methodological promiscuity."[10] In the shadow of methodological promiscuity it is imperative, even more than in non-interdisciplinary studies, to outline the applicable theoretical frame. However, the level of the analysis shifts, and very different theoretical frameworks will therefore be applicable. I start by describing phenomena at the brain level, moving to social interactions shaping constitutions and constitutional institutions at the macro-social level in different and formative historical contexts. Finally, I look into the interaction of specific constitutional law arrangements with social emotion regulation, which is partly legal theory (how emotions are handled) and partly social theory about the regulation of emotions in law. While I examine the specific emotions behind specific constitutional solutions, I try to refrain from developing predictions and related explanatory theories to determine how specific emotions generate or contribute to specific legal problem-solving.[11]

Is the rationality-based social theory of constitutional law sustainable? It is certainly useful when law operates under that assumption and tries to create safeguards for such operations. Even so, this is a risky and interest-ridden venture that is not, and cannot be, fully carried out; nor is it desirable to purge emotions from constitutional law and, in particular, from a theory that intends to understand the operations of constitutional law. In order to show the pivotal relevance of emotions in judgment, particularly in constitutionally relevant moral judgment, I rely on the currently available, rapidly changing conjectures neuroscience offers us. This is the closest thing to a factual rebuttal of the rationalism that pervades law and a great part of disciplines dealing with human decision. The available neuroscience information is sufficient to prove that human action and decision cannot be understood without giving emotion its due: and a lot is due. Of course, at this point in time, neuroscience data are inconclusive and cannot be aggregated meaningfully at the level of institutional design—but this is not necessary. We simply have to shift the frame of analysis, keeping in mind what we have learned about the role of emotion in cognition and decision-making. In the legal institution-building business, the emotionally shaped decisions become dependent on the meanings attributed to the situation and the social interaction which influences these interactions between emotion and higher cognitive function with its rewards, sanctions, and frames of reference.

The theoretical framework or tradition applied, especially in regard to moral judgments that I rely upon, is a very weak version of emotivism, in the sense that I allow moral intuitions and sentiments some explanatory power in the determination of morality. This is, however, only a small though indispensable part of the story. A few fundamental social stimuli are at work here, such as harming and fairness, which seem to have some evolutionarily confirmed power to elicit the emotional reactions that are neurologically preset. However, these natural facts have very little explanatory power and are to a great extent dependent on social perception and construction. The shared nature of the stimuli and emotional reactions points toward universalism, but it does not allow for a naturalistic theory of universal morality. Consequently, the assertion that human rights have natural (biological) universality, convenient as it may be, is unsustainable. Personality traits, cultural meaning, and interaction are to be factored in.

The neuroscience information is therefore placed in the broader scheme offered in psychology and social psychology. This broader perspective brings social cognitive and cultural elements into play. The cultural understanding and use of emotions change in history: in certain periods, including the one that shaped modern constitutionalism, sentiments were highly esteemed and, at the same time, were also considered (often by the same people) suspicious passions to be tamed. To what extent emotions were welcome in public sentiments and law's willingness to protect their display are a changing matter, depending on the social evaluation of emotions. Constitutional, and for that matter legal regulation of emotions are unfinished processes. The selection of constitutionally proper feelings is social conflict-ridden: emotional display forms are found protected or even mandatory because they fit into the dominant culture or into the culture of those who dominate and rule. They run into social resistance, and not only the resistance of those whose emotions and cultural traditions of display are hurt because these were selected out or at least were disregarded. The emotions of those who set the rules may run against their own feelings generated by the rules. Constitutional law sets into motion emotions which always remain an unfinished project.

At this point, scientific knowledge regarding the impact of emotions becomes decisive. Some scholars claim that the whole legal system has to be reviewed in light of the still tentative findings of brain science. I agree to a point: a scientifically informed theory of constitutional sentiments should provide enough knowledge to enable a critical approach to the assumptions about sentiments that prevail in constitutional choices.[12]

Using scientific data for a critical study of law, instead of using it in legal policy, is an important distinction, especially in light of the exaggerations and grave abuses committed in law and legal scholarship in the name of ill-digested science. However, a normative debate that disregards the emerging scientific understanding of emotional human behavior is equally impermissible because it would be irrelevant. Rationality helps social and legal accountability, but it does not justify legal and scholarly efforts to deny the presence of emotions in all human endeavors, including law. Sanitizing does not contain passions for good. The more oppressed by their denial emotions are, the stronger their revenge.

Are political and legal scholarship and practices going to use the lessons emerging from behavioral sciences? Law is an interest-driven practical activity. It is more than likely that interests will prevail in law in disregard of improved knowledge about emotions. Legal scholars and lawyers traditionally have put their bets on presenting themselves as the impassionate servants of a rational system. They may find it troubling when they are confronted with findings that indicate that emotions have an important place in law as in other areas of human behavior. This contradicts the prevailing misconstruction of the Enlightenment project (served by constitutionalism), namely that human progress moves from the medieval darkness of ignorance to the crystal light of reason. Emotionalism is not welcome, as it certainly undermines the foundational legitimating myth of law. As law and emotions scholar Susan Bandes has argued, "the idea that emotion pervades the law poses a threat to law's most cherished self-conception."[13] But I believe that better knowledge about emotions will enable us to protect some of the values of constitutionalism that are threatened by emotional fanaticism and fanatics' emotion: in order to do so, one can rely on other emotions or other combinations of emotion. There remains a concern: perhaps a better understanding of emotions will only add to the repertoire of legal manipulation. Feminist scholars offered important evidence regarding the role of emotions in legally relevant behavior, but the legal profession resisted the accommodation of that knowledge, because of, among other things, mental rigidity and special interests of domination.

The frame I use in this book is dictated by the logic of my approach: I am interested in emotions as far as they are relevant for constitutional institutions, and as far as public institutions can control emotions and emotion display in particular as part of a larger social regulatory function of law. It follows that the frame will be a "light" social constructivist concept of emotions, as summarized in Chapter 1, with an overview of scholarly literature in the Appendix, to be found online at yalebooks.com/sajo. The social constructivist approach is chosen because this can be linked in a meaningful way to institution-building. Once the foundational role of emotions in human thought and action is shown, I move toward the social aggregation of emotions in public sentiments to show how a unique formation of such sentiments contributed to the shaping of the institutional design of constitutionalism, including human rights. Here I discuss at some length the problem of moral judgment given the crucial importance of moral choices for constitutional law. This analysis is based on a summary of available neuroscience data, again with details in the Appendix. Given the power of moral sentiments in the shaping of human rights, it seems likely that human rights express some kind of natural human inclination. The outcome of the culture-nature debate is of considerable practical consequence for the universality of human rights: it indicates that reliance on moral sentiments as a foundation of liberal constitutional order is irresponsibly optimistic. The same emotions that were instrumental in the making of constitutionalism may undo it. Besides, not all emotions are equally constitution-friendly, and the emotional (as well as the rational) nature of man requires constant patrolling of human emotions, which wait, like Barbarians, for doors left absent-mindedly open in the Citadel of constitutionalism.

The broader, more theoretical discussion of the first chapter is followed by historical case studies, showing how specific constitutional institutions emerge in interactions originating in public sentiments, and also how constitutional solutions influence emotion regulation. Chapter 2 is a detailed sentimental history of the 1789 French Declaration of the Rights of Man, showing that specific emotions not only actually shaped fundamental rights but that they continue to reflect emotions which are frozen into the text. Chapter 3 specifically discusses fear as a fundamental constitution-making social experience that explains various constitutional solutions depending on what the constitution-makers are afraid of.[14] Here, the making of the American Constitution serves as the basis of the observations. Beginning with Chapter 4, I move away from a legal institution-centered analysis toward more emotion-centered methodologies. First, I look into empathy as an emotion and its socially construed forms (pity, compassion, sympathy), relying on the history of the abolition of slavery and discussing the social, legal, and cultural reasons why compassion failed to generate a comparable right in regard to the suffering of the poor or free workers. Chapter 5 and 6 are respectively devoted to the legal handling of emotions in free speech and demonstration, while Chapter 7, which is concerned with shame, is more centered on a specific emotion and looks into the emotion-legal regulation interaction.

1

FROM EMOTIONS TO CONSTITUTIONAL INSTITUTIONS

> Whoever appeals to the Austrian as a way of justifying Austria believes that the public mind is the sum of private minds, rather than a function intrinsically more difficult to calculate.
>
> —Robert Musil

This book offers a partial descriptive theory of the making and operation of the institutions of liberal constitutionalism; it puts the emphasis on the role of emotions, but it does not claim that emotions alone generate social and legal institutions. Emotions participate in building the constitution and a culture of constitutionalism, and then these creatures of constitutional sentiment patrol emotion display. This position contradicts the myth of law as reason, where law is presented as the result of conscious deliberation, or perhaps a horse trading of different plans and interests, but even so a purposive and rational venture. In the myth of reason, emotions are presented as separate from reason; passions' interference in reasoning, even if irresistible, is only a troubling external nuisance. Law is described as a mechanism to counter such interferences, institutionally reinforcing reason's shelter. This isolationist position, based on the reason-emotion divide, is unsustainable. The scientific evidence indicates that reason and emotion operate interactively in human decision-making and in the actual process of legal institution-building. This book aims to describe how the high level of emotionality in human decision-making is translated into legal, and in particular constitutional, institutions as part of social regulation. I will highlight those features of emotions which are crucial for social reputation.

Emotions are not momentary personal feelings, headaches to be forgotten as soon as the pain goes away. Emotions scholarship has demonstrated that emotions contain social information, contribute to social coordination and are culturally regulated. Emotions are social, because they pertain to a species that is "*obligatorily gregarious*."[1] (For a more detailed summary of the relevant emotion scholarship, see the Appendix.) In the process of social institution-building socially interacting emotions become patterns; the relatively stable social clusters of these emotional patterns become facts of social life in the form of public sentiments. Moral judgments and moral sentiments lend to public sentiment the emotional power that enables these sentiments to shape constitutions. The legal myth is that law embodies natural moral sentiments. In fact, moral sentiments are competing and what is accepted in law is the result of social conflict and selection. Nevertheless, the core elements of constitutionalism, human rights in particular, find inspiration and echo in fundamental moral sentiments.

How do constitutional sentiments (the specific constitutional and public affairs-oriented part of public sentiments) contribute to constitution-building? Beginning in the eighteenth century, public moral sentiments singled out certain claims which were later incorporated into constitutions. This recognition has created a new social reality. Modernity means that people act with the consciousness of rights holders. The emerging rights consciousness was effective because, among other reasons, it corresponded to "natural" moral sentiments, for example, feelings of justice. Moral sentiments served as centers of gravity in the formation of constitutional sentiments, while primary emotions like fear or anger added weight or selected out these moral sentiments, contributing to their consolidation in constitutional institutions, rights in particular. The transformation of constitutional sentiments into foundational institutions of constitutionalism could not have occurred except in a specific cultural setting where the available ideologies, prevalent language, and concepts (including concepts of law) attracted and shaped these sentiments and their interaction. However, the ultimate choices were choices of power (see the emancipation of slaves in the United States) where public sentiments are part of force that constitutes power, and the powerful followed, beyond their interests, the dictates of public sentiments and understood their interests through public sentiments.

Certain influential theories advocate that law should follow emotions and moral intuitions in particular. I argue that modern societies are emotionally and morally divided and that constitutions approach public sentiment in a selective way. However, there is a deeper level of neutrality underlying liberal constitutionalism. This is what constitutional sentiments of the late eighteenth century stood for, reflecting an experience of fear of cruelty and oppression (a matter to be discussed more in detail in Chapter 3, where I deal with the role of fear in constitutionalism). These emotional components of constitutionalism, which formed the *genre* of the modern constitution, remain crucial.

The emerging constitutions became tools of emotion management. We are not passion's slaves, and yet reason needs cunning for success. It is possible, at least to some extent, for humans to exercise cognitive control over emotionally dictated choices. This neural control can be externally and socially influenced. "Individuals can construct the contingencies of their lives in order to exert control over their emotional reactions."[2] The second-order control over emotional reactions is partly exercised by social institutions, including specific regulatory institutions of the state. Government, "which tho' composed of men subject to all human infirmities, becomes, by one of the finest and most subtle inventions imaginable, a composition which is, in some measure, exempt from these infirmities."[3] Human nature (passions) may not change, but situations do, generating emotional control and change, and situations can be shaped institutionally. Hence new constraints on passions arise even at the individual level.

This statement sounds dangerously similar to naturalist or emotivist positions. To attenuate such emotivism I will present evidence that highlights the culturally shaped character of public sentiments and corresponding human rights.

According to an important trend common to the theory of human rights, cultural anthropology and psychology, there are universals in human emotions. These, together with universal moral intuitions, as well as with other universal psychological traits and basic needs, constitute the basis of universal human rights. But anthropological and neural universalia, whatever they are, cannot provide humanity with a compelling standard of rights.

Emotivism has clear limits although this does not preclude the necessity and legitimacy of such standards, which find echo in human sentiment.

The public sentiment of constitutionalism had been frozen into the idea of the modern constitution, but this does not mean that, once in place, constitutions bar the influence of changing public sentiments. Emotions continue to shape constitutional law, even where law conceives itself as a mechanism to filter out and disregard emotions and public sentiment. Here, I sketch a model of the transfusion of public sentiments into constitutional law through judicial activities.

A caveat is needed here: constitutional sentiments were instrumental in shaping modern constitutionalism but there is nothing talismanic in human emotions and moral intuitions that would predetermine constitutionalism. Constitutionalism and the broader culture of our civilization should be alert all the time, ready to counter anticonstitutional passion. Morality is inherent in human nature, in the sense that it is the result of selection in the evolutionary process, but what is selected, for example, altruism or the capacity of revenge, may be destructive of human civilization.

1. Emotions and Their Cultural Regulation

In a desiccated tradition political institutions claim legitimacy, boasting that they are able to operate rationally, hence efficiently. Contemporary constitutional systems are typically presented as if they were operating according to rationality. It is believed that this is achieved by successfully exiling emotions.

Constitutional institutions claim respect and obedience because they allegedly enable rational behavior in society, which is made possible thanks to reason that animates the master plan behind the constitution. All the above is in line with the centrality of reason, the alleged core assumption of modernity. Judges tend to rely on the reason/passion opposition, claiming that only reason shall command decisions.[4] Quite a respectable position indeed; after all, the preference for reason is the first step to possessing it.

The emotion/rationality opposition and subordination are complicated by the multilevel meaning of rationality. "The word *Reason*, and the epithets connected with it—*Rational* and *Reasonable*—have enjoyed a long history which has bequeathed them a legacy of ambiguity and confusion."

"Rational" may refer to, among other things, being logical, or consistent, or finding an optimum means-end relation (where the end, for example, a value, might be irrational or detrimental to the actor). The rationality assumptions of modernity are "that all men have one true purpose, and one only, that of rational self-direction; . . . that all conflict, and consequently all tragedy, is due solely to the clash of reason with the irrationality or the insufficiently rational—the immature and undeveloped elements in life . . .; finally, that when all men have been made rational, they will obey the rational laws of their own natures, which are one and the same in all, and so be at once wholly law-abiding and wholly free."[5]

The master narrative underlying the cult of reason is this: "the history of the West is the history of increasing emotional restraint. The modern period (variously defined) brought with it self-discipline, control, and suppression."[6] From the mid-nineteenth century, emotions were dethroned and were forced into the ghetto of private life and intimacy, a sphere reserved to women whose greater sensitivity needs shelter and incapacitates them for political participation. Emotion becomes inferior and subdued but, like all slaves, it still remains suspicious in its reason-built chains.

Scientific observation contradicts these assumptions of opposition and inferiority. The emotion/reason separation disregards the nature of emotions and their impact on reasoning and moral judgment in particular. The proper understanding of the role of emotions and of moral judgment as an emotionally endorsed process is crucial for the understanding of the operation of constitutional sentiments and constitutional law. On the basis of brain lesion and various brain scanning studies, including functional Magnetic Resonance Imaging (fMRI), one can say with a high level of certainty that certain brain areas (domains) are activated when emotions can be observed and feelings are reported, while others are crucial for higher cognitive functions resulting in judgment that is considered rational. Contrary to the rationalist model of reasoning and decision-making that prevails in law, emotions are quite often present and decisive in mental activities, which are described as reason-based. (Emotion here refers to activation of emotion-related brain domains.)

The prevailing accounts of reasoning rely on a dual process model. System 1, where emotions and association play a very important role, coexists with System 2, which is a more reason-oriented analytic system.

Most cognitive activities including evaluation of perception and decision are primarily nonconscious, and about 95 percent of our acts are taken on autopilot.[7]

To counter the one-sidedness of the rationality myth, emotions are the hero of this book. Emotions are relevant as part of *social cognition* and social communication, and I will refer to those features of emotions which play a crucial role in these processes.

When we experience emotions, specific associations between brain domains (regions) occur. Emotions are events at the level of neural pathways and neurochemical reactions but this does not rule out the "cultural" nature of emotions. They add *salience* to the objects of attention enabling information selection. (Salience means that something stands out, attracts attention; this is indispensable for handling the otherwise unmanageable richness of the information that is generated by the environment.) Emotions are implicated in social reasoning—that is, in reasoning about social relations:[8] they provide us evaluative information about the environment and about the place of the person in that social world. Emotions make humans into "social animals." People have a representation of other people's feelings: they operate a *theory of mind* that represents the emotions of another person. This is crucial in the understanding of interpersonal sensitivity. This is how we receive information about the emotions and intentions of other humans enabling ourselves to react adaptively to such information.

Beyond evaluative information, emotions provide us crude action plans in the form of feelings.[9] Contrary to "pure" cognition, they move (e"*motion*") the person: emotions generate "action tendency." In the case of moral emotions the action tendency may translate itself into prescriptive power: anger felt at injustice compels to morally proper judgment and even behavior, especially if this prescription is socially reinforced.

Another function of emotions to be mentioned in the present context of social regulation is *signaling*. For example, fear is part of social cognition, leading us to warn others of nearby danger and solicit help. Emotions function as "commitment devices" in situations where temptations of defection are high which makes signaling to others credible. Because of the commitment signaled by intensive emotions, people can count on others for future cooperation.[10]

According to a widely accepted distinction humans have a few basic emotions—fear, sadness, etc. Complex or secondary emotions are combinations of these basic emotions. Most emotions are blends of the related feelings and cultural ascriptions; that is, a complex of the blend receives a common name which has feedback and other regulatory consequences. The blend reflects cultural influences and is organized by the self-concept of the person. Framers of the American Constitution relied on a basic emotion of fear that was related to the experience of English tyranny (the object of emotion); the complex emotion of fear of tyranny was reflected in their own identity as lovers of freedom. Obviously, for complex emotions social meanings and categorization are necessary, which are learned with the culture.[11] The categorization changes with culture. The cultural categorization of emotions ("affect labeling") may have direct regulatory impact on emotions. Where a feeling and related action are labeled "revenge," and revenge is esteemed or required, the emotion will be displayed, and not inhibited. It is not enough to consider what people feel or how they represent their feelings; the form of, and, the reaction to, the expression of emotion is socially relevant. "Feeling rules" or "emotion rules" indicate how to feel and how to express socially prescribed feelings, and prescribe the appropriate feeling at the observation of other people's emotions, and the way they are expressed.[12] Social sanctions and rewards including socially prescribed emotional reactions may also have regulatory impacts at the level of stimuli categorization and at higher level cognitive control (reflection). Social cognition matters; it is this cognition that makes emotions social, including their social-emotional evaluation. For example, social pain is pain generated by exclusion, where exclusion is not limited to formal and informal prohibitions and shunning practices: it includes negative emotions like contempt. In these circumstances the feeling of social pain will be construed as humiliation.

For the proper understanding of the constitutional handling of sentiments, it is of particular importance which emotions are prescribed or proscribed, and what are the techniques of categorization of emotion and of emotion display management. Display provides the actor with additional cognitive control and enables emotional reinforcement from the social environment. Where the display of outrage regarding slavery was culturally improper, antislavery sentiments were unlikely to develop. Further, culture contributes to emotion management by setting cognitive frames of perception. You will be angry at the person whom you perceive as causing injustice; concepts of causation will depend on socially construed frames.

Culture sets situational rules of emotional display, and the proper behavior at the display is culturally scripted.[13] Cultural scripts may simply deny that people actually have certain feelings: higher-class women in Vienna, before the advent of Freud, could not have anger (except perhaps vis-à-vis servants), only hysteria. Cultural scripts prescribe what to do with one's emotions, at least when a feeling becomes conscious, in specific situations, including the handling and display of emotions that are otherwise simple bodily states waiting for recognition and management by the person. These rules have further impact on how emotions are communicated and hence reinforced.

It is a matter of culture and of technique of social domination how much emotional display will be permitted/has to be permitted in a society organized under the cult of rationality. At least some forms of emotion display are legally sanctioned. For example, the proper display of love is judicially considered in child custody cases; well-expressed distress of victims is honored in greater legal recognition of victims' rights and even in their compensation.

An institutional structure may solidify emotion categories and concepts and display rules as mutual expectations, supported by social sanctions: departure from "proper" expected emotional behavior requires punishment, for example, by ostracism or other negative attitudes. Too much grief results in being labeled extreme, or even crazy.

Emotions can be outlawed with different techniques, not only by imposing social or legal sanctions on the display. A legal sanction applies where prohibited emotions are counted as aggravating circumstances of crime, as is the case, to some extent, with hate crimes. Of course, it is not the emotion itself but its display in relation to a protected target that is prohibited. On the other hand, husbands' anger used to be a mitigating factor in sentencing crimes of passion in much of the patriarchal nineteenth century.

Obviously, if emotions are scripted, there will be place for a higher cognitive evaluation and influencing of emotions. But there is no guarantee that the scripts will be rational or fair. The labeling part of the script often helps to legitimize the display of otherwise highly problematic emotions in a changing cultural environment. Today, at least for the time being, talking about revenge is anachronistic, at least in European high culture, but retribution is a perfectly welcome attitude, and it legitimates the same anger and sense of punitive justice (counter-aggression) declared culturally despicable as revenge.

Personal moral attitudes are contributing to the formation of public sentiments, and are influential in accepting or rejecting the constitutional solution of moral problems of the society. Contrary to rationalist theories of morality, moral sentiments are highly influential in the shaping of moral judgment, but this operates in conjunction with higher cognitive processes, most likely in some kind of dual process where emotions and higher cognitive control interact. In real life personal factors (for example, identity), personal interactions, and cultural frames are involved in framing the moral decision. Moral judgment and behavior might be emotionally shaped, but such emotions can be influenced by, and submitted to, enhanced cognitive control. This enables the intervention of institutionally designed cognitive corrections in emotionally driven moral judgment. Is this to say that cognitive and cultural control will prevail and emotions are tamed in morality? This seems unlikely: emotions are an integral part of human thought. Emotionalists claim that morality is based on, and even hardwired in, emotional responses and emotion-driven moral intuitions; moral intuition is an emotionally induced mental process, and it includes unconscious reasoning about matters that are culturally understood as "moral."[14] Although moral sentiments and intuitions may push for specific moral judgments, which may thus serve for preferable solutions for morality and are therefore influential components of public sentiments, their influence can be countered by institutionally driven cognitive impacts. Moreover, they are very much stimulus-dependent, and therefore harming or other "natural" events are not capable of defining the reaction of moral sentiments.

2. How Do Public Sentiments Shape and Interact with Law and the Constitution?

2.a. The Nature of Public Sentiments

The regulation of emotions and moral intuitions in particular is not a one-way top-down action. Emotions influence their own regulation.

Social institutions of emotion regulation are shaped by public sentiments. At least from the dawn of modernity, emotions and moral intuitions relied on the public expression of public sentiments, with quite some self-regulating effect.

Sentiments traditionally referred to private and interior feelings. We do not have to pass judgment as to what extent emotions have to be personal and communicated in a private setting; it seems that this depends on the emotion and the culture. The fact is that public sentiments have originated in a private and interpersonal setting,[15] and they continue to maintain intimate relations with the private sphere and actual individual emotions. Beginning in the eighteenth century, with the recognition and respect of sentimentality,[16] sentiments became a matter of publicity; their expression and evaluation were public acts. Sentimentality became politically correct. Publicity increased emotional interaction. The emerging channels of public communication, and of visual mass communication later on, facilitated large-scale and increasingly simultaneous emotional influencing, including in matters of politics. This publicity has gradually changed and homogenized sentiments, at least in regard to those emotions which were to be displayed. The emerging public sentiment was captured cognitively: there is a lot of reflection on what is the proper public sentiment; the exchange of these reflections tends to unify and consolidate it. Public sentiments are emotionally elaborated: people reflect emotionally what they see as the emotional reaction of the other, and in particular what is believed to be the prevailing sentimental mood.[17] You participate in public outrage with similar outrage—or with disgust. This will reinforce your emotions and the shared emotions, which, once displayed, function as social facts.

In consequence, (specific) emotions became a fact of social life in the form of *public sentiment.* La Rochefoucauld claimed that vanity (the desire for self-esteem) is the sentiment that holds (his) civilized society together, while compassion seems to have cemented nineteenth-century industrial societies.[18] Public sentiments privilege certain emotions and sanction others by emotionally evaluating them.

Public sentiment is different from individual emotions that constitute it: it is more than their aggregation. It is a structured (often manipulated) reflection of these private emotions. It reflects public (social) concerns which are expressed publicly as feelings, and which often receive emotional and cognitive reinforcement or sanction. The publicity of sentiments has the advantage of making emotions transparent, where transparency contributes to their pro-social management. British abolitionists met and exchanged their horror and outrage; then, they referred to these common sentiments as a source of community and used them as justification. A shared emotion is a comforting sign of appropriateness where the latter indicates truth.

Once emotions became public, they could interact beyond the private sphere. The interaction of moral judgments creates a prevailing majority; a moral judgment will emerge as that of the majority, which in turn increases its influence: thanks to conformism what is believed to be the majority sentiment will have the normative power of the factual.

Together with other emotions whose display is considered appropriate, this is then recognized and legitimized as public sentiment. The feelings of others act as a normative point of reference by becoming public. However, conformism is not the only reason for accepting public sentiments. Their normative power is due to their relation to individual moral judgments. Moral intuitions do not count for public sentiment as long as they remain momentary emotional inclinations, nor will a cultural endorsement of an emotional dictate turn it into a moral judgment. What matters for the constitutional incorporation is that it occurs as a moral choice: constitutions make selections that make people feel good as opposed to being wrong or bad;[19] hence the importance of public moral sentiments which tell the constitution-maker what will make people feel good. The dictate of the moral sentiment is felt binding because it was endorsed on moral grounds, as an expression of public morality. Some of these public sentiments are directed toward shaping the political structure through law. There are constitutional sentiments. Constitutional sentiments are public sentiments which concern the political structure and the constitution, and which are reflected in them. They emerge in a historical situation where the organization of the political society is understood to be shaped around a rather easily identifiable object, namely the constitution; for this reason constitutional sentiments are relatively distinct within public sentiments. This was certainly the case at the writing of the American and French constitutions at the end of the eighteenth century.

Constitutional sentiments are particularly effective where they serve the affirmation of an emerging national identity. It was for this reason that Pitt and the conservatives appropriated constitutionalism: ". . . we are in the possession of peace, of happiness, and of liberty; we are under the guidance of a mild and beneficent religion; and we are protected by impartial laws, and the purest administration of justice: we are living under a system of government, which our own happy experience leads us to pronounce the best and wisest which has ever yet been framed; a system which has become the admiration of the world."[20]

Having the right feelings or feeling good does not necessarily result in action, but it does contribute to ethical pressures.[21] Once a corresponding social or legal institution is established in conformity with the moral sentiment, the proper sentiment will contribute to its consolidation. Those in America who felt compassion for the suffering slaves but did nothing to undo slavery were ready to endorse emancipation and the Thirteenth and Fourteenth Amendments. In many regards, moral judgments which do not trigger the obligation to act in a certain way are still constitutionally relevant when they contribute to the consolidation of a constitutional sentiment. Feeling the right thing about a public matter becomes a matter of morally right, an "ought" that has to be respected and reflected in constitutional law.

As Montesquieu noted, specific public sentiments become foundational for specific political regimes as principles of government: for him virtue is the prevailing passion in the republic, honor is in the monarchy.[22] Constitutionalizing the dictates of public sentiments helps to sustain and extend the cultural environment that provides interpretive schemes to sentiments. To the extent moral and other emotions are cognition-dependent, such constitutional measures help the emotions in conforming with the "official" sentiment by reinforcing the common frames of interpretation of life situations. Public sentiments become normative patterns through constitutionalization. It is a social choice of modernity, and of foundational importance, that moral sentiments are turned into legal rights. This does not follow from moral sentiments, which are primarily about the right conduct;[23] further, moral rights in the sense of attributing to each other what is due are not enforceable.

The constitutional solution, be it in the text of the constitution or in a judicial decision that embodies rights, finds echo in the public sentiment. It is by reinforcement in public sentiment that the constitutional arrangements and fundamental rights will become "institutional facts" in the sense John Searle used the term. Once fundamental rights are recognized, people will act armed with fundamental rights as common reference: they do "something . . . as part of our doing something."[24] The best-case scenario of this "our doing" is the constitutional enthusiasm: here, the constitution successfully offers values for public identification.

Public sentiments are crucial for social and cultural change, because they contain an emotional reflection on the unfinished,[25] an element of desire. Moral sentiments "imply conceptions of what we might or should become."[26] Hence their relevance for the making of constitutions and for the development of constitutional law: public sentiments constitute and reflect upon a process, moving from private to public expression, of what is felt to be realizable as a public project. The public sentiment, expressing normative expectations of justice, confronts injustice with hope and proposes alternatives to rigid experience. Notwithstanding the centrality of conformism and moral anchoring in the shaping of public sentiments, they remain in a state of indeterminacy. Public sentiment remains an "indefinite fact," not only because of its uncertainty and malleability, but because it also emerges in the competition and exchange of emotions. People have different emotions and moral judgments in specific situations, hence public sentiment can be construed selectively by those who rely on it. The public sentiment of the abolitionists that was animated by outrage and compassion entered into conflict with the anger and disgust of slave-holders. The antislavery public sentiment that prevailed at the end of the decades-long campaign was the result of a selection, formalization, reformulation, and consolidation of the victorious abolitionist sentiment: a matter of choice of the public at large and, in particular, of those who could decisively influence selection.

Because public sentiment is unstable, intensity of the sentiment may counter diffuse majority sentiments and conformism. The strong and persistent emotional commitment of a small group of antislavery abolitionists could prevail in Britain against majority indifference. Consider also the cases of the Chevalier La Barre and Jean Calas, the emblematic instances of eighteenth-century maladministration of justice and religious intolerance in France. Voltaire felt indignation at the cruelty and treachery of the authorities, and successfully communicated his sentiments to his larger audience. Once public sentiment reflected Voltaire's sympathies, the humanistic criminal-procedure movement got off the ground. The same public sentiment found torture abhorrent, although a few years later the guillotine could not generate enough popular disgust, as repulsive as it was; contempt toward the guillotined has prevailed thanks partly to the sanitization of the event: the enlightened public appreciated in the machine the victory of scientific rationalism.

In the formative years of modern constitutionalism, poorly developed as it was, public opinion was of limited importance, and the population, whose attitudes had to be taken into consideration, was influencing the political process emotionally and much less intellectually. The publicization of private sentiment preceded and prepared the emergence of public opinion.[27] These two phenomena remain interrelated but separate till this very day. According to the prevailing Habermasian understanding, public opinion[28] is formed in a rational and prejudice-free discussion, in a sphere that is neither a subset of the state nor that of private interests. Public sentiment and public opinion regulate the state and the public sphere. In the case of public opinion this is intentional, while in matters of public sentiment it is a rather spontaneous public emotional reaction and emotionally driven action that shapes decisions, with or without the mediation of public opinion.

Contrary to public opinion where cognitive manipulation is common and formal, and institutions like the press play a central role in the shaping of cognition, public sentiment is more diffuse and it relies on emotional mobilization. Public sentiment can certainly change public opinion; vice versa, the cognitive components of public sentiment, like attribution, might be influenced by public opinion. In fact, public sentiment is the soul that moves the machine of public opinion: the relationship is illustrated by the influence of images on politics in modern democracies. Images affect public sentiments through their primarily emotional impact.[29] "Images, marked by positive and negative affective feelings, often guide decisions; . . . these images can be consulted more quickly and with less effort then it would take to form a judgment through normative routes."[30] Imagination is ignited by images, even if they need a whole culturally set framework of interpretation; words have a less dramatic influence, unless they totally capture the vocabulary. Thoughts and the mind are controlled if the language succeeds in taking control over the frame of interpretation. However, this is a long-term project, and the single image has much more power than isolated speech. There is more "salience" in an image than in words: it has incomparable attention-gathering power. Images drive public sentiment which influences and even changes public opinion.[31]

2.b. Moral Emotions Feeding Public Sentiment

What makes public sentiments so powerful in the shaping of constitutional sentiments? Public sentiments influence institution-building by setting normative frames, in particular moral frames. These moral frames, which animate the moral solutions of constitutional law, reflect moral emotions. It is the power of interacting individual moral judgments and the rather strong influence of underlying moral intuitions that animate public sentiments and, through these sentiments. constitutional sentiments. How does the transformation of moral judgments into public sentiments, and then into legal institutions occur? Here we face a methodological difficulty: moral judgment is an actual individual mental process while public sentiment is a collective event. Emotions are individual phenomena, but they are not molecules in a Brownian motion: individuals with emotions interact, and not only at the level of mirror neurons and empathy; emotions to a great extent follow social display rules. There is some socially and even biologically set similarity or pattern in emotional reactions: socially sad events cause sorrow to many people. Emotional interactions and social narratives about emotions result in widespread and repetitious individual feelings, which become socially observed and recognized as normative public sentiments.

Given the prominence of emotions in human thought and behavior the question arises: what is the role of emotions in morality?[32] This is of particular importance to law, given that it is prohibitively difficult to sustain law against morality, and because the congruity of moral intuitions with fundamental rights enhances the legitimacy of constitutional law.

As Kant famously argued, morality cannot be *based* on moral intuitions: an act performed merely out of sympathy instead of duty does not qualify as moral. Hume proposed an alternative source of morality. He compared moral judgments to those of aesthetics and argued that reasoning is and should be guided by emotions. In the sentimentalist (emotionalist) tradition moral intuitions form our moral judgments: "The final sentence . . . which pronounces characters or actions amiable or odious, praiseworthy or blamable . . . depends on some internal sense or feeling which nature has made universal in the whole species."[33]

Advances in neurosciences indicate that emotions do play a crucial role in moral judgment and moral behavior. Moral judgment is not a unified psychological or neurological phenomenon: harm-centered and fairness-centered moral judgments involve the activation of different neural pathways. Because of the high level of variance in the research design, instead of describing different parts of a moral elephant, we replace various moral animals with a single moral unicorn, a nonexisting single moral entity. Nevertheless, we have enough communality in the available experiments regarding fairness, harm-related and other social norm-breaking situations to say that moral judgment is not deductive or other propositional reasoning from deontic propositions ("what is permissible") that concern matters considered moral. Moral judgment is emotional processing, in the presence of some form of cognitive control. What remains contested is the role of moral cognition in this process and the possibility of conscious correction of the process (though not exclusively by stepwise reasoning). The debate concerns the primary causal or steering role played by either one. However, some data indicate that parallel but *interacting* neural pathways are activated in moral judgment, with only one of them involving higher cognitive regions.

Moral thinking is broader than judgments: it operates in a social interaction and it reflects public morality (and conflicts between moralities as ideology). When confronted with choices that might qualify as moral, the individual has to structure the problem. The structure and meanings are attributed as a function of self-understanding and agency, but at the same time the meanings are culturally generated. Morals in everyday life are mostly heteronomous, but morality is understood as autonomy. Fundamental psychological needs and social dictates of conformism set limits to and animate this autonomy.[34] Culture is learned in emotional processes of identification with the group that holds the ethical and other concepts, beliefs, and most importantly, representations that are applicable in moral judgment. Ethics (which includes conventions) is learned and "moral" behavior is often conformist imitation only. This does not preclude moral judgments that depart from conventionalist ethics, although even the forms of departure (at least for ulterior rationalization) are culturally shaped. When one finds that a specific harming is not wrong, the justification will rely on schemes of culturally relevant attributions—for example, lack of causation or concepts of group solidarity (see social killing).

Moral emotions have motivational consequences, a fact that explains their relevance to individual social behavior and social regulation, but they alone cannot explain normativity. "One needs some social buttressing of moral norms because the motivational forces of morality, though existing, are limited."[35]

Moral judgments influence constitutional arrangements via their contribution to constitutional sentiments, which reflect socially prevailing moral judgments, and they contribute to the social regulation of these very judgments and related emotions. Both Kantian deontology and utilitarianism presuppose a top-down, reason-based (higher cognitive) approach to moral judgment. However in the neuroscience perspective, fundamental differences in moral theory represented by these approaches become irrelevant, as none of them seems to be supported by neuroscience data. They might be relevant, only in particular situations where people are externally confronted with alternatives and are forced to deliberate. Such confrontation is also provided in law, thanks to, among others, constitutional institutions. How successful this confrontation is, and to what extent the moral judgment will remain emotionally shaped, is a different matter. In this regard, the best summary of the relevant emerging brain science knowledge was offered more than two hundred years ago:

> . . . reason and sentiment concur in almost all moral determinations and conclusions. The final sentence, it is probable, which pronounces characters and actions . . . praise-worthy or blameable . . . depends on some internal sense or feeling, which nature has made universal in the whole species. For what else can have an influence of this nature? But in order to pave the way for such a sentiment, and give a proper discernment of its object, it is often necessary, we find, that much reasoning should precede, that nice distinctions be made, just conclusions drawn, distant comparisons formed, complicated relations examined, and general facts fixed and ascertained.[36]

In the case of moral dilemma there are no clear-cut rules, only conflicting and quite often nonarticulated principles, which are easily replaced by intuitions. This malleability is limited by legally produced conventions that are followed habitually. Further, it is possible to construe environments where intuitions will follow the institutionally imposed consequentialist pseudo-utilitarian bias. This control mechanism is of particular importance for courts with specific legal/institutional instructions and mechanisms of supervision for judges and juries.

The dictates of moral intuitions are often challenged in the judgment process, especially if an external factor intervenes in the process. Even if moral intuitions might carry the day, a different dualism emerges where alternatives, and in particular consequentialist/utilitarian alternatives, are explicitly offered or socially signaled in a moral judgment situation. Here, brain regions associated with abstract (controlled) reasoning are activated at least for those people who choose the utilitarian alternative.[37] Social institutions tend to impose such utilitarian-conventional alternatives to moral intuition through institutional design and by the routine patterns of everyday life, for example when the mother asks her child about the appropriateness of a morally reprehended planned action of the child. An institutionally designed mental supervision in the form of direct confrontation of the decision-maker with consequentialist arguments may trigger higher cognitive activities.

There is a fundamentally cultural precondition for the operation of moral emotions: we think "morally" if we find the problem to be moral. Where the situation is qualified as moral, this will act as an "added value" in the sense that the moral frame itself is an emotionally shaped valence with normative power: the preferred act is seen as good or bad. Alternatively, the individual may simply exclude a situation from the realm of morality and disregard the weight added by the moral nature of the situation. But framing can be externally influenced, which is one of the fundamental ways culture and legal rules can manage emotions and moral judgment. "Focusing participants' attention on actions that violate moral rules promotes deontological preference, while focusing on the consequences favouring violating the rules promotes utilitarian preference."[38]

At this point, it is fair to say that moral judgments and moral behavior are to a great extent emotional, but cognitive elements do shape the impact of emotions on judgment and may shift the judgment away from what would be the dictate of emotion. Cognitive frameworks matter.

Once a situation is construed mentally in moral terms of right and wrong (though not necessarily as a "moral" problem), additional social schemes and tacit (not necessarily conscious) knowledge will emerge in shaping a moral judgment. These constructs do shape moral judgment but can be precluded and directed by emotions. A situation has to be evaluated in terms of agency for feeling shame, anger, or embarrassment. Moral cognition (consciously or not) brings causation and attribution into the judgment process. Here I refer to only a few elements of the attribution-emotion interactions. One can feel anger without a target, but for relatively lasting action tendencies, one needs a target. To be angry at a person we must perceive that person as having caused the wrong that makes us angry at him.[39] If you do not see harm being caused by yourself, you will not feel guilt. However, even if the observer did not cause harm, she may feel guilt. When she observes suffering which generates strong emotions she may feel that she personally contributed to the suffering that she did not cause in any "ordinary" sense. This results in guilt, including pathological guilt.

Assuming that there is some correspondence between moral sentiments and fundamental constitutional institutions like rights, and even further, if constitutional and human rights law reflect the dictates of natural moral sentiments, then these rights will be emotionally binding for all humans. As a consequence of human emotional nature, human rights will be universally valid as part of human anthropology. But such assumptions can be made only if the following questions are answered in the affirmative. Are there specific elements in the social environment that trigger emotions leading to moral judgments? Are these emotions different from other emotions; do we have specific moral sentiments? Are moral stimuli (dilemma) essentially different from other emotion-arousing stimuli?

According to some scholars emotions are elicited by specific consequences of acts, in particular harm or injustice. Harming and harm, including presumed harm, seem to be of outstanding importance for the individual. They are obvious candidates for defining morality. But even if harm were the natural ground of morality in the sense of triggering moral sentiments, harm in itself does not necessarily generate moral judgments. The harm has to be evaluated; the feelings need transcription into some kind of social norm.[40] Circumcision has all the elements of being classified as "causing harm." As such it should result in intuitive moral condemnation, but given its religious or scientific (health) classification, there is no moral condemnation attached to it, at least not in the community that shares the classification, even if some negative feelings may arise at the sheer image of the operation. In terms of intensity and consequences of intrusion, the nature of the tissue affected, etc., female genital mutilation/"manipulation" (FGM) differs from circumcision: however, the stronger harm and pain are unable to change the related feelings of those who find it to be a normal identity-enhancing practice. The polarized emotional evaluation of the practice shows the centrality and power of the classification of the "natural" event when it comes to moral judgment. Classification indicates the relevance of culture and of (not necessarily conscious) cognitive activities. However, at least prima facie, there is a "natural" element in these situations which may trigger moral sentiments and intuitions. Without the anesthesia of the cultural classification, the "observer without culture" (a person not bound by the cultural interpretation given to the harming act) would feel disgust at the sight of the cutting of the flesh from sexual organs. She will feel empathy with the imagined sufferings of the young girl or boy (in initiation rituals), even if they are proud of what happens to them and show (and perhaps feel) no pain.[41] The "observer without culture" will have the same feelings of disgust and outrage at the sight of a highly appreciated life-saving operation or when medical students practice with a cadaver. The "observer without culture" remains a poor fiction.

At this point, it will suffice to recall a fundamental nineteenth-century debate between Nietzsche and his despised contemporary, Professor Dühring, in order to show the interaction that exists between moral intuition and cultural selection resulting in fundamental constitutional arrangements. Nietzsche attacked the Professor for claiming that a moral sense of justice is what determines what is just and unjust. Nietzsche, in a somewhat positivistic fashion, held that only law will determine what is just. Nietzsche believed that law pre-existed injustice. "To speak of just or unjust *in itself* is quite senseless; *in itself*, of course, no injury, assault, exploitation, destruction can be 'unjust,' since life operates *essentially*, that is, in its basic functions, through injury, assault, exploitation, destruction and simply cannot be thought without this character."[42] However, at least in principle, in any given society, specific injuries, assaults, and exploitations may generate shared emotional condemnation even if the law says something different. If the conditions are right (the emotions are strong, repetitive, and culturally reinforced, and if group interests did not oppress or delegitimize them) the law will (selectively, of course) codify the emotional reactions, and indirectly, the underlying public sentiment. The specific injury (or the like) will be felt as unjust, and increasingly so as a result of official condemnation. The sense of injustice will try to cement in law the dictates of shared emotion. Constitutional sentiments are the set of shared emotions that triggers the feeling of injustice where the subject relates the injustice to governmental action. Human rights incorporate mostly specific (in)justice-related moral judgments. The incorporation reflects practical social experiences. It is unlikely that the differences in the underlying emotions explain the selection, but the intensity of the related emotions is an important factor. Bodily harm-related injustice seems to be a stronger impetus than concerns of care, which typically emerge in a private setting.

Specific emotional inclinations support privileged claims of action that are then recognized as human rights. The emotional attractiveness of human rights is more palpable where these emotionally supported claims are blatantly violated. Negative emotional reactions at the sight of injury and suffering that occur in the frame of norm-breaking are psychologically hard to avoid, especially when such violations are actually observed. The violation of norms triggers anger that increases action tendency in favor of the victim, and in certain situations against the violator, even where this does not serve personal interests (punitive altruism). Emotions at the denial of human rights generate condemnation of oppression, which reinforces rights consciousness and the belief in human rights.

The moral sense and the emotions behind it do participate in the shaping of fundamental rights. It is not easy to describe this relationship because both the relevant emotions and human rights are complex and operate in unstable interactions where feelings and public sentiments are easily manipulated. Given this complexity, the sense and feeling of injustice cannot be identified with specific constituent emotions, for example, anger or disgust. Most likely the sense of injustice and related moral outrage are elicited where the suffering is related to some kind of departure from a norm (in the sense of regularity) or norm-breaking. Even if such causation of suffering may fit into existing norms, there is at least a parallel norm that makes the act problematic. Torture was not contrary to the prevailing law of procedure of the eighteenth century, and it was felt normal. Once it went against norms of cognition which were becoming increasingly accepted outside the law, for example in science, it became more and more problematic, and as such it became capable of generating intense feelings of dislike and moral outrage.

The sense of justice shapes fundamental rights in a contradictory way. It may well be that the sentiments expressed in law as rights (what is "just" in the sense of being due) is the victory of the ressentiment of the weak, as Nietzsche claims in his magisterial attempt to delegitimize rights. This may make Nietzsche unhappy, but the weak have their power too, partly because of emotions. Constitutionalism is about restraining the powerful, and this project is motivated—in certain regards—by intensive majoritarian sentiments. There is strength in shared majority emotions, even if they come from the weaker parties;[43] resentment undermines certain prevalent claims to the benefit of others which were earlier disregarded. Given the human propensity to conform,[44] majority sentiments matter a lot for public sentiments and emotion management. Conformism is a primary human attitude rooted in human evolution, and it does have impacts. One such impact is that it emotionally excommunicates the otherwise powerful elite minority. The elite tend to resist the majority cognitively, emotionally, and in social encounters, and thereby sanitize themselves against compassion and majority sentiment.

"Natural" emotional reactions to specific (primarily body-related) stimuli remain important for the shaping of constitutionally relevant moral sentiments, but they offer a very thin foundation or point of reference. Individuals react differently to events which have moral judgment-eliciting power. Some people are angry at norm violation, others are not; some people are disgusted by homosexuality, others are not. Perhaps they are of a different character, choleric versus phlegmatic, etc. Or they manage somehow not to see the norm violation. Therefore the allegedly natural sources of moral emotions cannot have more than a limited and mostly negative role: where the culturally provided categorization of acts violating bodily integrity disregards the "natural" (evolutionarily selected) reaction, where it intends to neutralize this feeling, it will be more vulnerable, as the classification is not supported emotionally unconditionally. FGM remains emotionally more contentious than a practice of noninvasive healing. It is contentious even for the cultural pluralists, but certainly not to those who practice it as a matter of identity affirmation. However, women may and do turn against their own culture because of the harm suffered and because of the related humiliation, at least where they can turn to another community where they can afford such feelings.[45] It is also telling how easy it is to mobilize emotions against new invasive medical technologies, which are not yet culturally accepted (see organ transplants, stem cell research, or use of animals in research).

Besides, not all morally relevant threat is about bodily integrity: there are other resources, which are recognized as morally relevant (for example, environment).[46] The threat of bodily harm may activate moral emotions and intuitions for moral judgment, but not all harm is impermissible: self-defense and even war are culturally acceptable, though they need some justification in moral and legal theory, at least when and where justifications serve category shifting. The category shift is facilitated by very strong counter-emotions, like fear or hatred in self-defense. All this indicates that either not all bodily harm triggers moral judgment, or the moral emotion can be reshaped.

While there can be no direct correspondence between specific stimuli, moral emotions, and the moral substrate of the legal order, moral intuitions can certainly serve as ground for legal assumptions and presumptions. For example, in matters of euthanasia, courts find that "the law stands on the side of life,"[47] which does not necessarily preclude letting people die after complicated procedures. But the emotional construction of public institutions remains a limited project. Often, and with formal success, law engages in anti-emotionalist projects, hoping to repress moral intuition, or at least the moral intuition that does not fit into the project of those who have the power to shape culture and society.

3. From Constitutional Sentiments to Institutional Control

3.a. Transposing Moral Sentiments

Having identified the emotional components of public sentiments we turn to actual impacts public sentiments have on the formation of the modern constitution. Chapters 2 and 3 will offer a more detailed genealogy; here I only refer to one of the central "discoveries" of constitutionalism, namely fundamental rights. The concept of a rights-based political-legal community found its echo in public sentiment, but in a public sentiment that became effective being embedded in the social conflicts of the day.

Beginning in the eighteenth century, modern western society has been conceived in public sentiment increasingly as one where individuals are rights-holding subjects. Constitutionalism has been embedded in this rights culture. With the consolidation of the constitutional state, an increasing number of people in ever more senses saw themselves and each other as entitled to act without official authorization. Constitutional entitlements triggered corresponding duties of respect by others (in particular the authorities) with the increasing possibility of legal enforcement, resulting in restrictions on government action. It is in this context that fundamental human rights[48] have emerged in law and politics. They were held fundamental for the social organization of the market,[49] in the sense that natural liberty had been understood as the precondition for the operation of private interests which could maximize social welfare only under the conditions of this liberty.

Fundamental rights serve as preconditions to other rights because they define relations with the state—the most important coercive power. A social system where individuals operate with a rights consciousness is certainly different from one where this is not a fundamental assumption. It is a characteristic feature of modern society that its citizens operate with the shared assumption that they have the right to will.

To a great extent, rights are culturally shared conventions and mutual expectations.[50] Rights as beliefs can be shared because of not only a commonality of interpretation but also one of emotions. The commonality of emotions presupposes culturally shaped meanings of emotions. When the claim to freedom of expression emerged, this presupposed that an originally small but critical mass shared the desire to express their views and receive information without censorship. This desire and need were conceived and felt as something due, which in the emerging rights culture became a matter of strong expectation. This expectation grew stronger, to the point where any disregard of the expectation triggers a sense of injustice. Such feelings of right regarding freedom of expression were unthinkable (for example) in the sixteenth century when the Protestants claimed the privilege of having their materials printed because this was required by their religion. They claimed it because they wished to print the truth; access to the Bible follows from divine command. A right to print other materials, especially materials critical to their teachings, would have been the last thing on their minds. The restrictive attitude was of course shared by Catholics, except that they had no interest in providing access to the Bible for the masses.

The rights-culture-based constitutionalism offered a fundamental novelty: it was increasingly felt that the right to will (to act freely and independently) is something evident and obvious. ("I have the right to do this or that without authorization.") This situation is the result of revolutions in public sentiment, where the sense of justice (related to outrage, shame, dignity, and revenge) as a shared emotion played a mobilizing role. The emotional preferences (moral intuitions) and specific action plan claims supported by these emotional preferences were selected as rights. The selection occurred within the given cultural setting which favored some emotion displays to the detriment of others. But the preference for rights was not only a matter of sentiment. The prevailing language was particularly important in the cultural shaping of emotions. For the construction of human rights, a sufficiently influential critical elite that is engaged in a (human) rights-based language game was quintessential. For the founders of the United States, "birthright" was the common "natural language." However, no language, no ideology could have carried the day without emotional mobilization. It is no surprise that this language prevailed when constitutional sentiments tried to find a form of expression and communication. For people with individualistic aspirations and a remarkable level of personal independence and faculty of self-determination, grievances, hurt feelings animated by injustice, were expressed better in terms of rights than in terms of complaints of "injustice" consisting in the violation of alleged feudal duties. Classic human rights reflect fear of state-inflicted painful coercion originating from a specific concentration of power in the hands of the state; constitutional rights reflect a collective (shared) emotional reaction to threatening state practices, especially those which result in distress. Distress of others is amplified and becomes part of public sentiment.

Self- and other-directed feelings mingle here. Consider the sentiments leading to freedom of religion. The empathy with distress felt when our brethren cannot follow their religious beliefs is certainly stronger when we too feel threatened in our own free exercise. Where one's own religion is comfortably protected, there is less interest and emotional urge to stand up for freedom of religion (of others). It is perhaps no accident how little sympathy was available for Catholics and Jews in liberty-loving Britain in the eighteenth century when their civil rights were restricted on grounds of their suspicious religion.

The transformation of basic emotions into fundamental constitutional arrangement too had to do with the specific interpersonal formulation of these emotions in the public sentiment. Fear and disgust have existed before and throughout history, but it was during a change in social relations and perceptions in the eighteenth century that emotionally driven people acting in a new frame of reference could emotionally interact. In these interactions they followed the impetus of these emotions, and started to abhor cruelty systematically, ultimately crystallizing this sentiment in the prohibition of torture. Likewise, the empathy that supported some fundamental rights was a social reaction to specific distress; such empathy could socially consolidate itself only at a given historical moment when consolidation was feasible politically and viable economically. Emotional reactions which were previously isolated, like the abolitionist attempts of the Quakers and the teachings of Enlightenment philosophers, finally could reinforce each other, shaping a new public sentiment. The original sentiments and related concepts became relevant, even compelling for institution-building, as they recognized themselves as "normal," "supported," and legitimate in public sentiment.

Such consolidation has preconditions. One does not display her emotions unless she can expect some emotional support for it. Empathy with the victims of the regime enables the favorable communication of widespread personal emotional experience. Emotions became widespread once the conditions of communication turned in their favor.[51]

The conditions of emerging modernity enabled individuals to react to state-inflicted pain and other emotional distress in a legalistic way. Distress may be experienced at all sorts of pain, but there is a socially selected version of pain that becomes important enough to receive specific legal treatment, namely state-inflicted pain and, in particular, any such infliction that is felt and regarded as cruel. Cruelty and extreme ferocity create stronger feelings of distress than simple pain of the same magnitude. Such singling out would not be possible without specific cognitive attributions, namely that the causing of the pain can be attributed to deliberate intentional humiliation (see Chapter 3).

Fear based on past experience increases the intensity of distress. Past personal experience matters particularly if the personal experience is one shared by many others. In the formative years of the liberal state, certain forms of systematically imposed distress were singled out as important in view of shared past experiences. The constitutional consolidation of past distress and injustice helps to sustain the sentiment that had been generated by the actual suffering. Legal institutions serve as collective memory. They can replace, at least to the extent necessary for emotional support, the shared personal experience and the emotions contained in it. Where the experience is forgotten, it is more difficult to feel empathy toward past suffering that caused specific distress in different circumstances.[52] Quartering was a humiliating and stressful experience at the time of the American Revolution, and it was important enough a decade later to enter the Bill of Rights. Today there is little emotional support for the prohibition and it is absent from contemporary constitutions.

The 1789 French Declaration and other foundational human rights documents codify a social preference for a set of emotions and resulting action plans. The Declaration endorses emotions that demand liberty, which is the emerging form and condition of individualistic social cooperation in an increasingly nationalist, market-oriented and modernizing society. Liberty is also crucial for a new kind of emotion management, as it serves the identity needs of the constituents of capitalist society and for the actual operation of that society.

Of course, there is no single sentimental genealogy of modern constitutionalism. There were cultural (national) differences in the evaluation and resulting selection of constituent sentiments which were taken into consideration in the constitution-making process. Further, the character of the constitution-making differs too; as a result the way public sentiments interact in the constitutional process will be different.

Consider the historical and intellectual difference in the conceptualization of fundamental rights and liberties in Britain and France in terms of their emotional roots. In the British tradition of human rights, the moral sense which was claimed to be common to all, according to Hume, necessitated an extension of rights—or at least liberty—to slaves. Abolition did not reflect a universally shared moral intuition, but it was held as necessary because all humans were believed to be endowed with moral sense. Abolition was considered an act of compassion and benevolence and it was directed toward individuals as moral beings; it was not concerned with abstract entities like humanity. It was personal. In Adam Smith's view, the compassionate person imagines himself in the position of the other. Rousseau, however, cared about pity, not benevolence. Pity means "to be sorry without being touched in the flesh."[53] Compassion and pity are different (and troubling) roads leading to universal rights. While compassion cannot be touched by the suffering of mankind, pity cares about humanity's predicament and the sufferings of the entire people and of mankind. Benjamin Constant, who outlined liberal constitutionalism as a negation of all the Robespierrian excesses, described morals a matter of suffering and resulting compassion.[54] Here a shared ("universal") emotional reaction serves as the basis of rights.

As mentioned, the role of constitutional sentiments in constitution-making differs also because of the specific path of constitution-making. Remember that this is a process, not a single event. Today constitution-making is a rather centralized technical process and remains a matter of intimate elite dealings. Not so in *decentralized constitution-making* where constitutional sentiments appear naked and the dynamics of emotions are more important than in centralized processes. The making of the American Constitution was a *long-term* decentralized deliberative process, originating partly in local changes that predate the Revolution. It consisted of many disparate events, even if the actual drafting could be located at the Philadelphia convention. Constitutional-foundational choices were made along the road, and not only at constitutional conventions or through formal amending processes but through judicial interpretation and reinterpretation, even before and beyond the centralized constitution. Moreover, the mandates of the drafters were shaped in popular assemblies (albeit partly disregarded), and were ratified in popular processes where passions run high in face-to-face encounters.[55] It follows that constitutional sentiments represent a malleable and unfinished project and without a clear vision of the final structures.

Great Britain offers a famous example of the decentralized constitution-making process. For example, freedom of expression as an institution has been legally constituted in common law seditious libel cases, like *Wilkes*, *Gerrald*, and *Hone* (and in *Zenger* for the colonies). In all these cases jury sentiments (animated by and amplifying public sentiment) were decisive in establishing new boundaries for political speech; the cases and the resulting principles mobilized public sentiments in their support.[56] Many of the constitutional changes that occurred in common law in the eighteenth century have simply reflected changing public sentiment. In fact, a certain shared sentiment of liberty across social classes, emerging in poorly coordinated local events characterized Britain and its constitutional sentiments even beyond the eighteenth century.

Public sentiments continued to play a visible role in the shaping of core elements of the English Constitution well into the nineteenth century. The modernization of the political and welfare system in the 1830s and again in the 1860s reflected once again a "profound shift in sensibility," and "all this took place against a constant sensation of fear—fear of revolution, of the masses, of crime, famine, and poverty, of disorder and instability, and for many people fear even of pleasure."[57]

3.b. What Can and Cannot Be Done with Constitutional Sentiments?

The founding fathers of the American Constitution considered public sentiments a compelling fact that determines the content of the Constitution and that can be manipulated but not disregarded.[58] It was believed that constitutions and laws might fail if they radically disregard moral sentiments, even if only those of the minority, or they would at least perpetuate popular dissatisfaction.

Some constitution-makers believe that they have a right and even a duty to impose moral truth and proper emotion display rules on society. It is argued that the choices of law in matters of emotion are between appropriate and nonappropriate emotions, for example, that display of anger is wrong and destructive whereas care is sign of moral perfection, etc. Cultural and ethical wars are fought in terms of the propriety of sentiments. Vicious emotions are to be excluded from social life, expelled from the human psyche via education, suasion, and psychoanalysis, like the unclean spirits whom Jesus Christ got rid of by sending them "into the swine."[59] This power to choose or impose might be based on democratic legitimacy, privileged possession of truth, or any other prevailing theory of authority. Certain revolutionary constitution-makers and other moral entrepreneurs are intent on imposing their moral vision and choice of respectable emotions on society. Auguste Comte's program is exemplary in this regard: "The greatest problem, then, is to raise social feeling by artificial effort to the position which in the natural condition is held by selfish feeling." "To me this is like saying, the great object of mechanics is to alter the laws of gravitation," commented Sir James Fitzjames Stephen.[60]

Other approaches reflect more prudential considerations, keeping in mind prevailing preferences, with lesser emphasis on their appropriateness. It is often suggested that shared moral intuitions and public sentiments, including those on emotion display, should be taken into consideration and be *transformed* into law (the transformation thesis). Law has to be pragmatically moral, and for the purposes of law, moral and emotional consensus indicates a morality to be legally respected. "Disgust when sufficiently widespread is as solid a basis for legal regulation as tangible harm."[61]

According to this widely shared legal dogma the "first requirement of a sound body of law is, that it should correspond with the actual feelings and demands of the community."[62] It is argued that law and other regulatory systems should reflect human nature and sentiment. The claim goes back to natural law, and it played an important role in shaping constitutionalism in the late eighteenth century.

To claim that laws cannot avoid relying on widely shared emotions is close to the naturalist fallacy,[63] as it assumes that the alleged commonality of emotional reactions *mandates* legislation. It relies on the risky assumption that emotion display rules and intuitions expressed in public sentiments are *really* shared, or are at least accepted in the culture by all citizens. Of course, there may well be commonalities in human thinking and feeling about moral matters, irrespective of cultural differences and class conflicts of morals and emotions. In a few situations, most mentally competent members of a community do actually *believe* that they *should* or *must* act in a certain way (even if they often fail to do so). There are no natural facts compelling such behavior, but there are neural and other biological mechanisms, as well as culturally shared contents that make us think with some uniformity that such obligations actually exist. The theory of constitutional sentiments is not a naturalistic one: it assumes that emotions, even with long-term biological stability and cross-cultural presence, are culturally scripted and culturally interpreted. Culture (through the representation of events, including one's own feelings) and history shape emotional understanding and emotion display. A changing number of events and expectations fall within rights. From the perspective of emotions, rights are contingent. Beliefs concerning rights are not necessarily shared in society, and they remain socially contested.

In a contemporary restatement of naturalism, Christina McKinnon states: "Given their nature, humans have certain quintessentially human needs and human abilities. . . . The normative component of ethics will be seen to emerge from certain natural facts about human beings and from the ways in which these facts constrain what counts as a good human life."[64] However, as McKinnon adds to her plea for considering natural facts (which are not really natural, as they need a background theory of what counts as well-lived life), these considerations serve only to *rule out* certain choices. "Even Hume would have agreed that there are some 'oughts' that are definitely ruled out by some 'ises.' "[65] This is exactly what human rights do.

It is undeniable that moral judgments and sentiments are powerful (because, among other reasons, of their power at the neural level). The problem is that while moral emotions might dictate social action with some regularity, moral sentiments suggest conflicting approaches in divided societies and in complex situations. According to the transformation thesis, the constitution-maker or the legislator has to determine what is "sufficiently widespread," especially where the community's emotions do not dictate specific action. Disgust about certain types of sexual practices is not specific enough for official action to be undertaken, at least in most Western societies, where no compelling ideology endorses a specific disgust-related morality. An emotion may generate strong *personal action* tendencies, for example disgust may breed contempt and ostracism (avoiding contacts with homosexuals or people with AIDS), but this is not easily translated into legal action, although punitive or discriminatory legal action will most likely be welcomed by an emotionally biased public sentiment.

I would offer a nonprescriptive approach. As this story goes, constitutional sentiments are undeniably influential, in particular because they reflect moral intuitions. Such moral intuitions underlying public sentiment result in the selection of institutional rules and decisional heuristics (rules of thumb). Let's take the example of the presumption of innocence. The underlying moral intuition is that innocents shall not suffer. At a historical moment when too many innocent (and not completely powerless) people became victims of maladministration of justice, this became socially troubling and threatening, generating widespread empathy. When public sentiment endorsed this intuition, it became a legal precept. It may well be, however, that in a different historical situation where too many unpunished criminals at large increase anxiety, and where public sentiment is animated by concerns of failed deterrence and a moral concern about the injustice of impunity, a different heuristic would prevail, reflecting the moral intuition that wrongdoing demands punishment. (Failure to punish is what increases punitive attitudes the most.) Constitutionalism as we know it has a tacit and vague corrective to this kind of heuristics, which is partly expressed in rights and institutions related to personal self-determination: humans, including criminals, should not be treated as means to an end. The constitutional freezing of the public sentiment makes fundamental emotional revision difficult but far from impossible.

While certain emotions, supported by public sentiments and habit, set limits to what can prevail in law, public sentiments based on moral judgments have strong normative power. It is a social tendency of the public to invest "its own preferences with the character of moral laws." Moral policing that encroaches on liberty "is one of the most universal of all human propensities."[66] In a few but fundamental instances, the select moral sentiments produce moral rules which are more or less directly transplanted to and codified in law, as in the case of not punishing the innocent. Innocence means—at least in the contemporary understanding—lack of causal intentional relation to harm, and it is obviously a construct of higher cognitive activities. Widely shared moral judgments are summarized and fixed as vague values and principles of the constitution and set constitutional priorities. These priorities are needed to solve otherwise hard-to-treat complex problems. The priorities as represented in public sentiment are determined by the intensity of emotions (including emotions generated by moral intuitions), but also fear, etc., or perhaps primary emotions add weight to moral sentiments. This is how emotionally stringent concerns of equality or liberty (of the accused, of speech, etc.) are selected out. A constitutional value prevails first in the intuitions, and is then consolidated in various will-formation processes including by a majority vote, and/or in the intuitive preferences and calculated interest of the decisive power groups. Values animated by moral sentiment have specific regulatory power here:[67] moral values preclude the consideration of some of the consequences of value-driven decisions. Protected values operate as emotion-backed constraints on choice. The constraint often takes the form of moral emotions precluding interest-based or other consequentialist calculation: cost-benefit reasoning about values often elicits outrage.[68] ("You can't put a price on human rights!") Where "family" or "nation" is the highest value, the consequences of acts will be seen from this emotionally endorsed perspective only, while negative effects outside the sphere of the value are disregarded as externalities.

Notwithstanding their regulatory power at the level of individual judgment, moral emotions never operate in a social vacuum, and they never generate rights or other social institutions in their biological brutality. Human rights that seem to satisfy moral emotions are social institutions serving specific social functions, and they are sustained because of these functions. They are conventions of social assurances against risky (or other costly) acts like panic or unmediated anger-driven behavior or socially "expensive" altruism. Fundamental rights might have been emotionally powerful in given historical circumstances, but their selection cannot be explained exclusively in terms of the power of emotion: they were socially and culturally selected to a great extent following the dictates of culturally scripted and reinterpreted emotions where the script and interpretation reflect social interests and power relations.

Even if the transformation thesis, that is, that law must incorporate the prevailing moral sentiments, is excessive, or impracticable, in view of the above power of moral intuitions law cannot be sustained against prevailing moral sentiments in society, or at least sustaining it will be very costly. Therefore, law is better off if it refrains from offending public sentiments by curtailing action tendencies resulting from shared emotions. "To rely on any change which is hereafter to take place in the sentiments of the people would be trusting to too great an uncertainty. We know only what their present sentiments are, and it is in vain to propose what will not accord with these."[69]

Legal regulation can not simply disregard considerations of emotions as preferences, even if such preferences contradict the moral consideration of the legislative elite.[70] For example, to force people against their emotional dictates to maintain social relations with others who are ostracized in the public sentiment is very costly. Constitutional sentiments of one group may prevail for the group members, even if upsetting very strong and lasting emotions of other groups. This is the lesson of Reconstruction in the American South, of the enforcement of civil rights in the South after *Brown*, and of the constitutionally mandated protection of the untouchables in India,[71] where Indian law had to criminalize the denial of a handshake to a Dalit.

Notwithstanding the striking power of public moral sentiments, it would be wrong to assume that culturally and socially shared moral intuitions or dictates of shared feelings are an unequivocal "natural" basis of constitutional law. References to the "genuine sentiments" of the community often serve as attempts to alter the life form of minorities in the name of an imaginary emotional community. Most modern societies lack the "community of character" the Austrian social democrat Otto Bauer (1881–1938) dreamed of.[72] Heterogeneity makes the constitutional choice among moral preferences particularly difficult. "Far from sharing a common understanding, the citizens of a modern state are culturally disparate and often deeply hostile to one another as individuals and especially as members of ascriptive groups. A modern state . . . exists to mitigate by lawful coercion the murderous proclivities generated by racial, ethnic, and religious solidarity."[73] Constitutional sentiments operate in such heterogeneous societies, many of them possessing a political culture that discourages solutions with clear losers.[74] The emerging system of liberty of modern constitutionalism with its new emotion display rules had to overcome considerable political and emotional resistance. In a way, those whose interests and sentiments favored the new system of market-based relations mobilized a natural "instinct" long repressed through complicated learned rules. Traditional culture scripted specific emotions according to social status. Revolutionaries on the other hand were prepared to recognize all conspecifics as equal, disregarding the stratified rules of emotion display which, for example, had organized compassion along religious lines regardless of equality.

The selection of public sentiments is a *choice* among those groups which hold these sentiments where "choice" often means *imposition* of the sentiments of the victorious. "The morality between Spartans and Helots, between planters and negroes, between princes and subjects, between nobles and roturiers, between men and women, has been for the most part the creation of these class interests and feelings: and the sentiments thus generated, react in turn upon the moral feelings of the members of the ascendant class, in their relations among themselves. Where, on the other hand, a class, formerly ascendant, has lost its ascendency, or where its ascendency is unpopular, the prevailing moral sentiments frequently bear the impress of an impatient dislike of superiority."[75]

Constitutions through the endorsement of public sentiment participate in the social regulation of emotions. It is a matter of choice which emotions and public sentiments are permissible socially, either as foundations of legitimate action or simply in terms of display. Nevertheless, the possibilities of lawyers, ethicist-educators, psychologists, and social regulation in general are limited when it comes to the prescription of emotions: people feel what their neural pathways dictate and what their conditions allow them to feel. At best, regulators may influence cultural representations which will frame and direct these emotions.

Legal regulation tends to select those emotions which conform and cater to the prevailing interests and beliefs.[76] A status-based society will favor emotions that reinforce status privilege, such as honor-related pride, and law will be keen to protect these favorites. This kind of choice fits into the logic of social regulatory mechanisms.

Legislators are not necessarily without prudence and they often realize where the limits to regulation of emotions and moral intuitions lie. Norms are not pre-set straitjackets for emotions. The regulation, with all its values, principles, and norms, succeeds because they sufficiently reflect the already existing and culturally shaped emotions including emotions generated and endorsed by public sentiment. You protect honor successfully where honor is emotionally endorsed. Regulation contains hidden and overt preferences that help sustain certain forms of emotion display.[77]

The constitutional selection of emotion is not only a (temporary) solution to the social conflict among public sentiments and their holders. It is inevitable because of the uncertainty of sentiments. Morality needs the help of positive law. Emotional makeups are malleable and "are molded to various ends, *ends that may or may not be normatively sound*."[78] Individuals often have self-conflicting and uncertain moral intuitions and judgments, which are subject to external change and pressure. Moral intuitions may dictate one thing (equality), and its opposite too (the outgroup is different). Sometimes moral intuitions generate strong emotional conflict within a single person. For example, a victim's suffering generates compassion, while fear of becoming victim pushes toward denial of victim status and hampers identification with the victim, and hence, there is no sympathy. Law helps in the finding of a standard solution. It solidifies specific moral judgments, it in fact solves a specific problem of moral intuitions, namely that of their facility and fuzziness. Positive law may abuse this situation "when the public of this age and country improperly invests its own preferences with the character of moral law."[79]

While public sentiments are a matter of consideration for the constitution, constitution-makers meet the expectations and desires of public sentiment selectively: constitution-making is an act of biased choices, although in some instances the constitution deliberately refuses to choose (see, e.g., the reluctance regarding slavery and fundamental rights in 1787).

It follows that at a superficial level it is simply not true that constitutions represent *the* public sentiment (a commonality of emotions). On the contrary, they reflect privileged moral intuitions; the specificity of liberalism is that these intuitions are permissive, allowing much divergence in public sentiment. Certain emotions will be respected, especially those which the majority, or the majority of the powerful, believes to be the right feelings; others will be rejected. The actual conflicts at the making of constitutions clearly support the thesis that public sentiments were conflicting. American state constitutions disregarded the constitutional sentiments (loyalties) of the loyalists—not to speak of Indians, slaves, and the poor. The French Declaration and the 1791 Constitution can be seen as products of handpicking select sentiments of different publics, clearly disregarding, for example, the feelings of the die-hard monarchists (many of them had to die for it, swiftly). There might have been a rather strong antislavery sentiment (at least a feeling of guilt) among the American founding fathers, a sentiment perhaps acceptable to the majority at the Convention, but one that could not prevail even though slavery conflicted with the accepted sentiment of equality.

4. Neutral Constitutional Choices

Constitutionalism reflects choices of fundamental moral judgments affecting in a fundamental way the behavior of the state[80] through shaping the behavior of individuals who constitute the organizations exercising state power. Notwithstanding the fact that the constitutional incorporation and enforcement of public sentiments is selective, constitutions incorporate certain public sentiments that are not divisive in a deeper sense. The freedom of choice is limited by the function of the constitution and by the specific historical experience that continues to animate it. The upgrading of specific feelings and claims to fundamental rights occurred when the taming of state power was high on the public agenda. It was emerging individualism and the increased power of social actors against King and state that enable the selecting out of rights-supporting sentiments. The ideal type of the constitution that emerged in the formative years of modern constitutionalism contains and reinforces constitutional sentiments that can be shared by all people living in a political society. It is for this reason that certain divisive sentiments and their dictates were disregarded or left unresolved. The American Constitution left undecided the permissibility of the morally often condemned and debated institution of slavery, practically sustaining it, with the hope among those with bad conscience that the future would work for abolition with compensation.[81]

There is a layer of the constitutional state that is accessible to all citizens: at this neutral or thinly construed level, people share a neutral or "denaturalized" citizenship that has no particular cultural character. In this sense constitutionalism is cosmopolitan: it satisfies the needs of rootless people, equally cut off from their homelands.[82] Georg Jellinek claimed that law contains the norms of a society that enable the continued existence of this society. "Law is nothing else but the ethical minimum."[83] This might contain a kernel of truth as far as the expression of shared moral intuitions is concerned, but this is a very thin communality.

There is a minimum of constitutionalism serving all members of society, without reflecting special (group) preferences. Certain underlying principles like basic human rights (fundamental rights), separation of powers, government by the consent of the governed, and the rule of law are endorsed, or at least not rejected emotionally by an overwhelming majority and are compatible with the interests of all people. These constitutional sentiments are shared even by the majority of those who actually oppose the given constitution or even fight against it, as happened in the case of the American loyalists. Loyalists and patriots had shared sentiments concerning birthrights and the rule of law, but the loyalists had also accepted (British) Parliamentary supremacy (not a neutral matter).

At their heart, constitutions and human rights are *neutral* (impartial, politically not biased) institutions of power management. The neutrality of the selected constitutional sentiments relates to the shared need to live in a common state, where there is protection against arbitrary power and against socially destructive emotions. The selected sentiments are neutral in the sense that they all offer arrangements that serve all members of society equally, at least in an ideal world, behind the veil of ignorance.

Neutrality has become an increasingly attractive virtue of the liberal state. The noninvolvement of the state in certain matters that were dividing the society in a fundamental, identity-shaping way is seen to be the guarantee of social peace or truce. In a way, social peace by neutralization lies at the heart of Madison's dream of constitutionalism. He sought to find the panacea against governmental factionalism in governmental neutrality. Neutrality is often used as meaning "state impartiality," which explains the concept's attractiveness. After all, impartiality satisfies a minimal morality. Impartiality is satisfied if "the rule serves no particular interest, expresses no particular culture, regulates everyone's behavior in a universally advantageous or clearly correct way. The rule carries no personal or social signature."[84]

Human rights and separation of powers are neutral in the sense that (in principle) they protect all the people who are weak or vulnerable, in situations where in the face of overwhelming coercive state power anyone and everyone is a potential victim. Rights not only promise protection; they do so in a way that empowers all rights holders. Rights allow claiming (instead of begging), which "makes for self-respect and respect for others, gives a sense to the notion of personal dignity."[85] The neutrality of human rights, in the sense of not favoring people on any specific ground, is expressed in modern human rights law through the centrality of dignity. Dignity means lack of favoritism (neutrality): it promises a win-win position where no one loses when other people's dignity is recognized. Dignity is always compatible with other people's equal dignity. This is not always felt so because people, especially when their identity is group-based and status-oriented, will be concerned with maintaining status (honor) which is hierarchical; the equality that comes with dignity is offensive to status-related feelings. However, the concept (the social representation) of human rights allows for the opposing groups to articulate their differences within the common frame, to find commonalities and negotiate opposing identities within the frame.[86]

Neutrality implies that constitutionalism rules out the influence of certain destructive emotions. Intolerance, humiliation, and the sense of being humiliated are often part of the emotional repertoire, but they cannot serve as the foundation of constitutionalism. Humiliation may be elevated to respectability and into political argument, especially in our culture of democratic narcissism, but claims based on humiliation (more specifically claims to respect identities that demand recognition and privilege in the name of having been humiliated) undermine constitutionalism.[87]

The tolerant and neutral handling of religion illustrates the operation of public sentiment that enables constitutionalism. The public sentiment of religious tolerance suggests equal respect for all religions, even where gut feelings find the religious practices of others (that is, believers in other creeds) appalling. In fact, constitutional law is understood as a bulwark against intolerance. In the constitutional state, emotions which would deny tolerance will not be officially endorsed, and religious hatred and contempt even less so. Tolerance, as a constitutional principle, indicates that only peaceful faith-based emotional antagonism will be tolerated, but not faith-based oppression: "Mere public intolerance or animosity cannot constitutionally justify the deprivation of a person's physical liberty."[88] Neutral arrangements that disregard beliefs and gut reactions of the majority (or of a religious minority) are often despised by many to whom neutrality is outrageous. Fundamentalism and the associated emotions continue to challenge constitutionalism empirically and emotionally. The acceptance of social commonality in constitutional neutrality contradicts our expectations of bias in constitutional politics. After all, power-holders are in the position to favor themselves, and it seems to make little sense for them to impose self-limitations. But the revolutionary period of the late eighteenth century was a rather unique counter-intuitive situation,[89] and such unique conditions allowed the selection and reinforcement of neutral constitutional sentiments. While in ordinary constitution-making the power-holders are in a position to impose their interests, sentiments, and values on the state as if these were those of the majority, in the American and French revolutionary processes the emerging power-holders were carried away by public sentiments, and, more important, they were weak: they were not in full control of the political power (yet). The constituency behind the change was not a small group (of let's say generals); it was "the people" with guns, knives, and stones at easy reach. "We, the People" were encompassing groups, and the applicable incentives for large well-armed groups are "dramatically different from those facing an organization that represents only a narrow segment of society."[90] Further, the founders were in need of public support, not only because "the people" were powerful, but also because of the uncertainty they were facing in the setting up of a never experienced system of government. In this uncertainty, the intuitions embodied in the public sentiment promised some certainty and protection. The constitutional sentiments of the armed people, which animated the classic constitutions, were concerned with the *abuse of political power*.[91] A large segment of the society felt threatened by governmental abuse, and the sense of abuse could therefore become central in the constitutional sentiment. The prevailing norms were losing their legitimacy both in the American colonies and in the France of the *Ancien Régime*, as members of the community observed a systematic violation of the norms and the victimization of some of their peers.[92] The emerging constitutional sentiments expressed fear and outrage regarding past practices of abuse; in the frame of these emotions, moral intuitions proposed new arrangements to curtail government power. These unique sentiments have animated the universalistic claims which were accepted in the new genre of written constitution.

Beyond the historically established basic mechanism of constitutionalism that reflects emotional experiences about gross abuse of unlimited government power, there are additional constitutional sentiments which can be shared by all those who would like to live together peacefully in a state. Harming, causing harm (especially intentionally) elicits strong intuitive moral condemnation. Fear and anger related to bodily integrity are very strong primary emotions. Other moral judgments reflected in constitutional law, namely fairness (distributive justice), that are not closely related to bodily injury also influence constitutional values. Equality, with the underlying sentiment of indignation felt by those who are treated unequally, a sentiment that is shared by some of the people who benefit from it, is also to be mentioned.[93] The rule of law is another, at least partly fairness-related neutral constitutional value. The rule of law may also be seen as a technical safeguard against state arbitrariness that threatens bodily integrity, so it is in a way a reaction to the fear underlying moral judgments. Its principles (for example, prompt access to justice—Habeas corpus—, judicial impartiality, clarity of the law, *audiatur et altera pars*) emerged prior to the consolidation of constitutionalism and have long-recognized roots in legal technicalities that were known at least since the glorious days of Roman law. But they became crucial only once endorsed by public sentiment.

5. Constitutional Emotion Management

In the transformative period of classic constitution-making, the previously established emotion display prohibition rules lost their power and meaning, partly because they were seen as illegitimate impositions, and partly because they simply could not manage the strong emotions constituting public sentiment. The new constitutional regime had to handle and even repress some of the sentiments that had created the very institution. Even so, constitutions cannot annihilate public sentiments. More important, they do not intend to do so. Constitutional law is more about the *manipulation* of sentiments, and relies less on their direct suppression. In their better moments, constitutions offer mechanisms to cool down passions that endanger the constitutional system. (This, of course, includes oppressive mechanisms that serve the maintenance of the political status quo.) Constitutional pre-commitments, the difficulty of constitutional amendment, and gag rules are some of the examples. Passions may result in social instability: institutions offer solidarity and permanence. Once established, institutions increasingly disguise constitutional sentiments. Reference to emotions becomes embarrassing for the legal profession. "The dead weight of institutions, which have a life of their own, then gradually tames the impetus" of the original sentiments.[94]

Now we have a sketch of constitutional sentiments: public sentiments influence constitutional design, even directly in some cases: equally important, many constitutional arrangements are designed to anticipate and cope with what the drafters imagine or observe as popular sentiments. Constitutional decisions (both at drafting and in the judicial creation of constitutional law) are operating with assumptions about the current and anticipated sentiments that will be generated by constitutional design. Once the initial selection of public sentiments is in place in the constitution, the choices will begin to influence both legal decisions and the public sentiment in its constant reformulation.[95] The institutions of the state can directly (through display rules) and structurally (by institutional arrangements that shape human relations) shape emotions and their interaction in public sentiments. Institutions that separate people hamper compassion and contribute to a learning that either favors or restricts emotions. Because constitutional law has to keep all citizens, if not happy, at least not rebellious, law as a moral and emotional regulator may attempt to bypass affective processes of moral judgment, partly in search of uniformity, partly because certain moral judgments might be seen as counterproductive for the dominant social institutions and powers, and partly because law follows its own agenda and therefore often disregards emotions. The disregard of certain emotions may become part of a conscious legal program: "The instinct for retribution is part of the nature of man, and channeling that instinct in the administration of criminal justice serves an important purpose in promoting the stability of a society governed by law."[96]

"Any enduring political regime must establish as an essential element a normative order for emotions, an 'emotional regime.'"[97] Constitutions, as minimum safeguards of living together in a political community, might reflect fundamental emotion-control strategies. To the extent that constitutions serve to unite society or at least provide a living space for coexistence, emotions which endanger this fundamental stability are prohibited. However, at the risk of emotional and moral Balkanization (fragmentation), constitutions may allow decentralized models where different local normative and emotional orders coexist.

The constitutional choice of emotion management may reflect the prevailing cultural position against destructive emotional drives. The political community wishes to restrict these on eminently rational grounds in order to maintain social co-operation within the state. For example, the constitutional monopoly on punishment within the concept of the rule of law (punishment for crime only) expresses strong dislike of instinctive personal vengeance, a "natural" emotional reaction. Similarly, the ban on cruel and unusual punishment stands up against cruelty. These instances of emotional self-restriction were made possible by frightful emotional experiences of vengeance and torture, even if they reflect the interest of the state in maintaining a monopoly of constraining power. (Time and again we have to recall that the public sentiment is only one of the many factors that interact in regulation.)

The regulation of emotions is a subtle matter (is compassion or retribution welcome or is it prohibited?). Culture offers frameworks to perceive and classify events that trigger emotions, and frames and rules of emotion display. Law participates in this regulatory process by emotion categorization and by setting cognitive frames (for example, causation) and limits to and uniformity in emotion display and for emotion-driven acts, even if this is not a central concern of law. Further, certain patterns of problematic behavior are understood as emotion-driven. Given the state's interest in maintaining its monopoly of constraint and given the social interest in reducing social violence, certain distress-related actions are to be avoided. One way of such avoidance is to offer legal alternatives to personal violence in the form of remedies, which will satisfy emotional needs. Without state-provided action, outrage generated by cruelty and injury might result in private revenge; outrage at injustice might result in retaliation. Without the legal manipulation of public sentiments, without the handling of private emotions, the private satisfaction of such private sentiments would undermine the coercive monopoly of the state and its public order.

Beyond participating in the support and oppression of emotions, constitutional law is particularly concerned with moral sentiments. It manages and changes them by selectively sanctioning some while increasing the "availability" and legitimacy of others[98] and shaping the cognitive regulatory elements of moral judgments.

Constitutional arrangements contribute to social emotion control as part of long-term social design. An emotion is socially prescribed to the extent that it is a standard. A society, or a definable group within a society, maintains coercive attitudes toward basic emotions and their appropriate expression and "institutions reflect and encourage these attitudes in human conduct."[99] A choice of an institution (monogamy, "out-of wedlock," same sex-partnership, capital punishment) means also the institutional reinforcement of an emotional preference behind it. Where the death penalty is constitutionalized, it reflects the reinforcement (the "appropriateness") of the underlying emotions of fear (anxiety) and revenge (outrage).

The primary tools of law in emotion-management are normative framing and institution-building, in two senses of "institution." First, law sets into motion mutually reinforcing expectations and interpretations that have impacts on emotion display, as well as creating bureaucratic mechanisms which are designed in constitutional law to contribute and sustain the above institutions as expectations. Secondly, display rules contain preferences and hidden prohibitions: permissible legal arguments (references) preclude the use of emotions as arguments and encourage moral disengagement. (That suppressed emotions come back with vengeance is a different story, and a tribute to Freud.) Constitutional law is rich in display prohibitions, supported by the denial of the legitimacy of arguments that refer to emotional consequences in legislation: see, for example, the contemporary American rules of jury instruction. The same applies to the expectation that rational discourse—as opposed to emotional or religious appeals—about the permissibility of the death penalty will "encourage moral disengagement and discourage empathy."[100]

Constitutional law provides attitude-shaping values and rules of thumb for decisions (similar to heuristics for decision-making). Both values and decisional heuristics contribute to the social evaluation of emotions. For example, a strong constitutional emphasis on dignity undermines the legitimacy of emotions pushing for unchecked anger, cruelty, etc. Some of the counterintuitive constitutional biases, like the protection of free speech, help certain forms of emotion display or intend to counter emotions (when free speech is allowed to counter sensitivities).

Constitutional emotion management remains auxiliary and of limited success. This is not surprising given that such management is a by-product of a regulatory logic that follows other goals. Moreover, the regulation occurs in a context of conflicting emotions. The constitutional choices which affect emotion display reflect the outcome of social and political conflicts among groups with conflicting emotion management strategies.

I will use the example of transitional justice to show the difficulties and uncertainties of constitutional emotion management. As mentioned earlier, the social conflict among public sentiments continues at the stage of constitutional emotion management. Law simply cannot disregard the prevailing emotional expectations of the folk psychology of the day (the common-sense assumptions about how one's own and other people's mind work, for example, assuming a certain cause for an act or feeling). Where the public sentiment is structured along lines of atonement or of healing, or where the impermissibility of impunity prevails, these concerns will aggressively demand to be reflected in law.

The constitutional solution that grants the possibility of pardon and amnesty, banking on generally accepted emotions (empathy, mercy), and as such, satisfying conditions of neutrality, often has conflicting emotional consequences; it is the specific use of the institution that makes it emotionally controversial.[101] When, for pragmatic reasons, amnesty is granted (and/or pardon and amnesty are constitutionally permissible), this seems to follow the dictates of forgiveness. But unpunished crime triggers lasting feelings of injustice and anger. Whatever is the (dubious) utilitarian advantage of social peace by impunity, the emotional tensions due to the original crime remain.

Where victim status has become part of the self-definition of the person, pardon or amnesty to the perpetrators will deprive past victims of a fundamental and defining element of their identity. It is a widely shared hope of contemporary post-conflict justice that apologies, truth and reconciliation commissions, and perhaps compensation will help emotional and social healing. The institutionalization of one or another mixture of these measures is the preferred liberal constitutional solution.[102] The beneficial psychological effects of apology on the person expressing sorrow are obvious in terms of personal distress reduction. But what about past victims? It is hoped that the recognition of injustice will comfort the wounded self, and the legally endorsed formalistic process adds an element to the cognitive control over emotions (in this case the hurt feelings, degradation, and anger pushing for revenge). This assumption fits into the model where emotions are subject to social cognitive control. However, in view of the modest success of public apologies, and notwithstanding their importance for social confidence-building, one has to admit that apologies may not have the wished-for emotional effect.[103] Past victims may consider apologies another form of imposition or consider the expression of sorrow a denial of responsibility.[104] Constitutionally permissible or prescribed, politically reasonable designs may fail to regulate emotions, notwithstanding their conformity with fundamental constitutionally endorsed values. Constitutionally sanctioned forms of social conflict resolution that intend to mobilize or constrain emotions may not satisfy the public sentiment, though they might promise social peace.[105]

Such differences in handling past injustice and threats would generate differences in public sentiments and suggests differences in constitutional design. For example, where the culture labels past atrocities a non-issue, one cannot mobilize sentiments and people around them. Cultural restrictions of emotional sharing are efficient barriers to the communication of emotion. In the context of international justice, such differences may cause lack of effective communication. The claims of a victim nation to get reparation or apologies for past mass atrocities committed by another nation make little sense emotionally in the perpetrator nation if trauma is not a matter to be shared.[106]

6. Naturalism and Universalism

If constitutional law is embedded in human emotions, and in particular constitutional arrangements, then this might serve to legitimate constitutional law. This has normative implications: constitutionalism would be binding as it corresponds to the dictates of sentiments. Moreover, these sentiments are now elevated to the rank of reason. Most theories of moral sentiments that served as a background for human rights had more than a love affair with innate moral sense.[107] References to nature and human nature were standard provender of human rights. The natural-law tradition made its own contribution to naturalism. At least in some versions of the natural-law doctrine, human rights were natural rights in the sense that they did follow from a nonspecific human nature. Human rights should be respected as universally valid natural claims.

Naturalist emotivism claims that facts, including emotions, prescribe a certain social or legal arrangement. However, the presence of emotions in constitutional arrangements, including fundamental rights, does not imply a naturalistic assumption of the constitution, or at least of the moral order behind it, if there is indeed one (or more) behind it at all. Even so, the danger of naturalism looms large for any emotionalist theory of constitutionalism, especially when it comes to the issue of human rights. Some contemporary human rights theories claim that human rights correspond to specific basic human needs. Some of these theories tend to interpret needs in a social sense, while others, like Maslow's, made an attempt to create an entire rights hierarchy based on a biological needs hierarchy. Nevertheless, even Maslow had to admit that "man's instinctoid tendencies, such as they are, are far weaker than cultural forces."[108]

Naturalism, in the context of human rights, assumes that faculties or inalienable features that are embedded in human nature—the rational and/or the emotional composition of human animals—necessitate recognition of these faculties. An emotivist theory could argue along these lines that certain human rights satisfy emotional needs together with other biological needs.

A theory of constitutional sentiments does not have to commit itself to the naturalistic fallacy of needs theories. It does not replace needs with emotions, and it does not claim correspondence between emotions and rights. Correspondence between emotions and key human rights is certainly not the way emotions shape rights. Emotions influence fundamental rights in much more complex ways: the same emotion family, in interaction with other emotions, does contribute to a whole series of different rights (see Chapter 7 on shame), while rights as institutions manage emotion display and contribute to the social scripting of emotions (see Chapter 5 on freedom of expression). All that a theory of constitutional sentiment claims is that in the process of incorporation into the canon of human rights and in their constitutional acceptance, emotions (particularly fear and empathy) play an important role. This in no way diminishes the role of cognitive processes in the selection. Rational arguments do play a role in the shaping of rights; cognitive processes in fact contribute to their successful selection.[109]

The selection of human rights from among public sentiments is a historically contingent event, but the binding force of human rights is commonly related to their universalism. Universalism is intellectually very attractive, even irresistible. In eighteenth-century France, universalism of rights was related to universal reason—and reason, to be unconditionally binding, had to be universal: "Reason is the same for all thinking subjects, all nations, all epochs, and all cultures."[110] Human rights were the universally valid dictates of universal human reason. For the modern rationalist moral agreement, universal moral norms, and human rights are possible because the agreement results from rational argumentation which presupposes at least a common, universal capacity of understanding.

Universality means that one does not have to negotiate norms. This is cognitively economical and therefore advantageous: universalism enables maximum coordination. The precondition for the mandatory applicability of human rights is a naturalist universalism: here, it is assumed that the wish for, and respect of, human rights are a universal feature of human nature. In a sense there exists an anthropological unity of mankind: Hume, whose intuitions are vindicated with some regularity by contemporary science, believed that "nature has made" the moral sense "universal in the whole species."[111] After all, most species, from rats on up, are fundamentally inclined to recognize their conspecifics. It is argued that human rights are universals that reflect the anthropological and even biological unity of the species. If this is true and if human rights are reflections of universally shared moral intuitions, can't we assume that human rights have a universal validity and binding force rooted in the communality of moral emotions? Alternatively, the assumption of human psychological universality can be construed as cognitive: "human psychological universals are core mental attributes that are shared at some conceptual level by all or nearly all non-brain damaged adult human beings across cultures. The assumption of human universals is a foundational postulate of psychology."[112] In a Kantian mood, common cognitive structures would lead to shared moral conclusions demanding universal binding force to these conclusions in the form of rudimentary human rights. In both instances, the alleged empirical observation of anthropological unity transforms itself into a normative statement: since human rights are universal due to their origins, they are to be respected everywhere and in regard to all humans.

It is a sustainable assumption that basic emotions are universal, in the sense that these are shared by all humans as a matter of shared neural structure.[113] The variation that is observable among different people is generally found to be a function of cultural diversity (scripting). To the extent fundamental rights reflect fundamental emotions, one could argue that these are common to all humans and may reasonably be universally respected. Already Francis Hutcheson, in his refutation of Mandeville, emphasized the primacy of innate benevolence over interest and reason, on the basis of the universal presence of the moral sense in all men.

The universalist assumption is that once the emotions overcome cognitive barriers or cognitive barriers disappear, they will exercise similar dictates, resulting in the wish for similar rights. Wherever abolition of slavery becomes a social possibility, many people will feel slavery to be abnormal given their negative emotional reactions to it.[114] The similarity of human nature, and in particular the resulting moral emotions, may serve for a similarity of moral judgments that underlie fundamental human rights. However, there are anthropological, historical, and even biological objections to this naturalistic emotivism. Moral intuitions and related emotions do not generate specific human rights. Specific human rights depend on local cognition. Humans create and sustain cognitive barriers which preclude the uniform and transcultural working of emotions.

Universalism in human rights may refer to quite different sentiments and concerns. Rousseau and Marat advocated a pity-based universalism of human rights while Hume and Smith believed in universal compassion. The universalist claim has a rather dubious genealogy. The French commitment to the universality of human rights originates in specific national or social identity problems. They found this new identity in the universal mission of France which is to bring (universal) human rights, the fruit of universal reason, recognized by the French genius and presented as a noble gift to the rest of the world.

Beyond differences in human rights genealogy, there are actual differences among human rights concepts that directly challenge the universalism thesis. Locke denied universal morality on grounds of empirical observations, claiming that if one looks beyond the make of his own chimney no universal moral principles will be found.[115] Today, we notice that human rights with a universalistic claim trigger emotional resistance in millions of people who see in these claims an attack on their identity, and feel humiliated and disgusted when imagining the practices that such rights would bring into their community to the detriment of the prevailing conventions and emotion display rules—equality of women into a patriarchal male-chauvinist society, for example. The emotional reactions are well preserved by the interests of male domination.

As to the biological community of human nature, Rom Harré concludes radically: "There can be little doubt that, even if there are some universal emotions, the bulk of mankind live within systems of thought and feeling that bear little but superficial resemblances to one another."[116]

The difficulties of the naturalist universalism begin with the fact that human rights are often treated as a single entity or bundle. It is a quasi-normative expectation that human rights be interdependent and treated as a single intellectual universe. Lawyers tend to boast that human rights have a stable and clear meaning for them, at least in a given period. However, even in liberal democracies (let alone other cultures), human rights exist as contested mental representations. Human rights trigger action plans that are handled according to conventions which remain socially contested. Even where the meaning attributed to a human right is more or less shared in a given culture, individuals and groups position themselves differently according to their social anchoring.[117] Although there is a common legal and institutional logic that applies to human rights (for example "trumps" enforceable in court), the uniformity assumption is not fully legitimate from a psychological perspective. Contemporary reactions to human rights indicate that these rights are emotionally multidimensional.[118] Human rights show differences in their emotional genesis and are quite distinctly related to differing combinations of emotions; different human rights violations trigger different sets of emotions.

Even if one accepts that there is at least a core agreement regarding a few universal human rights (for example prohibition of torture, respect of dignity) it is difficult to find universal emotions that would serve as their emotional foundation. The lists of basic emotions differ inconveniently.[119] It is contested that emotions are of a "natural kind" that is based on fundamental functions of social animals (mating, defense or avoidance of predators, and social affiliation). Ekman and his colleagues claim that basic emotions are universal in the sense that facial expressions are transculturally recognized; however, cultural variation may exist in display rules, that is, when and how it is appropriate to express emotion. Own-culture emotional expressions are better understood relative to other-culture emotional expressions.[120] Other scholars argue that emotions are culture-specific and their universality consists in having "common" emotions as inter-translatable names.

The very idea of universal human rights is relatively new in history, not to speak of the recognition of the concept. Of course, this in itself is not fatal to universality. The legalism and individualism of human rights can be seen as a specific form that protects emotionally driven (universal) common moral intuitions that existed all the time. Certain common elements of human nature have generated proto-human rights, but the conceptual apparatus of their expression and the means of protection (for example custom, habitude) were different. Within the limits of the civilization and of what the socioeconomic conditions of human action have allowed, moral intuitions did play a functionally similar role to what they do in the age of rights; only that the psychological inclinations of respect of the other resulted in different norms. One could find functional equivalents of human rights in culture and civilization, but without the unconditional individualism and legal binding force that characterizes human rights today. Understandably so, as the society was incomparably simpler, and the available (limited) means of protection of the person were different and primarily nonjudicial. Already the ancient Romans and Greeks abhorred and condemned (even in law) certain forms of cruelty; and cruelty was perhaps condemned by other otherwise "savage" cultures, although many of their acts seem today prescribed, mandatory cruelty. The proto-human rights of the moral, religious, and legal concerns that reflected select humanistic emotional needs (emotions that dictate some kind of respect of the other) were construed within the community, and their validity was based exactly on this localness. In particular, given the relative isolation of most of these cultures, there was no interest in conceiving the emotionally driven concerns in terms of universality. However, to the extent that there was interaction among local cultures, elements of a concept of transcendent humanity emerged because of the practical needs of interaction. The Greeks had elaborate rules to protect alien visitors. On the other hand, early Christianity offered a vision of universality and even the community of all humans, but in a transcendental sense; attempts to apply it in worldly affairs, the recognition of equality of all bodies containing equal souls, repeatedly failed.

Cultural localists object to the possibility of universality in human rights. In their view, proto-human rights are not conclusive, and the similarities across cultures do not prove that common psychological needs are at work with a potential universal commonality of rights. Culturally shaped differences in cognition make "universal" human rights different for different people. Irrespective of a common human neural and psychological structure (for example, all healthy people try to avoid unwanted pain and reduce fear, or to protect their group-based identity), humans are primarily social, and they live in the society of like-minded people.[121] Like-mindedness is local. Understandably, universal human rights were irrelevant in earlier ages. Even where there is intense interaction among cultures, this "ethnocentric" localism (being bound by ingroup concerns) remains a fundamental psychological (and socioeconomic) barrier to universalism. Localization is the predicament of homo sapiens. All people condemn humiliation, but humiliation means different things to different people; likewise, there is agreement on freedom of religion, but one's own religion implies specific freedoms. Instead of imperative universalism, we have an empty overlap and agreement without content.

On the basis of evolutionary localism, reinforced by systematic abuses committed in the guise of universalism, universalism appears shallow, and even fake in the eyes of many of its contemporary critics: "The universal-one-species dogma has, of course, been the dogma of colonialism in all its guises—that everybody everywhere could be the same if they were given the same cultural opportunities, the ones *we* have on offer. Beneath the compassionate surface of this ancient dogma lies the belief that Homo sapiens everywhere is capable of reading and appreciating what others in the human species have in mind."[122]

No doubt, the empirical data, as if they were commissioned to prove Locke, indicate that universal human rights are not particularly attractive to people, even to those people who otherwise support their own minorities,[123] at least not all the time. In terms of international human rights, there are very strong empirical disagreements as to which rights have universal value. Even where there is some formal agreement across cultures, there are bitter debates about content (is FGM inhuman and contrary to equality? does respect of women's dignity mean that they should live a secluded life at home, etc.?) and meaning (what exactly amounts to torture? is disrespectful or hateful speech protected, etc.?)

Other relativists argue that the very occurrence of repeated mass-scale human rights violations would indicate that there is nothing universal in human rights, and therefore normative claims that are based on universalism cannot be legitimately made. After all, if facts may turn into norms, facts may instead also deny the possibility of norms. Universal human rights claims such as "the innocent shall not be harmed" cannot be reconciled with facts like the overwhelming presence of repeated genocide.[124] It would follow that what we have is human rights *talk* only, i.e. an imperialist pretense to universal language usage, a peculiarity of modern political interaction of the last sixty years. In fact, human rights and constitutionalism became a powerful industry that tries to counter the closed mindset of emotional ethnocentrism by generating a self-referential ideology. Universal human rights exist as institutional facts which require "continued collective acceptance or recognition of the validity of the assigned function."[125]

The universalistic extension of human rights—a far from unilinear process—may reflect sentiments about the conspecific, but it can be understood only in light of specific political needs that demand or make use of the extension possibilities. In escalating social conflicts, there is always a need to widen the support base and increase mobilization. Such mobilization, especially in the transformative revolutions and wars of independence, is impossible without granting an identity to those members of society who hitherto could not identify themselves with others on equal grounds. Members of the French Third Estate who insisted on being equal in all regards with those above them unleashed general equality in order to pull themselves up. The promise of equality was inevitably a promise of political participation in the political community of the new nation on equal terms, even if full equality—and especially the extension of its definition to include voting rights in the late eighteenth century—endangered the political survival of the revolutionary elite and even that of privileged personal liberty.

The bourgeois loved equality for all, as long as they had enough subordinates, but equality became sour once there was no one below their ranks. Where certain groups of humans are successfully framed as different, equality is easily curtailed. Such compartmentalization can resist the challenge of empathy for quite a while. Legal and constitutional provisions contributed to the containment of empathy. But once unleashed, feelings of equal identity and compassion could not be contained; they seized the day, and they have remained active since.

The idea of equality gained popularity and influence, beginning in the second half of the nineteenth century. This happened for a number of reasons, such as the need for a larger qualified work force and army, political competition among the elite, which in turn resulted in a search for new social support—as in the case of Bismarck, who extended electoral rights and introduced welfare rights for like reasons—, new techniques that allowed the elites to retain power even in mass democracies, still following the hard-to-resist logic of the original promise of equality. With the emergence of (liberal) nationalism, equality received a new emotional source in collective identity; identity projects have been changed and moved toward localism, but because of the continuity with the earlier self-definitions, universal human rights remained part of the social self-definition. National identity-related rights (for example self-government) were often presented as universal rights, and human rights became a fact of national cultural (civilizational) supremacy. They were used for purposes of an imperialist imposition of a specific reading of universal values ("white man's burden," "*mission civilisatrice*").

Then, however, there emerged a new source of intellectual resistance to equality: science. The way scientific knowledge is interpreted and applied (even at the level of research orientation) is culturally and organizationally shaped in accordance with deep-seated psychological needs. Theories of racism and of the crowd were quite successful in advocating differential treatment of people; later on, scientific theories of class struggle would have a similar impact on the denial of equality and human rights.[126] It was quite easy (and convenient) to deny empathy toward other races or criminals, where such denial was corroborated by the science of the day; the treatment of scientifically different people could depart from standards of equal dignity. Justice Holmes had no difficulty relying on scientific theories of hereditary moral depravity in upholding compulsory sterilization.[127] This was certainly not human rights-generating, although the language of rights and obligations remained in (ab)use. It was the right and the duty of the Nation to purify itself.

The mass violation of human rights by the Nazis which was supported by perverted science indicates the poverty of constitutional sentiments which remain the toy of other human passions and of cognitive framing that dehumanizes. Nazi ideology relied on race theory as a source of a collective right of the German nation and the Aryan race to cleanse itself. But this is an abuse of the concept of right; the abuse originated in the transposition of the individuality of rights to mythical collectives. The relative ease of not feeling empathy, even in face-to-face encounters with mass extermination, shows the power of dehumanization and the fundamental need to reinforce human rights through law in order to be able to resist not only passions and base interests but even the most ordinary and otherwise "respectable" emotions.

After World War II a return to the universalism of human rights was felt to be the appropriate belief and mechanism that provides protection both mentally and institutionally. The troubled history of putting groups outside the human community explains the strong desire and even the intellectual and emotional need for universalism that contributed to the spreading of the naturalist concept of universalism of human rights. But human rights do not correspond to specific emotions, and they seem to be rather contingent. The various historical references to universalism served peculiar identity needs.

One possible answer to these empirical objections to universalism is that many of the empirical differences and deviations are simply departures from what human nature dictates, or that they are applications of natural emotional dictates in the wrong circumstances. Alternatively, one could say that notwithstanding actual differences, a minimal agreement about certain norms that apply in a community of all humans is possible on nonemotional grounds. Even with imaginary communities in mind, interacting cultures are capable of generating mutually accepted norms for actual communities, without the need of shared moral intuitions or emotional similarities rooted in human nature. But what is the postal address of such all-encompassing humanity? It is true that a community of risks (collective vulnerability) will strengthen the acceptance of risk-diminishing universal humanitarian norms across group boundaries: it is a common fate and future, and not a shared evolutionary past, that creates the human community with a universal potential.[128] After all, it was shared collective vulnerability—a globally shared experience that seemed to capture the mind for a while after World War II—that inspired the Universal Declaration. The Universal Declaration relies on the recognition that a denial of human dignity—for example, racism—may destroy all humans irrespective of their community . . . Dignity is a clearly universalistic concept. This is what remains (to be respected) whatever happens to humans. This is the psychologically, even emotionally, desperate answer to a situation of total exclusion from society, to a situation where the individual is denied all membership, except what pertains to those who wait together to be massacred. Dignity-based human rights mean an inclusion into the (hypothetical and universal) moral community; it is an ultimate act of moral inclusion into an otherwise immoral body politic. Dignity is a-psychological, it does not reflect emotional or other psychological needs, and it does not provide identity, except the fundamental one of equality of the self, irrespective of status, that is, irrespective of everything social. (Fundamental psychological needs like living without fear and humiliation make dignity emotionally credible and attractive, but they always run the risk of localism, that is, ingroup applicability.)

The dignity-based universal human rights concept of modern international human rights law relies on an implicit sociology and an implicit anthropology. "The implicit sociology views all biological and historical differentiations among men as either downright unreal or essentially irrelevant. The implicit anthropology locates the real self over and beyond all these differentiations."[129] The self-fulfilling prophecy of a universal community that enables the acceptance of human rights as universals is a reality, that is, a self-reinforcing belief. Moreover, there are institutional facts that reinforce and realize the belief: for example, states engage in human rights-enforcing interaction. Nevertheless, most people continue, and in their social situation have to continue, to think and feel in ingroup/outgroup terms. For this reason, even if the increasingly shared belief of universal human rights were to create a universal community as reality, that reality could be undone.

There is a second, more empiricist and emotivist approach to universalism. In a different reading of Kant, human rights were perhaps the reflection of specific moral intuitions. It is argued that even if empirically these intuitions are not shared by all humans, they have moral and intellectual supremacy over other customs or concepts of rights in the sense of being *universalizable:* they are compatible with similar rights of all other people, which is not true of other intuitive claims or customs. Such universalizable human rights may expect that, in favorable conditions (that is, in the absence of the oppression coming from ignorance, fanaticism, tribal parochialism, and despotic power), they will be met with emotional resonance or even identification. Unfortunately, they do not always command such actual emotional support, (which, of course, does not rule out the legitimacy of the project). For example, it is most likely that all "abstract" women (like all humans) would prefer "not being subjected to male power" to "being in submission." However, there is no abstract woman in the world and therefore the relativist will argue that human rights and constitutionalism "would not be welcomed by most of those who live under their traditional customs, even if these are as cruel and oppressive as the Indian caste system. . . ." Real women who actually find their pride and identity in a system that institutionalizes male supremacy will not find the nonsubmission option psychologically attractive. To which Judith Shklar, the hero of this book, answered: "Unless and until we can offer the injured and insulted victims of most of the world's traditional as well as revolutionary governments a genuine and practicable alternative to their present condition, we have no way of knowing whether they really enjoy their chains."[130]

To conclude: the moral intuitions that animate human rights, even if they were universal, are too weak and nonspecific to generate human rights universally, nor do they have enough motivational power to make human rights claims valid in all local cultures, even if they might have some universal presence across cultures. The intuitions that support human rights easily fall prey to identity concerns and locally determined cultural framing. Emotional and anthropological communalities or even universals do not command universal human rights-based solutions. This is not to say, however, that human rights are only a local cultural product with negative consequences for many societies.

The lack of a strong (naturalist) emotivist support for human rights universality does not mean that human rights can be simply disregarded as irrelevant in a cultural relativist mood. This book is not about normative propositions, but it remains within the boundaries of description to say that the universal human rights position is logically superior to the cultural relativist one, in the sense that its universalizable prescriptions make no abstract moral person worse off, while local ethnocentric systems promote arrangements which are simply unacceptable unless one first accepts local cultural conventions, which most often assume submission and do not care about external effects. The only logical position against human rights is radical ethnocentrism: a denial that outgroups are relevant, that humans are similar, and should therefore be treated (at the level of biological reality) as equals. Hence the relevance of human universality. In order to say that what applies within the group is not applicable outside and, more important, that what happens outside the group is irrelevant for ingroup relations, ethnocentrism has to deny that humans are one single species. In the logic of ethnocentrism, there cannot be cross-cultural agreement on cruelty; therefore whatever is found cruel outside the culture will be irrelevant for the culture. Eating people is abhorrent and therefore morally wrong, but outsiders do not count as they are not "people." Empirical interaction may exist, but this is pure happenstance without normative relevance. However, once it is factually proven that humans are fundamentally the same species, the ethnocentric position will turn into a matter of logical contradiction, a purely pragmatist concern of survival.

While a universalist theory of human rights might be superior to relativism, and hence have additional convincing power, this intellectual supremacy is insufficient to make it accepted. In the absence of actual cross-cultural acceptance of human rights norms they lose some of their normative power within an otherwise rights-favoring culture or state: one cannot argue that a certain claim is just on grounds of its empirically observed universality. The normalcy of the disregard undermines the norm. What helps the acceptance of human rights is actual or quasi-habitual observance: here human rights will be endorsed with the normative power of the factual. If a claim is universally accepted all over the world, it is difficult to disregard it: a universal acceptance has strong intuitive normative power as it has characteristics of natural facts. The universalist argument of the naturalist goes like this: look, this human right is accepted all over the world; if is accepted then this is what follows from human nature; those who disregard it will disregard universal laws; they are acting against human nature, and therefore in an unnatural way.

Given the uncertainty surrounding human rights, they are in need of constant legitimation, hence the constant reference to their universality against a hostile empiricity: for this reason, human rights are institutionalized internationally as a self-justifying mechanism, whereby a universalist ideology, relying on and remindful of a moment of naked universal vulnerability (the shared disasters of World War II), is institutionally reinforced. But with other, more mundane interests in growing demand, strong countertendencies emerged, denying the legitimacy of the universalist argument. Human rights are articulated in contest, challenged and in conflict with regimes that neglect human rights, and in the competition of different human rights regimes. And it is in this competitive context where emotions, moral intuitions, and public sentiments play such an important role—not necessarily supportive of human rights. Consider, for example, how culturally reinforced disgust resists equality, and humiliation resists respect. Nonetheless, it is in the competitive interaction of public sentiments and different cultures that a chance for at least some cross-cultural human rights emerges. The state-bound local cultures have to interact in the global world, in new power relations, where traditional power disparities seem to diminish. Because of the needs of interaction, the different cultural practices not only confront each other, but they have to find commonalities; in fact they have to negotiate commonalities. Once commonalities are recognized, they may act as a new frame of reference: once cruelty and torture are recognized as bad and only their borders are debated, this offers a new frame for domestic disputes. If torture is now, in view of universality, domestically condemned as a matter of principle, it will be more difficult to sustain a police practice that requires that persons taken into custody shall be beaten up first thing, as soon as feasible. Beating of people who cannot resist and who did nothing to deserve the beating is abhorrent, and people can be sensitive to the resulting suffering (which might await them too). Empathy and fear might mobilize public sentiment against such practices—once there is a cognitive and even a legal frame to rely upon.

The international power equations may undermine human rights as we know them, as human rights-based hegemonistic political aspirations are subdued in favor of the recognition of the power of states which profess anti-human rights politics. The negotiated commonality will be vested with the convenient label of contemporary international human rights. The fact that the negotiation of the legal frame takes place at the level of intergovernmental interaction is not encouraging, because having access to new markets makes human rights vulnerable. Human rights violations in the commercial partner's country are often less important to governments than to their morally principled citizens, and even morally principled citizens may prefer cheap goods and job opportunities to their moral intuitions. One can only hope that the moral intuitions which are culturally streamlined and often hijacked in the prevailing cognitive frames will remain open for new frames of reference, frames which are closer to what enables human rights, frames which are less ethnocentric. However, this remains a hope only, and some developments indicate that the intergovernmental interaction is working in a different way, primarily because of the strength of identity-related emotions.[131]

7. Frozen and Changing Public Sentiment and the Living Constitution

So far, we have considered public sentiments primarily as active or constitutive elements in the context of the making of modern constitutionalism in the eighteenth century. It is historically more common, however, that the public sentiment confirms the choices of the constitution only *ex post*. Given that most of the fundamental constitutional choices of the formative era, except the issue of slavery, did not depart in principle from moral intuitions, there was little morally troubling in accepting the inherited scheme elsewhere or later. There was enough ex post facto support for sustaining the myth of a shared constitutional sentiment.

Once formulated under the pressure of public sentiments, constitutions became emotionally sustainable without much emotional involvement. Once fundamental rights are relatively well established in the culture, at least as venerable conventions, the violation of convention-based rights may generate less vivid emotional reactions than it otherwise would. The reaction will not refer to immorality and sin, while at the same time departure from convention is also a less frightening, painful, or otherwise emotionally disturbing matter.

Constitutions single out and privilege moral concerns and values and turn them into habits: a rule or a principle will be respected and emotionally endorsed as convention, without raising the issue of moral appropriateness. In prevailing moral theories, there is a clear dividing line between moral judgments, whatever they are, and other normative positions, primarily convention- or habit-based decisions. Michael Oakeshott, however, considered both forms part of morality. He distinguished between a type of morality that is "a reflective application of a moral criterion" and one which is "a habit of affection and behaviour."[132]

The legitimacy of conventions originates in their formal constitutional recognition. The moral underpinnings, the impact of constitutional sentiments are hidden behind the constitution's technicalities and the conventionality of its prescriptions. The moral element might continue to operate, but conventions are considered exemplary and binding because they are part of the social order and not for their moral truth. Habits (conventionality) help in the acceptance of public sentiments inculcated into the constitution, even where these were initially met with resistance by groups which did not share the sentiment. People acquiesce because of a strong status quo bias: the world is believed to be just, and any given arrangement that does not make one's life chances worse off is fundamentally acceptable, irrespective of the nature of the arrangement.[133] What really matters (even for a Rousseauist theory) is that the public sentiment emotionally echoes what is expressed in the constitution and some fundamental laws, and thus authorship is not a must. Moreover, over time, people are born into the constitutional culture. They will find the constitutional arrangement as granted and given, a kind of "natural order" without which order cannot exist for everyday life, even if increasing multiculturalism challenges these assumptions. The law that incorporates moral sentiments operates within a folk psychology "that focuses upon the expectable and/or the usual in the human condition. It endows these with legitimacy or authority. . . ."[134] Constitutional prescriptions, as conventions, represent conventional wisdom. The status quo protective power of conventional wisdom results from the emotional and cognitive costs of challenging conventions, not to mention the costs of social condemnation. Privileged emotions prevail in conventions as normal and habitual. "Folk psychology is invested in canonicality. It focuses upon the expectable and/or the usual in the human condition. It endows these with legitimacy or authority."[135] Because of habits, people will be less likely to be seduced into passionate action against the one-sided morality behind the convention. To challenge what is made accepted by authority as a fundamental belief or even part of the established order of things results in indignation, outrage, gut feelings, and rejection by others. Attacking previously unchallenged beliefs calls for indignation that will result in ostracism and other sanctions.[136]

Turning moral intuitions and ethical principles into conventions and simple rules of behavior is advantageous in terms of mental economies: moral judgments are time-consuming, uncertain, and emotionally often burdensome. The (emotional) costs of conventional decision-making are minimized; rule application is swift and effortless. People follow institutionally established default rules simply because they are not "programmed" to stand out and break ranks.[137]

Norms as conventions are learned, but the effect of the learning varies. After all, conventions differ from morality in terms of emotional reactions emerging at the breaking of the respective rule. Conventional rules as such do not generate feelings of guilt at their breach. This would make such rules vulnerable to moral indignation. Moral intuitions are turned into legal conventions; the direction can be reversed, even if there are ways to sustain strong support for conventions. Acceptance is a normative force and not only because of inertia.[138] "By publicly advertising and affirming the rightness of the new convention, the law can increase the perception that an existing illegal practice is unjust, add momentum to private indignation, and provide a focal point. . . ."[139] Moreover, conventions, or at least some, have moral reserve and backing: the closer the convention is to being harmed, the stronger the emotional support it may generate.

Where morality exists outside the institutions, the very institutions can be challenged in the name of the moral norm. Even a socially prevalent moral judgment remains open to contestation. The transposition of moral intuitions into legal-institutional conventions has the fundamental advantage of reducing the possibility of such contestation. It is for this reason that human rights, which at an initial stage were affirmed as satisfying moral ideals, need legal transposition: human rights violations must be found through legitimate formal procedures, which means institutionalization.[140]

As mentioned above, constitutions, by transposing the original public sentiments into convention and habit, diminish the original emotional resonance that has supported them. It is through the transformation into public authoritative sentiments, and from there into decisional heuristics and elementary institutional designs, that emotional dictates and moral intuitions are accepted in the legal and social practice, and in constitutional sentiment. Of course, such acceptance occurs only after emotionally salient experiences have already changed contrary sentiments. Emotions cannot be changed by argument, at least not directly, but the emotion of other people, amplified and communicated in public sentiments providing an emotional point of reference, can work miracles.

Moral judgment will be replaced by convention, even if the latter would sometimes contradict the dictates of the then prevailing (typical, common) moral judgment. Of course where constitutional choice dares to counter prevailing public sentiment, it runs a considerable risk, but it might be successful, especially by generating additional emotional support or if it can deny the moral relevance of the imposed rule. Even deontologically wrong acts may be construed, and successfully represented, as simply prohibited, resulting in acceptance of habits inhibiting the questioning of the underlying rules and assumptions, especially where such challenge imposes serious emotional costs and the community sanctions the challenge. The breach of conventional rules (be they moral or immoral) will be judged by the subjects as moral violations only if they "are considered wrong regardless of local conventions, if the violations are disgusting"[141] or generate other strong negative feelings. However, the very display of such negative feelings is made difficult: the conventionality of a constitutional arrangement means that it will be simply inappropriate to raise the issue of moral rightness or wrongness, except in exceptional circumstances where the uncertain constitutional value or principle does not give guidance against intensive emotions.

Conventions acquire further regulatory power once they become part of group identity as symbols.[142] Many Americans stand up for free speech because they consider it part of their American identity. The emotion felt at an attack of identity symbols is often described as anger, and the reason offered by the subject is based on some presumption of symbolic harm: there is a feeling of harming the (imaginary) community in the national symbol context.[143] Conventions may even become associated with taboo. Breaking taboo typically generates disgust. This is the case, for example, with desecrations of flags and other national/tribal symbols, where disgust is felt at the norm violation.

In the somewhat static perspective that we have applied so far, public sentiments and emotions were relevant in the shaping of classic constitutions and modern constitutionalism; however, it looks as if, once the constitutions have consolidated public sentiments, these seem to have been at least partly replaced with conventions which sustain the constitutional arrangements with the power of habit. Constitutional law seems to be institutionally sanitized against public sentiments and the role of emotions is relevant only in the sense of contributing to law observance. But public sentiments do not go away, and continue their conflicts. New sentiments emerging in the public try to capture public institutions. Changes in public sentiment (including changes in the social management of emotions) will result in restructuring rights, their meaning and scope, and in particular the circle of rights holders. The circle of rights holders—people whose suffering and sentiment matters—has been extended in the last two hundred years, but not without important reversals.

Once in place, the constitution, and the legal institutions that it has unleashed with all the power of constraint and habit, consolidate and police public sentiment. However, public sentiments, only some among them temporarily privileged and reinforced, follow their own dynamics. Norbert Elias's magisterial study of shifting thresholds of embarrassment describes the change of the emotional culture as a slow but often centrally initiated and enforced process. Some would object that "we come prepared to be disgusted by certain things and not others."[144] There is an element of truth here, but the object of disgust can certainly be culturally and legally transposed and moved away, as the example of homosexuality indicates. Nineteenth-century Victorians would have certainly fainted at the sight of contemporary "gross indecency," a Victorian gut crime that is legally protected today. The authoritative and centralized positions on morality offered by constitutional law integrate, expedite, but also conflict with the slower and diffuse shaping and changing of emotion display rules.

Learned disgust at homosexuality will be reinforced by false assumptions about its harmful nature, which is contained in prejudice like "homosexuals transmit disease, are child molesters, undermine public morality, and invite divine wrath." Constitutional law is reluctant to block such emotional processes, except in a few instances where it is inclined to create or reinforce taboos (prohibition of torture, slavery, right to life) claiming their absoluteness. Constitutional moral choices remain rather malleable emotionally even after the constitutional decision of codifying specific emotional claims. The changing emotional culture, and public sentiments with it, continue to compete and destabilize the status quo according to emotional dictates, while judicially created rules try to reify them by turning them into a petrified system of hierarchical ordering through constitutional precedents, only to be undone by other judges and other constitutional actors. This ordering and the attitudes related to it influence the cognitive frame. While the constitutional cognitive frames may to a great extent reset or channel the emerging public sentiment, to the extent that lawyers can afford to disregard or at least deny the relevance of such sentiments in emergency situations, emotions can mobilize for a dramatic reinterpretation of the meaning of the constitutional text by shifting cognitive frames.[145]

It follows that public sentiments continue to participate in the shaping of constitutional law even after the enactment of the constitution. The long-term support for existing constitutions comes from habit and custom, but this is not to say that public sentiment cannot be revitalized, changing the shape of the constitution and constitutional politics. Emotions remain an important source of social change after institutionalization: intense emotions may in a sudden cascade change public opinion, break down prevailing perception, and mobilize large-scale action. For example, the My Lai atrocities generated disgust and shame to the extent that most Americans abandoned their support to the Vietnam War, which led to the troop withdrawal. As part of the transformation, American free speech law has constitutionalized very aggressive emotionally disturbing displays of emotion.[146]

It should be added that, notwithstanding its interest in a uniform and unequivocal order, the constitutional system is designed to remain to some extent open to adjustment to emotional changes. Even emotionally endorsed constitutional norms allow for departure. The constitution is full of open texture and value statements. The consolidation of moral sentiments in constitutional values offers the advantage of flexibility: it reflects a position of the public sentiment prevailing at incorporation, but it also allows adaptation to changes in public sentiment. For example, the commitment that the free exercise of religion is to be respected leaves too much undetermined to qualify as a rule: one cannot write laws or decide disputes regarding free exercise on this textual basis without additional considerations of a given situation, as it is not obvious per se that one or another specific religious manifestation enters the protected sphere of free exercise.

Compared to the highly abstract formulations like "things cause damage" that characterize modern private and criminal law, the texture of constitutional law is less clinically sanitized in regard to emotions. Constitutional categories such as "life," "marriage," or "dignity" do not rule out emotional claims *a priori*: in constitutional discourse emotions as arguments are not *ab ovo* discredited, though some negative impacts of "passion" are precluded. Constitutional law in its textual and political openness recognizes that courts cannot fall out with prevailing sentiments. However, it sets limits and frames for change. It designates institutions of authoritative change, like courts and parliaments—and public sentiment is certainly not one of the privileged actors or sources in this design.

The open texture of the constitution may accommodate new, emotionally shaped cognitive frames which enable emerging intuitions to prevail. Stem cell research and its application, which many people found disgusting or repulsive,[147] seeing it as an act resembling playing God, may be socially reclassified thanks to changes in public sentiment. In the new cognitive environment new intuitions will apply.

The incorporation of the dictates of the emerging public sentiments takes place in (public law) legislation, referenda, through judicial interpretation, and by constitutional amendment. Substantive constitutional amendment for adaptive purposes is exceptional; it applies when there is no other way to accommodate public sentiment or a new sociopolitical equilibrium. Neither politicians nor judges can stand out for long in disregard of the public sentiment of the day, especially in a democracy. Consider the recent changes in privacy rights due to an emotionally charged social reinterpretation of disgust in regard to abortion and gay rights in many Western societies. Once gays were able to reduce disgust and anti-gay bias that relied on that disgust, antisodomy laws became unsustainable. On the other hand, resistance of public sentiments may undo accepted international human rights law in countries where primary feelings of disgust, reinforced by religious identity, militate against the legalization of sodomy.

Legislators and courts may successfully disregard some emotionally widely supported and culturally prevailing moral judgments in favor of other sentiments that fit into their legal ideology. But after initial negative reactions and resistance, constitutional sentiments may change; as a result a new constitutional solution will become conventional. Consider the abolition of the death penalty in countries like France. At least since the French Revolution, there have been people like Robespierre, Victor Hugo, and Albert Camus who were disgusted at public execution well before the law abolished capital punishment. On the other hand, public execution combined with torture used to enjoy great popularity, indicating that there was nothing naturally repulsive in it, or that repulsiveness is attractive. How could one explain otherwise the great *applause* of the crowd that greeted the public dismemberment of Damiens in 1757, when he was drawn and quartered for hours by horses for the attempted assassination of Louis XV?

The death penalty was decreed abolished by French legislation at a time (1981) when a considerable majority of French people were still in favor of executions. The demand for capital punishment was probably more a matter of public opinion than of public sentiment; public sentiment was divided and attitudes were torn apart by inconsistency. The inconsistency that results in cognitive dissonance is this: bodily harm, including that of the death penalty, is emotionally rejected as fearful, while revenge is wished for. Empathy is felt both for the executed and for his victim, depending on how one structures the situation. Where public sentiment is uncertain, the cognitive changes resulting from legal change (legal *fiat*) are sufficient to create a new convention, and the habit of convention leads to an inhibition that makes the conflict-ridden emotion powerless. In Western Europe, where capital punishment was abolished in many countries a long time ago, the majority is now against capital punishment as many people find it emotionally troubling (disgusting).

As always, a word of caution is needed: public sentiments are to be placed in a wider context. The constitutional influence of public sentiments does not entail that sentiments alone can explain constitutional change. Abolition of slavery was not the result of a sudden compassion epidemic: it was the result of long-term processes (including those changing economic competition), with group dynamics that speeded up certain cognitive changes which then enabled the reframing of slaves as being humans. Citizens' power has been further increased where they coordinated their actions through predictable rights-based constitutional law.

Once again, the process of change is one of conflict between various groups animated by distinct public sentiments, or at least of a conflict between new public sentiments and those which were frozen into the constitution. All prevailing cultural regulatory systems are in constant struggle with what Alison Jaggar has, in a social constructivist mood, called "outlaw emotions," that is, emotional responses that do not follow or support the values and norms we have been taught to accept. Outlaw emotions "challenge dominant perceptions of what is going on (for example, that welfare payments are a generous gift to the undeserving) and dominant values (for example, the unequal worth of poor persons' lives or their lack of entitlement to basic necessities)."[148]

Outlaw emotions operate to a great extent within culturally and even legally set rules of conflict and change. This is not some rough and tumble catch wrestling conflict. "While a culture must contain a set of norms, it must also contain a set of interpretive procedures for rendering departures from those norms meaningful in terms of established patterns of belief."[149] Outlaw emotions have to fight an uphill battle, particularly in law. In the determination of fundamental human rights, judges may be inclined to find emotional considerations improper, perhaps referring to the rationalistic legal maxim that our system stands for a government of laws, not men. As if laws were not made by human sentiments!

The fear of sentiments is partly attributable to the professional fear of personal caprice in judicial decision. Justice Frankfurter warned that the consideration of emotions will turn into "enforcing . . . private view[s] rather than that consensus of society's opinion, which for purposes of due process, is the standard enjoined by the Constitution."[150] Recognizing that judicial emotions are legitimate would depart from the canonical sources of law, even if endorsed by public sentiments. After all, judges are expected to be faithful to a specifically designated body of norms which is identified with "law" according to one or another authoritative theory of legal sources. For example, at one point in time, most Justices of the Supreme Court expressly rejected that emotions such as sympathy with applicants' suffering can be a source of influence in legal decision-making. In the few cases where judges openly take into consideration public sentiments, in particular sentiments of public morality, most judges support select social feelings as being *the* authoritative public sentiment of the community, although the expressions of public sentiment are multilayered. There is no place for outlaw emotions here.

Legal ideology, the institutional supervision of judicial activities, and accountability for decisions in the form of quashing judgments and verdicts are conditioned against allowing personal feelings to guide decisions. Law is, at least *prima facie*, sheltered against considering emotional considerations and consequences.[151] As Justice Blackmun stated, courts tend to purport "to be the dispassionate oracle of the law, unmoved by 'natural sympathy.'" This consideration prevailed paradigmatically in Joshua DeShaney's case. Because of the beating he received from his father, little Joshua suffered brain damage so severe that he was confined for the rest of his life to an institution for the retarded. In this case, the Supreme Court (a majority of six Justices) admitted: "Judges and lawyers, like other humans, are moved by natural sympathy in a case like this."[152] But before yielding to that impulse the Court considered the conflicting consequences of the application of the due process clause and found that the clause was not violated by the inaction of the State to intervene. Professor Tribe objected that it is wrong to construe the meaning of the Constitution without allowing sympathy to work: emotions are legitimate in the interpretation of the text.[153]

Justice Blackmun's much criticized compassion-driven approach did not intend to replace the law with a personal intuition-based concept of good and bad. His clearly emotional position was a matter of interpretation, an approach that Justice Blackmun found appropriate and applicable only in the context of open texture and unclear precedents. The majority in *DeShaney* did not deny that they were touched by sympathy; they just found it a personal matter of no relevance in the application of the due process clause. But what about the emotional reaction of most people in such a case? It is quite likely that most people would feel sympathy with poor Joshua (and find the Supreme Court decision heartless). Is this consideration irrelevant in constitutional (judicial) choice? What happens when public sentiments, consistently and intensively voiced, stand up for Joshua's compensation? Are the underlying moral intuitions—reflected in public sentiments—to be taken into consideration? Consider the very strong involvement of divided public sentiments in the Terry Schiavo case (and many other cases concerning euthanasia and abortion).[154] There are very convincing arguments that law should follow its own path and disregard the conflicting message of public sentiments. However, for a descriptive theory of constitutional sentiments, what matters is to what extent the judicial handling of public sentiments stands up to its own promises of "disregard."

Law and judges seem ready to promote an apparently false folk psychology, in order to disengage from emotions. Jury decisions are normatively described as being moral judgments without emotions. As Justice Sandra O'Connor stated, a jury decision is "a moral inquiry into the culpability of the defendant, and not an emotional response to the mitigating evidence."[155] But moral inquiries do trigger moral intuitions and behind them moral emotions. Such judicially exhorted exclusion of emotions cannot hold water; there is no moral judgment separate from emotions. The result of the denial of emotions is that emotions (including anger), even if suppressed, may still prevail in the sanitized and "rationalized" law where otherwise existing external control is nonexistent, as emotions are not disclosed and cannot be negotiated, or criticized. Emotion control by exclusion and denial is self-deceptive and rather inefficient. But intellectual and institutional constraints may matter in a different way. It may be the case that people, when they are systematically confronted, at least in highly controlled legal settings such as courtrooms, with sanctions for display of emotions and with arguments that would mobilize alternative emotional processes, will shift categorization and allow propositional logic to operate. Moral emotions may dictate a certain "just" outcome, but it is more difficult for emotions to dictate legal decisions against organizationally controlled admissibility criteria. All the compassion for a plaintiff will fail to do its work if she submitted her application late.

Time and again the author and the reader have to be reminded not to be carried away by sentimentalist naturalism. The fundamental emotional contribution to moral judgment is countered by (not always rational) institutional control, which of course mobilizes other emotions of the subject. Constitutional law is concerned to a great extent with institutional design intended to supervise emotions, to filter the impact of moral intuitions. Very often the constitutional concerns are more about the proper role of the court in matters of morals, the identity of the highest court or of the judge, and the framing of the problems, and less about moral intuitions.

Moral intuitions are most directly relevant in body-related cases, even where they are denied. In constitutional adjudication problems are framed in a way that diminishes the impact of carnality: the confrontation with the body and its suffering is absent or at least the suffering or cruelty are mediated and distant. The very nature of the procedure in courts of last resort, its formalism, the diminished opportunity to *look* at actual personal suffering, reduce empathy. Besides, as a result of their socialization, judges are often convinced that they have to refute emotions; they may have a whole strategy, including mutual control, to force cognitive confrontation with emotions.

The prevailing discontent with, and mistrust of, public sentiments in judicially created constitutional law are partly misplaced. Personal feelings, like sympathy with one of the parties or her sufferings, are distinct, at least in principle, from public sentiments, which are social facts. The personal sentiments are relevant and legitimate as emotional reflections on the public sentiment. The fear of personal judicial emotionalism does not preclude the consideration of public sentiments as a normative source. Interestingly, not even Justice Frankfurter rejected the relevance of external social facts like public opinion in the interpretation of the Constitution, though public opinion is more "objective," more identifiable, and in theory, more the result of rational discourse rather than public sentiment.

The antisentimentalist judicial position is just one element of the process of the ongoing selective incorporation of public sentiments into the constitution of the day, where personal emotions of judges and situation-bound emotional influences do play a role. The false absolutism of the judicially enforced exile of emotions may result in arbitrariness and defeatist exceptionalism. Sometimes scholars get the impression "that the Court will draw decisive conclusions about viewpoint-basis grounded in little more than a gut feeling about a regulation."[156]

The real issue is whether private emotions and public sentiments as specific social facts not explicitly recognized in legal texts can be taken into consideration in constitutional adjudication. Irrespective of the normative answer, public sentiments are in fact transported into constitutional decisions that reformulate the constitution. Public sentiment and folk psychology assumptions about the emotional nature of humans come into play in the judicial development of constitutional law, even if it remains a legally contested and quasi-illegitimate matter. In the constitutional discourse of politics and in constitutional adjudication, emotions as arguments are underprivileged but not discredited by definition, though some negative emotional impacts of "passion" are precluded.

These sentiments lie outside the psyche of judges, and within limits, even judicial doctrines recognize them as something external and objective like principles of justice "rooted in the traditions and conscience of our people." While personal outrage is considered illegitimate for adjudication, it is held acceptable if replaced by a sense that a matter is "repugnant to the conscience of mankind."[157]

We have a whole jurisprudence that relies on "evolving standards of decency." These evolving standards of decency are to be measured by "objective factors to the maximum possible extent."[158] Nevertheless, they remain within the realm of public sentiment: "where a punishment is not excessive and serves a valid legislative purpose, it still may be invalid if popular sentiment abhors it." It was recognized that a constitutional court cannot be blind to changes in public sentiments and the judicial debate is more about what constitutes such change. As far as the Supreme Court is concerned, these public sentiments are often found in legal sources like state legislation, sentencing decisions of juries and experts, and, most controversially, public opinion as reflected in public opinion research.[159] It is a specific authoritative selection that makes the sentiment constitutionally relevant, but it is still a public (though distorted) sentiment that matters.

As the above reference to "repugnancy to the conscience" indicates, public sentiments as a summary of changing emotions have been actually recognized as proper judicial points of reference. True, the conscience of mankind seems a very general, even metaphorical reference, a catchall judicial abstraction, and for some it looks as if parochial sentiments were attributed the power and truth of universalism. However, such a sentimental abstraction is perhaps inevitable given the genuine concerns about an admittedly emotional reading of the Constitution and constitutional precedents.

Public sentiment as corroborated in legislation can overcome long-established intuition-related prejudice,[160] as well as fundamental moral intuitions. From the perspective of liberty, this overcoming of other sentiments remains a highly problematic possibility of emotional influence: disgust can be artificially mobilized, even "invented" against certain people or acts, even if only certain physical facts (sliminess, excrement, bestiality) generate disgust without social and cultural intervention. (In view of children's lack of disgust before being taught, even this assertion is problematic.)

The difficulty is that the textual constitutional arrangements and the tenor of judicial precedents which attributes normative force to the status quo suggest a single moral understanding of the constitution, a single position of uniform public sentiments. Conservative judges and constitution-drafters confidently close their eyes to competing assumptions of morality and proper sentiments and stand up for taken-for-granted single emotional settings with the naïve conviction that they represent the "general feelings of society." National and religious symbols were, for example, protected as a matter of course, representing an uncontested community of feelings; those who did not share these feelings were ostracized or even excluded as traitors from the national or legal community. Liberal legal ideology has gradually recognized that feelings are not a given fact; sometimes such acknowledgment draws normative conclusions from the incompleteness of public sentiment. "Recognizing that the right to differ is the centerpiece of our First Amendment freedoms, a government cannot mandate by fiat a feeling of unity in its citizens. Therefore, that very same government cannot carve out a symbol of unity and prescribe a set of approved messages to be associated with that symbol when it cannot mandate the status or feeling the symbol purports to represent."[161]

With increasing social and cultural pluralism and with the relative inclusiveness of the welfare state, differences in public sentiment became at least tolerated, and the pressure to constitutionalize or legislate a single prevailing moral sentiment has diminished. With the advent of constitutional tolerance and social relativism, dominant and authoritative feelings and practices are losing their normative grip. Or perhaps with more social heterogeneity, and secularism, and on the other hand with less zeal, such moral endeavors become more costly and lose their sex appeal.

8. Caveat: Anticonstitutional Sentiments

To avoid misunderstandings, let me stress that the above account of the constitutional incorporation of public sentiments and moral intuitions is not a plea for writing emotions into the law. I have no normative propositions to offer and would be reluctant to endorse the position that law should allow a most flexible operation of heuristics[162] and moral intuitions. True, there are good reasons to take public sentiments into constitutional consideration, but such incorporation, besides being partial and hence controversial, is not "objectively" good, and therefore cannot be compelling. The presence of emotionalism and the respect of (conflicting) moral intuitions in constitutional law do not safeguard legitimacy. Quite the contrary, while the influence of constitutional sentiments is a fact of life, constitutional emotionalism can be detrimental to the very values that build constitutionalism, to those institutions which once were selected under the pressure of specific public sentiments of liberty.

When I argue that constitutional arrangements reflect moral intuitions to some extent, I don't mean that specific intuitions must be reflected in constitutional law. Emotions are not unconditionally good; in fact, they have destructive potential. A democratic theory that accepts the legitimacy of emotional dictates in the name of genuine popular support disregards the epistemological preconditions of democratic theory.

A public morality based on moral intuitions and consisting of feelings has already been criticized by John Stuart Mill. The moral intuition is solipsist in the sense that "[there is a guiding feeling] in each person's mind that everybody should be required to act as he, and those with whom he sympathizes, would like them to act." Mill claimed that unreflected moral intuitivism governs people: no public reason is given. This empirical state of affairs led to tyrannical and irrational consequences. However, he admits that strong emotions are hard to overcome: "Whenever the sentiment of the majority is still genuine and intense, it is found to have abated little of its claim to be obeyed."[163]

Democratic institutions reflect public sentiment in a selective way and set in motion a mechanism to regulate emotions, especially their display. By institutionalizing democratic legislation, constitutions create channels that bring into legislation poorly filtered public sentiments. Representatives are expected to mediate all sorts of emotions. In modern politics, it has become accepted to refer to the feelings of people. From the perspective of liberty, a poorly filtered reflection of emotions is a highly problematic influence: for example, disgust can be artificially mobilized, even "invented" against certain people, groups, or acts.

The constitutional values selected by liberal constitutionalism reflect specific, historically determined choices. Under different circumstances, different emotions could be and have been selected as constitutional, reflecting a morality that would not count as moral by Kantian, utilitarian, or contemporary human rights standards. Depending on cognitive frames, the same emotions that formed constitutional sentiments will generate inhuman moral judgments. In other instances, humanitarian moral emotions, even if constitutionally endorsed, will fail to resist evil, partly because of psychophysical numbing and partly because of the operation of emotion-blocking cognitive frames. Consider the Nazi legal system, where disgust, contempt, and hatred were mobilized against racially inferior groups who were blamed for all sorts of difficulties. The Nazis had some difficulty taking up the burden of inhumanity, but they found psychologically sufficient reasons (motivation) for doing so in the name of protecting the supreme race. Obligations (loyalty) to race, nation, and the Führer replaced fundamental rights.[164] Changes in perception and problem presentation allowed otherwise repressed emotions to prevail. These cognitive changes channeled existing public sentiments, which did not support constitutional values in the minds of a growing number of Germans. They became overwhelmed by destructive emotions after World War I and during the Great Depression in particular.

The fact that emotions have served evolutionary fit (adaptation) does not prove their appropriateness in our industrialized cultural environment. Perhaps harm avoidance as a natural stimulus of moral emotions might serve for a thin universal morality that all humans could accept in principle as it is acceptable to all, as long as we were the ones to be harmed. However, the theoretical acceptability of certain moral intuitions cannot guarantee that this moral emotion will inevitably guide us, nor would it be a good enough moral command in practical terms. Most emotions are unreliable. What feels good, like hating the criminal, is neither socially constructive (except in the Durkheimian sense of finding a community-building scapegoat), nor morally convincing.[165]

The constitutional institutional design, emotionally influenced as it may be, contains elements to counter emotionalism, and in particular to restrict democratic emotionalism and related populism. A number of constitutional arrangements insulate public institutions from the emotional public process.

Insulation means that social decisions are taken by experts instead of being decided by politically accountable institutions or directly by the people. These theoretically neutral experts deliberate on the basis of allegedly professional considerations. Nonaccountable judges and "neutral powers" (independent regulatory agencies) are designed to be less exposed to the influence of public sentiment, enabling them to counter emotionalism.

Constitutionalism contains emotion management choices that point in the direction of diminished aggression and suffering, although such emotion management may cause frustration, as in the case of frustrating feelings of vengeance or when protection against outbursts of disgust is denied, etc. "The denial of the desire for vengeance may well be analogous to the Victorian denial of sexual desire, and a similar psychological price must be paid for it."[166] At the price of individual frustration and resulting disorderly discontent, law may produce a relatively efficient social control of "destructive" emotions. (Unfortunately, no emotion is perfectly constructive or destructive; even suspect emotions like disgust or envy have positive functions, where positivity is culture-dependent.) There is no guarantee that the selected (preferred, "domesticated") emotions and constitutional sentiments will remain in the service of humanism and humanity. The construction of public sentiments is never-ending, and there is no guarantee that the individual liberty-enhancing arrangement cherished in constitutional sentiments will not be replaced by a communitarian system of a sort where love or hatred, inclusion or exclusion will be the norm, where duties are not bound by rights and self-determination, and choices are replaced by an all-encompassing welfarism of do-good. Constitutionalist arrangements reflect the experience of abuse of government power, and they provide some institutional protection against such abuse; they may as well reinforce a constitutionalist public sentiment. However, there is nothing talismanic in the emotional structures of humans that would guarantee respect of these constitutionalist structures.[167] Notwithstanding constitutional design, the human psyche and brain remain open for moral intuitions of hatred and vengeance that we fear today. There is enough "natural" emotional foundation for tyranny. Therefore we have to cultivate our garden of constitutionalist institutions vigilantly to counter these emotional drives that are waiting to find political endorsement in forthcoming historical contingencies.

2

A SENTIMENTAL *DÉCLARATION* OF THE RIGHTS OF MAN

True principles, rationally determined . . .

Human thought cannot be described without emotions. Social institutions like a constitution—and constitutionalism—are emotionally determined. To justify this assertion, we have to look at the role of the emotions in the creation of fundamental constitutional institutions. From the standpoint of modern constitutionalism, the defining documents are the American Constitution and the Declaration of the Rights of Man and of the Citizen from 1789 (henceforth "Declaration"). Anyone discussing constitutionalism or human rights on the continent in the last two hundred years will have used the grammar of the Declaration, the French Constitution of 1791, or the American Constitution of 1787. Subsequent constitutional history has largely been a history of intelligently grounded (and occasionally mechanical) borrowing from French sources, and sometimes from American ones. The focus of the present analysis will be the French Declaration.

The legal scholar's response to the constitutional sentiment thesis is that the Declaration's influence was limited to the debates surrounding the 1791 Constitution: namely, reference was made to it in debates on electoral rights, the equality of Protestants and Jews, and the liberation of the slaves. The Declaration, together with the Constitution of 1791, lost all validity as texts applicable in the law within a few months.[1]

Perhaps the legal scholar is interested in the creation of the Declaration merely as he considers its history to be an interpretive aid; for him what is important is the final fact of the Declaration, namely its text; as a source of law, it has not existed for nearly two hundred years. The act of the document's creation is over once the text exists. From this point on, what counts is its supposed meaning. The force behind the text—and its magic, so to speak—are rarely even noticed, and then only as somewhat dubious interpretive aids.

As a text, the Declaration is, like any text, an attempt at closure. Still, the Declaration is not simply the closure of a debate between principles, but also part of an identity-forging process crucial to modernity. Its subject: who counts as a human being and citizen and why, as well as the ramifications of this in France and beyond. Through a description of "man" and his place in political life, the National Constituent Assembly marks its own place within the political constitutional system. Hence despite the legal scholar's efforts to portray the Declaration as a mere text susceptible to analytical interpretation and appealing to Reason alone, it remains in fact an unending source of emotionally rich meaning.

I will provide historical evidence that the solutions gathered in the Declaration are concentrated and emotionally dictated responses to intense collective emotions. This is how the genius of France managed in just a few hours to distill experience it had hardly been able to gain over centuries.[2] The rights of man gather up the strands of emotion. The making of the Declaration is an act of emotional bootstrapping: constitutional sentiments gain power through their very capacity for emotional resonance. After all, for astute and sensitive contemporary observers like Edmund Burke, this was "a revolution in sentiments, manners, and moral opinions."[3] But this reading clearly contradicts the prevailing understanding of the Declaration and of the rights it declares. In this perception the Declaration and the 1791 Constitution were the fateful poisoned fruits of abstract enlightened speculation. In light of the eminent role of sentimentalism in Enlightenment, this characterization is one-sided and reproduces counterrevolutionary accusations. The rights of man were conceived in terms of sentiments, and the denial of this emotional component is part of the rationalist strategy that prevailed in legal and political ideology.

1. The "Noble Intoxication"

1.a. The Search for Identity

National bankruptcy is a stern taskmaster.

With the Royal Council's resolution of July 5, 1788, Louis XVI called a meeting of the Estates-General to be held on May 5, 1789. Fifteen months later, on October 5, 1789, and five months after the assembly convened, His Majesty was compelled by the pressure of revolutionary crowds to approve the basic principles and some institutions of modern constitutionalism.

These fundamental institutions were not invented by the Revolution. Indeed, they pop up as early as the convening process itself, with many of them consolidating as early as then. The decree on the election to the Estates-General considers a representation of the entire nation as desirable.[4] The problem was not any lack of vision regarding fundamental constitutional institutions, but rather the uncertainty that surrounded them. The *cahiers de doléances* (lists of grievances) reveal isolated impulses redolent of the conflicting dominant principles of the eighteenth century. On one thing the delegates agree: "Our constituents want regeneration of the state. But some expected that it would come about through simple reform of abuses. . . . Others have looked upon the existing social regime as so defective that they demanded a new constitution, and with the exception of the monarchical government and forms, which every Frenchman cherishes and respects in his heart . . . they have given you all the powers necessary to create a constitution."[5] There is no resolution, much less any unified conception, of the makeup of the constitution or the nature of renewal.

Most of the *cahiers* and the overwhelming majority of the constituents agree that the nation makes the laws. For many delegates nation and King were one. For others the nation makes laws with the approval of the King, who as one of the representatives of the nation is the trustee of executive power; he participates in the legislative process with the "other" representative of the nation that is the assembly. It is a shared belief that the representatives of power are responsible for their actions. The delegates also agree on the question of the sanctity of property.

According to the King's program of May 5, 1789, included in constitutional "renewal" are freedom of the press, reform of criminal law that provides security of rights to the individual, and public education allowing access to the achievements of the Enlightenment. There is naturally no place for extremism (*exagération*). Anyone whose profession is useful to society is an honorable member of one large family; given this, even equality before the law is a possibility. Necker proposes the "equal distribution of taxes," probably as part of a general sharing of the public burden.[6]

All this is heart-warming for constitutionalism, but what really matters then and there is what affects self-esteem. The Third Estate, by the will of the King and to the astonishment of the delegates, is compelled to sit in a separate chamber. The representatives of the people cannot vote individually, though *within* the Estate selection was in theory made according to the principle of proportional representation, meaning that the number of delegates for each constituency would be roughly proportionate to the number of voters. The concept of representation is still incompletely formed. It was not clear that the vote in the chambers will be individually (*par tête*) or that each estate chamber would have one vote. The mandate is binding, and most of the voting bodies are privileged medieval corporations. In addition to constitutional renewal, credentials of the delegates of the Third Estate call for a nullification of innumerable feudal privileges. This was the "electoral" idea of lawyers working on their own election, and was doubtless attractive to their constituents.

Necessary above all for the acceptance of the modern constitution was an identity for those who would take it up. Before the constitution comes the creation of subjects who are entitled to make and accept it. Delegates must decide in the first place who they are and what their charge is: they must create themselves. The representatives of the Third Estate are taken up with this self-definition. Self-definition equals the making of the self. The constitution becomes a function of social identity, and collective identity has a psychological and emotional component. Before determining the identity of the nation, the representatives' own identity crisis must first be resolved.[7]

Sieyès's pamphlet from early 1789 identifies the Third Estate with the nation itself. It would be the task of the representatives to demonstrate, through the words of the future constitution and its institutions, that they were the true representatives of this nation, in contrast to the nobles, who were marked as a hostile caste. The nation, in turn, would come into existence through representation, and through constitutional recognition. At the beginning of 1789, Sieyès writes of a nation, but the nation of the Third Estate is at this point just a prospect. Relying on universal and abstract principles, he forms conclusions in the name of "the recent science of societal condition." Yet "the triumph of the pamphlet lies less in this learned reflection than in what it offers, with brilliant simplicity, to anti-aristocratic passion. Public opinion is burying the years of contempt under a rediscovered equality, which has once more become the natural principle of every society. . . . It celebrates . . . its own deliverance from social humiliation. . . . He touched the *fiercest passion* of public opinion."[8] The biggest motivating force of the Third Estate and of the whole Revolution was an emotion: the hatred of nobility.

The French Revolution, characterized by many as an inflexible implementation of abstract truths and a tyranny of intellectual constructs, was in fact a matter of the liberation of passions. In this, primal emotions unleashed shape individual and community identity. The citizen possessed of a new self-image can become a subject of the Constitution. Can the nobles be greater than the rest? What is the place of the citizens of Paris, *sans* (silk) *culottes*? Is the slave a human being—or the Jew? Without running these questions through a mind shaped by fundamental emotions and passions, they will find no answer. The new institutions shaped by those who assembled in the summer of 1789, who took part in clubs, demonstrations, calumnious pamphlet-making, uprisings, and arson, cannot be understood if we ignore the emotions that shaped their identity.

The identity of the French was originally an estate-related status tied to a feudal order. We should speak of the heart filled with inferiority as we may hardly speak of the cold rationality of the marketplace in a country where successful tax farmers would give the bulk of their wealth just to see their children married into the nobility—a nobility whose most important characteristic was a sense of superiority. "In France, distinctions of status form the keenest subject of interest; obviously, no one objects to the pecuniary advantages to be gained, but it is the tactful handling of ideas of superiority which satisfies the most active feeling."[9] Against this background, more than one of the original drafts for a declaration of rights set before the Constituent Assembly mentions dignity to all as one of the most fundamental human rights (as does Sieyès). The right to honor, affecting all as it does, is an understandable object of the catalogue of desires formulated in the hearts of the masses of the Third Estate.

Of all the history-making assemblies, it was the National Constituent Assembly that stands out for its disinterestedness. For many of its participants, the will of their constituents was the prime consideration even in August of 1789. In such circumstances, where self-interest is heroically neglected, personal emotions have an even more powerful effect. One need only compare this chaotic crowd of the Assembly to the dynamics of the small isolated group that met in Philadelphia two years earlier to draw up a constitution. The American founding fathers may have shown a greater unity of thought and common interests, yet still they could not ignore the particular, local interests of their states. Though they may be united by common fears, the concrete solutions they forge are born of intelligent commercial give-and-take. There is little for trade in 1789.

Let us survey the well-known fateful events from the standpoint of group dynamics. The delegates arrive to Paris on their own, isolated, with only their few provincial acquaintances to rely on. Groups of uncertain shape spring up over a few weeks, primarily according to political or personal sympathies. In the lonely crowd of the Constituent Assembly, mass psychosis is hardly "resisted" and reason had little chance to dictate. Meeting first on May 6, 1789, in the chamber designated for them, members of the Third Estate await the representatives of the other estates—to no avail. They are at a loss primarily because they do not know what their body might be. In the days that follow, the subject of debate is this: Has the Assembly in fact been formed? The answer depends on whose assembly we are talking about. Was it in the capacity of the nation—and its representatives—that they expected the others to join them, or should they accept their uncertain role to be determined by the King? Emboldened by the gradual accretion of clerical and noble representatives, the Third Estate's chamber constituted itself a National Assembly on June 17, with the practical demand that their Assembly be granted the right of voting on taxes. On June 20, they found the debating chamber locked to them; then came the Tennis Court Oath. With one dissenting vote they proclaim their intention to prepare a constitution and hold themselves to be indissoluble toward this goal. Here we have the seeds of a new identity:

where the representatives are, there lies the nation. They choose the term "nation," proposed by Mirabeau, in contrast to "people;" the term shapes discourse not as an unyielding blueprint but metaphorically, a feature of vocabulary.[10] Clearly, these men are galvanized by an outrage of wounded dignity, and fear: sources quoted by Taine suggest that insufficiently radical representatives had been unremittingly threatened for weeks by street mobs and those in the gallery. Not a day passed without a high priest or aristocrat being greeted by a hail of stones. Only the gallery is incorruptible, writes Desmoulins: these faceless shouts are the people, the creators of the Constitution. As Taine sees it, every major decision of 1789 was tipped toward the well-known outcome by outside pressure. Reading Taine, one can have no doubt that the majority and the King were driven to accept the solutions offered in the Constitution by threats to their lives from hungry—or power-hungry—wild, blinded hoodlums.[11]

On June 23, the King receives the delegates of the Estates-General, but the representatives from the National Assembly are left to wait in the rain for an hour. Surrounding them is a conspicuously numerous and threatening military honor guard. The King declares the National Assembly to be unconstitutional; after that he retires. In the chaos that follows, Mirabeau, stirring the public outrage, makes reference to their charge given by 25 million Frenchmen, not to be overlooked. He is interrupted by the Marquis de Brézé, representing the King: "Gentlemen, you have heard the King's intentions!" "Go and tell your master that we are here by the will of the people, and nothing but bayonets shall drive us out," thunders Mirabeau in reply. Following this, "a deathly silence reigned in the chamber," writes the parliamentary scribe. In the minutes that follow, the inviolability of the representatives is declared. Another new constitutional institution is born.[12]

On June 27, the King ultimately accedes to the incorporation of the Estates into the National Assembly. Simon Schama attributes this to the fear of the aristocrats and the court.[13] After apparently accomplishing nothing for eight weeks, the Assembly has by now rejected an English parliamentary structure preserving feudal distinctions and accepted the exclusive right of the nation's representatives to draw up a constitution. They are now past the initial debate between unbounded people's sovereignty and constitutionality—so much so, that Mirabeau is now describing people's sovereignty as dangerous if unbalanced by the King's veto.[14]

Between June 30 and July 14, debate still remains centered on the binding force of the mandates. Much time is lost in long vetting procedures.[15] Given that the sessions are open to the public—and owing to the horrible acoustics of the place—only a few full-throated speakers can count on being heard. But proceedings are immediately put into print; thousands of flyers debate every position thereby accessible. Taking shape only slowly is a parliamentary procedure that would leave most preparatory debates on the constitution to randomly assembled committees of varying composition.

While the representatives are absorbed primarily in consolidating the legal standing of the Third Estate, disturbances erupt around the country. News of these events reaches the chamber of the Assembly.[16] The source of greatest concern is the increasing concentration of troops, and later the violence involved in the storming of the Bastille. While the Paris uprising of July 14 does preserve the Constituent Assembly, still daily reports of violence interfere with its operations.

On July 7, the first constitutional preparatory committee is formed. Two days later, between news reports of military threat and the daily public disturbances, Mounier submits the constitutional committee's report, in the light of which it is not yet clear what would be considered a constitution.[17] One thing is certain: arguments for the renewal of an old, now-collapsed order, and the return to an uncorrupted historical constitution—a position that was popular a week earlier—are now untenable. While the institution of the monarchy is beyond question, a monarchy in which spheres of power overlap and mix is not something that can be built on. The relationship between the King and the nation must be clearly defined. As the minutes put it, executive power would be the sphere of the King, but local self-governments (municipalities) would also participate in executive power in their own right, while the legislative process would function entirely separately from these. Legislation could only occur once a constitution was implemented—in other words, the troubles of compatriots would have to wait some time for relief. A good constitution would have to be grounded in the rights of men; such rights would serve as the basic principles for the foundation of society. The basic principles formulated in a brief, simple, and precise declaration could not, however, be philosophical ones: if abstract elements are not associated with direct consequences and guaranteed solutions, this opens the door for disturbing speculation.

But even this minimal agenda proves unsuccessful. Until the moment the Declaration is ratified, the representatives spend their time debating the necessity of a declaration on rights at all—and if it is necessary, whether it should appear before the Constitution or after it. Those opposed to the idea say that the hitherto-enslaved people would become delirious at such an abstract declaration, with anarchy being the result—in contrast to America, a nation of free people. Mindful of the public disturbances, Lally-Tollendal proposes first and foremost the creation of laws fostering societal stability; the declaration of rights would only agitate the society of the hungry.[18]

However, it would seem that by July 11, advocacy for the priority of a constitution and a declaration of rights has held the upper hand, thanks to Lafayette's motion. In Lafayette's view, the object of the declaration of rights is to calm the populace through the force of intelligence. As he sees it, the power to influence the sentiments is the future Declaration's primary positive force. In Lafayette's conception, the Declaration "can speak to sentiments that nature has engraved in the heart of all." In order to love freedom, a nation need only know it. Moral feelings are a given; all that remains for reason is simply to stir them. This releases a flood of drafts on rights of man. By mid-August, some 30 drafts for a declaration have come before the Constituent Assembly, each containing the "uncontested truth" about the rights of man.[19]

The ongoing debate about the constitution becomes interwoven with daily reports of mass disturbances and threatening troop movements. When the King dismisses Necker, or when actions are taken against the disturbances, the Assembly finds itself repeatedly tempted by an alternative arrangement of the branches of power: the notion that they themselves might act as an executive authority. They debate specific questions concerning the distribution of power. Does the King possess unlimited authority to dismiss ministers? Should not the threatened Constituent Assembly assume executive powers—take an active role, even in the direct maintenance of order?[20] After July 14, given the lack of any true executive authority or obedient military, the Constituent Assembly is particularly tempted to do the governing itself. To this end, it creates two executive committees at the end of July, whose spheres of authority prepare the way for the later Jacobin Committee of Public Safety. The Comité des Rapports deliberated on the legitimacy of local authorities (as created by local revolutions), while the Comité des Recherches exercised the legal authority of a secret police, including the opening of letters and house search without a warrant, and long-term detentions.[21]

The delegates of the Constituent could not isolate themselves from the passions of the crowds even when there was no screaming from the gallery, or from directly before the president's podium. On July 14 the Paris crowd came to the defense of the Assembly, but the way the "protection" was granted was deeply troubling. When word was received that Governor Launay's head had been stuck on a pike, the parliamentary minutes of July 15 recorded that the Constituent Assembly, deeply disturbed by the public crises, was unable to pursue its normal planned procedure.[22] We must imagine hungry crowds regularly stirred up by the likes of Desmoulins or Marat—or Loustalot, the editor of *Révolutions de Paris*: when the young journalist reaches the point in his account of the slaughter of Bertier de Sauvigny, intendant of Paris, where the man's still-beating heart is ripped out of his poor breast, he remarks, "Despots and ministers, what terrible lessons! . . . Frenchmen you exterminate tyrants! Your hatred is revolting, frightful . . . but you will, at last, be free."[23]

On July 20, once again a blood-curdling report, this time from Poissy, of the attempted lynching of a grain merchant in the presence of a delegation from the Constituent Assembly. Lally-Tollendal speaks of flowing streams of blood, and would settle the masses not just with a declaration, but with the civil guard as well. On July 23, the delegates listen to a naturalist account of the lynching of former minister Foulon and his brother-in-law. To those expressing horror, Barnave retorts, "Gentlemen, they wish to soften you with the report of bloodshed yesterday in Paris. Was this blood they have shed so pure?"[24]

Day by day speakers denounce conspiracies. Reports of arrests of representatives on the highways, and aristocrats in disguise making an escape are daily staples. Should the Constituent take up these individual cases? There are reports of suspicious letters opened locally. The majority view holds that postal secrecy is *still* inviolable. "A people wanting to become free cannot employ the methods of tyranny."[25] Here the choice of values is still determined by a *rejection* of the Monarchy's tyrannical solutions. Delegates Volney and Rawbell—in a foreshadowing of the views that would dominate the days of the *Terreur*—would not grant rights to the enemy.

How can there be time to deal with matters of state—with the Constitution? Finally, on July 27, the second constitutional preparatory committee (the "Committee of Eight") submits its summary of desires for constitutional renewal appearing in the *cahiers*. The Committee agrees with the necessity of the Declaration of Rights, though some members of the Constituent Assembly dispute this again. They fear, among other things, that a proclamation of rights would only create expectations that could not be fulfilled, and thus only heighten the passion of the crowds. Driven by a lack of confidence in the King—and in each other—the majority ultimately supports the Declaration. There is need to "remind" authority, and themselves, of rights. The necessity of rights originates from a genuine need for self-restraint.

"For the rest, they discuss nothing in their Assembly. One large half of the time is spent in hallooing and bawling."[26] On July 28, to relieve the turbulence in the Constituent, standing orders are adopted; with the clarification of the principles concerning a majority resolution, a new constitutional institution is born. The procedural rules are violated the very next day.

The delegates are restless. They would like to accelerate the process of formulating a constitution, but vote down a motion to restrict speaking time. Debate is now centered again on the necessity of a declaration of rights. Fear of the crowds steers them toward caution. If rights are bestowed on a people accustomed to barbarity and superstition and unfamiliar with the application of reason, the result will be confusion and further disturbance. "The fear, voiced explicitly by the comte de Sinety, was that by talking only about rights men would be encouraged to display their 'natural leaning' towards egoism, to the detriment of their fellows and of society as a whole."[27]

Meanwhile, Clermont-Tonnerre speaks of popular rage that threatens his 80-year-old uncle, and requests for him a letter of protection from the Constituent. Within moments, two further such requests are received.[28] Then some of the conspiracy theorists come to the floor, frightening one another with mobs of looters and the idea that "the enemy" is playing the city of Brest into the hands of the English. The Great Fear that runs like an epidemic throughout France has reached even the Constituent Assembly.

On August 3, speaking for the report committee, Salomon informs of burning castles. The law is no longer backed by compulsive force. "It is a war of poor against rich," cries an unidentified representative, calling for consistent punishment. Delegate Malouet proposes the creation of local employment and aid bureaus to soothe passions: if humanitarianism and a sense of justice are not enough to bring us hurrying to the aid of the sufferers, then we are bound to it by the interest of liberty.[29] The Constituent still fails clearly to see its place in the structure of the branches of power. Some feel that threatening events call for action—in other words, that the legislative body should assume an executive function. Others caution against legislators' interfering in judges' authority or taking over rights from the executive.

In the morning session of August 4, amid greater than usual shouting, the proposed declaration of obligations is voted down 570 to 433. The proposal was pushed for primarily by the priesthood, partly due to religious considerations and partly to settle the masses. At the second session, which began at eight o'clock in the evening, the drafting committee presented its proposal, consistent with its previous views, about "the security of the Kingdom:"

"Considering the fear filling people's minds that has been created by the disturbances and violence—events that lead to the most extreme assaults against the most enshrined right to property—[we proclaim] that until the Assembly determines otherwise, the earlier laws [in effect] shall be valid and applied, and present taxes are to be paid as they have been in the past."[30]

But before a vote can be taken on the proposal, the Club Breton goes into action.[31] The Vicomte de Noilles is the first to request the floor, and argues that the uprising cannot be impeded without knowledge of the reasons underlying it. No constitution, he says, can alleviate this problem. The people must be soothed. All should pay taxes proportional to their income, while personal services and seigneurial rights affecting the land should be abolished. Communities could supplant feudal privileges. This was easy for Lafayette's brother-in-law to propose, as he had nothing but debts. But the Duke d'Aiguillon, one of France's richest men, joins him: "There is no one who must not groan over the scenes of horror which France at this moment exhibits."[32] The uprising may be criminal, but its participants are victims of persecution. The feudal privileges must be redeemed, he concludes. There follows a proposal that considers the precise value of said redemption, since ultimately feudal privilege is just property—and property is inviolable.

Dupont de Nemours attempts once again to convince the Assembly to respond to the rioters with the punishments required by criminal law, but emotion wins the day over legalism. The doubters are jeered. Nobles, priests, and delegates of cities one after another vie to renounce their estate's privileges. At about two in the morning, feudalism is largely finished. The fundamental societal and legal questions of the new constitution have been decided, though the practicalities remain contested for a long time.

Although they will return to the Declaration only later (on August 14), the night of August 4 saw an irrevocable decision on equality under the law, and on equal opportunity for access to public office; the rule of law takes shape, as does the unicameral parliament. Even if Mounier (advocate of the English-type constitution) fails to notice it, with the abolition of status-related privileges there is no longer any prospect of a bicameral legislative body that would offer separate representation for the aristocracy.[33] The abolishment of the sale of public offices and venality is simultaneously a laying of the groundwork for new public administration and free administration of justice.

On this night, no one points to primal, abstract principles; it is emotions that guide decisions. Acceptance of such a new order demanded renunciation of ancient habits, which is inconceivable without the passionate involvement of the emotions. Duquesnoy, in his diary entry of August 5, notes that "if some brilliant man familiar with the French spirit should draw up a constitution to make us happy, he should pass it on, drunk and enthusiastic, without weighing it, to the National Assembly, [even if] the exaltation of its brilliance would take us past our goal."[34] For his part, Mirabeau writes of the night of August 4: "High-ranking lords called for the abolition of feudalism . . ., which inspired universal expressions of approval. Mere high-sounding expressions received their daily undeniable tribute of patriotic emotions. Anyone familiar with large assemblies, with the dramatic emotions that stir these up, with the heady power of applause, with the honor of personal selflessness, and finally with that noble intoxication that accompanies the outpouring of generosity—anyone who considers all these elements coming together will regard everything that appeared exceptional at this session as being in fact merely pedestrian. The National Assembly was caught in an electric whirlwind, with emotions following hard on one another's heels."[35]

At two in the morning, the monarchist Lally-Tollendal proposes, successfully, that they recognize the King as the restorer of French liberty. At this point he declares that his "heart is drunk, gentlemen, with your patriotism." Intoxication, enchantment, and a screaming gallery—but fear is still the determining force behind the motions drawn up.[36] Fear dictates the objective and makes it acceptable. No one dares to challenge the frenzy of the competition of magnanimous light-heartedness.

Some historians are inclined to see a conspiracy in the actions of members of the Club Breton, a tactical seizing of the opportunity. But even if it were true, would equality of rights and the Declaration be merely the dictate of conspiratorial reason, the adoption of some abstract schema? According to French historian François Furet, other considerations were at play in the decision of the Club Breton: they did not wish to rely on the army—the sole body capable of setting down a violent uprising—since this would only reinforce the King's power. "But in the eyes of 'patriotic' deputies the first proposal [that is, to use force] had the disadvantage of committing the Assembly to a course of repression and thus restoring force to what remained royal troops while at the same time putting the king in the position of arbiter."[37] They may not even have been confident that armed action would be successful, since troops were defecting en masse to the side of the uprising not only in Paris but in the countryside as well.

Lord Acton blamed royal panic for the success of the Club Breton: the court would have encouraged the nobles to save themselves through an immediate resignation of their rights.[38] In a similar spirit, the Marquis de Ferrières on August 7 encourages his noble constituents in the countryside to abandon all resistance, since "it is impossible to stand up to the tide of the revolution." According to the Marquis, the impossibility of resistance—as well as the force of patriotism itself—led to the nullification of feudal rights on August 4.

To summarize, then: some wish for the events in process, while the majority think there is no hope for resistance when "150 castles are in flames." "Severed heads were frightfully instructive."[39] The effects of the threat, though, are perceptible in everyone; the difference lies in the way emotions are processed. The members of the Club Breton, after weighing the situation, propose a solution that even suits their own material interests: they emphasize the principle of redemption of feudal rights, as a form of property. Still, the arguments used by the Bretons on the night of August 4 do not come from a cool head. It is emotions they stir up, emotions they yield to, and emotions to which they appeal. They cite inflammatory, sometimes invented examples of feudal injustice: "The first speaker who intended to pay tribute to the public interest expressed only what everybody already felt. There was need neither for discourse nor for oratory to have accepted what the great majority of the mandates of the nation has already accepted."[40]

Reason is heard only during the debate on the redemption of feudal privileges. All regarded feudal rights as a form of property. The King had only stated the obvious when speaking of these privileges in this light back on June 23.

The new institutions come to be accepted through a collective interaction, a group-dynamic process in which collective feelings (including the hysteria based on fear) play a determining role. The Bretons who were led by their *hatred* of the nobility developed a plan. They were a minority, making up at most 10 percent of those in attendance, but they acted in a concerted fashion to create the illusion of a majority, and proved capable of achieving a fundamental change in mood within the diffuse, anxious crowd of delegates. Mass psychosis, experienced as altruism by those competing to offer their resignations of privileges, can be explained as a cascade effect—compare Mirabeau's "electric whirlwind." This is what makes the resistance of the legalists, the proponents of legal retribution, who would apply force against the rioters, hopeless in the face of passions.

Fear paired with the exaltation of self-sacrifice. Some were influenced by a bad conscience, others by rage. Other emotions, like envy and hatred, also played a role. When Bishop Lubersac proposes the renunciation of hunting rights, the Duke of Châtelet, a passionate hunter, mumbles that "the bishop deprives us of hunting; I will take away his tithes."[41] Of course, passions did not sweep away absolutely all influence of reason; considerations based on interest remained. While talk proceeds on the resignation of privileges of municipalities and the provinces, most of the Breton delegates oppose this step, pointing to their mandate. The delegate from Languedoc stresses that "it is acknowledged that the ancient rights are grounded in the most solid foundation, as far as their privileges are concerned."[42]

The workings of fear and mass psychosis are followed by a period of sobering up. But during the August 5–12 debate on formulating the text on the abolition of feudal privileges, the light of day was not enough to nullify the work of the emotions of the first night.[43] Sieyès would place expenses for the maintenance of the Church on the shoulders of the landowners, since tithing had hitherto been applied to land ownership. Landowner-delegates remain recalcitrant. "You want to be free, yet you are unable to be just!" rumbles the outraged Abbé. The response he received to this was that since all take part in worship, it is the responsibility of the state to find a common source for funds to ensure its provision.[44] Lanjunais and Sieyès might argue against the redemption of tithes and certain feudal privileges, but the nobility insists on the redemption scheme that is most advantageous for them. The priesthood puts itself under the protection of the nation, for lack of anything better—in other words, it expects its funding to come from the budget. This is another frame of thought for the French constitutional system with lasting influence: within the church/state relationship, the dependency of the Church is institutionalized de facto, in the spirit of Gallicanism.[45]

To sum up: what will later become the "basic principles of the Constitution" are already present in the resolutions of August 4. These pillars of modern constitutionalism are legal equality, general and proportionate taxation, administration of justice without financial charge, access to public office, and the rule of law. There is no place for corporations. The individualism that was imagined and so longed-for in the various drafts of a declaration has now become fact. "What came into being was a modern society of individuals."[46] Not only is the Declaration of the Rights of Man now possible, but its primary elements have in fact already been ratified. The abolition of the feudal system, argues Mirabeau, is part of the constituent process, since there is no need to seek the King's approval for the abolitionist decrees involved.[47]

Other constitutional questions too will be decided before the appearance of the Declaration—or at least constitutional solutions will become possible. The King loses his monopoly on armed forces, since the oath the soldiers take, as specified in the August resolutions, binds them to the nation, and a nation is more than the King. The separation of church and state is formulated side by side with support for the Church. A definition of property in the modern sense appears here too. Property is protected by compensation for full value, something that remains part of constitutional law to this day. Property as a right to full compensation was an uncontested idea, at least among the delegates, and they might have omitted the right to property from the Declaration altogether, as indeed almost came to pass, without losing sight of this fundamental principle and right. The shared experience of August 4 only reinforced the inviolability of property. Those who did not share in that common experience, especially that of owning something—even through their delegates—were members of the Fourth Estate (the subsequent *Enragée*), who continued to destroy property.

These, then, were the events and emotions that, through the normative force of common experience, appeared as self-evident facts during the drafting of the Declaration that began a week after the night of the Great Fear. Every element that ended up in the Declaration could now become obvious in the wake of August 4; before all else, this included the notion that the French were free individuals equal before the law. Yet the things that were so evident after August 4 had found no majority support before that date. The melting pot of shared emotions produced a shared conception of social justice, while previous proposals pertaining to the rights of man had been "obvious" only to their proponents.

1.b. The Declaration

The breakthrough of August 4 did not much alter the state of the country. Disturbances persisted. Feudal obligations that were still technically in effect continued to be ignored—true, no one was forcing this issue, given the news of the August 4 resolutions, and the lack of a military force. While the Assembly had regained its legitimacy in its own eyes, since it had broken free of its complicity with feudal tyranny, the country nonetheless remained unsettled. In the State Treasury, it was not collections piling up, but rather unaccepted letters of debt. Steps needed to be taken, and it was seeming increasingly important that whatever those steps were, they should reinforce the power of the Assembly. An expedient ratification of the Declaration would not only settle the popular rage, but also allow the Assembly to consolidate its position vis-à-vis the King, since that body would be the exclusive creator of the Declaration and the Constitution.[48] As a result, the Declaration not only takes up the rights of man but also responds to questions of what constitutes the right to govern—and primarily *who* is entitled to lead the state. The Declaration describes the kind of person who must be respected within the Constitution, and decides the question of who shall make up the Constituent National Assembly and whom this body is to represent.

The suspended drafting session of August 4 resumes on the 12th of the month. We should recall that 56 requested the floor on August 1 to set forth which rights belonged in the Constitution; by the middle of August some 30 written proposals are received. Self-evident truths are listed in abundance, but there is agreement only on one point: that in light of external circumstances the Declaration must be formulated as quickly as possible, and then the drafting of the Constitution must be taken up.

Forcing a majority vote becomes a more and more frequent means of closing debate. What rights will ultimately make their way into the final version, and in what words, is largely a function of the personal ambitions of individual authors: if someone strongly insists on his own version, the others acknowledge this with indifference or haste. The delegates—and the gallery even more so—have had enough of arguments, particularly ones they have by now heard more than once. How fortunate that those insisting on their own wording are either outstanding figures or can compel others to forge their thoughts so magnificently!

First they dispatch a committee—the "Committee of Five"—to knead together earlier texts. The report of the Five is submitted by Mirabeau, who is now uncharacteristically unsure of himself. His words lack enthusiasm. He is compelled to admit, or confess, that they had discovered no universal truths that could be expressed in the Declaration. With a sweeping majority, the restless delegates choose the less-than-inspired (or inspiring) previous draft produced by the Sixth Committee as their starting point for a text, against the disquisitions and maxims of Sieyès.[49]

Ten days later, little is left of the Sixth Committee's compromise text. There is hardly any debate on what in fact constitutes rights of man and why, perhaps because historical grievances made a natural selection among the self-evident points of natural law. No one has any use for freedom of assembly and association at this point. This is really no wonder in the given circumstances, where the cult of the individual is strong, together with the desire to break away from corporations—not to mention the fear inspired by the crowds. Social rights and the right to honor[50] are forgotten and lost in the shuffle. The obligations that balance rights have hitherto failed to pass through the filter of previous votes of the Assembly; to settle the crowds, a restriction of rights in the formula of "respecting the rights of others," proposed by many, has taken the place of obligations. But the final refuge of "moderation"—the main barrier—is that rights are determined by the law. It is true that this law is not yet sovereign, it is not yet the unrestricted act of the will, since it can restrict only acts damaging to society. We can see the hand of fear at work again in the turn to law, for this is the refuge of the emotions stirred by anticipated unruly events. "The remedy against 'popular despotism' is respect for the laws." Mounier—like Madison who voiced similar concerns a year earlier—referred to the difficulty of countering the arbitrary power of the majority. On August 12, in terms that in four years' time will appear prophetic, he described the deliberations of passion-driven popular assemblies. The danger of assemblies is that eloquence arouses the passions of the audience. People will turn into crowd. "Man cannot enjoy liberty and security . . . where a simple suspicion is sufficient to endanger that liberty and security and not even people's sympathy will guarantee it."[51]

It would seem that the general will and national sovereignty have potentially won the day at the expense of the rights of man. The Declaration at any rate embodies a tension that proves fatal for liberty in the years that follow. Only the slow consolidation of the ideal of constitutionalism will be able to limit this unrestricted popular sovereignty in the long run. This purely intellectual corrective—constitutionalism that restricts popular sovereignty—will emerge from the persecution under the *Terreur*: fear is at work once again.

The sessions formulating the rights of man are sometimes indifferent, sometimes unexpectedly vehement. The observers and speakers alike are impatient. The only substantive decisions remaining to be made concern rights that have been omitted, like freedom of the press (Robespierre's proposal), the right to bear arms, and freedom of religious practice.

During the passionate debate on freedom of religion, even the pretense of rationality dissolves. Majority support for the Catholic position was a result of the makeup of the Assembly: representatives of the Catholic Church were well aware of the dangers threatening the Faith if every denomination could freely practice its creed. The Vicomte de Mirabeau (Mirabeau's younger brother and a staunch royalist) argues thus against religious pluralism: "To allow all denominations is to create the religion of circumstances. . . . Everyone will choose a religion that corresponds to his passions, and Turkish religion will be the creed of the youth."[52] Yet even the vicomte accepts that religious feelings are natural, and hence that no one is to be disturbed in the practice of his religion. In other words, this right is based on respect for natural feeling: *rights of man satisfy a basic emotional need.* The more traditional defenders of the privileges of the Catholic Church also point to the emotional components of human nature: in the absence of regulation of passionate religious feelings, order will be destroyed. Others, relying on the same anthropological assumptions, make reference to the "bloodbath . . . that springs from intolerance." De Laborde adduces the horrifying persecution of the Quakers, expressing his wish that the "feeling" (*sentiment*) of tolerance guide the delegates in their discussions of religious freedom, since impatience drips tyranny into men's hearts.[53] The Protestant pastor Rabaut de Saint-Étienne, arguing for equality of denominations, also cites injustice, religious persecution, and the suffering and humiliation endured by Protestant and Jewish victims resulting from their second-class citizen status. He closes his moving oration with an apology "for being compelled to use this kind of language and awaken the interest of your humanity by way of your emotions after I had attempted to achieve this by reason."[54] However, it is in connection with a phrase in Article 6 (on equality, including equal access to office) that the most scandalous debate arises, a veritable battle of emotions regarding the definition of civil equality.[55] Who has the right to what public positions and offices? Members of the Third Estate, jealous of status, insist on the right of all to fill all offices, something the original text might not have prevented anyway; still, the lack of self-confidence is paranoid.

"Anyone would be mistaken to imagine an optimistic exchange of ideas leading to a glorious text full of eternal principles. On the contrary, the debates of August 20–26 felt like an attempt at a breakup under pressure of events, often with prematurely arrived-at results. The effect of the Great Fear cannot be overemphasized here, and the ratified text met with criticism almost immediately."[56]

Here we see the convergence of the Great Fear, natural rights, and the hazy teachings of reason and general will (in fact the prevailing commonplaces of the age): rights are recognized, but only so that they may be properly restricted. Not one proved exempt from the effects of the prevailing clichés. This drew public thinking down a predetermined track, release from which would come only at the cost of bloody experience and the dictatorship of thought and practice. July 14, August 4, and October 5–6 (when the royal family was dragged to Paris) showed that the cliché of the common will can be accompanied by the reality of compulsion. In the months that followed October 5, the commonplace of general will proves irresistible. The general will is the litmus test to uncover suspicious characters and hidden enemies. Since rights can be restricted, they may be forgotten. But the cliché of rights (reinforced by Thermidor) lives on: "rights of man" and "popular sovereignty" were struck from the dictionary under Napoleon by the *idéologues* and under the Restoration by Catholic counterrevolutionaries, but constitutionalism could no longer exist without these expressions; at most, it might have offered a reconfiguration of the concepts.

A thorough look at the unfinished Declaration reveals that, despite appeals to reason, the rights it discusses have radically opposite origins and are very difficult to reconcile with one another. Fundamental, shared emotional demands are guaranteed in its text under the rubric of "rights," such as self-esteem, religion, self-expression, and desire for security (including the security of ownership); these had all been regularly affronted by the monarchy. Consensus, to the extent it exists, follows shared *intuitions* and language. As Gouges-Cartou writes in his draft declaration, almost the entire world recognizes the justice of these principles, "but we merely feel them," and they are arbitrary.[57] Commonality of reference is fostered by the vocabulary developed in the Enlightenment. This language is self-evident for the socially and culturally homogeneous majority of Assembly delegates. Besides the reference to reason, the proud mission of the nation is another typical commonplace.[58] By contrast, within the text of the Declaration itself, this is mixed with natural-law considerations and expediency; all this may now be set in opposition to the fiction of a unified nation and its despotic sovereignty.[59] As Rabaut Saint-Étienne put it later, the Revolution as whole "had only one principle; that of reforming abuses: but as everything in this dominion was an abuse, the result was that everything was changed."[60]

2. Enlightenment; or What Was the Role of Abstract Principles?

To have a constitution and the rights of man are self-evident demands in the self-consciousness of the modern world. Our self-respect dictates that we have such things as members of some sort of progressive society. A closer look at the "self-evident" reveals that the constitution and certain fundamental rights belong to us as part of the world we acknowledge as our own because we have *created* them. Our creation is honorable because it is not haphazard; reason—our reason, that is—recognizes some sort of preexisting order in the structure we have chosen.

What is the place of reason in the Declaration? Clearly the document appeals to reason in its Preamble. In the form of simple, undisputable principles, it aims to *remind* us of natural rights, whose previous violation was made possible by *ignorance*. The Declaration was to be posted all around the country so that all might *know* their rights. (This also explains the need for public education.)

It is therefore no wonder that in the common perception the Declaration is the manifestation of reason's dictates, or at least reason led the delegates to the knowledge presented in the Declaration. Rivarol was already complaining about the "empty metaphysics of the Declaration"[61] in 1789. The prevailing image of the Declaration is that it was intended to be the summary and victory of the Enlightenment project, a project that "is imbued with a belief in the unity and immutability of reason,"[62] but many contemporaries were of a different view. Outside of the Preamble there is no reference to the role of reason. References made by the various authors of draft declarations—a variable list of rights packaged as self-evident truths—admit the influence of the emotions, at least on the level of metaphor.[63] Modern scholarship has demonstrated that the reason-sentiment dichotomy was an artificial creation that was consolidated in the Consulate period.[64]

In laying the groundwork for morality and natural rights in the eighteenth century, sentimental references came to play an important role. Of course, "*sentiment*" could indicate an opinion, but a society whose language and culture honors certain emotions is more inclined to give itself over to their power; here no one is slow to appeal to the emotions. Yet it would be an exaggeration to conclude from the frequent appearance of the term that all references to its power are indeed about emotions (just as it would also be a mistake to believe that users of a language cleansed of all emotion have no emotions within them). Nor is it conclusive that nearly every realization and demand in the eighteenth century seems to well up from the heart, or that the dictates of the heart are coaxed forth at every turn.

The frequency of references to *sentiment* and *sensibilité* is not necessarily decisive. It only shows that the authors interested in human rights were faithful to the prevailing language use of the eighteenth century. But language is culture and a culture that relies on a sentimental language encourages the use of emotions in social relations by creating display rules. The century had developed a culture of tears and pity, and the Revolution followed this tradition. The Frenchman of the eighteenth century was highly "emotionalized," which characterizes—and may simultaneously influence—society's use of the emotions. Enlightenment ideas about human rights were emotional in orientation, which is to some degree a function of the cult of the emotions and the development of modes of thought in the eighteenth century.[65] If the usage of the term *sentiment* is without decisive significance, the same should apply for the constant reference to "principles" as well, a word that, since the writers of the Counterrevolution, has traditionally been seen as the source of the Terror and the reliable mark of abstract, speculative reason. Principles are evident truths; their evidence stems from their coherence and timelessness.[66] Particularly since Rousseau, himself easily the greatest sentimentalist, the development of "principles" has been seen as the task of political-philosophical thought. The debate has concerned the distinction between good and bad principles—but it was only during the full-blown stage of the Revolution that the role of empirical, experience-based facts came to be delegitimized. The temporary victory of deduction from principles was the consequence of an ever-bloodier political and power struggle, rather than proof of an abstract rationalism that was already operating prior to 1789.[67] The Revolutionaries were the ones who thought good laws were written on the firmament of eternally valid principles—and thence they drew their solutions, dictated in fact by the pragmatic needs of the changing situations and by their passions, setting off the inflation of basic principles. For Marat, first his opponents' basic principles became suspicious, than the adherents to bad principles themselves were suspect.

Naturally, intellectual considerations pertaining to human rights and the future constitution played an important role, even outside the circles of later radicals. In the usage of the Enlightenment, reason has a special, if circumscribable role; considerations of reason hardly play an exclusive role in the formation of political institutions. In the debate on the Declaration, it is often said that rights are self-evident givens, while the solutions proposed in the Constitution are frequently portrayed as dictates of reason. Still, reference to reason, more than anything else, was intended to signal a break with the past. What the Assembly ultimately accepts is far from abstract intellectual principles or the unalterable and unambiguous commandment of God; it cannot be asserted that the strict logical dictate of intelligence is formulated in a given fundamental right. While it is true that many attempts are made at metaphysical connections deriving from traditions of natural law and philosophy in discussions of the rights in the Declaration, these ultimately become untenable when it is revealed that each delegate has a different metaphysics.

In the public thought of the eighteenth century the human individual acquires importance bit by bit, and even then not in the capacity of a thinking being but primarily as a body that experiences and feels. "What is absolutely necessary to an understanding of the figure of man of the Declaration, is that over the course of the seventeenth and eighteenth centuries, the human, precisely in its quality as fleshly and embodied, took on new meanings that made it central to the conceptualization of right. . . . The human body . . . as the locus of sensibility, of feeling, and consequently of sympathy began to intrude into and remake the political imagination."[68] When thoroughly groundless accusations of the murder of a Catholic servant are made against Jean Calas, a Protestant subsequently executed under horrifying circumstances, Voltaire and his readers are moved by his physical sufferings and the manner in which he preserved his noble sentiments throughout; this combination of pain, bigotry, and dignity is what is described as an injustice. There is no mention of *abstract* procedural rights being neglected—rights whose justification would be their instrumental rationality.

There is no need to be naïve. The monarchy did not lose its status because of a negligible number of arguments pitting its tyranny against principles of the proper ordering of the state; even the outrage of Voltaire and his companions failed to produce a breakthrough. Its delegitimation should be ascribed first of all to pornographic pamphlets and crude engravings full of lies. Cheap and deceitful woodcuts depicting the lasciviousness of the "Austrian whore" (Marie-Antoinette) were what truly affected public opinion, and this effect was surely not in the first instance an intellectual process. It was typically based in visceral emotions.[69]

Typical of the main current of the eighteenth-century Enlightenment was the elimination of prejudices, rather than submission to any dictates of abstract reason. Voltaire and his followers saw liberty as the prerequisite for this, in order to allow the free individual to pursue his own inclinations and choices.

While the rights of man might be "self-evident," their source is not to be sought exclusively in reason. The language of the rights of man might have been accepted in the Assembly, but the connection between natural law and rationalism—between natural law and the law of reason—is unclear. Of course, belief in universal natural law was widespread during the French Enlightenment, though everyone had a different understanding of its substance. In his *Letters of a New Haven Citizen from 1787*, Condorcet explains: "These rights are called *natural* because they derive from the nature of man; because it is a clear and necessary consequence of the very fact that a sentient being capable of reason and moral ideas exists that he must enjoy these rights and could not justly be deprived of them."[70]

In Condorcet's view it is the universal possibility of rationality that serves as the basis and prerequisite for natural law. This is at variance with the restrictive interpretation of rights in the Declaration, which seems to restrict in practice the circle of rights holders. To take an example: for Condorcet, the exclusion of women or slaves—or indeed any beings capable of understanding moral principles—from the enjoyment of such rights is an injustice, a violation of natural law. Furthermore, for Condorcet, the will of the nation cannot set standards against the rational convictions of the individual just as the nation[71] (or the community granting his mandate) does not bind the representative to anything. At least this follows from the assumption that universal reason must prevail (and reason cannot be anything but universal). Only universal rights may serve as standard. "The prejudice that various communities and territories have differing or opposing interests must be done away with—and even more so the still-more-dangerous view that delegates or representatives must vote not according to the principles of reason and justice, but according to the interests of their constituents."[72]

But the prevailing opinion was much more *sentiment*-bound than Condorcet's approach. The Marquis de Lafayette, who expressed and influenced public conceptions much more closely than Condorcet, thought the Declaration must express "what everyone knows and feels."[73] In his proposal of July 20, Sieyès also treats freedom of expression, human thoughts, and feelings together, considering them side by side as basic rights. The individual is not to be prosecuted for his opinions *or* his feelings, nor can the expression of these be forbidden to anyone.[74] Even the will of the legislator serves to communicate emotions.[75]

For a better understanding of the role of the emotions in shaping institutions, we have had to reconstruct here the events that transpired over the summer of 1789, rather than rely on isolated, conflicting legal justifications. These events, though, cannot be understood in themselves, without considering the competing mindsets of the day that had been developing over the course of long decades. A survey of the events of 1789 reveals that the assessments of the situation and the solutions dictated by it, grounded in principle, were largely shaped by the emotions of the participants: fear and jealousy. The debates, which reasonable rules of procedure proved unable to contain, were marked by the mood of the moment, by spontaneity, and by egotism. Given the terrible acoustics, it was feelings and gestures—rather than arguments—that required interpretation and understanding. Constitutional and institutional solutions that might seem to have been guided by reason were in fact shaped by feelings. Driven by the hatred and vanity within him, Mirabeau ignored the rules of press censorship;[76] his desire to publish, which would have drawn a severe punishment a few months earlier, went unpunished amid the tumult, and it found adherents immediately. Doubtless there had been for decades issues of principle that called for the elimination of censorship, but it was ultimately bold action driven by emotion, and not speculative principles that brought this about. In the given circumstances, freedom of the press became the accepted practice even without its consecration in the Declaration. These developments were portrayed as the demands of reason only *after the fact*—or at least the previously ineffective rational arguments became convincing through the power of emotions. When the constitutional agenda was accepted through the Tennis Court Oath, this happened thanks not to the earlier speculative arguments of Sieyès, but rather to the delegates' wounded feelings of pride and outrage.

Chaos, fear, and passion led to the Declaration; given the actual events, it would be difficult to assert that the Tennis Court saw the workings of reason toward the fulfillment of its Enlightenment agenda. The horrible din drowned out most reasoning, and abstract argumentation was generally seen as dull. According to eyewitnesses, only emotion and passion had any effect in the theater of the Constituent Assembly. As theater, the Assembly had the task of transmitting the intense emotions of the Revolution's participants—rather than any abstract ideas—to the millions who were not present. Enhanced emotions, presented in theatrical form, were perfectly suited to move the crowds. This made it possible for them to participate in the community of emotions as if it were some new religion. "The French Revolution was made up of *tableaux vivants*, crystallizing in theatrical form the intensity of emotion experienced by its participants. Only with this dramatic license could its message be communicated to the many millions who could thus share its euphoria, engage themselves in its outcome and so bond themselves to its alliance."[77]

"THE GREATEST OF ALL REFLECTIONS ON HUMAN NATURE": THE CONSTITUTION OF FEAR

Battle not with monsters, lest ye become a monster, and if you gaze into the abyss, the abyss gazes also into you.

—Nietzsche

My claim is that constitutions reflect a selection of the emotional experiences of a given community. What is seen in constitutional law to be the expression of rational considerations, and is legitimized as such, is to a considerable extent the interplay of emotions reflected in public sentiments, and in particular fear. The rationality of a constitutional solution[1] originates partly in its capacity to handle constitutional sentiments—passions in particular. It is a means/ends rationality although the solutions offered may serve, among other ends, emotional satisfaction. Moreover, constitutions are not only reflections upon public sentiments: constitutional institutions offer emotion management by reducing the frequency of, and damage caused by passion. Such arrangements often reflect folk-psychology assumptions about human emotions.

This may sound odd. Most constitutions deal with the technicalities of power-sharing among public institutions. Even if one adds fundamental rights-related provisions, constitutions do not look like the children of sentiments. But the claim that constitutions have emotional foundations and effects does not exclude the relevance of other approaches which perceive constitutions as the incorporations of prevailing beliefs or interests.

To prove my point I will consider the available empirical evidence of classic constitution-making. By this term I am referring to the American and French experiences of the eighteenth century, the period in which the fundamental arrangements of liberal constitutionalism were consolidated. (For some French experiences see also Chapter 2.) But even if the reconstruction of constitutional sentiments is successful and their importance is demonstrated in these historical contexts, serious objections remain to be addressed. After all, modern constitutions and their fundamental amendments are most often the work of impassive technicians of law and power. Many of these constitutions are copies or mixtures of existing constitutional solutions, while many serve simply as certificates or decorum of state existence. Constitutional sentiments are hardly visible in most contemporary constitutions or in their making.

1. The Constitutionalism of Fear

1.a. The Role of Fear in American Constitution-Making

Acknowledging that constitutional sentiments (those of the framers, and of the ratifying public at large) were at work in constitution-making is not to deny that constitution-drafting is an exercise in problem solving, to the best knowledge of the participants. To a great extent this is an interest-driven process. What counts as "interest," how constitutional "problems" are identified, and what is considered an "acceptable" solution will all depend on the prevailing constitutional sentiments of the day. Consider the American experience: According to the uncontested authority of Bernard Bailyn, the American Revolution that began in 1775–1776 was a reaction to British abuses of political power, which were seen as part of "a settled, fixed plan for enslaving the colonies, or bringing them under arbitrary government, and indeed the nation too."[2] Responding to this threatening vision and a sense of sometimes purposefully provoked outrage, the revolutionaries began very early on to create their new institutional arrangements for governing the revolutionized political communities. Relying on Bailyn's authority, one can fairly say that the establishment of institutions at the state level was dictated by a fear of excessive government power. Though its drafting took place many years after the formative experience of the British abuse of power, the national Constitution was animated by similar concerns. The emotional experience of fear was publicly expressed; a shared public sentiment reinforced existing feelings.

The Philadelphia Convention was hardly a place for polite exchange of scholarly theories of government. It was a forum where, as Gouverneur Morris said later, the "fate of America was suspended by a hair." "Feeling ran high at the very outset," indeed so much so that Franklin felt it necessary to interpose a motion that 'prayers imploring the assistance of Heaven . . . be held in this Assembly every morning.'" The founding fathers were acting with the threats of Shays's rebellion and "the turbulence and follies of democracy"[3] fresh in their minds, and anticipating a new war that they would be unable to wage. Fear, specifically of concretely anticipated arrangements, was an important *argument*. For example, Madison noted on June 1: "Mr. Pinkney was for a vigorous Executive but was *afraid* the Executive powers of the existing Congress might extend to peace & war &c., which would render the Executive a monarchy, of the worst kind, to wit an elective one. . . ." As for Randolph "he next reviewed the *danger* of our situation, appealed to the sense of the best friends of the U.S.—the prospect of *anarchy* from the laxity of government everywhere; and to other considerations." Gerry "hoped he should not violate that respect in declaring on this occasion his *fears* that a Civil war may result from the present crisis of the U.S. . . . In Massachusetts there are two parties, one devoted to Democracy, the worst he thought of all political evils, the other as violent in the opposite extreme. From the collision of these in opposing and resisting the Constitution, confusion was greatly to be *feared*."[4]

The sad experiences of governmental abuse under George III loomed large in the public imagination. "The Framers were virtually obsessed with a fear—bordering on what some might uncharitably describe as paranoia—of the concentration of political power."[5] The popular source and breadth of executive power were perceived as frightening. Not surprisingly the election of the executive was not given in trust to the people; the Electoral College was thought to counter the passions of democracy.

Fear explains to a considerable extent the *selection of issues* which were held important enough to be included in the Constitution. Even strictly interest-dictated issues, like the powers retained by states and state voting power, reflect fear-dictated concerns of the interested communities. ("What will happen to our small state in case of a conspiracy of bigger states?")

The texture of the Constitution had steered clear of strictly structural concepts and arrangements; it was a texture that served the desire to create an acceptable but efficient central power for a new nation. It is certainly a masterpiece of utilitarian calculus, or, in less respectful terms, of able horse trading, including the "dirty compromise" that reconfirmed slavery and the slave trade in exchange for the commerce clause.

The Constitution was intended to provide an institutional device for interstate cooperation and nation-building; yet still, within its structural arrangements, we suddenly run into concerns related to personal security. The recurrent appearance of said concerns stemmed from fear of oppression and cruelty. The framers, whose majority thought it unnecessary to incorporate fundamental rights into the 1787 text, still found it necessary to include the protection of habeas corpus (disguised as a matter of competence) and the prohibition against bills of attainder and titles of nobility. Likewise, the Contracts Clause reflects the founders' outrage and fear regarding the confiscation of financial interests by legislative impairment of contractual obligations, which threatened them personally in an imagined democracy. The fear generated by Shays's rebellion granted power to the federal government to "suppress insurrections" and to keep a standing army in peacetime.[6] Further, the selection of the rights in the Bill of Rights was intimately related to the fundamental fears of the general public. Shared emotional experience, rather than some grand theory, dictated the choice of specific concerns, as in the case of the otherwise odd appearance of the prohibition of quartering in the Third Amendment. The rights granted in the 1789 Amendments are those which had been commonly violated or denied by the British colonial administration. It may indeed seem odd that certain constitutional solutions are so strongly influenced by experiences of past injustice and fear during the creation of a new design. But this predominance of past experience is much less surprising when we consider that some of the same brain regions involved in the recall of past events are also activated in envisioning ourselves in the future.

It was the constitutionalism of fear (here I paraphrase Judith Shklar) that has animated the consolidated model of modern constitutions. Of course fear is not the only important public sentiment in the eighteenth-century American constitution-making process. Personal pride, anger or outrage, empathy, and enthusiasm all play a role in the process of self-definition of a new nation and its citizens. Other emotional concerns were dictated by considerations of interest, such as those of the communities delegating the constitution-makers. But it is fear for bodily integrity and loss of personal status that looms larger than life. In the Revolutionary period the American public concentrated on birthrights, not so much out of some abstract respect for liberty as because of personal insecurity. Furthermore, the colonists struggled with anxiety over a possible loss of status.[7] The threat to one's social status generated anxiety, fear, and anger, and these sentiments resulted in the "discovery of rights." The colonists considered themselves equal to their brethren in England by birthright; lack of parliamentary representation, and the increasingly aggressive disregard of their social status in the administration of justice by British officials in the colonies, threatened their status. The related emotional reactions of indignation, outrage, and a sense of injustice are all voiced in the words of the Declaration of Independence, with its long litany of grievances and injustices committed by the Crown, including attacks on life, limb, and property, quartering of troops, trial without jury, burning of towns, "waging war against us," plundering, and "bringing in the merciless Indian Savages."

Fear may have been at work in 1776, but it had to operate within the framework of existing mentalities and self-understanding. The colonists, good Whigs that they were, took their privileged legal status for granted. The grievances were about the British re-interpretation of their birthrights in unheard-of ways: "The British . . . during the early 1760s . . . 'discovered' the right against general search warrants and made that right a major issue in contemporary politics. They did not, of course, discover the right. What they discovered was that it could be abused in ways previously not suspected or not understood. The seizure of John Wilkes's papers from Wilkes's home under the authority of a general warrant caused the alarm, but reaction to the seizure did not lead to the invention of a new right. In legal theory and in the minds of common lawyers, the rights had always existed. They just had not entered constitutional consciousness until threatened by the Wilkes precedent. The same was true for rights that Americans would claim."[8]

In the eighteenth century constitution-making was understood as an exercise in mass psychology. Common sense suggested that a constitution of liberty can work only if supported by public sentiment.[9] The Constitution was intended to handle the fearfully unreliable nature of humans, and that of their even more ambiguous assemblies. Constitutional government is about managing human passions by manipulating proper sentiments, a well-established view shared by Thomas Paine and his archenemy, John Adams. "Society is produced by our wants, and government by our wickedness; the former promotes our happiness *positively* by uniting our affections, the latter *negatively* by restraining our vices," states Paine in his *Common Sense*. The very same year Adams argued against granting all power to the representation of the people assembled in a single body because "a single assembly is liable to all vices, follies, and frailties of an individual—subjects to fits of humor, starts of passion, flights of enthusiasm, partialities, or prejudice—and consequently productive of hasty results and absurd judgments. And all these errors ought to be corrected and defects supplied by some controlling power. . . . A single assembly is apt to grow ambitious and after a time will not hesitate to vote itself perpetual."[10]

The founders had a strong shared view of the sentiments, inclinations, and proclivities of the people who would live under the Constitution. The Constitution was intended to provide a means for managing these sentiments. When it came to constitution-making in 1787, the delegates were of the conviction that constitutional solutions must manage a very brutish human nature, notwithstanding serious disagreements regarding the "nature of man"—that is, his psychological tendencies. James Madison famously advocated that the Constitution be written on the Humean assumption that "every man must be supposed a knave." Hamilton could not agree more.[11] The following well-known lines of Madison are also to be understood as reflections on an emotional experience that corroborated the Humean wisdom: "Among the numerous advantages promised by a well-constructed Union, none deserves to be more accurately developed than its tendency to break and control the violence of faction. . . . By a faction, I understand a number of citizens, whether amounting to a majority or a minority of the whole, who are united and actuated by some common impulse of passion, or of interest, adverse to the rights of other citizens, or to the permanent and aggregate interests of the community."[12]

I quote Madison at some length to show that the centrality of human emotions is clearly related to the fear of violence that results from uninhibited group passions; a fear that resonated among the founding fathers and many of the readers of the *Federalist Papers.* At the Philadelphia Convention, Wilson, Hamilton, Lansing, Mason, and Madison argued with one voice that passions should be controlled by institutional design, which relied on these very passions, including fear and envy.[13] In fact, the Constitution was the instrument of choice for managing public sentiments. Through passion management it exercises control over those who are susceptible to passion: namely, people. As delegate Wilson told at the 1787 Convention: "Every Government has certain moral and physical qualities engrafted in their very nature,—one operates on the sentiments of men, the other on their fears."[14] As it turned out, the Constitution controlled and contained passions by manipulation, and in masterly fashion. This then transformed it into a lasting social institution.

In Madison's view the problem of neutralizing passions is solved by representative government, separation of powers and federalism. This way "the [passionate] majority must be rendered, by their number and local situation, unable to concert and carry into effect schemes of oppression."[15] The solution is found in the constitutional manipulation of passions through proper institutional arrangements: "Ambition must be made to counteract ambition. . . . It may be a reflection on human nature, that such devices should be necessary to control the abuses of government. But what is government itself, but the greatest of all *reflections on human nature*? If men were angels, no government would be necessary."[16]

The Constitution's predilection for *representative* government is a fundamental choice in passion management. It rejects and excludes forms of popular and populist governments where "democratic feeling" would prevail. The psychology of counter-passion shelters class bias: uneducated poor bumpkins and back-country farmers might be part of the people and subjects of the constitution, but were not seen as capable of running the country. Excluding them from leadership is yet another possible component of the program of "fighting passions."

The institutional solutions to the passion problem are a mixture of cognitive bias and heuristics, both fear-induced. They prevail in the American state constitutions[17] as well as the federal Constitution, which seem nevertheless to be perfectly "rational" in an instrumental sense. Multilevel representative government is an efficient tool for handling the problem of a democratic multitude. Otherwise feeling-based politics in a democracy would allow decision-making by acclamation, which would open the door either to pure emotionalism or (equally bad) the will of the people "in the vital sense." In a way, the anti-emotional and "artificial" solution of liberalism, the statistical counting of votes, is the mechanical (or "rational") answer to people's power, which much later became grounds for criticism by Carl Schmitt & Co.[18] In this light it is no surprise that the referendum is not accepted at the federal level in the United States or (with one irrelevant exception) in Germany.

It would be an obvious exaggeration to assume that the prevailing constitution-making sentiment *always* reflects fear of loss of liberty and of status, or that uncertainty inevitably generates foundational anxiety. Nor do I claim that all references to danger or all threatening words arouse or reflect actual fear. Emotional references in constitutional debates are often purely rhetorical (in the sense of figurative speech). In the French context, references at the National Assembly to shared or collective sentiments often implied what later would be known under the rubric of "public opinion." Expressions like "I feel," "I fear," or the recurrent reference to the "jealousies of the smaller States"[19] at the Philadelphia Convention are forms that describe rational calculations, assumptions about rational behavior, and the like.

The fear-based scenario, though prevalent in America and at certain instances in the French constitution-making process during the Revolution, had its competitors in constitutional history. Other constitutional sentiments may carry the day, resulting in different arrangements. The alternative models were shaped by different sentiments which mobilized and relied upon different ideologies. For example, the Pennsylvania Constitution of 1776 reflected sentiments of equality prevalent at the time among the artisans and farmers of the colony; they originated partly in the religious doctrines and passions of the (First) Great Awakening of the 1730s and '40s. To some extent, the egalitarian aspirations explain the granting of overwhelming powers to the legislative body that was elected on the basis of nearly universal male suffrage and was answerable to the electorate through yearly elections. These sentiments of anticipated status equality and status envy regarding the local "nobility" were at odds with the fears of the upper classes concerned with a potential loss of status as expressed in birthrights complaints.[20]

Constitution-drafting and ratification seem to be disparate events. In reality the genesis of a constitution is a series of interrelated events, and the process cannot be identified with a prevailing sentiment in any one of its constitutive stages. In the process of constitution-making different emotional combinations emerge—including moments of enthusiasm, which block fears. Republican popular resistance to the ratification of the Constitution originated in a different emotional mix: it quite often stemmed from class hatred and resentment, and from mistrust of government common among farmers. The "apprehension that the liberties of the people are in danger, and a distrust of men of property or education have a more powerful effect upon the minds of our opponents than any specific objections against the Constitution."[21]

The above story of constituent fear is often read in a metaphorical sense. I have a more robust concept of emotions: constitutional institutions reflect the outcome of actual emotional interplay. The results may seem reasonable, but even these apparently rational solutions are to a great extent shaped in the actual interaction of emotions and higher cognitive processes. A considerable obsession with fear (originally a conglomerate of elite anxieties) has gradually come to prevail in the constitutional selection process over the last two hundred years. But what kind of feelings are we talking about when we refer to the verbal and written evidence of fear and other emotions cited above? Fear is a basic emotion triggered by perceived or imaginary threat, resulting in the fight-or-flight response. It activates the amygdala (at least in the case of fast-track fear). It is believed to be innate, and it is certainly hard-wired as evidenced by baby monkeys' reaction to snakes. Fear is described as being accompanied by specific physiological reactions, such as an increased heartbeat; its symptoms elicit the feeling or awareness of fear, and are associated with a specific facial expression.

The delegates at the French National Assembly were confronted with threats to life and limb. We have vivid evidence of their feasts of fear.[22] They were surrounded with the hot emotions of anger and hatred, enthusiasm, fear, and passions, and the delegates often shared or reciprocated these feelings among themselves.

The kind of fear caused by the direct threats to which the French delegates were subjected is absent in most constitution-making processes. At the American constitutional conventions, most of the automatic nervous system responses, such as the heartbeat famously required by William James for an occurrence of fear, were long gone (or were replaced by personal feelings of fear and anger elicited by other members). But beyond perceptions or memories, thoughts too may trigger emotions, and influence long-term memory. "Increased emotion at encoding facilitates retention," including where the stimuli elicit negative affect.[23] The constitution-makers of the newly independent American states and the founding fathers were not directly threatened at the time of drafting. They were responding to threats not of a direct physical nature. More important, they reacted to shared instances of past fear,[24] which had a formative impact on their thinking, and which were easily recalled and mobilized in the group dynamics of constitution-making.

In the absence of direct threats and physical danger, and of the physiological symptoms of fear, emotions may still play an important role in constitutional decision-making and human action. Meanings attributed to events are structured in emotional terms. Humans may be guided by stimuli even in the absence of physiological indicators of emotions (as in the case of a damaged amygdala, for example). Memories of fearful events and the experience of fear operate as "cold" fear. The emotional experience that feeds cold emotion will serve not only as a point of reference for the constitutional debate and its calculations, but will shape the subject's emotional condition of the moment.

Emotions are not only those phenomena that "are done within 120 milliseconds, the rest being mere aftermath and cerebral embellishment." There are strong arguments in favor of considering "states of mind" as emotions where "there are no signs of automatic arousal while subjects say they are, or feel, happy or anxious or angry. It is as well to take such subjects at their word, as long as their behavior does not contradict them." In other words, when Pinckney, or Randolph, or Wilson say "I fear," they mean it: and constitution-makers did say so quite often. Once you hear and accept that others are afraid, you will take the information seriously: it signals future thought and action. It makes sense to be afraid. The agreement of a number of people on this matter supports the notion that the fear is appropriate. As a consequence fear will become a shared emotional state.[25]

Constitution-making is a collective venture, and the drafting occurs in personal interaction where empathy is likely even if the participants are adversaries.[26] The emotions of others have a direct impact on one's own emotions. The impact of personal emotional memories and resulting feelings on others becomes even more obvious if we realize that strong emotions, and the language of fear and threats, signal real intentions. The (nonconscious) observation of the emotional state of another person activates a representation of that emotion (or a feeling similar to it), making the observer capable of understanding those emotions. In these circumstances people may feel the emotions of others, including fear, even if the original experience is not shared.

Imagination is crucial here. One can "enter an imaginative fear state as an automatic consequence of imagining a frightening situation."[27] Many people accept the prohibition of torture without ever having experienced it, or even having been in situations where they could at least imagine the possibility of being tortured and feel the concomitant fear, anger, and allied emotions. They can still envision the distress of other people being tortured.

Fear can be learned activating of the amygdala without a threat being experienced. Stimuli may generate reactions which are similar to those elicited by past actual threats, and verbal communication has emotional learning effects similar to the actual experience of fear. Learned physiological responses may guide behavior,[28] and therefore it is always possible that learned emotional responses are influential even in highly cognitive processes like the constitution-making situation.

The founding fathers shared the emotional experience of British injustice, humiliation, and threats, and the fears generated by Shays's rebellion, and of excessive popular rule.[29] Such experiences were accompanied by visions of a collapsing weak Confederation. These experiences, as well as imagined dangers, were the source of cold emotions. The intensity of cold fear might be less than of actual fear. Some of the processes in the brain may be different, but the impact of cold emotions on the rational process is comparable to that of hot emotions.

Likewise, some of those who participated in the "invention" of human rights as fundamental constitutional rights did not personally experience violations of these future rights. When Jefferson penned the Declaration of Independence, he did not need to confront "savage Indians" personally to feel afraid; stories he had heard earlier may have done the job. Actual emotional mobilization could have taken place at the constitution-making process even without the experience of something fearful on the site. The concerns of many people participating in the ratification were based on imagined or anticipated fear. Anticipated fear (fear about a possible occurrence) seems to have similar emotional impact to fear felt at an actual threat. The founders were informed about the emotional experiences of their peers in emotionally evocative ways. Other people's emotional experience influenced them. The cold fear of those who had personal fear recollection was contagious: "the sight of a fearful face elicits activity in the same regions [of the brain] as direct exposure to a fearful object."[30] Similarly, when "ordinary" people participated in these early exercises of constitutional ratification, they were moved partly by personal emotional experience and partly by empathy. Empathy enabled them to share other people's fear and outrage, relying heavily on other people's emotional experience.

The prevailing ideologies among the colonists, the shortcomings of the Articles of Confederation, or the influence of Enlightenment philosophers cannot explain the consensus on the relatively short list of constitutional issues and rights in 1776, 1787, or 1789. The agreement on these select problems is to be understood in light of the function of thought: "thoughts, whatever else they are, are telltale symptoms of emotions."[31] The similarities of thought in a situation of high uncertainty reflect shared emotions, which themselves enable shared thoughts. In Philadelphia there was great uncertainty about the future effects of the planned arrangements, and there was little common knowledge available given the conflicting theories of government. In circumstances of uncertainty, both at the closed sessions and at ratification debates, the emotion of other delegates was one of the primary pieces of available information. Social panic explains how other people's emotions function in situations of uncertainty.[32] If one sees other people being afraid, it makes a lot of sense to be afraid. Once fear became the prevailing emotion among the 1787 or 1789 drafters, this spread ultimately to define the mood and the common language.

References to danger like those used at the Philadelphia Convention are powerful precisely because they mobilize hidden emotions—fear in particular—or at least generally accepted convictions that consolidated under the pressure of fear, and possibly also of the related humiliations and anger that resulted from the denial of one's social identity.

The "rational" arguments and institutional solutions of the Constitution are rational because they promise efficient problem management where the problem is construed by emotions. The constitutional solution is "rational" insofar as it operates within assumptions dictated by fearful experiences. For example a bicameral, hence slow and ineffective, legislature makes much sense if one assumes that people will become tyrannical if left to decide matters in poorly structured groups with unlimited sovereign power. Limiting presidential powers makes sense if it is feared that a single strong person holding all executive power tends to tyranny. Such assumptions originate from fear; the solutions make sense only within the threat paradigm. This does not rule out the legitimacy and reasonableness of fear (given the statistical occurrence of irreversible damage) and the solutions it dictates.

The position, that fear would be prevalent in classic constitutions and constitutionalism encounters important objections. It is argued that the politics of fear undermines liberal constitutionalism. Most people are uncomfortable about the centrality of fear, believing that it enslaves us. They are ashamed of fear and fight it by denying it: then they call the denial "freedom." From a psychological perspective it can be correctly said that fear breeds suboptimal decisions. But this is irrelevant as to the *actual* role of fear: it is an explanation of the inevitability of certain shortcomings and also greatness in constitutional design. Certainly, fear makes risk-distorting bias acceptable, even attractive.[33] If constitutional arrangements are generated by fear-based group interactions, constitutions will be cognitively biased; they may produce socially inefficient arrangements. In this logic, if constitutionalism is fear-based it must be wrong, and fear, giving wrong answers, should not be allowed to play a role in human design. A famous line of thought of Justice Brandeis, representative of liberal constitutional ethics, claimed along these lines that the founding fathers' constitution-making act could not have been guided by fear:

> Those who won our independence believed that the final end of the state was to make men free to develop their faculties, and that in its government the deliberative forces should prevail over the arbitrary. . . . They believed . . . that the greatest menace to freedom is an inert people; that public discussion is a political duty; and that this should be a fundamental principle of the American

> government. They recognized the risks to which all human institutions are subject. But they knew that order cannot be secured merely through fear of punishment for its infraction; that it is hazardous to discourage thought, hope and imagination; that fear breeds repression; . . . Recognizing the occasional tyrannies of governing majorities, they amended the Constitution so that free speech and assembly should be guaranteed.
>
> Fear of serious injury cannot alone justify suppression of free speech and assembly. Men feared witches and burnt women. It is the function of speech to free men from the bondage of irrational fears.[34]

This position of Justice Brandeis may not reflect historical facts, but that is immaterial: it is a vision of constitutionalism as risk-taking, apparently based on disregard of fear-based considerations. But the normative position of Brandeis does not contradict the normative implications of the constitutionalism of fear thesis. The liberty-based strategy outlined by Brandeis, even if it were based on the denial of the presence of fear, is about freedom of speech, and perhaps individual liberty, and not about fear of the evil that government can be. The affirmation of free speech certainly involves risk-taking, given the possibility of social disorder and personal humiliation. Free speech is asserted, counter-intuitively if you will, against fear of speech. Speech and liberty are advocated precisely because of fear of tyranny, and because of the silencing power of "irrational fear" and superstition. Even if the founding fathers were not afraid of the consequences of free speech, they seem to be motivated by fear of censorship, even in Brandeis's attractive tale. In fact, free speech is to be protected because otherwise the state would restrict human imagination and thought.[35] Undeniably, here we have an example of overcoming fear in a rather specific way, but it is undeniable that this is an instance of fear management, shaped in emotionally influenced judgments.

In the context of constitution-making, fear has been a conscious and often-acknowledged feeling that mobilizes cognitive and social control. This kind of fear is not necessarily error-generating: indeed the display of fear helps to master it. The important thing here, regarding constitutionalism, is the type of strategy that emerges in the presence of fear. Emotionally charged public reflection on fear generates counterstrategies that tend to diminish the threat of the frightening conditions and circumstances and resulting anxiety and panic. The precondition of this reflection is the feeling and recognition of fear. Constitutional fear management can be associated with a sentiment of hope, often generated by self-esteem and pride, especially of the nationalist variety.[36]

Fear mobilizes preventive strategies, and even if these are biased, they certainly go beyond the primary "advice" fear offers, namely flight or fight. The emerging constitutional strategy does not rule out choices favoring liberty (at least in the sense of creating an institutional arrangement that may be beneficial to individual liberty).

1.b. The Foundational Fear of Cruelty

In light of the emerging understanding of the way emotions operate in deliberation, I claim that constitutional institution-building reflects an interaction of actual and imaginary (attributed) emotions, where fear, in combination with other emotions (such as the fear of status loss, outrage, and disgust) has a positive, structuring role. The constitutional centrality of fear cannot be attributed exclusively to the evolutionary primacy of fear that makes it stronger than the reasoning faculties of the brain. It has to do with the nature of politics: physical coercion and the possibility of inflicting bodily pain lie at the heart of political power, which is, therefore, threatening.

The late Judith Shklar argued that "liberalism has only one overriding aim: to secure the political conditions that are necessary for the exercise of personal freedom."[37] Freedom means decisions without fear and favor about one's own life. Constitutions that reflect this consideration serve constitutionalism.

Judith Shklar had no problem with a theory based first and foremost on the physical suffering and fears of ordinary human beings, and she accepted that the liberalism of fear of cruelty is based on emotions.[38] In fact there are solid neurological grounds for the strong moral reaction to cruelty and to fear generated by cruelty. The image or the imagination of intentional infliction of pain generates activities in those areas of the brain that are associated with moral reasoning.[39] But putting suffering and cruelty at the center of political morality is a matter of fundamental cultural and political choice. After all, there are other, legally less influential salient stimuli that also activate brain areas associated with moral reasoning.

In Shklar's view public cruelty is the principal vice to be avoided by human design. Liberalism of fear begins with the worst of our ordinary vices, namely cruelty.[40] The cruelty that is enabled by the concentration of coercive public power shapes the mind of a constitutionalist. Of course, abhorring cruelty does not in itself lead to constitutionalism: the hero of Shklar's essay is Montaigne, who did not go beyond disgust at the sight of cruelty. His disgust led him to skepticism regarding government. Fear in itself does not result in constitutional government: Hobbes's theory on the centrality of fear in government did not generate liberal constitutional positions. He advocated the centralization of power to diminish the fear of a brutish life. But the two considerations are easily combined, with remarkable consequences for government.

Cruelty is a form of total domination, a mobilizing force in the structuring of our culture, but it remains an elusive concept. Is it the deliberate or arbitrary infliction of physical and/or psychological pain of extraordinary magnitude that makes an act cruel? What is the role of the actors' intent in the infliction? Is cruelty a specific combination of emotions of the actor and/or the observer?

Is "cold" cruelty the same as the "hot" variety? This is unlikely, in view of the data from physiology and neuroscience. Is cruelty a special form of aggression? What are its advantages in adaptation?[41] Machiavelli finds cruelty attractive. Not that he was a cruel person: to him cruelty is simply the most efficient, least resource-demanding form of creating obedience through the paralyzing fear that cruelty generates. Of course, constitutionalism in all its long history is a refutation of Machiavelli and all those tyrants and tyrannical masses who act according to his advice.

According to Shklar cruelty is "the willful inflicting of physical pain on a weaker being in order to cause anguish and fear."[42] The kind of cruelty that became a matter of concern for emerging constitutionalism is related to an unlimited domination based on intimidation. Domination is total where fear whipped up by cruelty prevails among the citizens. This suggests that rulers are no longer reluctant to use cruelty, and have lost respect for personal identity and individuality. "Ultimately, cruelty is the moment when the integral dissolution of the 'I' must be decided . . . cruelty is necessary so that the 'we' and the idea become one, so that nothing comes to restrict the self-affirmation of the 'we.' "[43]

Cruelty is singled out culturally because it uses humans as *objects* by imposing excruciating pain. The dehumanization of course threatens everyone, as anyone might be turned into an object. The assumptions of arbitrariness associated with cruelty are also important: anyone can be its victim, for no reason whatsoever. Once again, culturally shaped cognitive framing is relevant for emotional reactions.

Cruelty is singled out emotionally too, partly because of the repugnant nature of the assumed emotions of the "cruel" actor and also because of the strong empathy correlated with the intensity of the suffering caused. The message of the cruel act may explain its evolutionary fitness, as an improvement in the reproductive status and personal survival potential of the agent of cruelty. The monopoly of power that grants permanent access to, and control over, the bodies of others inevitably triggers fear foremost; because it is the body that is involved, disgust, shame, and anger may come to have personal decision-shaping power. Shame is felt where we see ourselves exposed as valueless objects of cruelty; where cruelty or the imposition of pain is seen as breaking the norm, which triggers anger as well as outrage. While shame is related to one's own loss of self through the pain imposed, disgust and anger are elicited by cruelty directed against others.

Notwithstanding the naturalistic abhorrence of cruelty, the level of imposed pain alone does not define it; it must be a cultural concept, although an ambiguous one. In-group and out-group perspectives on pain differ; moreover, violence is called cruelty if directed against group members, while it may be a noble duty of conquest or self-defense if directed against out-groups. Given the human readiness to disregard prohibitions of cruelty when it comes to out-groups, constitutional law and international human rights law have developed specific rules to prevent the degeneration of specific social groups into out-groups; humanitarian rules are applicable to the handling of out-groups, and the law of war tries to limit cruelty and panic-ridden acts vis-à-vis the enemy. Such dehumanization would deprive the outcast and ostracized of the protection of what moral intuitions otherwise would offer. "A past history of devaluation of specific groups 'preselects' them as potential victims, who under certain conditions become likely objects of scapegoating and of identification as ideological enemies. . . . Less stringent moral values and principles are called into play, which allow harming them."[44] This experience of dehumanization explains specific preventive rules, sometimes at the expense of fundamental rights. In many Continental countries freedom of expression is restricted in the hope of precluding the process of dehumanization, especially when "speech" means the apology for war crimes and genocide.

Today culture changes relatively quickly, and with it the prevailing understanding of excessive pain and suffering may change too, independently of the level of pain felt. "Good or evil always implies a reference to will."[45] Certain acts imposing pain are culturally categorized as evil. Evil is attributed to someone in two senses. First, it requires a causal attribution, which is metaphorical and can be broken down as such, as for example with questions about soldiers being or not being responsible for atrocities committed under strict order. Second, it requires attribution of intent (or at least the impossibility of finding a reason for the atrocity) which makes it incomprehensible and therefore inhuman. But we are not talking about intentional pain only; harm's excessiveness is above all cultural, even if there is an emotional baseline of excessiveness, where gut feelings are elicited by cries and other signs of pain, blood, and the like. Excessiveness matters, as it can overcome otherwise socially acceptable or legitimate justifications of action; conversely, initial disgust caused by utmost suffering can be cognitively prevented or countered. Human rights law imposes a total ban on such cognitive strategies of justification in the form of the absolute prohibition of torture. What is called "torture" is so abhorrent for human rights law that torture is deprived of even the possibility of justification, and is construed as a wanton act. Wanton, unreasoned acts are perhaps the archetype of cruelty; such wanton injury opens the way to the worst in human nature. In the case of torture the actors' reasons do not count,[46] even if these reasons are otherwise acceptable, as where pain is imposed to fight the enemy in war or to save life, or against an internal enemy (communists, fascists, or other insurrectionists, guerillas, and the like).

The understanding of cruelty relies on an assumption about the perpetrator's theory of mind: the cruel person is one who has a clear picture about the suffering of the other; he is insensible to the other's state of mind, or even wishes the utmost humiliating suffering of the other, which is also part of the latter's objectification. This is what makes acts of cruelty *evil*: the evil resides in the person. There are competing theoretical and neurological assumptions about the personality of the cruel person. For some scholars, cruelty is the darkest part of human nature, generally hidden, which becomes operational where shame or other inhibitors fail. For others cruelty is environmental, that is, "torturers do not have a certain kind of personality, only exposure to certain kinds of psychological, social and political conditions."[47] Constitutional law treats cruelty as an environmental problem:[48] it attempts to create special institutional arrangements that reduce the occurrence of cruelty-enhancing conditions.

At least as early as the seventeenth century, an emerging demand for individual autonomy, together with the experience of political cruelty that was used to sustain despotic political power, and the brutality of religious wars, pointed toward what became a system for protecting human rights. This is how fear of cruelty (on the emotional basis discussed above) became crucial in institutional design. This concern animates general considerations of separation of powers, and more specifically rules about the civilian control over the military and police (the typical organizational settings for torture). Constitutional pressure may dictate specific public-law supervisory mechanisms which enable internal supervision of situations that invite cruelty, namely where the potential victims are at the complete mercy of physically superior government agents. Rules of due process for situations where cruelty is most likely to occur (arrest, evidence-taking, and the like) and the specific human rights prohibitions on torture and inhuman treatment contribute to the cruelty-prevention strategy. In a similar vein the French Declaration of 1789 tried to provide a limit to what can be defined and treated as crime.[49] The imposition of the label of "crime" results in the possibility of imprisonment, which always borders on cruelty per se, and indeed often remains a hotbed of state-endorsed cruelty. By procedurally and substantively narrowing the scope of crime, it is hoped to limit the sphere of public cruelty.

Further, constitutions recognize private spheres, originally in the form of the inviolability of the home and the body (search and seizure rules). Clearly this was intended to keep governmental constraint away from certain specifically designated areas (with the paradoxical effect of creating little kingdoms of private cruelty in the family). The boundaries are vaguely set, but in any given historical circumstances the transgression is more or less noticeable: Robespierre started his descent into dictatorship as early as 1789, when he concluded that the sacrosanct principle of the inviolability of correspondence must be abandoned for the general welfare. Regular governmental incursion into the private sphere marks the end of constitutionalism.

Fanaticism is another major source of cruelty; the way to preclude it is by banning fanatics from politics. Religions can easily turn into hotbeds of fanaticism, and hence of cruelty. The "separationist" move—namely, the separation of church and sovereign state that amounts to the respectful de facto subordination and (ultimately) the privatization of religion—intends to contain a major source of public fanaticism. In modern days banning fanaticism from politics has taken the form of a ban on totalitarian and caste-based political movements. Parts of the constitutional concern with equality are also motivated by concerns about cruelty: those human groups that are not considered equal may easily fall prey to (collective) cruelty, as they will be outside the circle of the protected—dehumanized, in other words.

We fear torture not only in our capacity as potential or past victims, but as potential torturers as well: we all have the potential to turn ourselves into cruel beings; panic and uncertainty only increase the wish to use cruelty as a quick fix. We protect ourselves against our worst through constitutional precommitment. Constitutional prohibitions are concerned not only with the passions of others; they also express a fundamental doubt about our own selves. The temptation to be cruel may be predetermined in evolution, and modern circumstances create endless rationalizations for cruelty. This is to be countered by unconditional bans which a priori restrain rationalization.

To conclude: experience with, and imagination of, cruelty generate a fear that can mobilize people, or at least make them resonate with the liberal constitution. When Shklar ranks cruelty first among vices, this implies that a liberal regime should fear a political system that allows and invites cruelty. Cruelty generates utmost anxiety among members of a political society that paralyses and consumes freedom. A regime of cruelty "makes political action difficult beyond endurance."[50] It follows that the right to be protected against the fear of cruelty is primordial, this being the precondition of the humanity of humans. Otherwise fear of cruelty would deprive citizens of autonomy and autonomous reasoning, as well as self-respect.

2. Committees, Bias, and Heuristics

At the end of the Philadelphia Convention an utterly exhausted Benjamin Franklin tried to convince his fellow draftsmen to accept the contested constitutional text. He argued in these terms: "I doubt too whether any other Convention we can obtain may be able to make a better Constitution. For when you assemble a number of men to have the advantage of their joint wisdom, you inevitably assemble with those men, all their prejudices, their passions, their errors of opinion, their local interest, and their selfish views. From such an Assembly can a perfect production be expected?"[51]

Franklin referred to what is described today as a fundamental difficulty of human reasoning in group decision-making. Contemporary studies on committee decision demonstrate that decision-making in a committee setting is particularly vulnerable to cognitive bias.[52] Cognitive bias results from the misapplication of decision-making rules, which may be otherwise valid, in other, different circumstances. Analytically, cognitive bias is to be distinguished from heuristics, which are rule-of-thumb tools applied intuitively or formed by intuition. Cognitive bias is often the misapplication of an otherwise helpful heuristic. Decisional bias is determined to a great extent by emotions, as (for example) bias in risk analysis is often influenced by fear, or even moods.

Fear and other emotions may be crucial in the agenda-setting for liberal constitutions. They bring cognitive bias into the constitutional decision-making process. When past fearful experiences dominate the constitutional discussion, the result is availability bias: the probability of fateful events will be exaggerated. Consequently the assumed risk pushes actors toward long-term institutional arrangements that are construed for extreme danger; this is clearly inefficient in ordinary political life. If, however, we consider tyranny and other fatal political events as *irreversible* and enormously destructive, and also as occurrences that escape rational prediction given their rarity, this excessive risk aversion in institution-building becomes much less a matter of decisional bias and distortion. Fear dictates a more rational long-term design than ordinary output-maximizing reason.

Are constitutions the irrational result of passion and panic? Do they simply and fatally institutionalize cognitive bias? The cognitive advantage of emotions consists in their salience: without salience there is no way to select the relevant stimuli from the thousands confronted. Fear creates a focus in problem-setting and motivates the constitution's makers to find solutions that will diminish fear. Mental executive functions do have the power to counter and direct emotions, albeit within limits. The constitutional answers of the eighteenth century certainly departed from perfect rationality, but given the great uncertainty of constitutional design in the early days, it was hard to say what would have counted as rational. The solutions were intended to be reasonably efficient, in the sense of reducing the occurrence of tyranny and cruelty. The constitutional tools of restricting arbitrary power were "invented" and applied in biased cognitive processes, where the bias originated in emotions. Bias helped to design lasting institutions and stable adaptive systems, partly by mandating additional cognitive bias. Bias ultimately became a constitutional intuition.

Constitutional intuitions triggered by the aforementioned constitutional sentiments provide a mechanism for handling future cognitive bias.

The following biases (a list that relies in part on Eskridge and Ferejohn) are particularly relevant in the constitution-making context:

- The committee may overgeneralize from dramatic and emotionally striking events (the availability heuristic)[53] or from small unrepresentative samples (the representativeness heuristic).
- The committee may anchor its decision-making on an arbitrary starting point and filter factual evidence through the lens of that bias (anchoring or cognitive dissonance reduction).
- The committee may impute its members' own views and preferences to everyone else, an assumption that reflects lack of empathy or understanding of others' different situations (the egocentrism bias).
- If the committee is composed of like-thinking persons, deliberation may tend to skew its conclusions toward positions more extreme than those with which the members started (the polarization effect). Conversely, more heterogeneous committees may tend to avoid the best solutions if they seem too radical (the extremeness aversion). In either event, there is a danger that committee members will go along with a proposal only because they think "everyone thinks this way" (the cascade effect).[54]

When constitution-makers select problems for the constitution, they are subject to framing bias. "One suggestion is that the framing effect results from systematic biases in choice behavior arising from an affect heuristic underwritten by an emotional system."[55] To solve the selected problems the constitution-makers create frames to fit the existing concepts, mindsets and language of law as dictated by affect. They are following an emotionally shaped path, and the framing choices they make both follow their own emotional conditions and rely on affect mobilization among those who will apply the constitution. "Findings suggest a model in which the framing bias reflects an affect heuristic by which individuals incorporate a potentially broad range of additional emotional information into the decision process. In evolutionary terms, this mechanism may confer a strong advantage, because such contextual cues may carry useful, if not critical, information. Neglecting such information may ignore the subtle social cues that communicate elements of (possibly unconscious) knowledge that allow optimal decisions to be made in a variety of environments."[56]

One should also consider vividness of information. "Vivid data are more likely to be recognized, attended to, and recalled than pallid data. Consequently, vivid data tend to have a disproportional influence on the formation and retention of beliefs."[57]

Most of the above biases were present at the Philadelphia Convention as well as at the French National Assembly and probably at other constitution-making assemblies. The composition of the Philadelphia Convention and the political realities in America prevented the polarization effect, while cascades played a role in the temporary radicalization of the Marais (the "swamp," or uncommitted majority of the French National Convention, 1792–1795). Extremeness aversion may explain the imperfections of the American Electoral College, while the availability bias, strengthened by the retention power of negative emotions, may explain why only negative experiences with popular representation were relevant for the founding fathers. The representativeness bias was at work when French or American delegates referred confidently to the available ancient Greek and other constitutional examples as sufficient and relevant. Dramatic single events provided a vividness of information and were shared by the drafting elite (and also by the ratifying majorities). Egocentrism bias prevailed in Philadelphia in the assumptions regarding human nature and mob behavior; it often operated in the form of class bias. Such egocentrism explains the ease in disregard of previously excluded groups in most early constitution-making. In contrast, the National Assembly was less homogeneous and had a more open nature. This may be one of the reasons that the egocentrism bias did not work and the previously excluded lower classes were taken into consideration.

Fearful experiences were decisive in classic constitution-making because of the availability bias. The accumulation of stories of pillage and lynching lead to the Great Fear of August 4, 1789, which crowded out most other considerations in the Declaration of the Rights of Man in France. Shays's rebellion[58] and the tyranny of George III were factored into the American Constitution according to the dictates of fear-induced bias, but the framing of the experience was more strategic than in France. In the American case constitutional heuristics stemmed to a great extent from fear-induced intuitions, and not just from panic envy and enthusiasm, as in France on the night of August 4. These intuitions contributed in Philadelphia to institutions *reductive* of cognitive bias, such as bicameralism. On the other hand the French experience of 1791 offers a tragic example of how the cognitive bias of constitution-makers can prevail through the institutionalization of decision-making settings conducive to further decisional bias. In France prudential considerations based on fearful experiences were increasingly sidestepped (as were those moderate delegates who were guided by these views), or were replaced by paranoia with its fantasies of conspiracy. Grandiose enthusiasm allowed a passions-based cognitive bias to prevail in the text of the 1791 Constitution (as evidenced, for example, by the unchecked legislative branch), while in the process that led to the dictatorship of Robespierre & Co., unmediated anticipated fear prevailed, together with allied suspicion of enemies everywhere. Madison feared group passions; Robespierre feared his peers.

It is through cognitive bias that emotions play an important indirect role in constitutional arrangements,[59] a matter that is not necessarily detrimental to decision-making. True, cognitive bias, especially if unaccounted for in the heat of constitution-makers' passion, has often contributed to clearly inefficient solutions that undermine legitimacy. But cognitive bias and the resulting inefficiencies of design may have alternative, constitutionally relevant advantages. For example, detrimental as it may be from a cognitive perspective, overconfidence (if successfully transmitted to the population) has often in fact *increased* the legitimacy of a constitution.

Constitutions cannot be judged only from the perspective of generating a means-ends optimum.

While emotionally induced cognitive bias seems to explain many shortcomings and some long-term efficiencies of decision-making within a constitutional committee, the high likelihood of bias raises further questions. How is it that such "irrational," suboptimal decisions were sustained for such long periods? Of course one could always avoid the issue by denying the relevance of bias and imperfection. The imperfections of constitutions originating from cognitive bias (and perpetuating it) show after all that we live in an imperfect world, one that cannot be fundamentally corrected; or perhaps constitutional imperfections do not matter, as constitutional vice is easily remedied by disregard.

In my view the actual shortcomings of the constitution due to bias are of secondary importance. Cognitive bias was present, but it often turned to be constitutional heuristics; that is, successful rules of thumb to be applied in constitutional matters: where you face passion-ruled factions, divide them and play their elements against each other. Where you see that religion in politics will increase oppression, remove churches from politics. And so on.

The transformation of bias into heuristics is partly related to the nature of constitutional choices. Constitutional choices worthy of that name are much more strategic than most legislative choices, and must therefore be sheltered from certain bias-producing public reactions.

Liberal constitutions are the strategic choices of a constitutionalism of fear. The constitutional heuristics of classic constitutions relied on assumptions about human nature, particularly regarding the way emotions work. What might be termed availability bias resulted, in response to the impulse of fear, in an institutional arrangement of power limitation that was beneficial when worst-case scenarios materialized or simply prevented such scenarios from developing. In fact, as Eskridge and Ferejohn argue: "One can understand or defend [constitutional] design choices after the fact as strategies to offset the most feared decision-making biases. Thus, the Framers' division of the legislature into two different chambers with the members of the 'upper' chamber having long and staggered terms ought to ameliorate the predictable operation of the availability and representativeness heuristics."[60] The founding fathers' minds were captivated by the experience of the abuse of concentrated political power and the resulting threats to personal integrity. Their concern may have been exaggerated, and the proposed relatively rigid institutional solutions might be termed disproportionate precautionary measures. Constitutionalism is another name for venerably disproportionate precaution and overcommitment.

Constitutional separation of powers may err by increasing the likelihood of worst-case scenarios, increasing (often prohibitively) the costs of governing. Because of the dictates of fear in the decision, governments may become delayed, paralyzed, and, consequently, expensive and inefficient. Consider for example the costs of separation of powers in emergencies, or even in ordinary regulatory responses to economic crisis or crime. Consider all the costly constitutional fuss about, and principled resistance to, delegated legislation, independent regulatory agencies, expedited procedures, and the like. Fear may preclude constitutionally viable alternatives: many constitutions, for example, expressly rule out or limit stronger forms of popular control through referenda as a corrective to government tyranny.

Constitutional design considers extreme, irreversible threats, and regards easy departures from the constitutional scheme as steps on a slippery slope toward tyranny. At least since Locke, the constitutionalist assumption is that one cannot trust government, even if it were one's own creature, and the way to tame it is through precommitment and precaution. The complexity of the draftsmen's tasks, and the uncertainty of the future that is to be regulated produce strategies that to some extent limit precommitment.

Precommitment. The prominence of fear in the shaping of modern constitutionalism generates availability bias, which would dictate excessive precaution (including rights restriction) against nonspecifiable attacks.[61] On the other hand constitutional heuristics, with their commitment to rights, affirm liberty through precommitment. Such precommitment institutionalizes a constitutionally mandated bias (in the form of overprotection of certain procedural rights, formal restrictions on emergency power, and the like), that helps to resist the "dread-risk" problem: risks that elicit visceral feelings of terror and of the uncontrollable.[62]

What constitutes efficient precommitment? This is the ultimate question at the constitutional quiz. Where articles of faith and covenants fail, a constitution must be a credible precommitment designed to counter the difficulty caused by social discounting of low-probability, nonvisible future events (primarily of a political nature). Institutions are designed to honor the commitments of the constitution. The rest is the work of institutional path-dependence. Institutional inertia that is added by a constitution's hard-to-change conceptual frame will sustain the commitment against insufficient historical memory and the myopic visions of ordinary politicians. Constitutional heuristics will impose the founders' "fear of loss of liberty" logic on future generations who do not share the founders' tragic and fearful experiences, and who have no interest in anticipating such events.

Path-dependence is not simply a matter of institutional self-interest and inertia; it is also mental. Concepts (and, to a lesser extent, categories), language, and authoritative reference can all shape institutional behavior and handle public sentiments. The constitution creates cognitive biases of its own—presumptions—by offering frames for problem-construction[63] (such as the presumption of innocence based on the notion that it is better to have 99 criminals go free than one innocent being convicted,)[64] concepts (venerated by lawyers as "principles"), or elements of a constitutional language. The fundamental lexicographic decisions of constitutional law will shape thinking about constitutional matters or, more precisely, allow for the shaping, categorizing, and framing of social-political events as constitutional events. Of course, constitutional impacts are also determined by institutional design. Constitutionally prescribed institutions, once established, will be programmed to impose their constitutional biases on other institutions and on social behavior. To some extent these biases are developed by the institution itself, as in the form of concepts developed in constitutional review. At least this is the master plan, but it is a plan that is fallible and indeed often fails. Understandably so: "For all our power to construct symbolic cultures and to set in place the institutional forces needed for their execution, we do not seem very adept at steering our creations toward the ends we profess to desire."[65]

Precaution. Constitutions institutionalize principles of precaution based on moral and cognitive intuitions. This, again, may not fit the utility model of rationality. But utility theory may have difficulties in handling low probabilities of irreversible large loss (harm). Besides, in view of the founders' experience, the loss of liberty was not a low-probability event and partial losses, once aggregated, increase the likelihood of a negative occurrence disproportionately.

Notwithstanding precaution, sudden and irreversible changes may occur, and these lie outside the constitutional frame. For such instances the design may allow temporary departure from separation and rights schemes. Constitutional heuristics are not rigid by design. "Rigidity and narrowness are not inherent features of our evaluative habits, but reflect defects in the social contexts that inculcate and trigger them. Properly structured reflection does not override our heuristics, but incorporates them as flexible inputs to deliberation."[66]

The institutionalization and mental consolidation of approaches that do not meet the high ground of reason and represent a certain sociocultural victory of emotions is not a bad thing per se. Emotion-based intuition is not necessarily an enemy of reason, particularly where complexity and uncertainty inevitably make rationality bounded. "The data suggest that decisions dictated by reason are not always good, while decisions dictated by emotion are not always bad,"[67] and this holds beyond the level of individual decisions.

Complexity and uncertainty. Constitutions handle problems of a complexity that partly stems from the uncertainty of future events and outcomes. "If the problem is complex, the committee may be overwhelmed and paralyzed (information overload) or driven away from correct but extreme positions (the dilution effect) by considering too much information, and may consequently be unduly deferential to other decision-makers (hypervigilance)."[68] If there are too many concerns entertained for consideration, there can be no optimal decision, or no decision at all, or decisions will appear arbitrary. One way to deal with complexity is through constitutional prioritization, as, for example, by setting value priorities and value-based institutional priorities, such as the primacy or importance of parliamentary supremacy or sovereignty in matters of legislation or members' immunity. These priorities orient decision as optimization.

In face of constitutional complexity one way to avoid information overload is deference to future decision-makers whose task will be to formulate specific policies. The constitutional text is left open enough to avoid compromises that will not work in the future.[69]

Uncertainty has aggravated the governmental complexity that early constitution-makers had to face. No one could predict how the new arrangements, like mass representation in a large territorial state, would work in practice. The same applies to federal executive power and elected presidency. Only the negative experience with George III's rule and a few years of experience with state governors was available firsthand. Keeping that experience in mind, and still fearful of it, the framers were able to overcome the negative impact of the availability heuristic, which was undeniably at work. They relied, in part, on a specific form of dilution (another cognitive bias): they deliberately left certain matters undecided, even at the price of diminishing pre-commitment. With few exceptions the power of the American executive was vaguely defined. This ambiguity did allow accommodation and development, though with important and inevitable conflicts. The much more rigid French separation of powers of 1791 failed miserably at the first crisis. The rigid handling of complex, unforeseeable situations might not have yielded perfect solutions from the perspective of the "perfect knowledge" of hindsight. But where constitution-makers opted to leave things undecided, they prevented their own cognitive bias from prevailing. A push for the imposition of some kind of specific solution would have implied the risk of cascades, and resulting extremism. "When the Framers were ambiguous or vague, the likely reason is that they meant to be. They intended their ambiguity and vagueness to be pregnant with meaning for unborn generations, rather than be restricted to whatever meaning then existed."[70]

The decisional difficulties resulting from uncertainty are similar to those caused by complexity. Constitutions have to shape the future, and optimization looks impossible at this level of uncertainty. As constitutions must guarantee that all people live together in a divisive society, constitutional law often leaves the prioritization unfinished. Open concepts allow an endless inclusion of additional human rights, resulting in rights inflation, or consideration of constitutionally nonendorsed or nonexplicit values such as security.

Complexity reduction requires rules of thumb, and morally significant actions demand "fast and frugal" heuristics.[71] Constitutional law contains a number of default rules, from procedural presumptions (such as the presumption of innocence) to opt-out rules (as in the case of organ harvesting). Some of these default rules reflect deeper moral intuitions which were formed in an intensively emotional process, others reflect cultural "intuitions" which at least do not generate moral outcry.

Constitutional heuristics as complexity reduction reflect, and at the same time shape, moral intuitions, as can be demonstrated in the context of different regimes applicable for organ donors. In France a presumed consent regime is in place with opt-out possibilities, while in the United States registration is required for one to become a donor. About 28 percent of Americans opted in, while in France about 30 percent of potential organ donors are not used for reasons of objection, mostly coming from relatives.[72] It is likely that the default rules reflect a prevailing cultural concept about body, religion, state-of-the-art health care, and the social understanding of medical services. But default rules are subject to emotional readjustment. For example, the French system underwent radical changes once public sentiment was mobilized against what was perceived as medical disrespect. In 1991 the Tesniere parents, who originally gave consent to some organ removal from their accident victim son, were shocked at the sight of the body of their donor child with oversized glass eyes in the morgue of Amiens hospital; the horror or outrage of this vision mobilized them to conduct a campaign against the existing law. After the Amiens hospital affair it became a matter of practice to ask for family consent, even if the deceased had not opted out. In the name of a catchall concept of dignity, family wishes are respected even against the needs of society as if they were the wish of the deceased.[73]

3. The Validity of the Model

Classic constitutions reified and set in (sand)stone the prevailing sentiments of successful social movements that shaped transformative constitutions.

Once the selection of public sentiments has been accomplished through their institutionalization, institutions set the frames of perception. The constitutionally frozen sentiments serve as content to be learned for individuals, for political actors, and for public sentiment and opinion.

Once liberal constitutions were in place, imitation could follow without the active support of constitutional sentiment. Learning as imposition can be taken for granted in the case of constitutional law that relies on well-organized servants of the constitution, dedicated to the enforcement of the institutional design. Institutional arrangements invite imitation and replication, and in the case of constitutions there are also external constraints that push toward imitation, at least within the country. Emotional structures can be transmitted intergenerationally with the help of a learned culture, and institutions can play a prominent role in bequeathing emotions. In the fundamental arrangement of these models there was little to antagonize public sentiment. The constitutional prevention of abuse of government power makes sense universally, as governments tend to rely on abuses similar to those that so animated the American and French publics in the eighteenth century. Human rights and constitutionalism reflect historical contingencies, but once they took their place on the ticket of universality they became a fact "proving" that these rights and principles are to be accepted as universal. Existing structures have mental colonizing power. (As it happens, and not without relevance here, states with civilized constitutions were successful colonizers.)

The classic constitutions that set the style, or indeed the genre itself, for modern constitutions were acts of emotion driven even enthusiastic creation. The participants in the creative process were aware of the lasting emotional impact their creation might have. They were playing and acting "with all the world watching." Constitutions codified public sentiment for posterity. The emotions "become codified in symbols . . . which evoke the supreme solidarity of the movement. The memory of emotional resonances of the French Revolution of 1789 were so strong that insurgent political movements tried to recreate that moment . . .; this was a guiding emotional imagery right down into the early twentieth century. . . ."[74]

Creation has specific power. I quote in this regard Derrida who reminds us that, even in regard to public sentiments, foundation is performative violence: "Its very moment of foundation or institution . . . the operation that amounts to founding, inaugurating, justifying law (*droit*), making law, would consist in a *coup de force*, of a performative and therefore interpretative violence."[75] What matters here, is the genre-defining power of the constitutional form, the mystical foundational violence; here lies the origin of the dominant interpretation. This is why the French Constitution of 1791 could serve as the source of inspiration for the 1814 Norwegian Constitution[76] and keep its power of dominant interpretation of the political structure in a faraway Nordic country with such different social relations from the more modernized France. But behind the creation there is a pre-foundational element, and notwithstanding the arbitrary violence of the foundation, pre-existing moral inclinations cannot be fully disregarded.

In the last two hundred years, several hundred constitutions have been written. Only in very few cases were conditions and concerns comparable to those that prevailed in the making of the classic constitutions. To a greater or lesser extent all constitutions imitate the genre that was accepted at the end of the eighteenth century. Although language like "imitation" and "intent to fit into the genre" may sound like belittlement, this is not to deny the presence of actual constitutional sentiments in the refurbishing act, and real emotional mobilization may occur from time to time even in copy-paste constitution-making. We are often proud to be able, finally, to copy (or "borrow") freely. After all, constitution-writing is a once-in-a-lifetime event, a matter of pride, and such situations elicit specific emotions even among dried-out lawyers and burned-out politicians. But the less intense the crisis triggering a constitution, the smaller will be the role of constitutional sentiments. Constitutions are written because a modern state must have a constitution and those in control of the drafting process seek the arrangement that is most beneficial to the perpetuation of their power. In such exercises one rarely has to consider public sentiments (except perhaps nationalist feelings).

In order to outline the role of constitutional sentiments in the different constitution-making settings I follow Jon Elster's typology of constitution-making. In his view these are the major grounds for making a constitution:

- social and economic crisis, as in the making of the American Constitution of 1787 or the French Constitution of 1791;
- revolution, as in the making of the 1830 Charter in France or the French and German 1848 Constitutions;
- regime collapse, as in the making of the new constitutions in Southern Europe in the mid-1970s and in Eastern Europe in the early 1990s;
- fear of regime collapse, as in the making of the French Constitution of 1958, which was imposed by de Gaulle under the shadow of a military rebellion;
- defeat in war, as in Germany after the First and Second World Wars, or in Italy and Japan after the Second;
- reconstruction after war, as in France in 1946;

- the creation of a new state,[77] as in Poland and Czechoslovakia after the First World War [or the Reconstruction of the South after the American Civil War];
- liberation from colonial rule, as in the United States after 1776 and in many former colonies after 1945.[78]

In the case of constitutional impositions, especially in times of (lost) wars and revolution, the frightened losers of wars will accept the dictates of the winners. The prevailing feeling is resignation.[79] This is not a creative constitutional sentiment. Fear is more creative in the face of an impending revolution after a lost war, it may result in anticipated expectations and it will push to accept the dictates of the anticipated. This was the case of the Weimar Constitution of 1919. Some of the fundamental solutions of the Weimar Constitution, such as that regarding a parliamentary system and even the republican form of government, emerged in the panic created by the loss of the war in 1918.[80] But in the Weimar Republic, once the foundational fear diminished and revolutionary hope was quashed, resentment prevailed and the constitution lost its public support.

The German Basic Law of 1949 reflects fears not only concerning the return of totalitarianism but also of the chaos of Weimar: it has an extended section on emergency legislation to overcome the kind of legislative deadlock that paralyzed Weimar, but Article 81 has never been used in the Federal Republic. However, the making of the *Grundgesetz* cannot be reduced to past-oriented fears. It reflects the pragmatic national and international need to reintegrate Germany into the Western alliance. Economic success did the rest.

Fear of governmental tyranny played a role in circumstances of crisis; fear of anarchy is in attendance at post-revolutionary constitution-making (specifically fear that the revolution might continue), and when attempting to forestall regime collapse. Some constitutions reflect specific fears, mistrust, hatred, and revenge regarding a political enemy, which might explain the very restrictive rules applicable to the clergy in the 1917 Mexican Constitution. Certain provisions in post-dictatorship constitutions reflect fears that totalitarianism might return, which explains the presence of rules regarding militant democracy, and tacit or explicit rules which deprive certain groups of political rights. Strong emphasis on human dignity and equality might originate partly in fear of past oppression. Certain arrangements of the Hungarian Constitution of 1989 reflect a fear that the communists would retain power through fair elections (hence the need for qualified majorities in legislation and the enhanced powers of the Constitutional Court).[81] The danger of civil war may have specific impact as well: this was the case in the formulation and acceptance of the 1958 French Constitution, including its emergency provisions, although the blueprint itself predated the 1958 crisis.[82]

New state formation is based on identity boosting and fear of denial of (collective) identities. This is the prevalent sentiment at nation-state formation which often triggers initial enthusiastic identification with the new constitution, increasing both its short- and long-term success. Fear surrounding issues of identity affirmation and related anxiety, or allied fears of the loss of identity and of status are crucial in matters related to language, religion, tribe, and race. These sentiments influence the constitutional recognition of self-government.[83]

But all these references to constitutional sentiments in the post-classic constitutions remain somewhat speculative except in matters of constitutional identity setting (such as nationalist feelings and racial liberation). Generally, we do not have the vivid display of emotions that was so characteristic of classic constitution-making. This is of course partly because the display of emotion became culturally less permissible beginning in the nineteenth century, or became simply disruptive in a legal culture where higher values were thought to have legitimating power. Sometimes fear prepares the acceptance of constitutional solutions, but this is not articulated: constitutional arrangements are understood as obvious, even "natural" solutions to the problems that may cause fear even without specifically evoking it. Constitutions are considered to be proven remedies for professional, intellectual problems. In our so-called age of reason the references in the political discourse have moved away from "shared sentiments" to concerns regarding legally manageable facts. Reference is made to the "state of affairs" in terms of, say, the "public order," rather than public sentiment. Those sentiments that can still bite, like ethnic and religious fanaticism and nationalism, are suspect; their constitutional accommodation and even their mere consideration are framed as highly troubling.

The language of sentiments is one of subjectivity, and such subjectivity can no longer be shared; it has been replaced by reassuring objectivity, or the promise thereof.

Contemporary constitutions are seen primarily as tools of instrumental rationality. Such instrumentality is quite salient when it comes to fundamental constitutional amendments and new constitutions that are part of governance modernization. Such amendments and new constitutions are written by existing institutions with an interest in self-perpetuation: parliaments, for example, will tend to write parliamentarism into the constitution.[84] There is little place for constitutional sentiments in institutional self-reproduction. In any case, little constitutional sentiment is required where the constitutional structure is intentionally superficial, and not a fundamental solution for future generations.

Contemporary constitutions are nontransformative. They affect the "assumed 'givens' of social existence" in a small way, and this is true not only in regard to what Clifford Geertz called New States, that is, postcolonial states, where "immediate contiguity and kin connection" might prevail.[85]

Constitutions became the tool of oppression and neutralization of sentiments: in fact the constitution's technical neutrality may be very frightening for those whose identity is not confirmed in it. This is hardly surprising if we look at examples like that of the European Constitution (a dreadful constitutional monstrosity to its opponents, but a necessary instrument of compromise for progress to its supporters). Ratification of a constitution may still trigger positive emotions, and there is some extra heartbeat where it reaffirms the identity of the citizens. But enthusiasm remains a passing feeling, without lasting identification.

Constitutions became a matter of self-referential legitimacy, with legitimacy coming neither from godlike framers nor from privileged and blessed moments of the making process. Legitimacy comes from public acquiescence, reinforced by the conventionalism that constitutional law is about. You do not need actual fear anymore, nor outrage or enthusiasm; the evocation of emotion is replaced by a desire to follow what is understood to be the sure safeguard against, and solution of, a nonexplicit or even deliberately hidden threat. Constitutions today fit into the civilizational project of hiding our own destructiveness, in a world where emotionality (beyond love stories) is troubling and suspect. Constitution is a *collage* of *what has the reputation of working elsewhere*, embellished by lawyers' and law professors' national pride. Constitutional sentiment and magic is replaced by cheap imitation that does not allow actual emotions to develop. Constitutions are accepted as part of a ritual. This is not to deny the importance of pragmatic considerations and interests, such as the pressure to conform that comes from occupation powers or needs of global fit. But constitutional sentiments are secondary to bureaucratically determined national interests of the powerful. It is no surprise that there is little constitutional enthusiasm today, except were the constitution serves nationalistic self-assertion, hardly a strong contributor to liberal constitutionalism.

Nevertheless, the mere fact that constitutions exist by imitation or simple convenience does not deprive them of residual emotional content. Constitutions embody some of those sentiments that animated the originals. Public acquiescence in the constitution (including acquiescence to the idea that the political sphere is to be organized through the constitution) is due partly to hidden identification with some of the fundamental guarantees against the fear of cruelty.[86] Ritualistic devotion to a long-dead God remains an efficient religion. The evolution-shaped, common moral intuitions of the brain, however important and helpful they are, are insufficient to push for a public sentiment favorable to constitutionalism. Constitutionalism reflects a peculiar historical constellation of public sentiment which in many regards tries to move away from the animality inherent to our brain. This public sentiment continues to cultivate itself with the help of entrenched constitutional institutions and their culture. This institutional setting has become widespread in the contemporary world thanks to the mental imperialism of constitutionalism, a sometimes honest desire to fit into the family of nations, a sentiment common among countries and people that wish to modernize or be respectable. In these instances constitutionalism operates through copying its past, read copy paste. The institutional setting of constitutional sentiments may survive, even if at the price of social insignificance, as long as the public sentiment of the day is not fundamentally contrarian to the original one. Where public sentiment remains unmediated through public opinion in a semi-modern world, where passions are taken for fact in the virtuality of television and YouTube, constitutional sentiments make little sense. How these prevailing public sentiments which are unconcerned with the public undermine constitutionalism remains a matter of prime concern. One needs a different book, one on anticonstitutional sentiments, to describe what happens in "societies so ravaged by violence and degradation that their people can only find refuge in lies,"[87] or where the only way to win recognition is to dwell in humiliation.

4

EMPATHY AND HUMAN RIGHTS: THE CASE OF SLAVERY

> Never apologize for showing feeling. When you do so, you apologize for truth.
>
> —Benjamin Disraeli

Strong emotions and moral judgments have considerable impact on the selection of fundamental rights. Human rights reflect considerations that reach beyond personal emotional concerns; they reflect needs of well-being of fellow humans. The taking into consideration of the needs of fellow humans is enabled by empathy-based mechanisms. But emotions alone cannot make a difference in society; the successful spreading of compassions presupposes favorable changes in economy and culture.

This chapter is a case study of the first hundred years of the abolition of slavery. This longer time horizon enables us to consider emotional influencing of constitutional law as an interactive process. Compassion played a crucial role in the emotional history of abolitionism; this happened within the conditions of modern economy and specific needs of warfare. In this context a fundamental counterfactual problem emerges: why did compassion for suffering not achieve emancipation much earlier, and, more broadly, why were only specific sufferings singled out for human rights protection, when other, comparable sufferings, like that of the poor, and child workers in early capitalism, were not?

1. Empathy and Its Functions

The emotional mechanism that takes into consideration other people's emotions and enables sharing emotions—crucial for their social (common or shared) representation—is empathy. Empathy is not a specific higher-order emotion, but a process of reproducing other people's emotions. It includes emotions generated by those of others.[1] Empathy enables us to feel what others feel. "The key requirement of an emphatic response . . . is the involvement of psychological processes that make a person have feelings that are more congruent with another's situation than with his own situation."[2] Of course, one can be concerned about the well-being of others without actual feelings of empathy as "fellow feeling," a feeling based on the activation of neural circuits similar to those the object of the concern has activated, although as a result of concern the feelings of the object are often imagined by mirroring the supposed feelings of the object.

Empathy requires taking the perspective of another person; on the basis of our imagination of the motives of that person we approve, exonerate, or disapprove his action. The imagination is based on the emotions elicited in us, which are based on the emotions of the other person. Referring to Rousseau, Alvin Goldman considers empathy the source of moral principles,[3] but empathy in itself is more a mechanism of emotional "comprehension," and it is in this regard that it generates moral emotions.

Empathy serves as the basis of concern for others through an emotional understanding of their feelings, thoughts, and actions; hence its importance for pro-social action. Indeed, empathy is about both sharing, understanding the emotional state of others in relation to oneself, and predicting their emotional response.[4] Social cognitive capacities include the ability to explain behavior in terms of intention. The same social cognition-related areas are activated even if the interaction is purely imaginary. Certain instances of empathy require a *theory of mind* (our assumptions about the other person's mental state). In addition attributions of causation will shape the feelings of empathy. In this process of attribution, emotionally determined assumptions like prejudice will play an important role.

The ability to empathize is related to a mechanism called mirror neurons. For example, in the case of processing pain, the firsthand experience of pain and the observation of others in pain show important similarities in the neural circuits involved. This is more than simple automatic resonance with the pain of a conspecific that characterizes rats too. In the case of humans, the pain of others (and some other emotions) is *understood* in relation to the self. A theory of mind goes beyond the feelings of the other: it contains a set of assumptions about the situation of the other person, for example, concerning her *intentions.* "Additional neural/computational mechanisms are at play when the situations involved a social interaction between two people . . . in which the pain was caused or alleviated by another individual."[5]

Empathy works in interaction with self-referential emotions. Consider the consequences of suffering caused by human action that violates norms, and in particular those that are caused by public authorities. The pain of others is felt through empathy. The pain felt through empathy, reinforced by fear of (anticipated) pain and suffering, animates the sense of injustice.[6] Anger (at others who cause harm) and guilt (for possibly harming others) generated by the empathically felt pain or by empathy with such feelings in the other person are additional elements of a sense of injustice.

Quite often (though not necessarily) empathy triggers self-awareness, that is, a cognitive reaction: the subject is aware of the fact that the emotion felt is other-directed and to some extent reproductive—that is, it is accompanied by the knowledge that the felt emotion is responsive to other people's emotion. This goes beyond cognitive perspective-taking, because it requires actual emotional involvement: "I feel his pain"; "I am angry as he is." In other words empathy is a fellow-feeling aspect of the theory of mind, "the affective state is isomorphic to another person's affective state" but it exists beyond mirror neurons, and "mirror neurons alone cannot produce or give rise to empathy." Even if one feels the emotions of the subject, the *reactions* to the emotion of the other might be different from those of the subject. Empathy-generated emotional reactions might be other-oriented (such as feelings of sorrow or concern) and/or self-oriented (such as feelings of distress). Other-oriented feelings may generate altruistic acts, while distress may result in avoidance and can become a sympathy blocker. "From a neuroscientific perspective this implies that distinct neural mechanisms may underpin different types of empathy-related responses" and empathy modulation depends on personality traits.[7]

The neuroscience community is divided regarding the automatic elicitation of emphatic responses at the mere perception of an emotional cue, and whether appraisal influences the empathic response *ex post facto* or emotional resonance depends on an evaluation process. Contextual elements including moral judgments and competing emotions may have a modulating effect even at the neural level, increasing or blocking emotion.[8]

Following Martin Hoffman, one can say that empathy may contribute to altruism and compassion for others in distress, because the way to reduce one's own distress (sometimes approaching actual pain) is to reduce the suffering of the other.[9] Guilt may be the reaction for harming someone where the distress of one's own victim is felt; such feelings may be generated by imagining such distress. Anger is directed at others who do harm. A sense of injustice emerges when the subject or others with whose deprivation we identify ourselves do not receive their due or where the distress results from some other norm-violation. But other rights-support mechanisms of empathy are at work too. When someone is confronted with news of torture she may feel herself vulnerable and have fear, or in case of identification with the "object"—the tortured person—she may feel sympathy toward the "object" and hence give support to efforts toward (for example) legal prohibitions that promise to preclude the occurrence of such events. Such action is comforting in more than one sense: it mitigates personal fears and has the effect of assuring that something good is done even if it will not much change the distress of the object. As with other instances of compassion, where help eases not only the recipient but the donor as well, here the occurrence of rights protection or even its abstract possibility serves as personal relief to the compassionate person. The availability of relief satisfies our hypocritical mind. Hypocrisy is the way to cope with the excess of injustice our world produces.

Empathy serves group coordination and in the evolutionary perspective it is closely related to it. It enables assumptions about other people's reaction, predicted from "emotion-reading." Moreover, it enables generalizations because of the need to conform with others. An assumption about the feelings of a significant other or the majority ("this is how people feel about it") has normative consequences. If somebody assumes that other people feel compassion, she may find acceptable a duty to help, or even insist that there be such a duty and expect other people or the state to be helpful. Similar assumptions may work for physical-integrity-related emotions (distress) or in situations that are described in terms of justice (distributive and retributive).

Altruism (helping others without reciprocation), or at least some of its forms, is one of the specific consequences of empathy which takes the form of compassion, which does not mean that altruism is always the result of empathy. In compassion the feelings of identification with the sufferings of the other transmitted by empathy may trigger *action* (help) that aims to improve the situation of the other. Altruism seems to contradict certain assumptions about human rationality, a contradiction that has inspired numerous competing efforts at explanation. Behavioral economics tries to connect what remains unexplained in theories of self-interest. Altruism may be a rational strategy for the individual where it increases group esteem or where some other reciprocation may be expected (for example, from the object). Arguably altruism satisfies needs of inclusive fitness: it pays for the herd to alert neighbors about the presence of a predator. But if the costs of helping are "greater than the benefit, attention can be directed away from the distress to control of subvert empathic processing altogether, making the desire to help less likely."[10]

The mental and somatic processes of empathy "can be augmented by cognitive capacities in evolution . . . so that empathy is possible in the absence of the object of distress, from imagination or effortful processing." The imagination of other people's distress may trigger feelings based on empathy. Not even the conscious awareness of, or assumptions about, other people's feelings is necessary. But the affective response is not automatic: it presupposes certain assumptions about the affective state of the other person. Brain imaging indicates that brain activation patterns of the sympathizer are overwhelmingly similar to those that exist in the subject. But this activation does not always happen in the presence of emotion cues. Certain (not necessarily conscious) cognitive processes are involved here, much as when one uses his theory of mind and also self-concept. The cognitive processes may be emotion-driven, like feeling love or anger toward the subject. This implies a contextual appraisal. Pain-related areas of the brain show less activation at the sight of pain in others when the empathizer knows that the pain is inflicted for purposes of cure. Whether observation of distress in others leads to empathic concern and altruistic motivation, or to personal distress and egoistic motivation, seems to depend upon the capacity for self-other differentiation and cognitive appraisal.[11]

Empathy is crucial for pro-social behavior. Darwin related empathy to mother-child bonding. Following this intuition it is argued:

> If empathy is a functional response to the perception of kinship, then—as a result of repeated association—empathy may come to serve as a heuristic kinship cue itself. The effect of empathy on helping may therefore represent a manifestation of overinclusive kin recognition. . . . It is more likely to be applied overinclusively (and thus to induce helping of non-kin) when the costs of helping are relatively low. Indeed, the usual empathy–helping relationship disappears when the costs of helping are made more substantial. . . . Another hypothesis implicit in this analysis is that the empathy–helping effect may be muted if there exists diagnostic information that strongly disqualifies a target person from being perceived as kin.[12]

In fact the struggle to liberate slaves centered on the kinship of blacks ("a brother") and whites. The alleged dissimilarity of victims was one of the main barriers to the recognition of their rights, as empathy failed to operate in regard to culturally outlying persons.

The contribution of empathy to pro-social behavior is partly moral. Emotions like fear, anger, and disgust are crucial for moral judgment and for constitutional sentiments, and they are spread and homogenized by empathy, but empathy also facilitates the cooperation necessary for a moral (or rights) sentiment to become socially shared and hence accepted. Because we feel what the other feels, we can morally condemn or support what the other person does: morality can be other-directed and general, even if produced "locally" in isolated moral sentiments. Even if empathy were not necessary to morality (and, through morality, for human rights) as it reflects self-directed emotions, it plays an important role in morality's formation, as it enables us to understand each other's emotions and will amplify the moral dictates of such emotions which cannot be efficient in isolation. The distress created by other people's distress will activate the observer to take altruistic action or participate in collective action with people feeling the same to reduce the distress felt.

Empathy plays a crucial role in pushing public sentiments toward fundamental rights, while personal concerns and interests are often interrelated with feelings for one's fellows. Fellow feelings and self-centered emotions interact in the shaping of constitutional rights. Identification often reflects concerns for one's own vulnerability. Empathy helps to explain the acceptance and endorsement of rights that concern and benefit people other than ourselves. Compassion is empathy in regard to other people's suffering, and is a crucial sentiment in the abolition of slavery; as part of the constitutional sentiment it did play a formative role in humanitarian action and the recognition of certain other-directed rights.

Identification with the victim and his suffering enables the emotional mobilization for fundamental rights. In case there is a deliberate element of identification, when one puts oneself explicitly into someone else's shoes the intensity of felt distress increases, which is more likely to elicit action tendencies.[13] Identification has played an important role in the history of the recognition of human rights. Other emotions that support rights are self-oriented, that is, the subject emotionally supports a rights claim because of her own emotional needs, for example, fear of status loss related to personal identity needs. When emotion display and emotion-driven social action became socially "affordable," intense emotions and empathy became crucial. After all, helping the slaves at the risk of persecution is excessively costly, even if one is concerned with her own salvation. But empathy makes other people's emotions accessible and relevant, and because of empathy, feelings are reinforced in interaction with people who share and admit similar feelings. These shared feelings, which reflect compassion for the distress of others and the outrage-based condemnation of causing suffering, will animate human rights movements. The example of the abolitionist movement as a mutually reinforcing emotional process with its own rewards demonstrates how emotions may change perception and rights culture.

Empathy plays a role in the conceptualization and acceptance of human rights because it enables the cooperation necessary in standing up for human rights; of course there are other emotional (for example, regime hatred) and rational (political or interest-based) grounds for standing up and cooperating for human rights.[14]

2. The Emotional History of Abolitionism

2.a. The Failure of Reason to Abolish Slavery in the Sentimental Century

At the dawn of capitalism, the bonds of newly discovered interests and commercial agreements appeared insufficient to hold political society together. Eighteenth-century moral philosophy attempted to find new cement for society. Moral sentiments were identified as capable of keeping society together in a natural way. Innate intuitions or learned benevolent sentiments toward fellow humans were expected to determine what is good and bad. Sensibility (that is, sympathetic emotional reaction to the psychological state of others) became a social expectation, even a virtue. In the eighteenth and nineteenth centuries, sympathy was the close equivalent of what we today call empathy. Adam Smith distinguished sympathy from compassion. For Smith sympathy meant fellow feeling toward other members of mankind, while compassion was a distinct "fellow feeling" for the "sorrow" of others. It was assumed that the suffering of others generates virtuous acts of benevolence through the dictates of compassion.

The intellectual recognition of the social value of sentiments and sensibility reinforced an ongoing change in social relations by changing the rules for emotion display. At the beginning of this (pre-industrial) transformation, family became a space for affection and a distinct private entity.[15] It became legitimate to be more "sentimental," more loving and caring in family relations, even at the level of the "lower classes." Political developments of the late seventeenth and early eighteenth centuries contributed to the trend. With the consolidation of central royal power the level of politically acceptable civil violence and rudeness was reduced. Sentiments of benevolence, compassion, pity and sympathy, and all allied feelings became legitimate beyond the family. The sentimentalism of the private sphere was gradually extended to more public spheres of life such as religion, literature, and politics; fellow feelings increasingly (though in very different ways) became central to various Enlightenment projects as a source of social solidarity. What used to be private feelings now became socially recognized, powerful public sentiments. Tears were elevated to the status of convincing argument, though to what extent and how remains a matter of cultural difference. The culture of sentimentalism not only enabled the display of pity and compassion but prescribed their favorable reception.

Perhaps as culmination of these different developments "an unprecedented wave of humanitarian reform sentiment swept through the societies of Western Europe, England and North America in the hundred years following 1750."[16] More and more people were concerned about prisons, torture, and other forms of suffering, including the miseries of madmen, especially in chains. The humanitarian sensibility applied to a wide range of misery from bullfighting to usury, and (though not always) to the conditions of poor laborers and their families. In the campaign against blood sports "the Man of Sentiment, or the Man of Feeling" appears as the ideal type of the age. The cult of sensibility was reinforced by enlightenment considerations but also by patronizing religious and social perspectives: the emblematic Thomas Clarkson, perhaps the most active organizer of abolitionists in England, and an admirer of French revolutionary egalitarianism, wished "to civilize [the slaves], to Christianize them . . . to make them better servants to their masters, and to make them more useful members of the community."[17]

The origins of abolitionism have to be seen in the context of this broader emotional and intellectual disposition, and its history must be placed within this humanitarian context. But the abolitionist sentiment was distinct from other humanitarian concerns, as compassion was lasting, large-scale and intense, resulting in action for fifty years in Britain and even longer in the United States. Abolition of slavery went on for more than a century. It began in the age of humanitarian-sentimental benevolence and continued well into the nineteenth century when sentimentality and sensibility were less important for folk psychology and prevailing ideologies than they had been in the eighteenth century.[18] But these sentiments remained a respectable part of the emotional repertoire, and abolitionists could rely on periods of occasional social outbursts of empathy, benevolence, and compassion.

Among the miracles of sensibility, perhaps the greatest was that of abolition of slavery. This humanitarian outburst—and abolitionism in particular—is somewhat of a puzzle. Slavery was an unlikely candidate to attract sensibility's interest. A geographically distant phenomenon, it was the least visible of the various forms of suffering. Very few people in Britain had ever seen a slave or a black person. More important, slavery was an accepted practice in most countries of the "civilized" and less civilized world of the distant colonies, around 1750.

Slavery was also a natural fact of history: "The ubiquity of slavery and oppression throughout human history leads one to wonder whether intolerance rather than tolerance may be the easier and more natural posture for most people to assume. . . . If one has sufficient strength and cunning to repel the enemy, one is inclined to do so unless one has discovered that, for some reason, another type of response is legally or socially required, or preferred."[19] It was this "natural posture" that had to be challenged.

A rationalistic explanation of human rights would assume that the abolition of slavery occurred in a process of recognition of its incompatibility with generally held, convincing ideas of personal liberty. But this is not the case. Slaveholders had no difficulty when they had to combine the generally recognized human liberty with their ownership of slaves as chattel. Voltaire, a proto-racist, gladly accepted that the ship of a slave owner be named after him, and speculated in slave trade. Intellectual consistency with the principles of liberty held limited sway in the recognition of the rights of slaves. In the age of Enlightenment "surprisingly few people saw a contradiction between freedom for whites and bondage for slaves."[20] The differing histories of abolition in Britain, France, and the United States do not support a rationalistic explanation of abolition.

My claim is that rational arguments and considerations might have worked where there was no major social or economic price to be paid, but general considerations of human equality and liberty failed in Britain, the United States, and France. The abolition of slavery is tied to a public sentiment that found slavery emotionally unacceptable. Emotions—empathy in particular—generated mass movements that would be instrumental in the political process that led to emancipation. The pressure of mass sentiment was not enough to change the law, but abolition, and its implied recognition of equal liberty for all, once declared, met with a constitutional sentiment that made the new right unquestionable.

Of course, rationalistic or rights-oriented considerations were well known at the time abolitionists started their campaign. At least some versions of natural law have long recognized general claims of liberty and equality, and these were used to show the injustice, and hence impermissibility, of slavery. Enlightenment philosophy condemned slavery on moral, religious, and humanitarian grounds. Montesquieu stated: "The state of slavery is in its own nature bad. It is neither useful to the master nor to the slave; not to the slave, because he can do nothing through a motive of virtue; nor to the master, because by having an unlimited authority over his slaves he insensibly accustoms himself to the want of all moral virtues."[21] He added practical and political arguments: slavery is detrimental to the constitutional order, and except perhaps in despotic countries, it reduces labor productivity; finally there is simply no justification for the right to keep slaves. But these general considerations could not make a fundamental difference as politics and law resisted logic and the great principles scored partial victories only.

In Britain liberty considerations came up in common law in 1772 at the latest. *Somerset*, an important commercial law case about a fugitive slave from the West Indies, indicates the law's ambiguity in the face of injustice. In fact Lord Mansfield expressly refused to consider moral sentiments: "Compassion will not, on the one hand, nor inconvenience on the other, be to decide; but the law."[22] Slavery was not supported in common law but it could have been supported by "positive law." He had no doubt that such positive law was possible, but in the current absence of such law in Britain there was nothing to enforce. According to Alan Watson "for Mansfield's own approach to law, Somerset is, and should remain, a slave. For this there can be no doubt. The issue, never stated but obvious, is one of conflict of laws." In Lord Mansfield's legal theory Somerset was undeniably a slave, but the property claim that would have been a valid one in foreign law was not enforceable on habeas corpus grounds in England.[23]

In practical terms, however, *Somerset* resulted in the freeing of all slaves on English soil. The freeing of the (relatively few) Negro individuals satisfied the image of England as home to liberty and the rule of law. Beyond the limited influence of the slave-trading and plantation lobby the strong public sentiment of liberty is the likely reason why the efforts to "legalize" slavery in Britain after 1772 failed in Parliament. But this sentiment of liberty originating in practical complacency is a proto-constitutional one at best. Freedom from slavery was not at the level of what today would be called (human) right. There was little talk in law about the inherent natural rights of blacks. Lack of a principled, constitutional approach to liberty in eighteenth-century Britain precluded the use of general principles of liberty and equality of humans.[24] Given the condescending social attitude among the British upper classes and their refusal of social equality, the abolitionists' strategy had to be an unprincipled one to achieve legislative reform. The abolitionists realized that the "upper-class Britons comprising [Parliament] might be moved by pity, but certainly not by a passion for equality."[25]

As to revolutionary France, the stereotypical land of reason and principles, where equality was a fundamental, popularly and constitutionally endorsed sentiment and even a principled right, abolition seemed to be a most compelling demand. The change resulting from the Declaration of Rights was, however, very limited: "Once the French Revolution erupted, merchants would promptly christen slave ships *Liberté*, *Égalité*, and *Fraternité*."[26] Notwithstanding the position of the Declaration, slavery was not abolished for five years. Perhaps there has never been a French public sentiment moved by the suffering of slaves. At least in 1780 Diderot had to remark that the Africans "are tyrannized, mutilated, burnt and put to death, and yet we listen to these accounts coolly and without emotion. The torments of a people to whom we owe our luxuries are never able to reach our hearts."[27]

The seemingly inevitable logical dictates of the Declaration of Rights of 1789 could not carry the day in the absence of mass sentiment. It took three years to grant citizenship to people of color, but only if they were free (April 4, 1792). The enlightened French abolitionists, members of the Amis des noirs group, remained a small elite, often contenting themselves with general declarations of principles, and ready to make compromises in favor of mulattos. Contrary to their British brethren, they did not (and amid the revolutionary turmoil, perhaps could not) rely on large-scale campaigns with images of slavery's cruelty, although "Mirabeau . . . in the debates in the National Assembly in early 1790 had a model of a slave ship built, which he was in the habit of using in his demonstrations of the inhumanity of the trade."[28] The French abolitionists used the language of horror and tears, and insisted on pity as a duty. Nevertheless, the abolition of slavery remained a matter of pure *Realpolitik*. In St. Domingue, a French colony at the time, a successful slave revolt began, inspired by (among other reasons) the metropolitan promise of equal liberty. In 1793 Léger-Félicité Sonthonax, the National Convention's *commissaire* in charge of the fight with the British and royalists, granted emancipation to the colony's slaves in order to mobilize the blacks to fight for the Republic. Sonthonax had an impeccable personal abolitionist record but his *ultra vires* gesture followed dictates of warfare; back in France he was properly arrested for his action. The French emancipatory legislation of 1794 only acquiesced in the 1793 measure by extending it as a principled solution applicable to all French colonies. Finally, with the *fait accompli* in St. Domingue now irreversible, the 1795 French Constitution prohibited slavery. Napoleon reintroduced it without much concern about humanity. But humanity has never been a concern to the person who closed the book of the Revolution together with that of eighteenth-century sentimental benevolence.

General principles and rational considerations of humanitarianism and enlightenment seemed to have had more success in some of the new American states. The Commonwealth of Vermont abolished slavery, drawing the consequences of its Constitution's liberty and equality clause in 1777. Pennsylvania did the same; the other Northern states abolished it gradually through legislation. But consistency with principles of equal liberty had its limits. Many leaders of the American Revolution had humanitarian objections to slavery; some of them emancipated their own slaves but were ready to accept the compromise of the Constitution. However, "[w]hat is significant in the historical context of the time is not that the liberty-loving Revolutionaries allowed slavery to survive, but that they—even those who profited directly from the institution—went so far in condemning it, confining it, and setting in motion the forces that would ultimately destroy it."[29]

After these early revolutionary enactments the principles of natural rights of mankind to freedom only sporadically won the day in American law.[30] In most cases the Supreme Court disregarded broad principles; human rights-based arguments like those of Tom Paine did not prevail in court. Prior to the Civil War it was an incontestable truism of American constitutional law that slavery was a matter within state powers. Northern states may have gradually abolished it, but compensation for lost property was given to past owners, and not to the victims of slavery for the deprivation of their liberty. Slavery might have been seen as conflicting with the logic of the general principles of equal freedom, but the slaves were not seen as rights holders.

Constitutional equality arguments were of diminishing force once growing racism made the claim increasingly problematic in a culturally and ethnically ever-more heterogeneous society. Northern emancipation did not mean equality. The growing racism erected serious barriers, including limits on voting rights outside New England. It was only during the Civil War that New York City, San Francisco, and other cities desegregated their streetcars.

2.b. Abolitionism in Britain

Abstract concepts of liberty and equality had only limited impact on the abolition of slavery. Enlightenment considerations which had a strong abolitionist impact in revolutionary America were of limited influence in Britain, perhaps because after a few years of litigation slavery was not a practicality on British soil. Although the enlightened members of the ruling elite like Fox and Pitt disliked slavery on moral grounds, they failed to take government action. Only emotions and empathy in particular were able to make emancipation socially acceptable.[31] The emotional history of abolitionism is rooted in empathy.

In a few years after 1770 a sudden shift in public moral consciousness occurred, especially in Britain. The changes began with the humanitarian outburst that started around 1750. At that time only a few individuals were ready to offer help to slaves. Glenville Sharp, a well-connected eccentric and deeply religious person full of enlightened concerns, exemplifies this early humanitarian concern. Sharp became interested in slavery through an accidental encounter with a cruelly wounded fugitive slave. When this person was later sold back into slavery, Sharp stood up on behalf of his protégé at considerable personal risk.

Those individuals who took abolition seriously had either some kind of personal experience, or very strong religious feelings that increased their empathy toward suffering and abhorrence of cruelty in the treatment of the slaves. From a theological point the question was one's own salvation. To what extent will the believer be held responsible on the Day of Judgment? What should the sinner do?

Theological concerns, namely a new understanding of sin[32] that was characteristic of a few religious minorities, like the Methodists and the Society of Friends, and religious sensibility opened mind and heart to the suffering of slaves. But even for these intensely religious groups, it took several years to conclude that slavery was immoral. Once the Society of

Friends finally recognized that slavery was intolerable, the Quakers became committed to follow the dictates of their conscience, which made abolition part of their systematic activities. They were ridiculed, and for this reason their empathy-dictated considerations did not "travel well" beyond their own ranks.

Religious faith was not alone in preparing the common man for greater sensitivity in matters concerning slavery. The popular abolitionist attitude was a mix of moral indignation and a sense of injustice. Consider the work of the evangelical poet William Cowper, who worked with John Newton, the author of *Amazing Grace*. In 1781 Cowper published "Charity," a poem much used in abolitionist propaganda. For Cowper liberty is a natural tendency that justifies the flight of slaves; he labels slaveholders morally corrupt. Slavery is shameful for Christians. "Canst thou, and honored with a Christian name,/ Buy what is woman-born, and feel no shame?"

The breakthrough occurred in Britain with the founding of the Society for Effecting the Abolition of the Slave Trade in 1787. With the formation of the society, non-Quakers joined the continuous effort of the Quakers. Between 1787 and 1792 the Society used relentless propaganda based on graphic evidence of suffering, unleashed religiously disposed empathy, and managed to mobilize the largest group of people so far for a single cause in England. This is even more remarkable in view of the strong resistance coming from slave-trading and plantation interests. Pro-slavery groups disposed of enormous financial and social resources and a network of influential politicians including the King's brother. But the abundance of visible evidence and oral testimony of slave suffering brought distant suffering home: distance and lack of knowledge did not provide shelter against the emerging compassion. The resulting national sugar boycott allegedly reduced sugar consumption by 30 percent.

The abolitionists were able to set in motion Privy Council and parliamentary hearings and reports. The hearings produced damning evidence. The stain of slave suffering became visible in the Empire of Liberty. The cognitive dissonance that emerged was difficult to withstand, both outside and inside Parliament. In a campaign of a few weeks in 1792, the abolitionist network succeeded in securing about 390,000 signatures on the abolition petitions.[33] The House of Commons voted for the *gradual* abolition of the nefarious traffic notwithstanding arguments about revolutionary troubles in France and news of slave revolts in French colonies. The bill stalled in the House of Lords, and when it came up for debate again in 1793, it was too late: the war against regicide France was already on. The pro-slavery forces successfully labeled abolitionist sentiments as unpatriotic and revolutionary. Abolitionism suddenly became politically suspect.

It took another fifteen years and a lot of cunning to achieve the abolition of the slave trade. The bill resulting in the Foreign Slave Trade Act of 1807 was not based on abolitionist considerations of humanity and suffering. In 1806 Wilberforce's annual bill to abolish slave trading proposed a ban on British subjects' participation in the slave trade to the colonies of France. It was a prohibition on trade with the archenemy. The draft sailed through the Commons without much public support and in fact nearly without attention in 1806; by the 1807 debates there was already considerable public support. Sir John Doyle, MP, presented in the plenary debate his personal recollections of the inhuman sufferings of a slave found in irons: "The rats had actually eaten off the greater part of both his ears." Of course, at this point in time, with independent Haiti in ruins France could no longer dominate the sugar market to the detriment of the British colonies. No one could argue that prohibiting British slave trade would only benefit French traders. The prohibition was in tune with public opinion as it did fit well into the British self-image in the early Industrial Revolution, where "Britannia occupied the moral high ground" and cherished a nation of free people, different in that regard from the rest of the world. This self-confidence made the 1807 prohibition into a booster of national pride, contrasting Britain favorably with Napoleon's France, where slavery had just been restored. While it was compassion, and behind compassion the psychological dictates of evangelicalism that mobilized public sentiment against slavery, its abolition "was a way of renegotiating national identity."[34]

The prohibition was unilateral, but the Royal Navy, interested in prizes, was in the position to enforce it on most other countries, many of which joined the anti-traders' club. The Navy continued its raids for many decades, liberating thousands of slaves. The unilateral enforcement became international law: slave trade was now considered piracy. But slavery was still not considered to be beyond the pale, and the freedom of slaves was not a right. For example, Britain agreed to the restoration of slavery for French colonies in 1814 at the Congress of Vienna. Emancipation of slaves in the West Indies seemed hopelessly distant. Moreover slavery was made tolerable in the public eye through the successful organized propaganda of the West Indian lobby, which sailed with the wind of humanitarian and religious benevolence and professed deep concern about the welfare of their slaves. In this new mood the government created the position of His Majesty's Protector of Slaves. This was in tune with the growing paternalism of welfare compassion: lack of freedom was presented as serving the best interest of immature slaves who would be worse off without the protection of their masters. The actual suffering of slaves was probably on the rise.

The abolition of slavery became possible only when public sentiment could be considered *directly*, that is, when public sentiment could choose the decision-makers through relatively democratic elections.[35] Around 1830, partly in reaction to news of increased cruelty in the West Indies, a new generation of abolitionists revived the movement, this time with a program of unconditional abolition. The Reform Bill of 1832 made representatives accountable to the electorate; many electors committed themselves to abolition. Indeed, at this first moment of modern British electoral politics the candidates were often vetted by the abolitionist movement to ensure their sufficiently pro-abolition stance, and apparently the abolitionists had enough support among the electorate to determine the outcome of many close calls. The 1833 parliamentary debates on emancipation were held in an atmosphere influenced once again by testimonies of suffering and cruelty. A very large-scale and orderly demonstration took place in front of the prime minister's office. Despite this moment of victory, abolition remained a gradual process. It was made possible not only because of the public sentiment of indignation when confronted with the actual cruelty of slaveholders, but also because the planters' lobby realized that they might be better off with a generous compensation for their loss of property. The compensation bonds represented 40 percent of the then national budget.

2.c. Abolition in the United States

The emotional history of American abolitionism is similar in many regards to its British counterpart. It began as a Quaker idea, and it was reinforced by Enlightenment philosophy. As in Britain, American antislavery arguments based on "the sentiment of Justice and Humanity"[36] did not result in mass mobilization. As in Britain there was a Quaker-Enlightenment organizational alliance, but given the direct interest in slavery in the Southern states its chances of success were limited, notwithstanding the political representation of abolitionists in legislation and their strong presence among the political elite. Where there was political representation for enlightened and other abolitionist sentiments in the new states, these carried the day, at least marginally. But when it came to the nation-building moment of preparing a constitution, the slaveholding interests of the Southern states prevailed.

Although the revolutionary equality arguments could not generate sizable support at the national constitutional level, both religiously motivated and Enlightenment humanitarianism-based abolitionist work continued after the ratification of the Constitution. In 1794, while being showered with abolition society petitions, Congress adopted by a large majority An Act to Prohibit the Carrying on of the Slave Trade from the United States to Any Foreign Place or Country. U.S. citizens and U.S. ships were banned from engaging in trade in slaves from Africa to the Caribbean islands and elsewhere. This was all that one could do within the straitjacket of the Constitution.[37] Even Southern states imposed trade prohibitions. This uniformity was the result of fear of the Caribbean slave revolts: Americans hoped to avoid the spreading of "confusion." Still, the trade continued, as the laws were poorly enforced.

The main arguments of the abolitionists until the 1830s were moral and humanitarian ones, with frequent references to justice and Christianity. But the immorality of slavery was not obvious to all. As Joseph Clay declared, "morality has nothing to do with this traffic," for "it must appear to every man of common sense, that the question could be considered in a commercial point of view only."[38] The Southern position simply denied the applicability of the rights of man to slaves.

The various abolitionist societies and relentless religious propaganda helped the cause of large-scale individual emancipation in the Near Southern states, where the economic conditions favored such a move. But slavery became untouchable in the Deep South, where the economy became dependent on cotton and hence on slave labor.

For many whites in the North, neither the continued sufferings of black slaves nor living with a growing number of blacks among their ranks was acceptable. Once the number of free ("visible") blacks increased, mistrust of the Negro race—these "promoters of mischief"—increased too. The fear that free black labor would compete with white unskilled labor was also of importance here. For people socialized in a world that promised equal liberty it must have been difficult to live with the cognitive dissonance caused by slavery. But prejudice involving the supposed moral and biological inferiority of the Negro and fear of rebellion successfully countered and tempered compassion. Colonization—that is, quasi-forced "repatriation"—to the newly founded Liberia gained popularity. The American Colonization Society (1816) dominated the antislavery movements, at least for a while. Needless to say, colonization did not reflect genuine respect for *human* rights. In the end, the whole colonization effort turned out to be impracticable. In the wake of the Nat Turner rebellion of 1831, the abolitionist move came to a halt. In response to the brutal massacres committed by Turner's men, the stereotype of black brutes was reinforced and once again the belief that slavery was God's will was on the rise.

At this point, when it seemed that humanitarian concerns could not change social conventions in the face of well-vested large-scale interests, a new religious attitude to slavery was already emerging within a sizable minority, changing the field. A young philanthropist by the name of William Lloyd Garrison burst onto the scene. His newspaper *The Liberator*, founded in 1831, relentlessly advocated unconditional abolitionist action. This was followed by the founding of the American Anti-Slavery Society in 1833. Garrison and his group demanded "immediate emancipation, gradually achieved." By 1837 the AASS membership had grown to quarter of a million.

The Society abandoned previous gradualism. Growing mass support for radicalism met with strong political resistance. When abolitionists continued to petition Congress, the House of Representatives decided to table the petitions automatically. The gag rule was made permanent in 1840. Only in 1844 did public opinion in the Northern states succeed in compelling their representatives to repeal the resolution. Notwithstanding the persistent mass appeal of abolitionists, the sentiments of compassion and outrage could not carry politics. "The manufacturing development of Massachusetts had been rapid, and a close affiliation had sprung up between the cotton spinners of the North and the cotton producers of the South—or as Charles Sumner put it, between 'the lords of the loom and the lords of the lash.' "[39]

The South, whose whole form of life had been at stake, mobilized national politics for its purposes, and the "immoral and irreligious" fugitive slave laws were enforced with increasing vigor. Abolitionist mail was banned and the abolitionists faced increasingly violent mob resistance and public dislike even in the North. Radical abolitionists took violent action against the enforcement of the fugitive slave laws, further polarizing the public. As Wendell Phillips put it, "We must trample [the fugitive slave] law under our feet."[40] The shared experience of action and violent mob reactions to resistance reinforced and hardened abolitionist feelings but contained the spread of compassion. The beliefs that hardened in confrontation went beyond what would follow from mere convictions arising from sheer empathy for suffering. Antislavery politicians, who like Charles Sumner "came to view slavery as the very antithesis of the good society, as well as a threat to their own fundamental values and interests,"[41] tried to push for a solution relying on democratic political process. Sumner's nearly fatal beating by Preston Brooks on the floor of the Senate in 1856 clearly indicated the limits of a peaceful political solution. Abolitionist sentiments might have reached the point of political stalemate, were it not for the outbreak of the Civil War.

In fact it was only during the Civil War, and resulting from dire necessities imposed by the war, that emancipation became acceptable to the northern elite and their supporters. Recall that even at the time of the Civil War the issue for the Republican factions was not human liberty. Freedom for slaves was conceived as a matter of taking from their masters, just as in Britain in 1833. Because the northern majority still believed that slavery was constitutional and its injustice did not change the Constitution, the debate was framed within the rule of law as it concerned the constitutionality of the confiscation of enemy property, which arguably falls within the Commander in Chief's power. The Union had still no right under the Constitution to legislate against slavery. After all, the Civil War was not a Republican initiative to end slavery. "While northern soldiers had no love for slavery, most of them had no love for slaves either. They fought for the union and against treason."[42] Military advantages of emancipation had become a major consideration for emancipation once the border-state considerations lost importance. The Emancipation Proclamation had to wait until the victory at Antietam, and the granting of equal civil rights required another century-long battle.

3. The Secret of the Success of Abolitionist Sentiment

"[Abolition] was not primarily a movement of Negroes asserting the rights of free people, but a movement to convert whites to the belief that Negroes ought to have those rights."[43] Where the persuasive power of convictions and rational arguments failed to a great extent, the job was done by emotions. Understandably so, as emotion-based moral intuitions cannot be changed by rational arguments. "The reasons that people give to each other are best seen as attempts to trigger the right intuitions in others," while social persuasion (conformity based mechanisms) is the other possible source of moral persuasion.[44] As Elizabeth B. Clark has stated, "only by understanding changing cultural and religious conceptions of the nature of pain, the value of suffering, and the duty of compassion can we understand how, by the later nineteenth century, legal standards came to incorporate (albeit imperfectly) the idea that to be free of physical coercion and deliberately inflicted pain was an essential human right. Graphic portrayals of slaves' subjective experience of physical pain emerged as common antislavery fare."[45]

The crucial emotions in the formation of the abolitionist mindset were compassion and outrage. These were elicited by experiences and representations of pain and cruelty. In Britain, from the early days on, Thomas Clarkson systematically collected evidence of suffering and cruelty, having done tons of interviews with sailors and former slaves. Storytelling, including reports by escaped slaves of the beatings they received, atrocities against their family members, cruelty against children, and rape, was regularly used. Beyond physical suffering other references, such as those to the deprivation of "normal family relations and religious life," also generated empathy. Visualization of pain is crucial here: the abolitionists' most famous trophy was the diagram of the slave-trading ship *Brookes*. The image of slave bodies amassed in the bottom of the ship in the middle passage "seemed to make an instantaneous impression of horror upon all who saw it."[46] Several thousand copies of the diagram were handed out.

In America the abolitionists were encouraged, and tried, to imagine themselves as victims of the same suffering the Negro had to endure, encouraging their audiences to imagine the same in order to elicit compassion among people who had never seen the actual suffering in the South.

"It is clear that the purpose of at least some of these articles was to force the reader to put himself imaginatively in the place of the slave. This would be the first step toward his learning that the Black man felt the degradation of slavery as he himself would. . . . The blood is moral: the blood is anti-slavery: it runs cold in the veins: the stomach rises with disgust, and curses slavery," wrote Elizabeth Margaret Chandler, the first woman writer in America to make the abolition of slavery her principal theme (and a Quaker, for that matter).[47] The language was very graphic. Images of whipped pregnant women were deliberately used, and blood was flowing everywhere. Similar blood-related emotional mobilization was used for pro-slavery purposes, especially in the wake of the Nat Turner rampage.

If compassion for suffering and abhorrence of cruelty were crucial for the formation of abolitionist sentiment, they were certainly not the only relevant feelings. Slavery was often condemned for the *arbitrariness* of slave masters. There were humanitarian arguments "that slavery denied the humanity of the Negro" too, but it was more important "to rouse Whites to anger." To stir up anger, the abolitionists emphasized how the North was being conquered by the South, and how Northerners were losing their rights and influence. On the other hand, "Southern slave owners increasingly articulated their sense of indignation, as had the revolutionaries of 1776, in terms of unjust political enslavement by the North."[48]

In addition, personal fear and anxiety were involved.[49] In many parts of England, pressing was a common practice: people were kidnapped to serve on slave-trading ships and later as soldiers in hopeless and deadly wars against revolted slaves in the Caribbean. Likewise, personal fear was used deliberately in the American moral war on both sides. Reacting to the fugitive slave acts, abolitionists intended to elicit fear by telling stories of slave catchers seizing whites. All that could not overcome pro-slavery public sentiments of the deep South, where slavery was vindicated as a positive component of the benevolent, humane, and racially superior Southern identity. Empathy was in a constant battle with a fundamental emotional barrier that originated from racism that relies on visceral disgust. Racism, at least beginning the 1830s, became a constitutive element of the identity of an increasing number of Northerners. This indicates the limits of abolitionist success based on the limited power of empathy: the vivid representation of distress might penetrate the fortress of prejudice, fear of losing status, and disgust only exceptionally. The moral outrage of the abolitionists and even the actual observation of the cruelty of slavery that often generated compassion could not overcome the anxiety that lived on nightmares of slave revenge, and in particular the feeling that the prevailing arrangement fits into the normal order of things.

And of course there was always the fear of damnation resulting from living in sin for allowing slavery, but also for rebelling against God's will that instituted slavery. Imposition of a sense of guilt (comparable to the use of sin in the religious awakenings in Britain and America) was part of the abolitionist strategy applied to mobilize Northerners. This seems to contradict the dictates of a successful empathy-based campaign but it must have been thought useful for deeply religious audiences. Abolition promised exculpation, getting rid of guilt (and sin) by purging oneself of prejudice and freeing the slaves.

There is convincing evidence that emotions triggered by suffering and cruelty contributed in a fundamental way to the formation of the abolitionist sentiment; further that the whole social conflict around abolitionism was fought as a conflict of public sentiments. In order to place sentiments firmly in the process of rights recognition, we have to answer counterfactual questions. If emotions are there more or less "all the time," why were rights not recognized earlier, or elsewhere? Slaves were in chains, flogged, and deprived of family five hundred or two thousand years earlier, and yet their suffering did not result in much compassion. Even if there was unease or distress, this did not aggregate into public sentiments. Why were constitutional sentiments less powerful or nonexistent in so many situations? Why, even where emotions were liberated by the abolitionist movement, did emancipation occur largely as the result of historical contingencies, and not under the pressure of public moral sentiments? Did these sentiments really fail or were they countered by other emotions and social and psychological tools of emotion containment? What made the breakthroughs in Britain and the United States possible and what made the emerging constitutional sentiments occasionally powerless?

Abolition and the public sentiment insisting upon it depend of the material conditions of the world where the emotions unfold and display rules are determined. In the eighteenth century the economic conditions of Britain permitted a new perception of slavery. Such framing of the problem had not been possible in earlier days of human history, and would have been a luxury to a great extent in other parts of the world even in the eighteenth century. For thousands of years in history, and in many places, slavery simply could not be seen as an anomaly. Where there is no alternative, there is no problem. Slavery was more than a fact of life: it was its precondition. Slavery was a matter of convention in ancient Greece, "life proceeded on the basis of slavery and left no space, effectively, for the question of its justice to be raised. . . . [In Greece] considerations of justice and injustice were immobilised by the demands of what was seen as social and economic necessity."[50]

With economic growth, compassion (for slaves) became more affordable. Affordability made these friendly sentiments less subversive for the mainstream. There was room for the new social conventions of social problem perception advocated by the new sensibility. We also have to look at historical coincidences. Plantation sugar and the slave trade were not decisively important in the abolitionist period of British history, and therefore little resistance to the abolitionist moral sentiment came from political power, while in the United States, Southern plantation interests created the most unfavorable conditions for abolition. In the North, economic, and resulting cultural, conditions were much less unfriendly toward abolitionist sentiments and, given the constant interaction between the South and the North, Americans were confronted with a parallel moral judgment coming from fellow citizens. Once the question of slavery's injustice had been raised, it became "quite hard not to see slavery as unjust, indeed as a paradigm of injustice."[51] Nevertheless, in the American South ordinary life made most people blind to the suffering of the Negro, even where the interracial interaction was daily. This is how Mark Twain, a committed abolitionist (and a Confederate volunteer for a couple of weeks) remembered his childhood experience:

> All the negroes were friends of ours, and with those of our own age we were in effect comrades. I say in effect, using the phrase as a modification. We were comrades, and yet not comrades; color and condition interposed a subtle line which both parties were conscious of, and which rendered complete fusion impossible. . . . In my schoolboy days I had no aversion to slavery. I was not aware

> that there was anything wrong about it. No one arraigned it in my hearing; the local papers said nothing against it; the local pulpit taught us that God approved it . . .; if the slaves themselves had an aversion to slavery they were wise and said nothing. In Hannibal we seldom saw a slave misused; on the farm, never.[52]

In such circumstances only people of extraordinary sensitivity noticed the underlying injustice; they could feel and see because of their extraordinary compassion. They could feel right, but in their isolation they could make only a limited, personal difference.

The issue is how individual sensibility to the injustice of suffering—the potential for empathy—translates into a mass movement capable of changing constitutional sentiments. Beyond the beneficial material factors, individual human sensibility requires emotionally favorable conditions, a world where sensibility is welcomed, and focused on suffering. The late eighteenth century is well known for its sentimentalist culture: this was hunting season for fellow feeling. In a broader sense, in European culture, suffering was no longer considered a theological matter, a way to salvation. The display of emotional suffering was not condemned; it was mostly lawful, even legitimate, and culturally not frowned upon.[53] If we trust sales revenues of popular sentimental literature, it was even lucrative.

A favorable emotional environment with favorable pain and compassion display rules may facilitate the public operation of compassion and other sentiments, but we have to identify what really attracted a growing number of people to these specific fellow feelings. In other words we must identify the psychological process at the individual level that led to a mass proliferation of the abolitionist sentiment. In this context the perception of the issue, "framing," is perhaps the key to emotional change. A new personal concept of religious responsibility offered a new frame of perception. Changes in religion changed the cognitive frames for moral emotions. In late eighteenth-century Britain, Evangelical and Methodist abolitionists were fascinated with personal sin, originating in a personal understanding of their religious responsibilities for the fate of the world. Their preoccupation with salvation made them concerned with slavery. Recall that among the twelve founding members of the Society for Effecting the Abolition of the Slave Trade, the three non-Quakers were Evangelicals; all of them shared a religiously shaped new frame. Almost all abolitionists considered slavery "a heinous crime in the sight of God."[54] By loosening the grip exerted by the written and rigid religious doctrine of the day that considered slavery acceptable, the new theology and humanitarianism exposed individuals to the very emotional influences that brought about such an opening.

Theological changes also played an important role in the revival of radical abolitionism in America. The liberal Unitarian clergy of the 1830s eroded Calvinist orthodoxy. It was part of the religious awakening to take responsibility for others. "Protestant ministers . . . preached the value of an 'interest in the sufferings of others who are at a distance from us . . .' "[55] This attitude helps to overcome physical and social distance, which is the primary reason for not feeling empathy. The rejection of cruelty was translated into a "universal entitlement to bodily integrity" pointing toward universal human rights.

Deeply felt religious convictions were instrumental in the change of emotion display rules. The expression of compassion, like that of other strongly felt emotions, became a test of the believer's sincerity. Testimonies "fulfilled the evangelical desire to hear of things close to the heart. In the evangelical framework, the measure of authenticity lay in the feelings, not the intellect."[56] Once religion welcomed, and even required, that compassion for suffering and for the pain of the slaves be displayed, the expressions of sympathy multiplied, sending reinforcing messages to others who felt the same way. The display enabled a veritable spiral of reinforcement within the closed religious community. Once there was a critical mass of converts to abolitionism through the good works of the heart, it was easier to spread the new mentality in the larger community where intense feelings and convictions were influential, even if the abolitionist position remained in the minority. Intensity of feelings can carry the day against passive majorities through a cascade effect.[57] But religion was not the only system of belief that contributed to changing the frame of perception that enabled compassion to work. With the emerging influence of medical science, which was gaining social prestige thanks to its effectiveness and increasing monopolization of the body, pain came to be viewed as not "normal heavenly punishment" but a matter treated by physicians.[58] As such, pain is wrong, and as such it is opened up for unconditional compassion. But science, as the emerging dominant ideology, and the argument of pain could be used for sustaining slavery too. Medical literature, at the time under the influence of scientific racism, held that people of African descent, together with criminals, were least sensitive to pain; their suffering could, therefore, be denied. To counter such science, religious universalism (which later was translated into a specific meaning of the universality of human rights) was therefore crucial for the abolitionists: they relied here on egalitarian teachings of religion: slaves were presented as "fully sentient beings with God-given physical sensibilities."[59]

In eighteenth-century Britain, where theories or false experiences of racial inferiority were not yet quite at work, empathy, once aroused, was difficult to resist. The slaves were successfully represented on the iconic 1787 medallion, designed by Josiah Wedgwood, of a kneeling slave in chains with the words "Am I not a Man and a Brother?" The kneeling figure became the emblem of the Society for the Abolition of the Slave Trade. At a time when most social classes were interested in equal liberty for themselves, it was hard to deny the dictates of empathy without serious cognitive dissonance. On the other hand, members of the British upper classes who hated equality but cherished liberty, felt uncomfortable when liberty was denied to slaves, and did not insist on this position.

We have seen how emotions emerged and were used to mobilize against slavery. Expressed emotions have emotional impacts and provide moral guidance by influencing evaluation. If I feel compassion with suffering that is reinforced by emotionally strong moral condemnation, where the moral sentiment is expressed strongly and convincingly, this will likely have a moral impact on me, and not merely because of conformism. The strong personal outrage felt at instances of slavery certainly had a further impact on others, as it offered direction or at least confirmation to the emotions felt by those confronted with the images and stories of cruelty and suffering. However, in order to create a lasting moral mobilization against slavery, the strictly interpersonal impacts and self-reinforcement due to emotion display are insufficient.

Emotions have to cluster into public sentiments, and such clustering needs social actors with sufficient organizational capacity. In the case of abolition the antislavery emotions emerged in the closed world of closely controlled religious communities and their clients; these communities became the carriers of public sentiments. A dramatic change in moral sentiment begins with the very strong emotion-driven commitment of a few people. But there are always people around whose strong sensibility produces moral sentiments. Why did these people fail to generate sympathy for their sentiments for so many centuries? Why is it so difficult to sustain emotion-driven social movements? After all, acts of heroism and dedication dictated by emotions—even the emotionally validated sincerity of an expression—have strong convincing power. But even these influential displays of emotions are mostly powerless outside small groups.

Religious enthusiasm acted as a facilitator of the cascade that followed the emotional breakthrough. How to get from emotional cascades in the closed interpersonal community to the "moral contagion" that reaches beyond the favorably predisposed believers and would change the moral sentiment of society outside the interpersonal community? The existence of small groups sharing certain sentiments and beliefs in a passionate way and acting in accordance with their beliefs is a fact of life that has an impact on outsiders, an impact that is stronger when the emotion-driven moral action affects others. A consumption boycott based on moral convictions may have an emotional impact on other consumers: the example may convey moral sentiments. It functions as an example of what is doable, and the more people follow this lead, the more it will become the norm with all the reinforcing advantages of conformism. Emotion-driven mass action may directly affect the unjust practice that triggered the emotion. In the case of slavery, the plantation sugar boycott had some impact but still could not bring the trade down.

Emotions, for example the display of outrage, act as a form of convincing information. They are convincing because of mechanisms of conformism: outrage triggered by slavery indicated a strong abolitionist commitment, and it makes little sense for a bystander to challenge someone who has made it emotionally clear that he is fully committed to a position, which, given the intensity of the emotion, is likely to be honest and true. But how does this emotional message of authenticity and "truth" reach the public? At this point we have to examine the conditions of effective social communication of emotional information, and of efficient social influencing. This perspective takes us to the organizational conditions in which sentiment is spread. When we feel empathy with those who condemn slavery emotionally, we may feel strong emotions which may change our perception and cognition. But in the absence of proper channels of communication the emotions, which do not travel with the ease of other information, will remain isolated at the level of face-to-face (small) groups. Once the sentiment and related beliefs are isolated in an interpersonal encounter or in a small group, it becomes difficult to sustain a common group sentiment in a hostile environment; at least the group has to isolate itself. This is what happened with many religious initiatives, which ended up as small closed sects cultivating inward spirituality. (See, for example, pietism in Germany.) Even where the community persists and institutionalizes the spreading of the sentiment, and (for example) sends missionaries to spread the "Good News," it is easy to contain the spread of emotions, together with the messengers.

After an intragroup reinforcement, the spread of emotionally driven information may succeed through well-established *networks*. It is through these that the general public will be confronted and mobilized by emotionally engaging images. Emotionally convincing personal dedication bordering on heroism seems crucial here. A minority position that emerged within face-to-face groups, supported by the force of emotions, through reiteration and a second cycle of societal mutual reinforcement, becomes a majority position (or at least a position and sentiment able to compete with others on equal terms).

Such is the cascade that made abolitionist sentiment prevailing. In the eighteenth century a few religious individuals found slavery morally repugnant, but most of them belonged to the ridiculed and isolated minority of Quakers. Their abolitionist propaganda was successfully contained. However, at this time some isolated members of slightly more mainstream groups, Evangelical and Methodist as well as some humanitarians, also nurtured feelings of abhorrence at the sight of slavery. Perhaps by accident some of them realized that there were others who shared these feelings of outrage; Clarkson found it electrifying when his Quaker friends explained him that he was not alone in his condemnation of slavery.[60] The personal isolation of abolitionist sentiments had now been broken. The mutual reinforcement of moral sentiments in frequent organized meetings and the nearly ritualized repetitions of Negro suffering helped "to assure members that they are part of a group with a historic mission, are not fighting alone, and have somewhere to go and others to turn to when public opprobrium weakens their dedication."[61]

After the arousal of strong intragroup sentiments and the formation of groups standing up for them, comes the task of taking the emotionally charged new cognition beyond the group. It is here that most religious initiatives and moral entrepreneurs failed, and this seemed to be the fate of abolitionism as long as it was contained as a Quaker idiosyncrasy. But once the Quakers managed to reach out, we can admire the workings of their well-established, very dedicated networks of enthusiastic people, relying also on additional networks of Evangelists and Methodists. Much later in the United States, free blacks created networks beyond religious networks. Moreover, the networks could mobilize politically influential mainstream players like Wilberforce in Britain and Charles Sumner in the United States, who made the abolitionist claims accessible to the political elite. Public opinion was at the same time systematically bombarded with abolitionist evidence.

Mobilization of large audiences was the third stage. The main tool of such mobilization consisted in generating empathy primarily by making suffering *visible*. It was increasingly difficult to avoid exposure to compassion and outrage-generating scenes of pain. Pain suffered by slaves came within the access of many. This is how the abolitionist sentiment reached broad circles of society: it was represented as a socially widespread sentiment, with the effect of mutually reinforcing emotions, thanks also to the constant confrontation with oral, written, and visual evidence of slave suffering presented by victims and observers. Slavery was no longer a hidden event occurring thousand of miles away: the evidence of cruelty and suffering inevitably aroused empathy, especially if there was no direct interest or intellectual obstacle to its perception and elaboration. Damning evidence of cruelty was systematically collected and used in major propaganda campaigns.

New techniques of communication facilitated the spread of emotional information. Faster diffusion of information became possible thanks to late eighteenth-century innovations crucial to the success of the abolition movement.[62] The increased speed enabled coordinated action, and coordination led to mutual reinforcement of empathy, implanting a new way of thinking about slavery. In the nineteenth century, speedy circulation of news and easy mass travel could be taken for granted.

Public moral sentiments, even if carried by strong empathy, cannot match economic interest and the force of external historical events, like the increasing fear of the French Revolution that became an element of politics and killed the slave-trade reform in the House of Lords in 1792 and the years to follow. Emotions could change the disposition toward slavery of many people; it would, however, be simplistic and even wrong to argue that the irresistible dictate of constitutional sentiments in the end caused the prohibition of slavery and a generalized prohibition of cruelty.

Historical accidents, namely the lack of the danger of French competition in the slave trade due to Napoleon's losses at sea and, ironically, the success of a slave revolution in St. Domingue enabled the British abolition of the trade. British naval supremacy was turned into international customary law of stopping slave ships. Legally, the prohibition of slavery was to a great extent the result of an emerging practice in international law.

As for the United States, here too there was a strong, emotionally driven abolitionist movement. But again the dictates of the constitutional sentiments generated by the movement failed to be transformed into constitutional rights. Only the brutal military conflict in the Civil War resulted in the imposition of the fundamental right of liberty through the Thirteenth Amendment. But without the emotional support among the victors there could not have been a constitutional commitment to the right. In fact, the sustainability of equal liberty (at least as a principle) was to a great extent attributable to the moral sentiments of the abolitionists. The right of equal liberty received additional support from below, from the experience and interest of former slaves. "Recent studies have made clear how the persistent agitation of Radical Republicans and abolitionists . . . produced the Civil Rights Act of 1866 and the Fourteenth and Fifteenth amendments—measures that embodied a new national commitment to the principle of equality before the law. But the conception of citizens' rights enshrined in national law and the federal Constitution during Reconstruction also came, as it were, from below."[63]

The political and economic happenstance could not have resulted in a principled abolition without the pressure of public sentiments, although these sentiments cannot be limited to abolitionist compassion and equality beliefs. The ban on the Atlantic slave trade was a matter of British national pride, as well as a calculated step in the legitimation of supreme naval power. In the United States, although abolitionist sentiment was important in the electoral victory of the Republicans who pushed for civil war, it was the war itself that necessitated the Emancipation Proclamation. In both instances, however, abolition reflected widely held sentiments which provided continued support for it and pushed for the international enforcement of the prohibition of the slave trade in the British case; after the Civil War it pushed for additional equality (civil rights) legislation, at least for a decade, in the United States. Public sentiments, once legally sanctioned, stood and stand behind the long-term emotional sustainability of the human right of freedom.

4. Limits to Compassion

4.a. Market Rationality against Compassion

Around 1705–1710 Anthony Ashley Cooper, 3rd Earl of Shaftesbury, came up with the idea that one gets to moral virtue through feeling certain emotions.[64] He and his followers (including Hume and Adam Smith) pointed toward a new, individualist source of moral knowledge that could potentially replace the revealed truth of Scripture. According to influential theories of sentimentalism fellow feelings, and compassion in particular, are capable of organizing and sustaining society. The emotional bond was seen as the source of sociability in France as well. "The magic of compassion was that it opened the heart of the sufferer to the sufferings of others, whereby it established and confirmed the 'natural' bond between men which only the rich had lost."[65]

Humanitarian sensibility enabled and required religious believers as well as enlightened persons to work for a good society of mutually benevolent individuals. As Adam Smith stated, sensible and benevolent people find guidance for action thanks to sympathy: "By the imagination we place ourselves in his [the fellow being's] situation, we conceive ourselves enduring all the same torments, we enter as it were into his body, and become in some measure the same person with him. . . . His agonies . . . when we have thus adopted and made them our own, begin at last to affect us, and we then tremble and shudder at the thought of what he feels."[66]

Notwithstanding their appeal, sensibility and the human tendency to feel compassion presented a major problem for social regulation and discipline. Some of the empathy-dictated actions might be "too sympathetic" to the underclass, undermining the dictates of interest and the institutions of the emerging market society. Benevolence may have detrimental effects in a society that has to be disciplined with vigor and force to guarantee that the disciplined live according to (certain people's) interests.

Moral sentiments and morality are unpredictable and unruly. "It is probable that there is no point of duty, where conscientious persons differ more in opinion, or where they find it more difficult to form discriminating and decided views, than on the matter of charity."[67] Moral sentiments of empathy may increase sociability but remain poor coordinators of social action; they give very imprecise and even impractical (or inefficient, hence irrational) guidance. Empathy with the sufferings of the victim of abhorrent crime runs against empathy with the future suffering of the convicted felon and his family. Compassion dictates different things to different actors. Emotions are not only unstable and conflicting within a single individual but are also so within society. Certain emotions are considered inappropriate by some groups because of the action generated by the emotion, while for others the same emotion serves as a factor for mobilization. Moreover, empathy is easily corrupted to result in the admiration of the rich and the neglect of persons living in poor conditions.

Mandeville was the first to point out the potentially detrimental consequences of compassion in an economy based on self interest. Workers would continue to be idle and lazy were they taken care of. Adam Smith as the author of both *The Theory of Moral Sentiments* of 1759 and *The Wealth of Nations* of 1776 struggled with the tension between benevolent moral sentiments and private interests. He pointed out that among proper conditions of *natural liberty* the social products generated by the self-interest of all, including that of laborers, will be more efficient than benevolence.[68] This is not to say that he did not believe in compassion's good work, but he considered it to be applicable in a limited sphere where natural liberty did not yet apply (as in the case of slavery) or where self-interest could not exercise a beneficial impact (for instance where wages of workers are too low). Given that he was writing before the full development of a market economy operating in a system of natural liberty, it is understandable that he was unconcerned about the need for compassion in a fully operative market system with its temporary inefficiencies and suffering. But Smith, who undeniably stood up for moral sentiments (particularly compassion) as the basis of justice and virtue, categorically rejected humanitarian benevolence as the basis of social organization. He was certainly aware of the inherent limits of compassion when it comes to social regulation and was worried about this. He was skeptical not about the strength of altruism, but rather about its scope or reach. He asks "how a man of humanity in Europe" would respond to hearing "that the great empire of China . . . was suddenly swallowed up by an earthquake . . .?" His answer was that "[i]f he [this man] was to lose his little finger tomorrow, he would not sleep tonight; but, provided he never saw them [that is, the people of China], he would snore with the most profound security over the ruin of a hundred million of his brethren, and the destruction of that immense multitude seems plainly an object less interesting to him than this paltry misfortune of his own."[69]

In the context of slavery (and Poor Laws too) Adam Smith relied on self-interest-based considerations. He was in favor of the gradual abolition of slavery on grounds that slave work undermined the efficiency of interest-motivated work.[70] However, utilitarian abolitionists of the Adam Smith brand denounced all forms of "false charity" that limited the free exercise of individual self-interest. "[*The Wealth of Nations*] makes it perfectly clear that man's benevolent feelings can be disastrous if allowed to interfere with public policy." Social philosophy and social regulation had to be "free from sentimental notions of charity and human rights."[71] Law and other forms of social disciplining were instrumental in limiting "false charity." But for certain actions, especially where economic considerations did not prevail, emotions (including compassion) could still have a legitimate role.

The regulatory dilemma of the emerging market society was to single out the proper subjects of empathy. Law (including fundamental rights law) is one of the tools for identifying these areas. Needless to say this process—the developing of socially acceptable uses of empathy—is a historical one, within which the display rules change. The identification process is a conflict-ridden social one: empathy is hard-wired, but its objects and the resulting display and proper social (or behavioral) reactions to emotion are socially construed. Some feelings of empathy were found acceptable in the emerging market society, even socially expected and respectful, and occasionally elevated to rights. Other instances of empathy, such as compassion toward the misery of the poor, had to be restricted and channeled, and in the long run even suppressed (or at least accommodated in forms of institutional care). Compassion for the workers' plight often resulted in outrage, and through outrage it led to revolutionary positions (especially outside England), instead of human rights claims. Contemporary efforts to elevate social rights claims to the status of fundamental and human rights try to mobilize culturally frozen emotions.

The working of the emotion selection and accommodation process can be seen in comparing the success of abolition (which transformed the prohibition of slavery into a universal human and constitutional right) with the handling of relief for the poor, which never generated the same amount of passionate compassion and never became a full constitutional right. In the case of abolitionism a fundamental right was gradually recognized during the early Industrial Revolution, and later even constitutionalized. When it came to the miseries of the poor, attempts to allow compassion for unemployed workers to work itself up to the level of a full social right were nonetheless rejected.[72] In fact, Poor Laws were to a great extent enacted to prevent fellow feelings, partly by providing conscience-appeasing regulation. One advantage of the work house and orphanage was that they hid misery. Slaveholders tried something similar: to accommodate compassion they boasted of "humanitarian treatment of slaves." But their effort failed, at least in the long run. American slaveholders, however, not only developed the lie of patriarchal benevolence; they also succeeded in successfully mobilizing growing racism to block empathy.

4.b. Psychological and Sociopsychological Empathy Blockers

The market rationality of the early capitalist period relied on self-interest. Consequently humanitarian feelings like compassion could not guide public policy.[73] But what was to be done once such emotions actually arose at the sight of suffering people, including workers and the poor? What to do with emotions that challenge the supreme rationality of the market? After all, in this sentimental age people excelled in sensibility. British workers used tactics that closely followed those of the abolitionists, with representations of suffering that the sensitive heart would find hard to resist. They claimed that the same feelings of compassion that applied to slaves could be applied to their miseries as well. In their view their sufferings were comparable to that of the chattel slaves, and hence they asked for the extension of public sentiments that applied to slaves. This was not an easy claim to disregard. Nevertheless many otherwise sensitive abolitionists were little touched by the visible suffering of workers or the unemployed and idle.

David Brion Davis has argued that, notwithstanding the cult of sensibility in the eighteenth century "middle-class Englishmen learned to screen out most of the oppression and suffering in their midst." Laborers' suffering did not translate into liberty or human rights. This is also true of other special groups of institutionalized sufferers, such as those in orphanages. For E. P. Thompson the screening out was close to self-deception: "We forget how long abuses can continue 'unknown' until they are articulated: how people can look at misery and not notice it, until misery itself rebels."[74]

How did it happen that compassion was largely limited to slaves, and how could it disregard workers? For a theory of constitutional sentiments it is particularly relevant how emotions are *prevented* from having an impact on the formation of social institutions. There are a number of mental processes leading to the disregard or neutralization of a phenomenon that otherwise may affect emotions or trigger their display. Avoidance techniques include the distortion or denial of facts, and other forms of intellectual manipulation of perceptions, including denial of victim status, or blaming the victim, and category change. These techniques are culturally mobilized through, among other means, the scripting of emotion display, but most importantly by determining the framing of social perception through the *reclassification* of suffering. Another technique of nonperception consisted of denial of facts. "Wilberforce and 'Saints' of Clapham . . . often contrasted slavery with the happy lot of British workers and craftsmen, who—except when led astray by French or outside agitators—were patriotically content with their place in the social hierarchy."[75]

The question is how focusing and denial occur in the social culture. These social and cultural processes rely on the psychological mechanisms that manage emotions primarily by structuring the stimuli that trigger these emotions. What is particularly important from a social-regulatory perspective is not that distress results in feelings through empathy, but rather how these feelings are *avoided* (through inhibition) or transformed. In other words, how is it that we avoid the automatism of empathy that would make humans and many other species themselves distressed at the sight of others in distress, and "act to terminate the object's distress, even incurring risk to themselves."[76]

Other people's distress is not irresistibly contagious. Professionals like medical staff are trained successfully not to feel empathy, and such training or socialization is common among those who regularly exercise coercive power like prison guards, policemen, and soldiers. The emotional culture of totalitarian institutions contributes to the sanitization of other people's suffering. Further, emotions can be countered by emotions and by framing the stimulus that would trigger the emotion. Consider cruelty, a most abhorrent, fundamental right-producing event likely to arouse disgust and fear. During the French Revolution Robespierre successfully reframed acts of cruelty into legitimate acts of self-defense. There could not be cruelty or violation of due process when it came to causing suffering to the enemy, at least in the minds of those people who accepted the mental frame of the Jacobins. The only thing Robespierre had to do was to deprive his opponents of credibility by representing them as suspects, putting them therefore beyond the reach of sympathy: "Terror is naught but prompt, severe, inflexible justice; it is therefore an emanation of virtue."[77] This was the immortal recipe for the disregard of human rights.

There are a number of social and psychological obstacles to the emergence of empathy. In an anonymous and fragmented society, the encounter with distress outside the circle of family and friends is unlikely, which facilitates the marshaling of cognitive inhibitions against empathy.[78] After the distress of the other has been processed, empathy can be controlled or its "resonance" degraded. Even if empathy works, there are many comforting behaviors that mitigate the feeling that the other person is in distress. For example, potentially comforting acts minimize the distress of the other, if only partially or symbolically.

Below I list some important empathy blockers which influence information processing, and thereby the emotional reaction itself, with particular relevance for compassion.[79] These are

- geographic and social distance from distress, and more generally from the intensity of its direct observation;
- psychophysical numbing;

- (lack of) similarity;
- framing (categorization and reclassification of the distress, its causes, or the person in distress); and
- familiarity.

Frames of cognition (for example, categorization) are social constructs. Socially generated framing, by hiding or deconstructing similarity, creates obstacles to the impact of other people's distress where such distress might mobilize for human rights and for humanitarian intervention.[80] Familiarity, and the lack thereof, are facts of social life. Socially influenced cognitive manipulation (social bias) may deny familiarity and/or create social distance that will alienate the subject from the person in distress. Group identity may suggest that the distress comes from people ("others") with whom one cannot identify: the "natural" emotional inclination will be blocked. It was held quite successfully in the nineteenth century that members of inferior races (who happened to be slaves) do not feel pain to the extent members of the more sensitive superior race do. While human infants respond to stress (cries) of other unknown children and rats respond to the stress of their conspecifics, human adults are capable of dehumanizing other humans and denying any community with them. The result is that one can avoid identification even in the presence of visible suffering.

Currently neuroscience cannot explain how humans manage to avoid the emotional consequences of the emotions of others. It may well be that subjects are genuinely "self-blinded" and do not observe the distress or manage to deny its relevance, especially where it occurs as a regular event, as in hospitals, prisons and other total-control institutions including (paradigmatically) concentration camps. Even if empathy forces humans to feel the distress of others, they manage to trivialize it. The feeling of other people's distress may turn the observer against the person who suffers: consider the common situation of blaming the victim. Techniques of denial are socially scripted and transgressions of the script may be sanctioned. But even without such sanctions, the personal need to affirm group identity may be sufficient for considering distress, especially where such identity is based on strong denial of equality for non-group members. Overt and covert display rules in formal organizations further counter empathy: "Through recruitment, selection, socialisation and performance evaluations, organisations develop a social reality in which feelings become a commodity for achieving instrumental goals."[81]

Other empathy blockers, such as attribution, operate at a higher cognitive level. Martin Hoffman emphasizes that "people spontaneously attribute causes to events and causal attributions shape one's emphatic response to another state. Furthermore, many events witnessed in life produce a rapid shifting of causal attributions from moment to moment."[82] Advance knowledge also sets limits to empathy: if prejudice or the prevailing culture and ideology already blame a potential victim for her suffering, her distress will not be regarded as such in the actual encounter with the victim; it will count as deserved punishment, or at least it will be easily neutralized. Likewise, advance knowledge regarding one's own identity will have an effect on developing or reducing empathy.[83]

4.c. The Social Screening Out of Emotions

In preventing empathy, psychological empathy blockers operate in close cooperation with social techniques which provide cognitive frames for avoidance. Social conditions and traditions prepare humans not to perceive events in a way that would trigger strong and painful or discomforting emotions. People are very good at reducing cognitive dissonance, especially where the prevailing culture and law allow it. Religion and other forms of ideology play an important role here.[84]

As Thomas Haskell has pointed out, there are cognitive preconditions for raising the issue of injustice. Humanitarian sensibility was not unlimited even in the sentimental century: it did not even appear where the sense of responsibility was absent; and responsibility is absent where the conditions for the social construction of such personal responsibility and agency are absent. There is no causal relation in the social sense where action is socially impossible and incomprehensible. Hence assuming or even envisioning responsibility for doing something about slavery, harsh as it may have been, remained beyond the socially imaginable for many, many centuries. Or to take another humanitarian concern: one can personally do nothing about other people's madness. In the Dark Ages even its treatment was seen as impossible and beyond the capacity of medieval physicians and caretakers. Once it was believed that science could treat and even cure the insane, or that there were rational ways and available resources to run asylums without chains, an increased sense of responsibility and compassion found an object. A cognitive change occurred, one related to enlightenment; this was the precondition of the change in personal responsibility and related feelings.

Likewise, the abolitionist movement became much stronger when the abolitionists realized that boycotting sugar (as most of it came from the plantations) and signing petitions might change the fate of slaves. The possibility of making a difference—in the sense of contributing in a causally sensible way—made personal responsibility meaningful. Without such casual relations there could be no responsibility, and empathy could not function, certainly not in any sustained way. A matter that cannot be influenced cannot result in relevant compassion, which emerges as sensible only where the suffering can be mitigated. This makes sense in terms of social psychology: if a person could not have done otherwise, we would not say that this person ought to have behaved differently.[85] We have already mentioned Adam Smith's famous example of an earthquake in China. Where tragedy occurs at great distance our compassion quickly fades as there is very little we can do about that suffering. But there remains value in feeling the right thing; limited faculty of action does not rule out moral intuitions and moral duties. "What enables us all—the abolitionists in their day and you and me in ours—to maintain a good conscience, in spite of doing nothing concretely about most of the world's suffering is not self-deception but the ethical shelter afforded to us by our society's conventions of moral responsibility."[86]

Social conventions apply not only to moral responsibility but to other elements of social perception and construction of suffering. The economic conditions and the new religious beliefs of the late eighteenth century and parallel Enlightenment beliefs in science and reason created a faith that mankind could influence its future. Empowerment was the basis of a new extended perception of causation and resulting personal responsibility. Empowerment broadened the scope of empathy, extending in the age of television to distant earthquakes and to "events" at Tiananmen Square in China. But "[a]s long as we truly perceive an evil as inaccessible to manipulation—as an unavoidable or 'necessary' evil—our feelings of sympathy, no matter how great, will not produce the sense of operative responsibility that leads to action aimed at avoiding or alleviating the evil in question."[87] True, in eighteenth-century Britain the suffering in the West Indies was geographically and socially more distant than other objects of humanitarian concern (like the insane, prisoners, orphans, and even the poor). But empowerment overcomes the psychological barrier created by distance.

In the sentimental century suffering was elevated in prestige to the extent that, in the public perception, it was a source of rights. Hence the language used by Charlotte Corday to gain admittance at her third visit to Marat: "I was persecuted for the cause of liberty, I am unhappy, this should be sufficient to have the right to your protection."[88] However, the poor and other categories of sufferers never received the same large-scale support and official remedy leading to rights that we have noted in the case of slaves, although the same groups were active in the various philanthropic ventures and in the abolitionist movement (for example, Methodists). Slavery became an object of far-reaching preoccupation, while other forms of allegedly comparable sufferings could not generate the same sympathy and resulting social recognition in the form of rights. Tom Paine tried it and failed. He considered the Poor Laws to be "instruments of civil torture." Now, torture is the ultimate suffering that ordinarily triggers a reaction expressed in terms of fundamental rights, but Paine could not elevate workplace suffering to the level of wanton imposition of serious pain. He suggested that the institutional care of the Poor Laws be replaced by relief provided as a *right* that is "inherently in all the inhabitants,"[89] but the idea never attracted the popular imagination in his day among those who otherwise felt sympathy with the misery of the poor.

The prohibition of slavery took its place among human rights, while other sufferings, notwithstanding some attempts, failed to be recognized as rights. As discussed in the context of slavery this difference is partly due to the screening out that was enabled by the prevailing conventions, particularly assumptions about (lack of) empowerment. While it was possible to mobilize compassion successfully against slavery, given the scarcity of resources and knowledge relatively little could have been done at the same time about the suffering of madmen, except removing their chains and (occasionally) beating them to take ice-cold baths; further, given the mode of capitalist competition, relatively little could have been done regarding housing and care of the poor.

There is also a genuine substantive difference between these suffering-based claims, even if the sufferings may have generated comparable compassions. Certain emotion-dictated claims of action are simply poor candidates for being recognized as rights, as the remedy does not fit well into judicially enforceable individual rights structures. The social and human problems behind the suffering were different too, and the causes of this suffering did not easily lend themselves to the radical treatment offered by a fundamental right. Recall that fundamental rights determine action hierarchies and priorities where resources are limited. Overcrowding of human rights undermines their steering capacity, as contemporary human rights inflation clearly demonstrates.

The suffering of the slaves was extreme, even by the standards of eighteenth-century poverty and illness. These standards reflected a legitimate distinction between suffering caused by deliberate human action and bad luck.[90] The injustice of slavery originated in a legally sanctioned, state-endorsed practice—and not just from what could have been viewed as nature's injustice, bad luck, or misfortune. From the psychological perspective compassion was combined with outrage directed not only against the cruelty of slaveholders but also against the state that authorized such cruelty. There was enough of moral and religious norm-breaking and hypocrisy in slavery capable of generating outrage and moral condemnation. Hence sentiments of outrage related to injustice could channel the dictates of compassion into public and legal action. The solution was construed in terms of rights because the concern for the well-being of distant others could be framed as an issue of rights. On the other hand, prison conditions were in the long run considered from the rights perspective, at least in the sense that cruelty and torture as punishment were ruled out. But most humanitarian concerns about prisoners like moral improvement, education, and the like never succeeded in becoming fundamental rights.

Contrary to other humanitarian concerns, the issue of slavery was the one that translated in the long run into human and constitutional rights; at least this was the concern that resulted in the genuine recognition of equal liberty for all human beings. This is crucial for transforming the emancipatory claim into a right to liberty.

Notwithstanding superficial appearances, emancipation was not an application of an already-existing general right to liberty or an exercise in human equality. In fact the history of abolitionism is the history of the failure of applying the abstract concept of the right to liberty. Abolition as it happened was more an *ad hoc* reaction to suffering.[91] For practical reasons the movement in Britain opted for requesting gradual change whose first step was the abolition of the Atlantic slave trade. In Britain only a few people, like Elizabeth Heyrick, asked for the compensation of slaves and not that of their masters.[92] The prevailing argument was not one of rights. However, radical abolitionism, especially in the United States, always went beyond the ameliorationism that characterized humanitarian sensibility, since it moved toward unconditional human rights. Once emancipation has taken place, the personal liberty of all people, and at least implicitly their equality before the law, became an incontestable right.

The process of constitutionalizing emotions (and compassion in particular) is a historical one. Objects of compassion may change with changes in misery and human empowerment (what can be done about suffering, in other words) and with evolving sensibilities. Humanitarian sensibilities have influenced professional practices, partly through legislation, affecting suffering other than slavery. Professional knowledge, not rights, improved the life of the insane. Some sensitivities related to apparently similar sufferings have ended up on the ever-changing list of universal human rights, while others failed to do so. This is often the result of "technicalities": some of the grievances were issues of international law, that is, they concerned empathy with suffering emerging in an interstate conflict where concepts of sovereignty precluded the emergence of a domestic claim. It makes little sense to constitutionalize at the national level the protection of wounded soldiers where only the victorious enemy would be in a position to alleviate their sufferings. Here empathy finds its way into international humanitarian law. Abolitionism itself was a borderline case, emerging in an environment of fluid sovereignty. The crucial step consisted in a one-sided abolition of the slave trade. This became international customary law only after it has been unilaterally and beneficially enforced by the hegemonic gunpower of the Royal Navy for many years. It became a domestic constitutional concern when it became a matter of domestic conflict in the United States.

Once the "Age of Rights" of the late eighteenth century was over, the perspective in Hegel's civil society ("*bürgerliche Gesellschaft*") brought social problems to the fore.[93] Reactions to other people's misery were not framed in terms of fundamental rights. The nature of the social problems, the limited possibilities for their solution (the level of empowerment), and the stakes they represented for the ruling establishment typically resulted in a combination of individual charitable action with compassion-animated public pressure on the government to contain and improve the most visible part of the misery through policies. Nonhumanitarian pragmatic considerations of protecting public order (such as public health, sexual morality, and safety from crime) were decisive here. It is telling that the first piece of British legislation concerning child labor (the Health and Morals of Apprentices Act of 1802) was motivated by fear instead of compassion: it was intended to contain a contagion that may have been caused by orphan children working endless hours in textile factories.

5

FREEDOM TO EXPRESS WHAT?

> The danger of free speech does not lie in the menace of ideas, but in the menace of emotions. If words were merely logical devices, no one would fear them. But when they impinge upon a moron they set off his hormones, and so they are justifiably feared. Complete free speech, under democracy, is possible only in a foreign language.
>
> —H.L. Mencken, 1929

The protections granted to speech look, prima facie, like guarantees granted to rational actors (hereinafter: the rationality paradigm). "Much of our current free speech jurisprudence is based on the assumption that . . . people will be perfectly capable of responding rationally to speech." This understanding is reinforced in a prevailing deliberative understanding of democracy. "From Kant to Rawls, intellectuals have unabashedly placed a high premium on deliberative, rational thought and by implication, rejected emotions and feelings as legitimate (although unavoidable) elements of politics."[1] Deliberation is about providing reasons, assuming that the force of the better argument prevails. In other words freedom of expression is about the protection of rational discourse among rational actors; it presupposes such actors, who react to rational arguments; it is dictated by the functional needs of such discourse. It follows that it should disregard emotions; communication of emotions is not worthy of protection and emotional consequences of speech are considered suspicious, even dangerous, for rational discourse. Free speech appears in many regards as an anti-emotional institution, a successful separation of reason from emotion. The constitutional protection of freedom of expression assumes a discourse among rational actors, but unfortunately most social discourse occurs among not always reasonable people who are inconveniently overtaken by "irresistible" emotions.

For a theory that emphasizes the importance of constitutional sentiments, the legal protection granted to reason-based speech seems to pose a fundamental challenge. But in fact freedom of expression based on the rationality paradigm is only a normative assumption that is intended to discipline and overcome emotions.

In a way, the rationalistic construction of the right to freedom of expression illustrates that constitutions and constitutional law are indeed the fruits of an imaginary rationality. Even if the rationalist paradigm of speech were, arguably, the prevailing and decisive one among the free speech justification theories, this paradigm has not been exclusive. Neither most rationalist free speech theories nor the actual constitutional protection of freedom of expression have been able to disregard the emotional drives behind communication. Constitutional law struggles to incorporate emotions into the protected sphere of communication and, at the same time, to disregard them. But emotions come back with vengeance, and with censorial power.

1. The Rationality Paradigm of Freedom of Expression

1.a. Rationality as Foundation of Speech Protection

For a theory of constitutional sentiments, freedom of expression is the grand attempt to build an institution on the assumptions of reason being a self-standing entity, in order to enable such isolated reason to create a rational world. In order to protect this world of interacting reasons, freedom of speech law bravely attempts to disregard and censor emotions, which are seen as existing separate from, and opposed to, rational speech and reason. In this approach the dualism of reason and emotion is taken for granted. The U.S. Supreme Court states, for example, that "[p]reventing unlimited display or distribution of obscene material . . . is distinct from a control of reason and the intellect."[2]

But this attempt at separation continuously fails both in theories of freedom of speech and in constitutional practice. Emotions are finding their way into the protected sphere of speech, and, at least in some instances, the legal protection granted to expressions of emotion reflects the psychological inseparability of emotions and reason. Nevertheless, for good normative reasons, freedom of expression operates within some inconsistent version of the rational discourse paradigm, resulting in uncertainty as to the management of emotions in speech.

As with so many other constitutional institutions, the strong emphasis on speech as rational act originates from Enlightenment efforts to rationalize the world. It satisfies the emerging Enlightenment aspiration to hammer out of passion-driven human beings reason (and interest)-driven citizens.

At least by the late eighteenth century, the idea of free speech appeared intuitively attractive to a growing number of people. Most people love to see themselves as reason-driven beings. Even in societies where religion is decisive and freedom of speech is not particularly cherished in the constitutional system, there seems to be a desire among people to be seen as rational beings who respond to arguments, though what counts as argument varies.

The foundational constitutional documents and later constitutions insist on the natural need for free speech: freedom of speech is presented simply as one of the sacrosanct rights of mankind. What is sacrosanct needs no further justification. But it took quite some effort of the Enlightenment to reach this point: freedom of speech, especially as lack of censorship, was understood as a means for reason to fight obscurantism. Those who argued for free speech wanted to get rid of censorship and preclude persecution for religious and selected politically critical opinions. The political implications necessitating free speech emerged only slowly and somewhat spontaneously, and, especially outside the United States it was not obvious that free speech is to be protected in order to avoid tyrannical rule. The positive functions of free public opinion for political (democratic-type, representative) decision-making were constitutionally recognized only gradually, as promoting *truth in politics.* In Hegel's retrospective summary the institution of free speech was socially acceptable as a rationality-enhancing institution: "The opening of this opportunity to know has a more universal aspect because by this means public opinion first reaches thoughts that are true and attains insight into the situation and concept of the state and its affairs, and so first acquires ability to *estimate these more rationally.*"[3]

Private opinions were instrumentally related to public opinion and hence were protected within the right of freedom of expression for a pragmatic reason: namely, that it is never clear where "public" speech begins.

Free speech protection in modern democracies assumes that access to information and the possibility of free expression of opinions contribute to rational political deliberation; in a democracy all people should have equal opportunity to express (form) opinions. Where the maximization of information is allowed, the rationality of the political decision will improve.

This understanding of speech as rational discourse is related to theories not articulated in constitutions, but generally endorsed in liberal constitutional systems. John Stuart Mill's theory of truth offers the most prominent and influential exposition of the rationality paradigm, though he discussed freedom of expression in the context of personal liberty. According to Mill, liberty needs and means personal choice, and the search for truth is part and precondition of the personal development project. Although Mill's interest in truth is individualistic and only indirectly political, his theory of truth serves as a foundation for many contemporary speech theories, including those related to democratic theory. For normative reasons that are compelling in a political system committed to modernity and democracy, the rationality paradigm that relies on the truth claim became central.

The Millian "rational discourse" paradigm does not provide substantive criteria of rationality or "truth." It is about guaranteeing a procedure that brings us closer to truth as reasonable choice. The preferred procedure is the one that emerges in a marketplace of ideas.[4] The marketplace of ideas and, evidently, speech as the product in the market, are to be protected because it is in the circumstances of the marketplace that truth is most likely to emerge. The assumption is that truth emerges because *rational* individuals will use the opportunities generated by the marketplace. Rational actors are capable of agreeing on truth, and false beliefs will be driven out. Truth "occurs" where rational individuals in an unfettered discussion come to agreement in the form of "acceptance." Speech serves informed choice in political decision-making because it enables the individual to make decisions about "truth" as far as possible, and allows the individual to get closer to truth in politics, whatever "truth" means in that context. (It may mean better information, better comparison, awareness of circumstances, refusal of uncontested authority.)

The assumption that one gets closer to truth in rational discourse may make sense in the political and academic spheres. Here speech may result in more speech and not in irrational, passionate action; as a result of arguments and counterarguments, rational considerations and socially acceptable behavior will emerge. But this may offer only a limited foundation for speech protection as it applies to very specific communication situations. As Laurence Tribe stated: "Expression has special value *only* in the context of 'dialogue': communication in which the participants seek to persuade, or are persuaded; communication which is about changing or maintaining beliefs. . . . Starting with this proposition, it is reasonable to distinguish between contexts in which talk leaves room for reply and those in which talk triggers action or causes harm without the time or opportunity for response."[5]

However, the rationalistic "acceptance" of the value of speech may have little to do with truth. A pragmatic justification of the marketplace of ideas arrangement does not require the assumption of truth; it may be justified as an arrangement that satisfies individual self-interest which, however, fits into Mill's theory of liberty as self-realization. Further, in instrumentalist concepts of free speech such freedom serves wealth maximization. In other words, the institution of free speech is rational in the sense of utility maximization. Here you don't have to assume rational speakers and audiences, but this comes at a price: restrictions of speech might be acceptable that would not be held admissible within a pure rational discourse paradigm.

The Millian justifications of free speech as rational truth search are contingent: they are sustainable only as long as the marketplace conditions are present. What happens if people are not as rational as that well-educated phantom of an English (upper) middle-class gentleman who seems to have served as point of departure for Mill? What happens if the marketplace of ideas fails, simply because there is no time for truth to prevail in an exchange of ideas? The truth-driven paradigm does not apply to emotionally driven people and the mob problem. Further, the rational marketplace paradigm presupposes institutional and cultural arrangements as well as a level of international stability that are not always in place. As Mill states in reference to liberty: "Liberty, as a principle, has no application to any state of things anterior to the time when mankind have become capable of being improved by free and equal discussion." Neither does the principle apply to people surrounded by external enemies.[6]

Finally, Mill accepts that there are consequentialist limits to liberty. This concern is formulated as the harm principle. Even rational speech may harm others. Mill admits that speech that results in actual injuries is not protected. This position remains contested in so far as his concern is limited to actual physical injury, even if broader free speech concerns offer strong reasons for such limited understanding of harm. Like all other elements in the free speech equation, harm is socially construed. The legislative equation that responds to emotionally determined concepts of harm necessarily departs from the "rational discourse" paradigm. What seems to be intellectual speculation about permissible risk of harm resulting from speech depends on broader sentiments of the public. For example, where fear prevails, people and their legislators will not opt for the disclosure of what is classified as sensitive information. "[L]egal doctrines and practices have buckled under the pressure of violent political events."[7]

Given the cognitive bias toward negative experiences which results in fear-induced risk-aversion, censorial precaution is expected to prevail in speech regulation. The constitutional institutions and the legal elite of liberal democracies may tend to counter these popular censorial considerations but cannot disregard them, even if social experience with governmental abuse will create disposition toward robust rights protection.

The "rational discourse" model with its truth-search mission serves as the acknowledged jurisprudential ground for the protection of speech.[8] Here the emotion management policy of free speech is laissez-faire; it disregards emotional consequences, and it enables speakers to manage emotions the way they like. But what happens if the participants of the social discourse are not rational? It is unlikely that such communication will aim at truth search. A closer look at constitutional restrictions of speech will show that the idea of free speech does not disregard the possibility of nonrational speakers, messages, and audiences. To force communication back to rational discourse, these "excesses" are to some extent discouraged. Certain forms of what is deemed irrational will be unprotected and even prohibited because it is believed that, in responding to otherwise protected speech, people may act under the impulse of passion or misleading information or belief. "Irrationality" here includes certain unacceptable consequences which may be instrumentally rational for the speaker but are unacceptable in their social consequences, as is the case of harm resulting from speech. As the paradigmatic example of Oliver Wendell Holmes indicates, crying fire in a theater results in stampede and is, therefore, rightfully punishable.[9] Further, not all people are reasonable, or they are misled; they are in need of protection when acceptance of opinions without "proper" reflection would result in self-destructive action. Advertising poison as medication or advertisement directed to children can be prohibited. Hateful agitation of violence may lead to actual violence and can be prohibited within the rationality paradigm. To an extent, the restrictions concern temporary excesses of panic or "stupidity,"[10] and one could claim that these are only exceptions to the basic and general human capacity of reason-directed opinion formation and decision.

Even where the Millian preconditions are more or less met, the nonrational elements still reach into the rational clearing in the woods of emotions and irrationality. Contemporary theory only half-heartedly admits that the Millian preconditions are often absent in communication. In well-established democracies all adults are considered to be fully rational for the purposes of (political) speech regulation and free speech is assumed not to result in the breakdown of the society. This might be a good *normative* point of departure for established constitutional systems with stable social order. However, given the nonrational and noncognitive elements in human reasoning and given fateful consequences originating in emotional reactions to speech, the legal paradigm based on rational discourse is constantly challenged. Censorship, on the other hand, is about preventing certain emotions and passions in particular, and also about sheltering and protecting certain emotions like religious sensitivities. A political system facing (or endorsing) strong religious or political fundamentalism may, however, conclude that free speech will result in unrest because of the passion-driven reactions of the believers. Indian law, which otherwise favors free speech, has very restrictive rules against offenses to religion and refuses to take risks where speech may stir disruptive emotions, irrespective of the otherwise respectable content of the speech.[11]

In the rationality paradigm free speech is protected under the assumption that it is socially affordable; that is, there will be no harmful consequences of speech. Socially disputed, disruptive emotional impacts and motives are not taken into consideration and the rationality paradigm prevails.[12] In the eighteenth-century liberal revolutions, at the time when free speech became an important tool of political conflict, the audience-related risks were accepted, at least in principle, by those victorious forces which relied on free speech, and envisioned politics as a free deliberative process. Speech was understood as a major tool of social action, but speech is irrelevant if there cannot be audience for it; therefore the risks had to be accepted. But a measured suspicion reminded legislators all the time that emotions may mobilize people to act contrary to the rationalist assumption of the Enlightenment. Beginning with the revolutionary practice of censorship during the French Revolution, law was inclined to depart from the risk-taking assumptions of the rationality paradigm.

1.b. Emotions Recognized as Speech (within Reason)

Emotions that are perceived as threatening and harmful to rational discourse are suppressed in law. Other emotions, and the very nature of the communication process, push toward the incorporation of emotional needs into constitutional rights. Given the difficulties of sustaining the rationality paradigm in view of recurrent irrationality of speech, speakers. and audiences, and their emotional nature, the paradigm is unable to resist emotional (nonrational) pressures, even at the price of great inconsistency, or even allowing for a double justification of speech, with the resulting uncertainties. The inclusion of select emotions in the realm of protected speech is related partly to psychological needs of identity expression and partly to the emotional nature of the communication process that is protected.

The incorporation of emotions into speech has a long history that parallels the protection granted to speech as rational expression. At the time of the 1789 Declaration of the Rights of Man and Citizen, sentiments and reason were seen as intertwined in communication, and it was common to claim freedom of expression as protecting both, jointly.[13] The tradition finds echoes in modern law. There are a number of instances when law and legal theory admit that the individual has the right to determine "to what extent his thoughts, *sentiments, and emotions* shall be communicated to others."[14] This follows from, among others sources, the social respect paid to certain "worthy" emotions. Emotions are selected for protection because of their social attractiveness, "nobility," in line with the tradition of Antiquity, especially the ancient Roman admiration of virtue: "The difference between the intellectual and the emotional is not the difference between heavy and light. There are solemn emotions, and there are frivolous ideas."[15]

When emotion display via unfettered speech is allowed, a deep psychological need is satisfied,[16] such expression being a primary tool of the speaker's self-assertion. It is through speech that one identifies herself with specific roles and groups, and it is through free speech that identity is generated, granted, or denied. Freedom of speech (and religion, extended to freedom of belief) enables socially the satisfaction of one's emotional need of identification with the group. It is for these reasons that Mill provided a second line of thought to justify free speech that was related to the concept of liberty; free speech serves individual personal development (self-realization).[17] The personal development concerns imply the protection of feelings.

This second line of justification emphasizes freedom of belief and free speech as *conditions* of individual liberty. Here liberty is understood as liberty of conscience that includes the freedom of feeling.[18] Additionally, modern constitutional law expressly protects emotions in contexts beyond rational discourse where they are seen as expressions of (culturally acceptable) personal identity. The expression of identity as part of *relational* discourse is a matter irrespective of "rational discourse" concerns. In this regard modern constitutional law that reflects changes of an increasingly individualistic Western culture caters to the identity needs of the self. Modern cultures are favorably inclined to self-centered individualism where the individual is publicly allowed to negotiate his identity as a legitimate central life project. (Expressions of an identity that challenges the majority identity are less likely to be protected.)

The self-realization aspects of free speech which require the display of emotions provide for the protection of expressions that do not fit into the rationality paradigm. Art is certainly more than sheer emotion; in fact, what is valued in art goes beyond the form of expression; its full protection would never fit into a rigid rationality paradigm.[19] Needless to say, it depends on the emotion display rules of the day what elements of the identity, which emotions, can be displayed within the protection of free speech; when protection for emotions as speech is denied, this follows from broader emotion management considerations of the culture. For this reason certain emotional displays in art were not protected at certain points in history, the argument being that such "distortions" and "ugly emotions" deprive the product of its artistic character.

Beyond the identity-related emotional display, expressions of emotions are included in speech protection also because of their inherent contribution to communication. Emotional commitment to an opinion is crucial to the *rational* acceptance of such views, even in Mill's theory. "[E]ven if the received opinion be not only true, but the whole truth; unless *it is suffered to be*, and actually is, vigorously and earnestly contested, it will, by most of those who receive it, be held in the manner of a prejudice, with little comprehension or *feeling of its rational grounds.*"[20]

Emotions signal the intensity of affirmation or negation of a view. The fact that an opinion is endorsed by a concerned majority may serve, at least temporarily, as a probabilistic confirmation of truth: the majority heuristics dictate that the more people agree strongly (where strong agreement may be expressed emotionally), the more likely the opinion will be true, especially if opinions are generated independently (the independence condition). In many regards, the intensity of affirmation or negation counts, particularly where one gets closer to a temporary truth through majority opinions, as is the case in politics. Intensity of the communication is also important where it signals sincerity of convictions and (in a way troubling to speech theory) commitment to future action. The emotional confirmation of positions facilitates coordinated behavior.

Emotions, in fact, convey and support ideas and opinions, even without adding arguments to the position.[21] The emotion-related communicative components of expression resulted in extensions of the concept of protected speech. In *Cohen v. California*,[22] the Supreme Court defends the emotional in speech. Here the protection is granted in order to make emotion communicable where the emotion gives credibility to the message. Likewise, Article 10 of the European Convention for the Protection of Human Rights and Fundamental Freedoms "protects not only the substance of the ideas and information expressed, but also the form in which they are conveyed."[23]

Notwithstanding the inevitable inclusion of emotions in protected expression, a cognitive versus noncognitive distinction prevails in constitutional law, and the noncognitive remains suspect. This position seems to be based on a distinction between speech that allows "rational" cognitive processes and "speech" which, at least according to folk psychology, appeals exclusively to noncognitive faculties. Quite often it is the classification of the content of the communication that will be decisive, irrespective of the emotion communicated or the emotions generated. First Amendment protection would be denied only to such sexual materials that have no "serious literary, artistic, political, or scientific value."[24] The emotional nature of speech and understanding, the emotional impacts of speech (as in hate speech), and the evidence of nonrational reasoning (bias, stereotype) are hardly compatible with the "rational discourse among rational beings" assumption.[25]

On the other hand, in some contexts the emotional impact is more important than the content of the message. In the context of "indecency" the legally relevant emotional impacts are disgust and outrage. To generate and express disgust and outrage is understood to be expressive activity without value, and such emotions and the ideas represented by these emotions may be deprived of relevance. Moreover, in certain cultures disgust and outrage are improper and should not be displayed, and people have to be protected against such impacts, hence what causes "impermissible" emotions is also impermissible. Nevertheless, as the Supreme Court admits, "indecency may have strong communicative content, protesting conventional norms or giving an edge to a work by conveying otherwise inexpressible emotions."[26] In the long run it is the specific social meaning attributed to emotions that turns the expression of arousal or emotions into protected speech, even where the law refers directly to the valuable content of speech. The expression of culturally endorsed emotions becomes a protected act. The emotional reaction to the communicated message, which seemed to be a "natural reaction," is also subject to judicial (re)construction. Consider the psychological mechanisms that accompany the reception of Delacroix's painting *Liberty on the Barricades.* The image of the bare breast in the painting might be called indecent, and in certain cultures it may indeed arouse disgust or cause sexual arousal (not a matter of rational communication). But the waving of the tricolor might translate the bare breast of the woman who represents Liberty into a celebration of freedom. An act of celebration is not a rational argument either, but certainly it is an intellectual position.

The "positive" emotions assumed to be behind the expression, which assert preferred values or emotional impacts that are understood as promoting positive emotions, like the use of symbols such as the national flag, are likely to be protected as speech. But from a psychological perspective these distinctions are not obvious and the legal classifications are somewhat arbitrary. Contrary to the dead certainty of folk psychology and medieval psychology, there is no such thing as per se positive emotion. Law relies, among other things, on cultural scripting of emotions and the alleged intent and emotions of the speaker which is retrospectively attributed to her.[27] The rational/nonrational (emotional) distinction refers here to differences in emotional consequences, but in terms of law the distinction is one of content, one of the most unreliable and therefore dangerous distinctions for freedom of expression.

The changing social evaluation of emotions as grounds for speech protection or their oppression reflects cultural changes in emotional reactions. The understanding and evaluation of emotions are not uniform across societies and times. Freedom of speech, like other rights, is a flexible policy and accommodates or denies emotions depending on how a given emotion is culturally structured and politically used.

In the world of changing standards differentiated handling of pornography and obscenity is certainly not surprising. Emotional reactions to sexuality and the body are reinterpreted as part of underlying social conflicts. In the contemporary Western legal handling of pornography, emotional reactions to sexuality are generated in a conflict where moral entrepreneurs and the pornography industry are pitted against each other. The political interests of moral crusaders who condemn pornography dictate that they reinforce disgust and indignation among viewers and people whose opinion might be decisive in the generation of a prevalent, legally enforceable public sentiment. Here disgust is consequential to the worldview that condemns immorality: the moral indignation would result from the all-encompassing identity of the anti-pornographer. The pornography industry on the other hand often refers to liberty values which intend to influence (neutralize) disgust and shame. Primary sexual drive may lend additional credibility to these respectable references. The pornography industry relies on the emotional needs of its customers, who may not have negative emotions at the exposure, or are fascinated by negative emotions. The same industry may attempt to change social perceptions, and lobby and argue on the basis of changed social perceptions in the legislative process. The fashion industry, too, can change emotional reactions and display rules regarding naked body parts.

However, given the way emotions operate, both these emotion mobilization strategies may fail. Constructs of social interpretation are of limited impact on gut feelings. Identity may offer a frame of interpretation but cannot determine what is and what is not arousing emotions.

We know relatively little about the mechanisms that determine the incorporation of sentiments in the protection of speech. Certain cultures, especially the American one in the last fifty years, became committed to an extended protection of emotion display within the rationality paradigm, where rational discourse is understood very broadly. This was promoted, respected, and reinforced by the American judiciary, and it was emotionally endorsed in the prevailing culture. Kuklinski claims that "the basic values that form the bedrock of American society elicit gut-level responses. . . . The slogan 'freedom of speech,' like the national anthem, commands an emotional, or perhaps more correctly, a knee-jerk, reaction from U.S. citizens."[28]

But not even the firm, quasi-religious veneration of the First Amendment, its incorporation into identity, can rule out the popular legitimacy of speech restrictions which reflect emotional dictates. This does not cause much cognitive dissonance: the communication of unpleasant "valueless" emotions and socially unacceptable emotional consequences are simply placed outside the rational. In reality, however, such displacement has to do with specific emotional reactions about certain speakers. Speech-restricting trends are rooted in the intertwined nature of affect and cognition. When American citizens had to evaluate the speech rights of communists, they were more ready to accept even blanket prohibitions. People's affective responses to communists may depend partially on their (perhaps unconscious) recollection of past events involving the group. References to negative consequences of speech rights (and other fundamental rights) dampen enthusiasm for rights.

To sum up, the truth theory of speech reflects a rationality paradigm, but it is not an exclusive theory of speech, and it lives in an ambiguous intimacy with the self-development theory that allows for the protection of speech expressing emotions. The truth theory remains a limited one, as it does not apply unconditionally where basic social and cultural conditions regarding rational discourse are absent. Such situations may be handled as exceptions in modern societies, but constitute the norm elsewhere.

2. Some Realism about Communication

In view of the strong presence of emotions in speech and its regulation it is time to consider the sustainability of the normative assumption that animates liberal free speech theories. The "rational discourse" among "rational beings" that serves as a paradigm for robust speech protection and that justifies the strong, nearly absolutist protection of speech is subject to a number of criticisms:

1. people are not rational, at least not all the time;
2. most communication is not about the truth; and
3. emotions and pre-existing audience preferences are effective barriers to communication.

The protection granted to freedom of expression is based on the assumption of human rationality. The experiences with totalitarian ideologies and actions carried out in their name raise doubts about the power and nature of human reason. The Enlightenment project had been demonized as an imperialist plot of oppression.

Today many critiques claim that irrespective of human reasoning capacities citizens in the post-industrial age do not operate according to the psychological assumptions of Mill: the self is manipulated to the extent that the search for truth is irrelevant. Under the pressure of advertising, in Giddens's words: "To a greater or lesser degree, the project of the self becomes translated into one of the possession of desired goods and the pursuit of artificially framed styles of life. . . . The consumption of ever-novel goods becomes in some part a substitute for the genuine development of self; appearance replaces essence as the visible signs of successful consumption come actually to outweigh the use-values of the goods and services in question themselves."[29]

In light of the orgy of contemporary consumerist irrationality, the conditions for the Millian marketplace are perhaps absent in our democratic societies. The rationality paradigm has been gradually eroded, though to different degrees in the various jurisdictions, in the context of politics too.

The *Zundel* case decided by the Supreme Court of Canada offers an authoritative summary of the shift that occurred at the governmental level: "In the rational connection portion of their analysis. . . . Cory and Iacobucci JJ. rely upon the Report of the Special Committee on Hate Propaganda in Canada, which impugned the '19th century belief' that man was a 'rational creature' who could distinguish between truth and falsity. We are told that '[w]e cannot share this faith today in such a simple form'—thus, a limitation of this type of speech is rationally connected to the goal of furthering racial tolerance."[30]

Insufficient human rationality, at least in the short run, is the leading argument why extremist or offensive speech should not be protected. This, however, remains a contested issue even among judges of the same court, and even if it is accepted it is not a sufficient reason for many judges to depart from the working hypothesis of the "rational creature" because of fears of a slippery slope.

The "rational discourse" paradigm disregards and disguises the fact that speech and communication serve functions only accidentally related to truth. Expression satisfies developmental, identity, coordination, and social cooperation needs of the individual and her environment. Most everyday communication is about coordination and cooperation, as in these utterances: "let's go" and "buy me a burger" (though this might become political and identity-related speech, like "Buy American"). Such speech is free mostly because of lack of legal interest and not because of the search for truth or other rationalistic considerations. Exceptionally, communication within the family that is related both to developmental needs and to coordination may be subject to legal restrictions: for example, certain parental or spousal expressions may be considered abusive and prohibited. However, such intervention is rather unusual, both out of respect for private sentiments and intimacy and because of the practical difficulties of enforcement.

Most everyday communication seems to be below the radar of law, and constitutional law in particular, as it is relegated to the domain of the private. For freedom of speech it remains a matter of irrelevant liberty. It is a sphere of intimacy where considerations of public order may apply. The role of constitutional law is limited to providing protection for these private emotional communications especially against the state, in the name of privacy. But most of the social communication remains outside law, both public (accessible to all) and private. Law provides only fences for the free flow of communication. This comes at a price for law. Because law is serving as a fence and it is constitutionally bound to noninterference, it will be seen as an accomplice to all the injustice caused by such communication. The nonintervention model that is embodied in freedom of expression allows for private monopolies of communication to prevail, which undermine the "rational discourse" paradigm.

The broadcasting market is particularly distorted, and it is here that the "rational discourse" paradigm is most seriously challenged. Many broadcasters operate in a dominant position. The mainstream media are not interested in viewpoint diversity given their interest in audience maximization. The consumerist manipulation that relies on means of noncognitive processes conflicts with the values of autonomous choice, but it is quintessential for the commercial success of broadcasting. This does not contribute to rational discourse either.[31] Broadcasting is primarily about entertainment (with troubling emotional consequences, such as generating fear and anxiety, or normalizing violence). Entertainment drives out rational speech because there remains less time (and sincere interest) for such speech.[32] "The economics and aesthetics of commercial television have profound influence" on political speech, and "the gulf between important political expression and pure amusement nearly vanishes."[33] Advertising on television exploits and promotes the public's pervasive pursuit of pleasure and entertainment.

Besides, entertainment is intimately related to advertisement, with its emotional appeal that hardly fits into rational discourse. In consequence a double standard emerged: in matters of broadcasting, the rational discourse approach is disregarded in favor of an ad hoc theory that allows the curtailment of free speech in the media in favor of audience emotion protection and corrections of market imperfections, in the name of pluralism. Of course, American law (like other legal systems) superficially sticks to the applicability of the First Amendment.

Notwithstanding the nonapplicability of the truth-oriented paradigm of free speech protection to many forms of communication, some expressions related to social cooperation and coordination are included in the freedom of expression domain. Conceptually, this is reflected in the category of commercial speech of relatively recent stamp that receives a certain level of protection in the United States, while it is incorporated into "speech" in Europe. Commercial speech is a primary tool of social cooperation and coordination. It is protected in the name of economic freedom and because it allegedly contributes to consumers' informed choice. This hypothesis allows its fit into the rational discourse paradigm although the improvement of consumer choice through advertisement is questionable.[34]

The rational discourse paradigm allows emotional manipulation, and this is what is protected in commercial speech. A similar emotionalism is present at the level of political discourse; the persuasion is largely playing on emotional or other nonrational cognitive processes. Further, the legally protected debate in politics is often about value choices that are accepted at least as much on emotional grounds as on rational interests. There remains little empirical ground for the foundational assumption that free speech protects rational discourse. The prevailing, though not uncontested, rationalistic legal theory about free speech has all the values of a myth, and it is successful as such.

Personal communication satisfies a number of psychological needs, including emotional needs. These needs include the need for self-expression as a personality function. Emotions need display, and speech plays a crucial role in display and also in the psychological reinforcement and shaping of the "other." The verbal communication of emotion receives little legal protection per se, other than what falls under liberty interests.

Ideas are often accepted not because of persuasion, but because of force and resulting intimidation: the application of force makes other people rather receptive to arguments and symbols, as the tragedy of the Weimar Republic indicates. Communication occurs in a space where not only ideas and preferences determine the spread of ideas, although this seems to be the assumption in constitutional law, especially in the United States.[35] The emotional environment, where the communication occurs is disregarded in the classic vision of free speech. Fear may spread dogma and (mis)information as epidemics, as in moral cascades. Of course, the answer of constitutional law is that the heuristics it offers are intended to preclude such epidemics. Further, constitutions offer structural protection to the public order through elaborate mechanisms of separation of powers, representative government, speaker protection, etc. Speaker protection (including lack of censorship and liability, as well as criminal law protection to provide safety to speakers) is particularly important as it allows speakers to counter emotions and preclude the formation of cascades. Nevertheless, one cannot easily discount Judge Richard Posner's admonition that the "fact that the propagators of vicious ideas are given to violence as well as speech, that their speech consists largely of persuading their audience of the delights of despoiling some other group . . . goes unmentioned"[36] in some suicidally absolutist interpretations of freedom of expression. Strong, politically channeled, and manipulated emotions act as a social fact. The legal importance of emotional reactions to speech lies in the fact that emotional reactions at the collective level may be used politically. This potential can have both short-term and long-term impacts on freedom of speech. The emotion-driven social concepts may result in category changes, and reduce (or, much less likely, extend) the sphere of protected speech. In the shorter term, the politics that relies on emotions may simply force society to expressly admit the legitimacy of certain emotion-driven concerns. Such concessions are granted, for example, in libel law[37], in group libel, and in the protection granted to religious sensibilities, for example in blasphemy law. Changes in emotion display rules will result in the delegitimation of certain contents if regularly accompanied by prohibited emotions. Once hatred becomes culturally suspect, speech that is regularly accompanied by disgraced emotions will lose protection.

The assumption of rational choice resulting from fair discussion may be of limited value where the speech counters a belief deeply held by a group, especially where the belief holds the group together. Group beliefs are considerable obstacles to the free movement of ideas.[38]

A marketplace of ideas concept accepts the existing preferences of the audience, and assumes that these preferences are rational or at least change rationally. However, this is not the case empirically. Speech affecting preferences is often "patrolled" by the group (or institutions of the group), depriving the individual of the opportunity to consider the new position offered by new (perhaps more rational) arguments. In fact, group members are socially forced to avoid opinions and facts that challenge the beliefs of the group. Such sheltered beliefs include hateful beliefs.

Hatred and prejudice constitute important emotional barriers to free communication.[39] Here I am not referring to the emotion-influencing impacts of hate speech that undermine the assumption regarding "rational discourse." Hate speech and hatred have lasting impacts on the audience of similarly inclined soul mates; prejudice and speech that reinforces it prepare groups to resist rational and emotional arguments. Hate speech contributes to the perpetuation of prejudice that becomes an effective filter to communication that contradicts the assumptions of the belief system, in particular concerning elements that would affect group supremacy (and inferiority of the "other"). Hate speech is also capable of silencing the voice of the hated group and its members. These disparities create additional skewing in the marketplace of ideas.

3. In Praise of the Rationality Paradigm

The above-mentioned examples indicate that the "rational discourse" hypothesis that serves as the foundation for the constitutional protection of the right of freedom of expression disregards important empirical phenomena. In many regards (most spectacularly in broadcasting law) the law openly departs from its own unsustainable assumptions. In other areas the communication of emotions is what the communication is about, and communication is regulated following dictates of emotions and cultural norms of emotion display. Given the centrality of freedom of expression to the alleged rationality project of the Enlightenment, the recognition of emotions seems to indicate the shortcomings of that project.[40] Likewise, where free speech absolutism disregards emotions, the Enlightenment project fails again, because emotions and passions seem to take their revenge at every point, forcing free speech to retreat, either by censoring passions in violation of its principles, or allowing them to bring irrationality to power.

Of course, the apparent revenge of emotions is not simply the result of an intellectual weakness, namely of the deliberate misunderstanding of human nature. The occasional legal recognition of emotions in the speech context to the detriment of the rational discourse paradigm results from a historically changing politics of emotions and politics of communication. In a culture that promises control over passions, free speech may go very far without running the risk of passionate reactions, for example, where honor is not felt crucial for identity. Here the defamatory criticism of politicians will be protected. The permissibility of offensive speech relies on the assumption that people are able to control their emotions, they will not get excited or, at least they will refrain from harmful action where passions run high. But there seem to be human limits to such social control over emotions. The abstract constitutional doctrine of free speech is applied in democracies with some disregard for the local emotional culture. Political and other developments, like the revival of strong religions, may undermine emotion control. Where passion (intense, socially poorly controlled emotions) comes back with revenge, the whole Enlightenment project of speech, and with it the secular society, may be empirically doomed.

I would argue that notwithstanding the psychological reality of emotion-driven reactions to speech and the empirical reality of emotion manipulation in the name of speech there are strong normative arguments to be made in favor of the rational discourse paradigm. Freedom of (rational) expression as a constitutional strategy deliberately operates with rationality assumptions that tend to neglect emotions. These empirically false normative considerations make pragmatic sense. The constitutionalized bias in favor of a normative theory of "rational discourse" may be a successful strategy of liberty, notwithstanding constant compromises and uncertainties about the domain and scope of protected speech. Such compromises certainly diminish the performance and extension of free speech, but may serve other legitimate social and psychological functions. From the perspective of liberty maximization, it is legitimate to stick to these normative considerations. Otherwise the scholarly description of the psychological insufficiency of free speech absolutism may be abused for generating unfounded criticism and attacks on freedom of expression. Certain emotions operate in disregard of free speech assumptions, but a constitutional speech policy that fully accommodates the emotional concerns about speech is contrary to the basic value choices of liberal democracy. Just because speech is emotionally disturbing, or because people are unable to draw rational conclusions, speech cannot be restricted in a liberal democracy that bets on the possibility of rational exchange. It assumes that proper social institutions can channel and properly mobilize conflicting and competing emotions that will prevent the destruction of rational exchange, or at least will not allow the social disruption that certain emotions like speech-induced anger and fear might dictate. Free speech is not about the lack of intense emotion generation, though it is to a great extent a categorical tool to disregard these emotions. Notwithstanding the presence of strong emotions resulting from passionate speech, the constitutionally induced bias in favor of free speech does not result in an emotional chaos undermining public order and civilization. Hatred, insult, contempt, and attempts to humiliate the other that are enabled by robust speech protection do not inevitably lead to an emotionally oppressed or revolting collective psyche. Emotions do challenge the negative message, but speakers' emotions are also challenged by other emotions. The boundaries of the emotion display can be changed—through law, among other things. What amounts to insult is not fixed and it is reinterpreted in a culture, and targets of defamation have techniques to shrug off insults without censorship and libel laws.

The protection of free speech based on "rational discourse" is necessary, otherwise the censorial nature of the emotional will prevail. Imagine a system of restrictions in social communication that follows emotional dictates like that of dignity or religious sensitivity (religion-induced disgust and anger). Such a system would selectively restrict speech in the name of audience emotions. Historically speech operated in an environment that was hostile to intellectual development; in this culture taken-for-granted truth was venerated. Emotional dictates, for example, public outrage and disgust, were mobilized against dissenting speech, in order to curtail the formation of critical public opinion. With changing cultural and political circumstances, the return of such a situation is not ruled out, especially because there is little interest in producing and freely communicating ideas. The vulnerability of the marketplace of ideas requires strong protection. Such strong protection implies that the psychologically unsound rationality paradigm be promoted. However, to the extent the prevailing culture respects emotions it will set limits to this attempt of overprotection.

The prohibition of prior restraint is the keystone of any constitutional recognition of free speech. Mill was very clear on the censorial consequences of social feelings: "Wherever the sentiment of the majority is still genuine and intense, it is found to have abated little of its claim to be obeyed" and the tyrannical *feeling* of the majority will impose "its own ideas and practices as rules of conduct on those who dissent from them."[41]

Historically, before the Enlightenment, the primary control over speech was ecclesiastical. Religion and custom controlled emotions in the sense of sanctioning display rules. They have created categories for emotion management, defining, for example, where and how the Christian believer should feel compassion, sadness, or fear, including above all, fear of damnation. Religion also tried to cultivate enthusiasm and defined appropriate anger and hatred against sinners and apostates and believers of other denominations. The control over these emotions determined choices of identity; monopolistic religious speech served control.[42]

The constitutional guarantee of free speech—sheltering ideas from legal censorship and to the extent possible from the tyranny of majority opinions—is intended to counter social and institutional forces (like that of the churches) that would like to restrict speech by mobilizing the emotions they tend to control. Academic freedom (though based on internal peer censorship) is another attempt to shield research from public sentiments (see the debate about evolution or genetic engineering).

In order to free communication from the dictates of emotional reactions that insist on legal protection, and thereby improve the chances of rational discourse, constitutional law institutionalizes self-deceptive assumptions combined with a pragmatic epistemological consideration. The possibility that a position is mistakenly characterized irrational, coupled with the likelihood that the government has specific interests in such characterization, suggests that the protection granted to speech on grounds of its rationality-enhancing capacity shall be extended to all speech, without consideration of the value (nature) of such speech. Otherwise, if only expressions of "certified" rationality were to be protected, governmental censoring would become the rule. If government is in the position to determine what counts as irrational, or dangerous to rational discourse, it may abuse such power, because it never knows what is really irrational. Moreover, given governmental interests in sustaining its power, it will abuse such power. To minimize this danger there is no such thing as a false idea under the First Amendment.[43]

When one reads contemporary judicial decisions that disregard socially esteemed emotional reactions to speech, one has the impression of a rational speech dictatorship. This impression is historically and socially quite misleading: speech-protective provisions that enabled rational discourse operated historically in an antirational social environment. It was an emotion-ridden (anxiety-ridden) *belief* in truth that dictated ecclesiastical and secular censorship. It took a long time to carve out a protected area of communication against emotion-driven oppression and obscurantism, even if such obscurantist positions claimed to defend a unique truth.

Note that emotions *privilege* certain communications. This is true in regard to politics and science and in artistic expression, too. A specific concept of public decency delayed the liberation of literature and art in the nineteenth century and supported a moral censorship well into the mid-fifties of the last century. Even today, speech is protected in Western law in a reason-unfriendly, emotion-driven social environment, where passions are currently less speech-restricting mostly for reasons of complacency. Emotion-driven censorship is common in democracies where ethnically motivated sentiments intend to undermine rational discourse, and favor emotionalism. Here the restrictive communication policy is arguably not shaped by censorial dictates of emotions, but is intended to prevent the escalation of emotions by incitement. It is argued that free speech is counterproductive in the context of ethnic or religious zeal. The more emotionally driven, intense communication is enabled, the less opportunity there will be for rational discourse. Censorship is presented not as an emotional dictate; it is a necessity of emotion management for the sake of public order and rational discourse. It is argued that once display of certain emotions through speech is permitted, speech opportunities for reasonable discourse will diminish; the speaker's intense display of menacing emotions generates fear. Therefore, proper speech policy would restrict speech in sensitive areas like ethnicity, and in particular, where the threatening or otherwise emotionally manipulative message blocks rational communication. It is assumed that arguments that seem to be dictated by reason, operating on the assumption that they may counter the emotionally driven speech, will not be heard. There is a lot of emotion behind this apparently reasonable approach, mostly fear, or emotions related to majoritarian identity. Whatever the emotional grounds of the preventive speech strategy may be, where emotions are clearly distorting the reasoning of both the speaker and her audience, censorship or other legal mechanisms conducive to self-censorship and silencing seem appropriate. The problem is that the standards of emotional communication distortion are not clear, and they are formulated in politically biased, emotionally compromised processes.

The above censorial policy misconstrues the dynamics of social communication and disregards the dangers of speech oppression. This position, victim of an availability bias, applies the lessons of very specific and extreme situations where the threatening message of the speech is credible because of actual violence that occurred in particular historical conditions. It assumes that emotional reactions to speech are mechanical and people have no emotional defense mechanisms. It underestimates the power of human reason, emotions, and personal interest. It is based on the assumption that the state is capable of singling out "really harmful" irrationality. Once government has the power to single out specific contents on the basis of potential emotional consequences (and their relation to the emotions communicated), it will have the power to single out what is politically inconvenient or what is troubling for the majority sentiment. Considerations of emotional harm can be abused, and those with power to control emotion display will abuse them. The more one allows taking into consideration the emotional effects of speech, the more likely it is that potential harm of speech will be assumed. It is for this reason that in negative theories of free speech, free speech is protected having in mind that government and majorities are unable to determine neutrally what kind of truth or whose self-realization is to be protected, because of their inherent bias.

It must be admitted that the "rational discourse" assumptions of free speech may be one-sided and exaggerated in their disregard of emotional consequences including harm, but this one-sidedness is dictated by the skewed nature of social communication where there is a political and sociopsychological bias against speech. This bias has to be countered. But how could law overcome the dictates of emotions? Social institutions are in the position to provide the individual with categories and meanings; by changing categories one can shift emotions. (See the Danish cartoon row case, *infra*.) Together with other social institutions, law is capable of channeling emotions and hence emotional reactions to speech.

First Amendment jurisprudence and robust theories of free speech rely on the rationality paradigm and tend to disregard emotion-based reactions to speech. However, this strategy does not exclude the possibility of incorporating into actual speech protection considerations of emotions and assumptions about *conduct* that result from these emotions. While finding irrelevant the emotional reactions to speech, it also maximizes the display of emotion through speech, which may be socially constructive. The verbal venting out of socially disruptive emotions like discontent, dislike, and anger has a sanitary effect. Of course, there is a risk: enabling these kinds of emotions may also result in socially disruptive behavior, as when it serves to reinforce destructive emotional dispositions and false beliefs in others.

Law is not the only regulator of social communication. There are social, institutional, and cultural interactions that enable consideration of emotional needs and consequences of communication. Social custom, education, and empathy help to make criticism or other communication restrained (polite) enough, without additional legal sanction. An absolutist protection of free speech does not necessarily mean the disregard of the conditions of meaningful communication where persuasion and competition prevail. Law may contribute to sustain these conditions with what U.S. law calls place, time, and manner restrictions. Freedom of speech creates a breathing space, but one does not need to make use of all that space in ordinary circumstances. There are, however, certain channels of communication where without the most robust protection of freedom of expression, communication as socially open discourse collapses. This is the case in politics, especially because of governmental interventions.

I referred already to the historical experience of religious censorship, where ideological dictates turned into psychological functions and psychological needs and were petrified as dogma. (At least some of these dogma served eminent emotional dictates like uncertainty reduction.) Such censorial control over emotions and reflection precluded human knowledge development. Certain emotions when managed by religious beliefs mobilize against modernity and secularism, and cannot be countered effectively without the strong and psychologically nonsensical commitment to freedom of expression (and freedom of belief of others). These experiences point toward the need for the absolutist constitutional protection which relies on distorted cognitive models where rationality prevails.

From the perspective of emotionally driven cognitive processes, constitutional law is primarily an institutional device to *overcome* a system of communication that would be dictated by what comes naturally (the spontaneity of gut feelings). In fact, the absolutist attempt to protect free speech as a rational enterprise is a large-scale framing attempt that produces simple heuristics and forces the public (through, among other things, authoritative judicial positions) not to depart from the results of the heuristics even upon consideration, where consideration means allowing emotions to come up with dictates.

The robust constitutional protection granted to speech that resists censorial sentiments is not contrary to the psychological interests of most people as speakers living in modern society. In Section 1 of this chapter, I referred to the psychological need to express oneself for reasons of identity formation and self-reinforcement. Freedom of expression means freedom of emotion display, but not its dictate. The legal protection of the borders of communication, through the symbolic and model-creating force of the law, has an impact on the process of social communication. However, the robust border protection is needed also because of the very nature of communication, because of the nature of the marketplace of ideas. In the marketplace vision, there are individual producers and distributors of ideas and opinions. The products (ideas) compete with other ideas. The recipients not only make choices of their own among these ideas, but also generate ideas and counterarguments. This contributes to their welfare maximization including psychological needs by rejecting or endorsing these ideas. The price paid for the idea is the effort, for example, the time spent to accept or reject these ideas, where rejection might be costly. Third parties and the society benefit from the production of such ideas. The benefits of speech are primarily externalities. A positive externality here is a positive impact on a party or parties who did not participate in the generation of ideas, for example people whose knowledge increases due to reading about an intellectual exchange among others.

The products in the marketplace of ideas are public goods. Richard Posner argues that this public good nature makes speech particularly vulnerable, as is generally the case with the production of public goods by private actors.[44] Typically, there is no individual return on an investment in a public good. Speech is a public good: an opinion informs about preferences and it is available free. Most speakers have little economic interest in their speech; at least they are not willing to invest in the proprietary protection of their speech. The audience is seldom ready to pay for the production of an opinion or idea by others; they are free riders when it comes to the contribution to social discourse; even contribution to the exchange of ideas through active participation is rare. Remember Dr. Johnson's admonition: "No man, but a blockhead ever wrote, except for money." Money is seldom paid for speech and writing: this turns speech as a product into an exercise of blockheads. The benefit for the speaker is mainly emotional (private pleasure, vanity, pride, identity affirmation, perhaps indirectly marketable products like reputation). Most self-realization through self-expression can be satisfied in private. *Ceteris paribus*, there is little market value for speakers in their speech, especially where the speech is not part of actual business or professional political activities which promise monetary gains or power, influence, etc., easily convertible into marketable goods.

While there is little return on it, speech is costly in terms of lost opportunity (consider the time needed for public expression). The generation and storing of social information is particularly costly, and there are only limited and expensive ways to recoup on such social information storage. By granting specific protection to ideas that reduces their additional production costs we try to diminish the resulting vulnerability in their production and storage.

The efficient production and distribution of ideas and other information presuppose a psychologically counterintuitive solution, namely the robust protection of free speech as rational dialogue. The institutionalization of free speech overprotection promises to overcome the difficulty that results from the vulnerability of the production of ideas. The costly protection granted to copyrighted ideas cannot be extended to all opinions. How efficient copyright and similar monopolies are for social innovation is contested. Hence the strategy of overcommitment to freedom of expression emerges. The strategy of overcommitment means that constitutional law frames speech in a way that favors speakers and is flexible enough to accommodate new forms of expression in the body of protected speech. The constitutional concept of freedom of expression allows for a very limited number of "exclusionary rules."[45] In addition, rules of consequentialist inclusion are also restricted in free speech law: the inclusion of emotional consequences in the legal, and to a certain extent social, calculus is thereby prevented.

Speech generates externalities, namely the harm caused by speech.[46] Only a few speakers may be ready to run the risk of social sanctions and even imprisonment for the inconvenience caused by their criticism. By extended speech protection, the emotional harms caused by the speech are disregarded in the sense that the speaker is not held responsible for these harms. Speech has to be free in the sense that the speaker shall not bear the cost of related externalities. Speech is vulnerable not only because of its inherent weakness but because of the psychological nature of the audience. Political and emotional interests seriously menace the production of opinions, and the censorship of majority opinions is powerful enough even where formal censorship is nonexistent, because of mechanisms of conformism and related ostracism. These mechanisms operate as efficient behavioral control and punish innovation and dissent. Consider the vulnerability of speech in the absence of specific actors with strong interests to be expressed. Add to it the weak emotional need to protect speech, and the actual interests in censorship, nontransparency, etc. Compare these speech-supporting forces with the broad social interest in not allowing silencing that would undermine the production of ideas. The balance tips in favor of silencing. This would undermine the socially efficient, inexpensive production of ideas.[47] It is this very disparity that dictates the strategy of speech supremacy.

Free speech is an institutionally endorsed precondition of *social* cognition. Once established in society, it acts like a heuristic or legal "intuition": "a heuristic, a way of framing and thinking about the regulation of speech, rather than an algorithm for use by judges."[48] The law imposes certain heuristics on people who are most likely to follow it in the hope that these will not only counter their emotions. The heuristic favors certain social actors who are especially important in sustaining a free space for communication (journalists, in particular). On the other hand, this is not the only heuristic at work. Certain emotions like resentment elicited in the context of religious and nationalist sensitivities create beliefs that "can serve as heuristic devices that threaten protected speech."[49]

Because speech is a vulnerable collective good, a strong, quasi-unconditional protection for speech emerges. The resulting rationalistic, speaker-biased model of speech rights runs against the way human personal and collective deliberation operates. The intuitive recognition of the necessity of strong speech protection originates in the original constitutional sentiments that animated the making of modern constitutionalism. The current American position seems to go very far in affirming speech heuristics. But the constitutional heuristics that favor speakers resulted in a complacent position regarding the First Amendment's quasi-absolutism.[50] The lawyers' comfortable position is that lawyers should be concerned only about speech as a rational phenomenon and resist the pressure coming from emotions (and political forces using emotions) by ignoring these emotions. In fact, such a position implies that law has nothing to do with the censorship dictated by private, worldview, or business considerations, and freedom of speech is only about government nonintervention.[51]

The long-term interest of all political competitors reasoning behind the veil of ignorance of the constitution-making would dictate a constitutional arrangement where all voices will be heard even if they happen to be in opposition or minority, as anyone may end up in such a situation. At the moment of the fundamental constitutional choice, the political branches had to give up, at least as a matter of principle, their claim to continued intervention in public communication; they are committed to refrain from speech regulation.[52] The power of intervention and regulation in matters of speech was partly transferred to courts, at least in most contemporary constitutional systems. The submission of controversial speech to a judicial process runs the risk of chilling effects, as even where the process results in the acquittal of the speaker; the possibility of a legal procedure is censorial enough.

Given the above vulnerability of the rationality paradigm and free speech in general, many lawyers, including American judges, prefer to provide categorical and quasi-absolutist protection, in fact overprotection. The advantage of this strategy is that it makes experimentation with restrictions difficult. However, the American categorical approach is not the fruit of some abstract conceptual consideration. The commitment to the categorical approach emerged only gradually in a trial and error process over fifty years, beginning with Justice Holmes's dissent in 1919 and consolidated in *New York Times* and in *Brandenburg*, in an age of increased domestic political stability, in a society that not only had a tradition of distrusting government, but in which such distrust was affordable.[53]

While First Amendment jurisprudence is ready to assume certain risks that come with overprotection, in other constitutionalist legal systems free speech may not have such a privileged position. In Europe, where courts rely on ad hoc balancing, it is argued that the resulting uncertainty is not censorial. Europeans are less concerned with the potential silencing effects of experimenting with the prohibition of speech that is deemed socially harmful.[54] However, a number of doctrinal techniques are applied to protect heuristics that endorse speech (though not against other rights) even in these systems. In case speech is criminalized for being offensive, generally there is a requirement to show that the speech was intended to be emotionally disturbing, insulting, offensive, in a way that oversteps the limits of objective and responsible discourse.[55]

Most liberal democracies consider emotional and other consequences of speech, though in a conflicting and undertheorized way, while in America the law disregards most emotional consequences. This has little to do with contemporary commitments to rational discourse, and it reflects a fundamental political concern of the American elites and many individuals: it reflects a fear of abuse of power by the central government. Government is seen as always ready to be taken over by fear. If there is an opportunity, it will venture into determining what one should think and believe, which includes targeting disfavored opinions. The techniques used are not directly censorial in the legal sense. Such opinions will be labeled unpatriotic and against decency. One of the governmentally endorsed techniques is that disfavored opinions are described as quasi-blasphemous, while God stands with the government. "Time and again Americans have allowed fear and fury to get the better of them (and) have suppressed dissent, imprisoned and deported dissenters, and then—later—regretted their actions."[56] Geoffrey Stone's observation indicates that even the constitutionally endorsed and reinforced heuristics of government mistrust cannot resist social fear outside normal stress.

As to the less absolutist continental systems, the prevailing position here is based on a different psychological attitude toward the state. European societies operate with the assumption that the state exists to do good things for society, and there is nothing wrong with the state standing up for certain positions. This is probably in gross disregard of European historical experience, but it seems that it is much more important that individuals are cultured to be less self-reliant (a difference noted already by Tocqueville), hence they have to trust the state more. However, partly because history still matters, partly because of the fear that benevolent state intervention in the marketplace of ideas will favor certain groups, a strong governmental siding with specific opinions in certain areas is not acceptable, although governmental support of privileged culture is not considered controversial in many democracies.

4. Emotions Challenging Free Speech

In a few select instances (hate speech, blasphemy, and libel) emotions challenge free speech in the sense that the presence of these emotions may force law to censor speech. Of course, the standard judicial reference to emotional factors is disguised by reference to constitutional values, like public order or protection of the family, privacy, honor. But in the case of the public order reference, it is quite common that the courts are concerned with acts dictated by anger, while the protection of the family against pornography and obscenity is about disgust or often serves as shorthand to refer to parental sentiments (including entitlements over child education in the name of parental love).

The economic vulnerability of the production of ideas necessitates overprotection in the form of constitutionally privileging the speaker's position, though primarily in regard to governmental intervention. However, speech has impacts that might be construed as personally or socially harmful, and harmful consequences generally legitimate government intervention. The presence of nonrational elements in expression provides some ground for speech regulation, even if one accepts the rationality paradigm: if the ideal of speech protection is that of enabling rational deliberation, the grounds for such protection do not apply to what is separated from the rational. Certain emotional reactions to speech may be seen as socially undesirable, typically because of painful emotional consequences or the disorderly behavior resulting from the emotions triggered by communication. The emotional consequences of communication may have normative implications, like censorship, that are neither fully theorized nor systematically handled in the law of freedom of expression.

Robust free speech theories find the objection of emotional consequences of little relevance: after all, where there can be counter-speech,

speech itself is the remedy, and emotional consequences allegedly will not carry the day. The response itself will heal the alleged emotional wound. Hence the constitutional paradigm of free speech remains within the assumptions of the rational discourse paradigm. Fears of slippery slope and concerns that considerations of emotional reactions of the audience clear the way to heckler's veto animate this inflexibility. Once again, such constitutional assumptions of free speech contradict or deny fundamental institutional and psychological realities. The emotional reactions to speech are very often elicited by the emotional components of speech; after all, emotions are far more responsive to other people's emotions as stimuli than to intellectual arguments. A statement of facts becomes an impermissible threat by interpreting emotionally the underlying emotions of the speaker as threatening.

The normatively grounded neglect of the psychological (emotional) reality of speech effects comes at a price: emotions that are offended by, and oppressed as result of speech may come back with a vengeance, with censorial or destructive impacts. Consider the influence of extremist speech, which is used today as the model for emotionally harmful speech. The overprotectionist argues that such expressions should not be banned. In her view it is easier to police hate, and criminalization would only push extremist speech underground. Lack of the opportunity to speak out publicly generates emotions of animosity and deprives extremists of reality control.[57] The slippery slope argument also applies: once censorship is found acceptable, though first only in regard to speech that is emotionally and socially obviously unacceptable, censorship will gain respectability and will be applied to critical views. By the way, who determines what speech is "obviously unacceptable"? There is always a dangerous inclination that will find criticism, especially if directed against the dominant preferences, "extreme."

Robust theories of First Amendment operate in a deliberate socio-psychological vacuum; emotional reactions to speech are disregarded. Such normatively legitimate self-blinding may make constitutionally protected free speech vulnerable in the sense of losing public legitimacy. The "unpleasant" impact of speech on larger sections of the population or on smaller sections with a loud voice often undermines the worth and therefore credibility of uncensored speech. Victims and potential victims become disillusioned about the value of speech, which is believed to be systematically used to their detriment, and freedom of expression is presented in the public opinion as protection for lies, and a pretext to offend and humiliate with impunity.[58] Freedom of expression remains important for the academic elite and the press only, as they are the ones who have a personal interest in uninhibited speech. Further, because of the social realities of the communication sphere and the difficulties of the psychological sustainability of robust speech that offends, the legal practice of freedom of expression is full of doctrinal exceptions and inconsistencies that amount to the violation of underlying principles.

Notwithstanding the constitutional commitments to free speech, emotions do constitute limits to speech in law. Incitement is prohibited because of the specific emotional arousal; verbal, undignified attack on politicians is prohibited if it amounts to "bestiality."[59] And, there is no protection for pornography—a "feeling" thing. But the emotional consequences are suspect where the speech itself is deeply emotional because such speech is likely to have strong emotional impact. In the language of law the emotion is "intended" to arouse emotions related to suspect ("impermissible") contents and action dispositions, subjects that are turned into taboos. Officially it is the intent that generates punishment, but in reality it is the intensity and nature of the expressed emotion that causes the consternation.

Partly for the sake of "realism," that is, in order to accommodate the emotional pressures, partly to maintain the dominant rational paradigm as a consistent legal doctrine, even contemporary American jurisprudence allows, sometimes even explicitly, for a limited consideration of emotional impacts. The category of "speech" is an open one. Such definitional openings allow for the consideration of public sentiment-based evaluations of communication effects, resulting in "declassifying" speech into unprotected utterance. This is particularly clear in the context of obscenity. The Supreme Court found that pornography is not speech in the sense of the First Amendment and is, therefore, subject to regulation, but it did not offer a clear definition, except within the context of its much-criticized and unclear concept of obscenity. Obscenity can be regulated (as non-speech) supposing that "the average person, applying contemporary community standards must find that the work, taken as a whole, appeals to the prurient interest; the work depicts or describes, in a patently offensive way, sexual conduct specifically defined by applicable state law; and the work, taken as a whole, lacks serious literary, artistic, political or scientific value."[60]

What does appeal to the prurient interest? According to American law, this is to be determined according to local public sentiment. So what is and is not protected speech is left (within limits) to be determined by local sensitivity (a matter that is hard to predict, especially in the age of the Internet).

The "rational discourse" paradigm is not necessarily unaware of the problems of emotionalism. But there are differences regarding the applicable strategy both within a country and internationally. First Amendment absolutism, for example, handles this problem mostly by disregard. European courts, on the other hand, often recognize emotion-protecting interests that are to be balanced against free speech. The way emotional reactions are taken into consideration in the construction of limits to free speech reflect the prevailing social construction of emotions; in the present case it is perception of emotions by the cultural and judicial elite that matters. Censorial sensibilities, expressed in general terms of neutral folk psychology truisms are often directed against minorities and express contempt and mistrust toward difference: the actual application of insult laws is often directed against minorities, including instances of minority self-assertion. "History has taught us that much of the speech potentially smothered, or at least 'chilled' by state prosecution of the proscribed expression is likely to be the speech of minority or traditionally disadvantaged groups."[61]

Emotional impacts are accepted as limits to speech where they are related to specific, powerful social interests or concerns, like public order. Without such considerations, even serious emotional distress resulting from speech will remain unprotected. Further, because of the socially construed nature of emotions, it is quite possible that speech that is offensive in a given situation or culture will not have similar emotional impacts on the audience elsewhere, simply because either the meanings are categorized differently or emotions cannot be legitimately displayed.

It is simply not true that social concepts of the sacrilegious or what constitutes an offense to honor, and the emotional reactions underlying or associated with these concepts are natural and stable. They have changed through time, with law playing some role in the shift. The perception of attacks on personal honor may change with every new generation. Once law successfully rejected that there is libel in false fact-based defamation of politicians, the general public no longer considered some of the offenses emotionally relevant. Profanity also was on the way to disappearance, both in the United States and in Europe, among other places, because in the public perception less and less is it rated as shocking.

Normalization matters for emotions. Emotions, of course, continue to operate in the communication sphere, but the categories that trigger them change as well as the display rules. Freedom of speech expands in a sphere that is emotionally less loaded, for example in academia. Once on its path, speech continues to expand its sphere of influence to spheres of communication where emotions were more able to hamper reasoning and the consideration of counterarguments. But all the time, behind the general theory of robust speech-protection and rational discourse paradigm there is an ongoing negotiation with emotional reactions that shape the understanding, interpreting, and evaluating of those communications. There is no unidirectional progress here toward uncompromised rational speech, and temporary intensification of emotional reactions and their social evaluation changes the equations. The current revival of religious sensitivity has already rewritten certain rules of communication with potentially restrictive implication for the legal protection of freedom of speech.

Constitutional law has a built-in mechanism for bringing in certain dictates of emotions. In line with the Millian approach, it considers various harms as grounds to restrict speech. Law considers as harmful actual consequences resulting from speech, like violence. The emotional impacts of speech fall outside the rational discourse paradigm and in principle should be disregarded; however, in reality often they are not; even if this means an extension of the Millian harm principle, where the consequences are the result of emotional arousal (incitement) and longer-term cognitive processes (like dehumanization through category change, resulting in genocide, rape, etc., triggered by inciting speech). In the modern experience, it is only exceptionally that the intensity of the emotion becomes decisive in restricting speech. Many of the non-harmful emotional and other psychological impacts are considered relevant for legal regulation, where the impact is both cognitive/normative and emotional, as in the case of identity formation. Of course, it is a matter of self-understanding of the polity to what extent it allows law to intervene in the shaping of identity by speech restrictions.

The rational discourse paradigm of free speech cannot incorporate and handle the problem of emotions generated by speech and has constant problems with long-term impacts of speech. Speech is suppressed because of its emotional impacts on the audience (and even on the speaker). The censorial emotions are such that the social elite that is capable of shaping public perception and legal evaluation, and even more the groups and institutions which endorse and feel those emotions, find them worthy of protection. Prudential considerations, especially fear of consequences, also point toward censorship. The emotions of the speaker are relatively easy to disregard in this context; however, the consequences are a different matter. To the extent these psychological consequences like humiliation are harmful, they may be excluded from protected speech, perhaps satisfying the Millian harm principle. Further, there are structural consequences of speech that may have negative emotional and social/behavioral consequences. By structural harm, I mean an emotional shaping of social relations that perpetuates objectionable power relations, in particular injustice. These structural consequences are emphasized in feminist jurisprudence, in the context of pornography.[62] The systematic representation of women as subordinated persons perpetuates such subordination through normalization and other mechanisms, both in the minds of the subordinated and those who have an interest in sustaining the subordination.

Feminist jurisprudence emphasizes that speech has socializing effects (I would call it normalizing effects) by defining the "expected and the permissible." In the case of pornography, it is not persuasion that matters. The socializing impact occurs through a noncognitive process because "[p]eople often act in accordance with the images and patterns they find around them."[63] This nonrational impact served as the basis for regulation of a famous ordinance of the City of Indianapolis, which classified "the graphic sexually explicit subordination of women" as pornographic publications. It is argued that because such speech does not allow for rational processing, it falls outside protected speech. Further, "[w]hile an isolated incident is not enough, the number of incidents alone is not determinative. . . . Conversely, incidents that are much less severe may constitute harassment in the context of a working atmosphere 'polluted' with racial tension."[64]

Likewise, a simple utterance of racial superiority is of little impact for the speaker or even the target, as it has limited humiliating or frightening effect, but racist discourse of supremacy and inferiority may have socializing effects on both victims and perpetrators.[65]

Among the utterances with destructive aggregate consequences, legal doctrine has singled out a specific class called "hate speech," a most unfortunate shorthand.[66] Hate speech refers not only to expressions that spread, incite, promote, or justify hatred based on intolerance, including racial, ethnic that is "nationality-based," religious, and sometimes sexual orientation- based intolerance, with or without potential violence, but even contempt.

From a psychological perspective the "hatred" in hate speech is a mixed bag. Expressions of contempt reflect an emotional state that is different from the expression of hate and anger, though in case of cold hate there may be some overlap, and very often statements directed against minorities combine all the above. Contrary to what the name suggests, the dominant emotion in hate speech seems to be cold anger and contempt against the outgroup, and the message that is legally categorized as hateful does not primarily act by arousing hatred but by contributing to a social dynamic of clustering by evaluating the outgroup. Of course, hate speech is often emotional, and tries to influence emotions, particularly those of self-esteem and fear, but this is true of most political mass communication.

Hate speech as a set of interrelated, learned, and sequential hateful messages results in cold anger and hate among those who support the stereotypical denigration of a group, while it causes loss of self-esteem and anxiety in the members of the target group. It goes beyond prejudice; it will become a source of emotional endorsement of harmful acts even without specific action tendency.

Though all hate speech concerns are related to divisions between ingroups and outgroups, the distinctions and discriminations based on race and ethnicity (and under specific circumstances, religion) are psychologically distinct from hate speech that targets other group characteristics. (In many societies ethnicity plays the role of race and the term "racist speech" applies to utterances against ethnic groups.) Race has the potential of total definition of identity and total mobilization against outgroups.[67] In terms of content and impacts on emotions, hate speech is differentiated. Racist speech (or speech directed against groups with immutable identity) is effective in arousing disgust against the target (but often against the speaker too, for racist speech is often felt to be repulsive). The message of this kind of hate speech is that the other race violates "our" *purity* (as understood by the group of the speaker). Compared to such speech, prejudice is simply a race (etc.)-related biased pre-judgment (like "members of group X are lazy"). Such prejudice-ridden speech hardly ever results in gut reactions originating in references to impurity.

Very often, the hate message is predominantly nonemotional; it intends to shift categories. For example, dehumanization is not about moral character and emotion-arousing metaphors like references to impurity, but is simply about category shifts. Racial traits are stressed in order to emphasize the otherness of the outgroups.

Irrespective of the understanding of hate speech (narrow or broad), the contemporary objection to racist hate speech is that it has led to discrimination and violence, and, if uncensored, it not only imposes a badge of inferiority on the target but it reminds "the world that you are fair game."[68] It turns the humiliating message that is related to immutable characteristics into credible attack. Immutable, socially relevant characteristics are integral to a person's identity, because the characteristics stay with the victim, if for no other reason. In some cases the trait can be hidden, but that results in feelings of personal betrayal and quite often feelings of guilt develop. Racist hate speech is a distinct class within the attacks on reputation (that is, within the general legal category of libel) because hateful or supremacy-motivated stigmas have more profound (shaming) impact on personal identity than most other attacks on honor.[69] Here the victim has little choice in his behavioral *repertoire* to counter the verbal attack, except, perhaps, racist counter-speech.[70]

These concerns combined tend to result in the legislative and judicial criminalization of racist speech: "Racism tears asunder the bonds which hold a democracy together. . . . Where any vulnerable group in society is subject to threat because of their position as a group historically subjected to oppression we are all the poorer for it. A society is to be measured and judged by the protections it offers to the vulnerable in its midst. Where racial and social intolerance is fomented through the deliberate manipulation of people of good faith by unscrupulous fabrications, a limitation on the expression of such speech is rationally connected to its eradication."[71]

Anti-hate speech legislation is animated by concerns about impacts on the audience and target populations, but here again contempt and hate have quite different impact, in particular when it comes to incitement to violence. In the folk psychology hate speech is deemed the author of hateful mentalities; people with such mentalities will move toward impermissible behavior. When hate speech is singled out, hatred is classified as a "negative" emotion, and both social and legal norms are mobilized against its display, a tendency that was expressly rejected by the Supreme Court. The inculcation of hatred is psychologically far more tricky than the above legal simplification would admit.[72] Hate speech intends and/or impacts individuals far beyond the target (victims). The impact on racists and "bystanders" is one in which emotions motivate imagination, and it is through imagination that the proposed categories (of supremacy/subordination and actions) become accepted and determinative of conduct. Quite often, racist speech that develops into hate speech arouses fear not only in the target (victim) group members, but also in the speaker and his audience. Sara Ahmed points out that white Aryan narratives are based on being threatened: the ("white") anger that is directed against the invasion of the others is generated by the threat. The result is that the "average white" feels love for other whites, and it is love that brings together Aryans with a "shared 'communal' visceral response of hate."[73]

Even within the secularized society that tends to satisfy the Millian preconditions of intellectual maturity, "rational discourse" runs into obvious difficulties when hatred or contempt regarding groups is communicated, especially with regularity that "promises" normalization. The hatred generated in the audience against a target, in particular against a group of people, typically selected on grounds of race or its equivalent (religion or sexual orientation), is hardly conducive to the search for truth and may contribute to the breach of public order. The standard objections to such speech include the impact on the self-esteem of the victim of the speech. Other concepts of hate speech refer to other nonrational consequences, for example, the ban on hate speech would protect members of the concerned group from fear, or it is related to the shame-related impacts of degrading speech. Even in the United States, though group libel has been found unconstitutional in the last fifty years, there are categories of hateful utterances that are not protected in light of *Chaplinsky*. These are, among others, the "lewd and obscene, the profane, the libelous, and the insulting or 'fighting words.'"[74]

It is argued in favor of hate speech restriction that the primary harm to be prevented and sanctioned is the hatred against other people, particularly specific vulnerable groups. This was the prevailing ground for speech restriction in Canada. The speech restriction was upheld as being necessary given the needs of a multicultural society in Canada, where multiculturalism refers both to resulting problems of public order and in particular to the needs of minority cultures. One could argue that even today American jurisprudence finds hate speech outside constitutionally protected speech, and it is only because of secondary concerns regarding the consequences of government censorship that the legislative attempts to criminalize or otherwise regulate hate speech are found unconstitutional. Justice Scalia's strong condemnation (and acceptance) of racist speech in *R. A. V.* is particularly telling in this regard.[75]

To sum up, anti-hate speech legislation intends to prevent that emotions construct a Manichean world of dehumanized enemies. Further, in some jurisdictions it also intends to protect special group sensitivities. Nevertheless, courts evaluate isolated acts of communication; this makes our understanding of communication impoverished. The isolated utterances are relevant (being amplified and amplifying) as part of a larger narrative but law has difficulties when it comes to the handling of structural problems. The doctrine of free speech is reluctant to handle problems of long-term aggregation of emotions,[76] especially as the resulting action tendency is not clear, even if disruptive emotions may accumulate, reinforcing each other, and can be mobilized by a single signal (sign, symbol) that was used to generate these emotions originally. In view of the complex structural and psychological impact of communication, the individualistic approach in law that looks only at the isolated impact of a single statement cannot grasp the problems resulting from speech protection. The public is concerned with aggregated consequences of repeated instances of degrading speech. Given the limited social support for free speech, politicians and judges influenced by public opinion will from time to time accommodate public, emotional criticism of free speech without a principled, reasonable strategy.

Speech often affronts personal identity (including group identity), in ways that commonly trigger emotions of shame and outrage. This is traditionally the area of libel law (both civil and criminal). Historically attacks on reputation were sanctioned not because of the emotional pain inflicted but because of loss of commercial reputational interests, and of honor in status-based social relations. I include here speech that affects collective identity, though in many regards the demand for legal restriction is not concerned with reputational interests and is only indirectly honor-based. The emotions triggered in the case of symbolic insult laws[77] are also group identity-related. Consider the specific use of collective symbols like the disparagement of national symbols or the use of prohibited symbols, and attacks on national honor; here the accompanying emotions include anger about victimization and feelings of injustice, which are often triggered by attacks on honor too, and shame.[78]

Speech has an impact on other people's self-understanding, partly directly, partly through the influencing of the external reactions to self-understanding. This impact is traditionally captured in the law of defamation and personality rights. Speech that enhances the speaker's personality may be detrimental to the target of the speaker. For Mill, preference should be given to the speaker, even at the level of communicative conduct, and one has to endure "the inconveniences which are strictly inseparable from the unfavorable judgment of others."[79] If a person displeases us, we may express our distaste. Without harm resulting from conduct there is no ground for intervention, and therefore feelings are free.

A person's self-understanding cannot develop without external reflections; in fact, allowing critical remarks regarding the individual makes the person socially conscious, reflective, and responsive. Without accountability there is no moral capacity, and accountability needs external criticism. On the other hand, there are important considerations in favor of "emotional protectionism." Consider the imperative need to build self-confidence. It demands that central attributes of personal identity should be shielded from contestation; therefore, in this reasoning, the cultural identity component (including religious identity) should be protected.[80] However, even if the development of personality would require a shielding of its central tenets, in liberal legal theory this requirement is addressed to the state, and not necessarily to individuals. Expectations in the welfare state may be more concerned with horizontal, interpersonal effects.

Law was traditionally reluctant to recognize reputational inconvenience and emotional distress in the tort of defamation beyond the allegedly quantifiable financial damage to reputation. Honor was socially construed as a nonpecuniary matter, and honor codes predominantly required private nonlegal restorative action for the restoration of honor. On the other hand, even in "honor societies," law and social norms tried to restrict the enforceability of redress for speech-related injuries to honor in order to avoid overburdening of the law (among other reasons). Nevertheless, the shame resulting from offensive, degrading speech continued to increase expectations of reparation, at least as German and French personality rights concepts indicate. In American constitutional law, *fighting words*, verbal attacks on honor at the level of action, are not protected.

Some of the emotion-based reactions of the target person and other members of the group are taken into consideration, especially when they are perceived as "normal" and reasonable emotions, worthy of legal protection to the detriment of speakers' rights.[81] Such normalized emotions are acceptable as "inevitable" (natural) and found therefore more important than the speech interest. Of course, in libel and insult law the insulting and/or libelous nature depends on the socially accepted and changing construction of self-evaluation and respect. The preference for "normal" emotional reactions includes certain sensibilities which receive institutional social confirmation, like the disgust-based reaction to profanity (in the form of religion-determined sensibility; see below). However, in regard to press criticism of public authorities ("public officials," public figures'), certain emotional reactions of the victim were gradually disregarded in favor of uninhibited speech.[82] In these contexts the position of the law quite often is that the emotional reaction of the victim can be disregarded or discounted as she deliberately submitted herself to public scrutiny, and further in this context negative emotions are "normal" in the sense of not being troubling: the political discourse is full of demeaning attacks and counterattacks anyway;[83] the discourse among politicians is emotionally driven and dirty and therefore without triggering the need for censorial intervention. Anger answering anger and insults answering insults are normal: there is no reason to intervene in the debate, and free speech emerges nearly unscratched.

Freedom of expression has a point and function in a political community operating according to the principles of modernity, where people dare to know only if the right to speak includes the right to offend and be mistaken. The European Court of Human Rights, which both reflects this prevailing European understanding of human rights and helps to form it, recognized this concept when it expanded freedom of speech to include protection of offensive and insulting expressions.[84] In fact, speech is meaningful only if it can offend; only then can it be effective for change. Otherwise, it remains of no account. The language of love and esteem builds community, establishes bonds, and reinforces the self, and it is wonderful, but it is of limited relevance in the search for truth. Speech has its full effect upon others, including the addressee, when it stirs visceral outrage; it is effective if the addressee or the audience wants to make the speaker disappear, because she says what we would rather not hear, because we are *exposed*. Speech is often a mask, but its value stands in stripping the masks of others. Without this exposing function and effect there is no point in talking about the beauty of freedom of speech, and certainly little reason to praise it, as noncritical communication is purely status quo-enhancing.

Nevertheless, to deter exposure of the self the prevailing culture insists on censorial sanctions in order to prevent and undo shaming. Is this a good enough reason for respect of the self-centered culture in the form of silencing shaming criticism? One cannot blame it on the speaker if the exposed person can counter the exposure only with violence, or by other socially destructive means; and the speaker cannot complain if he himself ends up exposed in the response. Freedom of speech is lost if we have to practice criticism in the least offensive way. It will result in self-censorship and abusive legal processes against speakers; in the unlikely case that the courts find that the specific statement was the least offensive possible, the process itself has chilling effects.

The alleged psychological realism behind identity-protective censorship is somewhat problematic. Most emotional impacts discussed above remain hypothetical and disregard the psychological needs that motivate the speakers. On normative grounds one can sympathize with the victims of racist, hateful speakers—I do, for sure—, but the content discrimination that hate speech policies entail remains problematic and invites abuse. A legal policy that follows censorial emotions is based on the assumption that if the expression of anger and hatred is silenced, the identity of others can be protected. Just as legally induced silence offers false security to potential victims, it is also unable to manage the emotions of the silenced speaker. There is, nevertheless, an empirical advantage to the silencing: it restricts the possibilities for amplification of the hateful sentiments.

So far we considered statements animated by/triggering hatred which damage personal identity. Fear of loss of identity and resulting anger may be per se grounds for speech restriction, and free speech theories will have difficulties facing such emotional concerns. But identity and the threat to it is a matter of sensitivity. Is personal sensitivity a sufficient ground for speech restriction if the speech was disrespectful and offensive?

In the last 15 years, even in societies that were moving closer to the model of rational polity, vigorous claims were made insisting on legal protection of religious sensitivities in a constitutional society. It is argued that behind the disrespectful criticism of religion there is old-fashioned hatred against the believers, especially against vulnerable minority groups, often migrants, who, perhaps because of their insecurity, are particularly sensitive and offended by various forms of criticism of their religion and religion-related life form.

The first contemporary reminder of the revitalized power of censorial religious sensitivities was probably the *Satanic Verses* affair in 1988–1989. At that time many Western societies realized that they were turning into multicultural societies. Such multiculturalism implicated the presence of strongly religious groups whose partly religion-based identity felt menaced by the majority value system. Globalization added to these concerns the claim that sensitivities of geographically distant nations are also to be considered because of the long-range impact of speech. By 2006—as the reactions to Danish cartoons in the Islamic world and even in Europe indicate—the assumption that speakers in democracies should be worried only about the reactions in their own country had become less and less sustainable. The consideration of multiple foreign sensibilities results in undermining the sustainability of the rational discourse hypothesis that is based on the operations of one's own secular society. In consequence, given that communication occurs interculturally, one has to see to what extent the Millian preconditions of free speech, namely not being permanently liable to hostile attack, intellectual maturity of the society, etc., are satisfied. This in itself raises issues about the sustainability of the prevailing free speech rationality assumptions. Change in fundamental legal values occurs not because an argument is stronger, but because changing social practices and beliefs have normative power. If intense emotions sustain a social practice for a longer period, it will come to be considered normal and even respectable; especially if there are political interests favoring it. It is quite possible that the understanding regarding the boundaries of free speech will shift in the case where there are enough people, even a minority, with a strong enough emotional motivation, commitment, and force to display beliefs that dictate some kind of censorship.

In case religious sensitivities are protected by government, public discourse is skewed to the detriment of nonreligious sensitivities—including but not limited to the sensitivities of atheists or believers who happen to be less or differently religiously sensitive. Sensitivity protection also skews the discourse in the sense that it favors those religions (and groups of believers) that are "more emotional." As a result, it pays to have a concept of religion that requires its believers to be more often or more deeply disgusted.

Offense to religious feelings of others is historically one of the crucial boundaries to free speech. The protection of religious feelings (and behind it, of course, the system of religion and religious institutions, including hierarchies, oppression, and denial of advancement of learning) was the defining consideration in matters of expression in nonsecular societies. Freedom of speech emerged to grant protection against religious censorship, first and foremost to allow competing religious speech; and the social importance of undisturbed, unchallengeable religious feelings explains the enormous difficulties of acknowledging freedom of expression even where other social interests clearly militated in its favor.

In light of contemporary blasphemy laws, the constitutional attempt to disregard the censorial efforts of religious sentiments that are used to serve institutional interests of churches was not fully successful even after secularization became established. Freedom of expression faces a new challenge with the global revival of religious fundamentalism. The censorial potential of religious sentiments was already crucial for Mill: "there is no parity between the feeling of a person for his own opinion, and the feeling of another who is offended at his holding it; no more than between the desire of a thief to take a purse, and the desire of the right owner to keep it. And a person's taste is as much his own peculiar concern as his opinion or his purse."[85]

This passage can be read two ways: the "stolen purse" may be the religious feeling that is offended by speech, or alternatively, the religious feeling is acting as a thief, and the speaker is the one who is deprived of his belief. This second meaning is referred to in the example given by Mill: he refers to "the disgust of the Mussulmans aroused by the Christians eating pork." He refuses to accept that any *conduct* that a group finds distasteful, and therefore an outrage to their feelings, would amount to injury. "[W]ith the personal tastes and self-regarding concerns of individuals the public has not business to interfere."[86] Note that in the free speech context the expression is not conduct, though for a bigot the blasphemous speech amounts to action. (The bigot is perhaps right: speech may be performative.)

The impact of religious sensitivities is well demonstrated in the 2006 Danish cartoon row.[87] The simplest construction of the facts in the case is that the cartoons, allegedly as part of a campaign against the Muslim minority in Denmark, offended core religious feelings and the identity of believers.

The Danish cartoon row is more than a simple paradigmatic case: it is an important component in its own right in the shaping of collective mentalities. It is part of a process that can challenge in a fundamental way all the assumptions that served to determine the very fuzzy and changing limits and boundaries of free speech as discourse among rational beings.

The anger created among the believers by the presentation of the image of the Prophet Mohammed, and European fears that the offense to religion might contribute to the demeaning of Muslim minorities, would dictate that the emotional consequences of offensive speech be factored into the equations governing permissible speech. The case is one where the religious sensitivity is inseparably connected with an identity issue. From the perspective of identity protection, given the intensity of the offense, and assuming that the publication expresses contempt of a religious minority in Europe and majority believers elsewhere who feel themselves victims of Western imperialist colonizers, such expressions should not be protected. It is not only the centrality of the religious belief that makes the attack offensive: here religion is most intimately related to an identity that feels threatened and is in need of affirmation.

It would be wrong, however, to assume that publishing an image of the Prophet is like crying fire in a crowded theater, for example, that such publications trigger inevitably uncontrollable passions. It would be a mistake to believe that here we have a dictate of spontaneous and intensive emotional reactions. The religious sensitivity and the anger that was observed and will be displayed time and again are socially construed through institutions. The outrage in the Muslim psyche was preconditioned by a specific interpretation of religious teachings in a local culture where religion is understood as the primary source of a contested identity. The outrage was the result of a long political process where the popular display of emotions has been shaped by decisions of political actors (including religious leaders).

For our purposes, it is important to note that censorship dictated by religious sensitivities is not limited to contemporary militant Islam. The religious sensitivity that was offended is not a peculiarity of Muslim believers, though the intensity of the reactions may have to do with the political conflicts in the Muslim world. Christian and Jewish religious leaders (who spoke of "provocation against religion" with one voice) and, for reasons of international and domestic politics, European politicians, too (crying "racist provocation") were eager to condemn the cartoons and insisted on press responsibility in the name of religious sensitivity. There is nothing new under the sun: the Vatican condemned the publication of Salman Rushdie's *Satanic Verses* too.

In fact, European legal systems and American public attitudes indicate a strong readiness to protect religion against offense. Blasphemy results in strong emotions, including anger, although the secularization process made these feelings less intense, and less and less speech was considered insulting to sentiments and therefore "offensive" to religion. Within the process of secularizing society, the boundaries of offensiveness were changing in conjunction with increased social and cultural permissiveness, and more and more expression lost its patently offensive character (a category change) in an increasingly pluralistic society. Churches had to keep up with the perceptional changes of the believers and had to accept, therefore, that religion cannot determine life in the public sphere. It is possible that we are facing a historical backlash in regard to the role of religion. In the Danish case the emotional power of religious identity, coupled with respect for pluralism, resulted in strong anti-speech positions.

Notwithstanding the need for strong constitutional protection of free speech, and the progress of secularization, many liberal legal systems have blasphemy laws on their books, and these provisions are applied from time to time. Secularism in Europe went very far, but it exists as a mode of pragmatic tolerance based on lack of strong commitments; it remains a matter of practical convenience without strong normative commitment. European constitutions were slow in abolishing state churches, partly because this status had lost its practical importance. European secularism was a matter of leaving things undecided. This attitude allowed for the protection of religious sensitivities where such sensitivities were claimed to exist. In the *Otto-Preminger-Institut v. Austria* case in 1994, the ECtHR upheld an Austrian court ruling that confiscated a blasphemous art movie and imposed punishment for its planned showing in a private club. The movie was not shown, but the Austrian authorities claimed that the religious sensitivities of the population were a sufficient reason for such measures, nevertheless. The violation of such sensitivities consisted in the knowledge that profane movies can be privately shown in the country.[88]

Because of the interplay of globalization processes, increased religious fundamentalism, and multiculturalism, a new standard of free speech seems to be in the making that reinforces the privileged consideration of religious sensitivities that is intimately related to the protection of the faith in most religions. This concern for sensitivity is the recognition of, or at least a tribute to, the psychological need of reasserting a religion-based identity and indicates that the Enlightenment-based secularism and its rather relaxed emotion management attitudes cannot be taken to be irreversible. Note that the reason for the strong endorsement of speech was related to the Enlightenment program of rational pursuit of truth by trial and error against the religious assumption that truth is given, which as such precludes all further search for the truth. If truth is divinely revealed, there is no place for such market-like competition.

In the *Otto-Preminger-Institut* case and in the handling of the Danish cartoons we see the beginnings of a typical cascade process in interpretation, where the motor of change is the intensity of emotions as publicly expressed. The important new development is that the source of the cascade is only partly endogenous: it is likely that it will result from international developments as part of globalization. In the aftermath of the politically generated furor about the real and fake cartoons, and relying on the geo-strategic power of Islam, there is a good chance that in many countries legislation or political correctness may impose new legal and cultural restrictions on speech in the form of the duty to respect religion. In practical terms, this means that there cannot be criticism of dogma or religious practices. Proselytism will be prohibited as disrespectful, and criticism of the oppression of women resulting from religious prescription will be disrespectful too. The cult of sensitivity, coupled with already strong religious fundamentalist pressures, brings us to censorship and self-censorship. Freedom of speech is, after all, socially negotiated, and it has always had an important open wound, or at least an Achilles heel, in the form of respect of sensitivity. Note that competing rights like personality rights or freedom of religion, or even parents' rights, incorporate and aggrandize emotional concerns limiting speech.

The above scenario does not come from science fiction. We are approaching a situation where the social norms of the global village will be dictated by local parochialism, where the most intense feeling (for example, the one with a highest likelihood of violent action) will determine the standards of publication. The feelings, including *ressentiment*, which seems to be the underlying public sentiment, are genuine and will not go away soon. Genuineness of the emotion is an argument in itself. Anger is genuine among many Muslims who would prefer to live according to the Shari'a, and this anger is transforming into the cold anger that we call hate. "My anger *is* that set of judgments . . . an emotion is an evaluative (or a normative) judgment. An emotion is a basic judgment about ourselves and our place in the world, the projection of the values of ideals, structures and mythologies."[89] One need not subscribe to the psychological theory that underlies these statements. For the audience, the emotion generally has a strong judgment-like message; it is understood as a sign of a judgment. Anger is condemnation, and it is generally assumed and felt that what is condemned by large-scale anger is wrong.

Is mass anger or even a sense of humiliation, which was mentioned as a justification of the rampage following stories about the cartoons, a good reason for changing our constitutional standards of free speech? Is anger to be taken into consideration beyond the obvious pragmatic reason that anger-dictated behavior endangers public order? From the perspective of the descriptive ambitions of the present work, what matters is that emotions actually and continuously, and in the present case globally, shape and redesign constitutional institutions. An individual reference to passion (for example, "I was beside myself with anger") is in a way an apology, a claim of lack of responsibility. It is an apology—at least in Western cultures. It may be troubling from the Western normative perspective to come to a point where anger is the sign of authenticity only: not an excuse but a legitimation. After all, authenticity is respected as a value in itself in Western culture.

The strong constitutional bias in favor of (offensive) free speech is based on the empirically sustained assumption that emotions can be institutionally channeled and contained. People learned to live with speech that hurts and even with the destruction of taboos. But now speech seems to affect cultures and communities of minorities where the containment of certain emotions is not socially enforced: quite the opposite. The emotional preconditions of constitutionalism—emotional restraint—are absent. The West is not in a position to determine the social construction of emotions in different cultures and political regimes. It has difficulties with the management of intensive emotions even at home.

What follows from this new situation? As a matter of principle, there is no reason to give up the strong protection of speech. However, multicultural societies may end up being different from the secular societies where constitutionalism was progressing. As mentioned above, all societies have to reflect the global society too. Of course, it would be legitimate to change the anticipated emotions of the fanaticized believers instead of changing our norms of free speech. It is legitimate, but it may not be possible. Fanaticism has social and psychological roots not necessarily in religion; after all, dogma alone never determines behavior. Strong emotions exercise a strong pressure, and constitutional law is probably not strong enough to withstand it. Americans are convinced that the quasi-absolutist protection of the First Amendment can withstand the challenges of religious sensitivities; after all, offensive speech is respected even among American religious fundamentalists. But categories erode quickly. Europeans tend to believe that there are more important things in a constitutional regime than speech: here the gates are open for further erosion of free speech, even without strong religious sensitivity.

Those who are ready to restrict freedom of speech for the sake of religious sensitivity forget that, in principle, speech has a distinguished role in Western society. The political community that Westerners imagine themselves to constitute offers a democratic political identity—a liberal political identity that presupposes freedom of speech at least to the extent that coexistence in society presumes the possibility for communication among the citizens. Identity is communicative: the citizen can acknowledge and express her opinion, since the opinion is the person herself. In this sense, there is no Western identity without freedom of speech.

6

THE CONTAINMENT OF PASSION: ASSEMBLY, RELIGION, AND POPULAR SOVEREIGNTY

> Thousands of men were present twenty-five years ago at the celebrated cavalry charge during the battle of Sedan, and yet it is impossible, in the face of the most contradictory ocular testimony, to decide by whom it was commanded.
>
> —Gustave Le Bon

Public gatherings are important opportunities for often-passionate collective emotion display and important venues of collective identity formation.

Freedom of assembly grants concessions to irresistible emotions which are, in exchange for recognition and protection, domesticated in the very process of recognition. Or so it is hoped. Freedom of assembly enables and regulates the display of "destructive" passions in gatherings. Nevertheless, any celebration of an unconditional legal endorsement of collective sentiments in recognition of the right to assemble would amount to the merest simple-minded naturalism. Assemblies are protected thanks to a number of happy historical accidents. Good theoretical justifications underlie this historical happenstance, primarily involving freedom of expression and related communication needs. While freedom of assembly is to a large extent a tribute to emotions, their relevance and ambiguity are hardly mentioned.

The chapter will discuss the ambivalent constitutional treatment of collective public display of emotions and passions. Passions are considered to be a particularly intense form of emotion display, the most damaging to reason. Passions are to be blamed for the bad reputation of emotions. In Section One I will demonstrate that crowd phenomena are managed according to prevailing folk-psychology assumptions based on historical experiences, prevailing scientific and political concepts of the crowd, and the tools available for crowd control. In other words, constitutional emotion control is to a great extent a reflection of the social construction of passions, which have only a limited direct influence on the legitimacy and regulation of their collective display. Section Two deals with contemporary judicial approaches to demonstration. In self-confident democracies the approach to large gatherings is framed with optimism about human rationality and self-control. But the experience with crowds still lingers larger than life, which explains certain restrictions involved and the loss of self-confidence underlying them. Specific privileged forms of collective behavior, such as organized manifestations of religion, voting, and other election-related activities receive better treatment. These are nearly unconditionally free, although an equal level of irrationality should have made them equally suspect. The organizations that control such activities (for example, churches and parties) are seen as capable of containing the passions of the relevant gatherings. Optimistic folk-psychology assumptions about human self-control in matters of politics raise concerns, especially in view of the problems that emotional politics creates. These resulting concerns generate the theory of, and to some extent the vocabulary and instruments of emergency. Constitutional restrictions on direct participation of citizens in the political process are expressions of similar concerns.

1. Crowd Mentality

Demonstrations are eminently suitable ground for the display of intensive emotions. Given the ambivalent role of passions in public life, such display and its forum (the assembly) are treated ambiguously. On the one hand, assemblies are to be protected as a forum for venting emotions and generating collective identity, while, on the other hand, behind the façade of a right hides an army of reservations. These are related to concerns and fears that passions will take over; they are articulated as "the danger of the crowd."

The permissibility of demonstration has always reflected the prevailing assumptions of the forces of order. We are dealing here with the folk psychology of a profession regarding crowd behavior and crowd control.

Beyond the very ambivalence of the notion of what constitutes a crowd, ambivalence is visible at the level of the standard constitutional language: only participation at unarmed "peaceful" assembly is protected. Armed assemblies are too risky. Until recently assembly in English law was a mere common-law liberty with ample discretionary police power to control it. In France, the freedom to demonstrate existed as a liberty; it received higher level constitutional protection as a "constitutional value" only in 1995.[1]

Freedom of assembly is an outgrowth of the right to petition.[2] Because of fear of unruliness and direct mass pressure, English law traditionally tried to limit the number of signatures and even more so the number of people who could assemble to present a petition to King or Parliament (see for example, the Tumultuous Petitioning Act, 1661). But petitioning remained the main and cherished form of expressing public sentiment in the proto-parliamentary age when only a tiny minority of the well-to-do had electoral rights. Because of the importance of petition, the corresponding right to assembly remained acceptable.

The right to assembly became increasingly problematic with the Gordon riots of 1780, which arose out of mass petitioning when the King Mob pressured for the repeal of the Catholic Relief Act by petition. Unruly demonstrations and riots were considered part of the ordinary politics of the day in eighteenth-century England, an unpleasant but inevitable fact of life. For the marginalized the only opportunity for political expression was to gather in a threatening manner.[3] With the increase in the intensity of eighteenth-century riots in England, assemblies were demonized: Hume, already in his 1770 edition of Essays, *suppressed* the following sentence that he used in the original version: "It has been found . . . that the people are no such dangerous monster as they have been represented."[4]

Demonstration became known more under the category of disturbance than of right, partly because the authorities did not have proper crowd control techniques at their disposal. When in 1819 the Peterloo demonstrators were massacred by the regular army, this was due to an insufficiency of civil power; for this reason authorities felt the need ultimately to resort to military force.[5]

However, with the increasing participation of lower classes in political life, demonstrations became accepted by dint of electoral politics and improved crowd control techniques available to the forces of order. The recognition of the normalcy of demonstration remained at the level of common-law liberty with nearly unfettered and often abused police discretion until very late. Characteristically it meant for Sir Ivor Jennings the same liberty as that "to go without a hat."[6] The standards of judicial review of restrictions had never been particularly demanding.[7]

The attitude to the right of assembly seems to have been different in the United States. Already in the October 14, 1774 *Declaration and Resolve* of the First Continental Congress, the people's "right peaceably to assemble, consider their grievances, and petition the King" was recognized. The Constitution incorporated the wishes of a movement that came to power partly on the shoulders of successful popular assemblies. But the recognition of the right to assembly also indicated the democratic commitment of the new nation. State constitutions like that of Pennsylvania expressly considered assemblies as tools of [democratic] political decision-making, beyond creating a forum for grievances.[8]

While the right to assemble was supported by historical right (as part of birthright), as well as by practice and the commitment to popular decision-making, certain forms of gathering remained threatening to the establishment. The same Madison who in 1789 proposed the inclusion of the right of assembly in the Bill of Rights was himself deeply suspicious of assemblies: "In all very numerous assemblies, of whatever character composed, passion never fails to wrest the scepter from reason. Had every Athenian citizen been a Socrates, every Athenian Assembly would still have been a mob."[9]

The French Declaration of Rights was created amidst (and thanks to) repeated mob actions. However, it did not single out freedom of assembly, though arguably this might be part of general liberty; the right to resist tyranny is expressly mentioned. The Constitution of 1791 affirmed in title I, § 2 that the "Constitution guarantees as natural and civil rights . . . the liberty of the citizens to assemble peacefully and without arms, in accordance with the laws of police." This formula was repeated in a declaration of rights preceding the Montagnard Constitution of June 24, 1793. It was omitted, as were other liberties except for personal security, in the Thermidor Declaration. After that, *liberté de réunion* and *liberté de s'assembler* was not mentioned in French constitutional documents until the 1848 Constitution, whose Article 8 guaranteed freedom of peaceful assembly within the limits of rights of others and public security.[10]

Peacefulness of assemblies remains a fundamental condition, and one unlikely to be always satisfied. The experience with the riotous and revolutionary *journées* in the 1789 Revolution and of all the demonstrations which brought revolution against the wish of the organizers looms large. It should be added that disorderliness of crowd gatherings was a matter of nearly daily experience in the first half of the nineteenth century in France, a matter that was true in Britain as well. Aurélien Lignereux reports that between 1800 and 1859 there were at least 3725 reported acts of local violent rebellion against the gendarmerie coming from a mass larger than three people, excluding incidents in Paris. Some of the mass gatherings had to do with the conflicts of industrialization, but the bulk of the violent clashes grow out of local cultural conflicts where traditionalist groups resisted centralized concepts of order. Violent mass demonstrations typically erupted at arrest and conscription, a matter quite different from the Peterloo riots.[11]

Notwithstanding the gradual textual recognition of the right to gathering, large multitudes remained suspicious. Multitudes continued to be seen as hotbeds of antisocial attitudes and behavior. Law and the authorities did not or could not (for lack of identifiable criteria) distinguish between spontaneous and more organized crowds.[12]

Nineteenth-century assemblies could turn into riots at any moment: the police were not in a position to be proactive. As the dramaturgy of the Peterloo massacre indicates, the classification of gatherings as riotous was a matter for police constables. Likewise to use violence for dispersion was a matter of opportunity, not rights. Anticipatory emotions (like guilt or empathy emerging at the carnage envisioned as a result of police or military action, or anticipation of political and legal condemnation, and resulting fear) could not play a major role, as the armed forces were socialized against such feelings. The legal uncertainty about gatherings increased the legitimacy of the intervention, and intervention-discouraging political outrage was not part of available experience. As to the latter, it was the death-related empathy transformed into outrage, especially among an already existing political opposition that helped to build up more respect for peaceful demonstrators. Given the lack of efficient police crowd control, there was little opportunity for courts to stand up for a strong presumption of the lawfulness of a gathering, except perhaps when it came to the criminal prosecution of the participants. With improved police control emerging at the end of the nineteenth century, preventive policing became a possibility and preventive action in the form of bans made judicial supervision more important. It was only after World War II that robust judicial protection of the right to assembly began to spread in advanced democracies. But the ambiguity of demonstrations (or the ambiguity of the prevailing social construction of demonstrations) still haunts the judiciary.

What is the psychological particularity of assemblies that makes their legal treatment so ambiguous? Does constitutional law single out for protection specific emotional displays and/or the display of specific emotions which necessitate protection at the high level of a constitutional right? This constitutional protection is somewhat accidental, in the sense that it partly comes from assemblies' historical association with petition, the most important organized and streamlined form of expressing the popular mood. It became part of the democratic structure and a form of popular will formation. Additionally, freedom of assembly became more important because of its role in identity affirmation and communication. As to the communicative aspect, it is a peculiar part of freedom of expression, serving the expression of the emotional intensity and collectivity of beliefs.

Nevertheless, it seems that from the perspective of emotion display, restrictions on the display are more important in the constitutional provisions than the right itself; its restriction reflects concerns about crowd passions and also fears that large gatherings may undermine the social and public order in a revolutionary or riotous manner. Here we have three emotional components for consideration: the emotional dynamics of the gathering, the folk assumptions about it, and the fear that emerges in the evaluation of actual demonstrations.

Undeniably, the action tendencies of the emotions that animate demonstrators and the "group mind"—particularly in large gatherings—have certain troubling aspects. The most problematic emotional factors of crowd behavior (which are, as we will see, often exaggerated for purposes of regulation) are a) imitation and b) loss of control over personal decision.

Imitation in the crowd remains fundamentally troubling for a civilization based on individual subjectivity. The concern was most famously argued by Freud, who discussed the problem in the context of psychopathology of young girls in boarding school. In his view the imitation behind what he calls "hysterics" is based on sympathy with the suffering of one of the participants. To Freud the problem with the "mental infection" is that the entire reaction results from (and is enabled by) a previously established significant analogy between two egos. The analogy may be misperceived as coincidence, and the identification threatens a dissolution of the subject's ego.[13] The analogy is at work in the "infections" that characterize mass phenomena of various levels of structuring and organization; it is present in randomly assembled demonstrators, assemblies of movements, and organizations and collectivities of religious believers, as well as citizens who share a strong national identity. Constitutional law deals with mass phenomena which run the risk of this pathological overturn, one that may destroy the ego. In less Freudian terms it incapacitates the citizen's self-determination.

Loss of control is attributable to the uncontrolled workings of empathy (partly as "imitation") in the presence of other people with strong feelings. There is an inevitable tendency for the feelings to become part of a mutually reinforcing process, especially where there is already a desire for mutual identification among the participants of the assembly. The above process limits or excludes the control function of individual reason, or in brain-science terms, the control function of the executive function. The loss of control is particularly likely when a charismatic leader conveys an emotional (religious or identity-enhancing political) impact, guiding the mutual empathies toward a specific single emotional goal. The emotionality of the crowd and the resulting loss of control remains a looming presence both problematic and controversial.

These "infectious" tendencies often pave the way for rampage and destructive violence. Given the intensity of the face-to-face encounter, emotional cascades are likely. As a result of the cascade, individuals easily lose self-control over the emotion display. The display-related control over emotions diminishes, and unchecked emotions reduce the control provided by the executive functions of the brain. Passions will run high, and consequently people will act in ways (including resorting to aggressive violence) that they hardly ever would in the conditions of ordinary solitary life. What was described by Le Bon as "regression" and has remained part of folk psychology from Roman days until today—that even rational and good people become bestial in assembly (*senatores mala bestia*)—can be explained as inevitable given the cascade effect. Given its randomness and rapidity, emotional contagion appears irrational to the outside observer. It may be felt as "irrational" by the demonstrator also, as emotional short-cuts reinforced by other people's feelings and action limit the use of his cognitive faculties. In the physical proximity of other crowd members, intensive emotions are transferred from others, thanks to mirror neurons. The human need to stick with the majority becomes irresistible.

The legal reaction to assemblies is not directly determined by the psychological specificities of crowd behavior. After all, the above dynamics do not fully develop in most large gatherings, and external factors to a very great extent determine the way psychological interactions occur in actual crowd gatherings. Depending on actors and their goals, cultural patterns, the level of momentary frustrations, the attitudes and resources of police, the mutual assumptions of the demonstrators and the authorities, and many other conditions and contingencies (like an accidental scream that triggers panic or makes a horse too nervous, resulting in a mounted police charge), demonstrations have a dynamics all their own. Constitutional and other public law texts give little guidance; the assumptions of folk psychology, social prejudice regarding demonstrators, and assumptions about the possibilities of riot control fill out the space between the words of the constitution. The actual protection granted in the name of freedom of assembly indicates how the social understanding and construction of emotions (as part of events) in folk psychology and the resulting jurisprudential assumptions can structure law and our understanding.

Historically freedom of assembly was shaped by the dominant perception that assemblies—especially of the lower classes, and of the hungry in particular—are easy prey to passion and consequently dangerous to the established order. Napoleon's Penal Code and the French gendarmerie saw rebellion as the work of violent people who follow their mean passions; they are then followed by the easily manipulable masses clearly distinct from the "good citizens."[14] The "bestiality of the mob" became part of public concern about assemblies. Lombroso elevated this prejudice to the rank of the scientific theory of "inherent crowd criminality." Reacting to the mass atrocities of the Paris Commune of 1871 Le Bon and other nineteenth-century masters of mass psychology produced a science (the irresistible frame of understanding in the age of modernity) that sanctioned this mistrust, although for Le Bon it was not innate criminality but the laws of social interaction that explained the disruption of the masses (crowds) through suggestibility and hypnosis.[15] These assumptions animated folk psychology; from there they found their way back to the police and the judiciary, framing the handling of gatherings in the nineteenth century. It must be added, however, that the folk psychology of the crowd was never uncontested, and opposition politicians and liberals in particular (notwithstanding the distaste for assembly so characteristic of Benjamin Constant) rejected the blaming and vilification of the masses.[16] With the passage of time, the dynamics of assemblies that served as the empirical basis of the crowd-mentality thesis started to change. From sudden and disparate acts of desperation and rebellion, demonstrators turned to action that was more integrated into existing, better-managed social conflicts. In time the civility of demonstrators (owing to the diminishing appeal of models of violence) and the technical preparedness of the forces of order changed as well, which enabled a better-managed interaction between police and the organizers of assemblies, who had better control even over marginalized demonstrators. The emerging forms of public expression of grievances through the press and elected representatives offered new opportunities to vent discontent. The demonstrators are "no longer the result of the breakdown of the former system;" they are the product of "*massification*, the mixing and blending of the social classes."[17] The demonstrations of these more "respectable" people might have been capable of the same intense destructive passions attributed (with some basis) to bestial mobs, but people at gatherings having more self-control hardly ever reached the point of unlimited passion display.

Social fear receded through more favorable experiences with demonstrations, and it became easier to imagine peaceful manifestations. Social and political actors successfully relied on assemblies and gained social respect and influence by mobilization. Freedom of assembly had gained middle-class and judicial respectability among other things for the following reasons:

- Labor and "rights" movement leaders clearly intended to use mass demonstrations as ordinary and legitimate pressure in the democratic political process, without challenging the foundations of the social system. Except for moments of radical political struggle, women in the suffragette movement and workers could legitimately use the tool of demonstration. The respectability of assemblies further increased because previously suspicious lower classes were now accepted and even welcomed for instrumental use by the upper classes.

- Later on the American civil rights movement and the European student demonstrations of 1968 successfully challenged the class bias that might have been applicable previously. At this time a growing part of public opinion sided with the demonstrators, who were often strongly associated with the majority. The demonstrators claimed to represent legitimate constitutional values against the violent and even brutal police, who could not claim specific values to defend and who were at the time often unprepared to handle demonstrations in a nonviolent and therefore nonrepellent manner.
- Demonstrations against tyranny in oppressed countries, beginning with the June 1953 demonstrations in East Germany, the images of Budapest streets in 1956 or Prague in 1968, were celebrated as legitimate expressions of people's stand for freedom.
- The use of police violence became a contested matter. After World War II the world became increasingly emotionally sensitized to violence, which delegitimized certain actions of the police.
- It became more and more credible that demonstrators follow rational goals, and therefore they could be treated as rational partners without running the risk of mob destruction. Police attitudes have to change where demonstrations cannot be construed as extremist ventures.

This new, comforting political perception was corroborated by, and partly originated from, the emerging social science of the twentieth century. The new scholarship, arising from the sociology of movements and also from political science, has delegitimized crowd psychology, labeling it a poor, racially biased, and scientifically unfounded construct of frightened bourgeois authors.[18] It became easy to ridicule the old paradigm for its reliance on hypnosis and somnambulism (which were the explanatory folk-psychology theories for Hitler's and Mussolini's success—all on display in Thomas Mann's *Mario and the Sorcerer*). Relying on a careful analysis of sources and actual events, the new movements' scholarship could show that descriptions of mob brutality and hypnotic imitation often came from the reports of police agents who were interested in a doctored version of crowd and police behavior. The authorities of the day willingly accepted the sensationalistic accounts of criminal savagery of the mob, as in the case of the 1870–71 Paris events, partly to justify their own brutalities and retaliatory measures and for purposes of exclusionary politics against class or ethnic enemies. Fear of criminal lower classes was an important component of middle- and upper-class identity.

The attack on crowd psychology has undeniable scholarly merits, but it too offers a one-sided perspective. The sociology of movements scholarship—often for reasons of personal sympathy with specific movements—and democratic political theory helped to elevate masses and demonstrations to the pedestal of disciplined, rational goal-seeking and to the status of regulatory paradigm, at the price of disregarding the fact that even disciplined masses may produce crowd behavior. Football hooligans and religious fanatics act as mobs and always did, even if their action is carefully planned for rational purposes by sinister minds. A purely rationalistic approach to demonstrations is well founded but unsatisfactory.[19] It may well be that demonstrators seek rational goals and act "rationally" when they selectively destroy police cars and other possessions of their supposed enemies; it may well be that football hooligans rationally seek out opportunities for violent encounters in specific, partly symbolic spheres. But it remains difficult or impossible to fit the display of emotions of hatred and acts of aggression (including disproportionate violence) against objects into a narrative of rational and individual behavior or into the rationality of a group or movement.

The rationalistic construction of mass behavior in movement sociology and (following it) in law disregards the troubling phenomena of Nazi rallies and contemporary populist gatherings. Schumpeter was aware of the limits of crowd rationality: the disappearance of moral restraints and other "gruesome facts that everybody knew but nobody wished to see. A serious blow to the picture of man's nature which underlines the classical doctrine of democracy and democratic folklore about resolutions."[20] While the choreographed Nazi rallies in Nürnberg or at the Heldenplatz in Vienna were certainly very orderly,[21] their transformative emotional effect remains deeply problematic. They served to mold a new collective identity: this kind of emotional collective identity formation—the exhibition of the multitude as a model and the suggestion that nonidentification is impermissible—hardly has a place in constitutionalism, and remains problematic for it even when not associated with racist extremism.

The shortcomings of the paradigm of the respectable and rational gathering are discounted in the prevailing legal discourse, which is concerned with the short-term public order aspects of mass phenomena and considers the anticonstitutionalist and antidemocratic implications of plebiscitarian identity politics to be beyond the legally manageable. The construction of mass demonstrations as rational acts prevails in a discourse where rationality still counts as crucial for legitimacy, and where the traditional way of delegitimizing demonstrations was centered on their irrationality. In this new approach demonstrations are alternative forms of genuine popular participation in a world of faltering representative and mediatized democracy. Once identity politics became popular, demonstrations and other collective presences were found more and more attractive in the name of the genuine emotional needs of group identity.

The above changes in social science and in the political use of demonstrations had a considerable impact on folk psychology. Once news about the rationality of the crowd reached political ideology and folk psychology, judges were freed to change their attitude for more protection of demonstrations and demonstrators. Note that this change occurred at the time of the civil rights movement and the 1968 student revolutions. In the age of television the sufferers were the beaten-up demonstrators, and the vision of suffering mobilized compassion for them. The police gradually learned their lessons, and received the resources for better policing, including training for appropriate police conduct before, during, and after demonstrations.[22] The burden of proof regarding the appropriateness and level of police intervention shifted to the police. The authorization and handling of demonstrations became increasingly judicialized, with stringent standards based on the assumption that the assembly would *not* get out of hand; if it did, the police would be blamed for lack of professionalism. In addition democratic theory animates a certain political correctness and projects it into the folk psychology available to public authorities: a democratic citizen is normatively assumed to be above passion, except when purposely incited.

2. Contemporary Legal Reaction to Gatherings

It is the combination of this new perspective on crowd behavior and of the possibilities of policing that animates the contemporary approach of the judiciary to freedom of assembly. The police are expected to provide a service for the demonstrators by offering them a safe public space. Of course these preliminary considerations are hidden behind the long-time prevailing legal doctrine that places freedom of assembly within the context of rational discourse.[23] It is protected as a special application of freedom of expression worthy of protection for the same reasons, and is understood as a special form of communication. But within this speech-extending paradigm prior restraint, a fundamentally unacceptable measure in matters of speech, is still found legitimate in the form of prior notice and even authorization.[24]

To some extent demonstrations are protected as the least dangerous form of venting passions. *Schmidberger v. Austria*, the emblematic demonstration case of the European Court of Justice, is quite telling in this regard.[25] The blockade of a major international highway was judicially considered to fall within the protected freedom of assembly as "all the alternative solutions which could be countenanced . . . would have been liable to cause much more serious disruption to . . . public order, such as unauthorised demonstrations, confrontation between supporters and opponents of the group organising the demonstration or acts of violence on the part of the demonstrators who considered that the exercise of their fundamental rights had been infringed."[26] This judgment makes explicit what many courts do as a matter of routine. Freedom of assembly is protected as a right (implying the imposition of serious costs on police and third parties) because this is the most civilized and overall the least costly form for expressing passions which might be destructive in less controlled situations.

There is one remaining element of uncertainty with demonstrations where the change in perceptions and related presumptions seems not to carry the day. Violence remains a possibility both under the rational action plan and in the mob contagion scenarios, though to different extents. In the rationalized understanding of mass behavior, violence is seen only as a premeditated act of a small criminal group (racists and fascists intending to intimidate; acts of religious fanatics, etc.) and not the consequence of crowd behavior or destructive animal instinct. This means that the violent group behavior of "certain groups" is predictable, and police restrictions and bans can be fully justified on the basis of such rational foresight. Often the assumptions about groups and their purposes will determine the preliminary handling of the demonstration: what can be presumed about groups will depend on the political characterization of their views, or on past behavior.[27]

I am not asserting that there are no objective criteria used here, or that past record of violence of a group is not an intuitively acceptable predictor of future violence. I am claiming merely that assumptions about risks of emotionality and violence are socially and culturally framed. Legal dogmatics is influenced by these frames, and also contributes to their shaping and selection. This ambiguity is also present when it comes to the evaluation of hate speech made in front of a large audience. The speech is unprotected, but not the gathering itself without the speech. At least outside the United States, the arousal of hatred is suspicious in law. As discussed in Chapter 5, even a negative impact on the identity or denigration of other people may deprive these utterances of protection. In folk-psychology terms, the ban on hate speech is a protection against speech that arouses fear and shame in members of the group concerned. But it is far from clear that gathering to listen to such speech and giving support by presence and acclamation to repugnant ideas and groups would be enough for the prevention or dissolution of such gatherings in these same countries, even where the speaker will be called to account. The gathering will count as an exercise of identity expression.

There is something odd in the legal and social handling of hatred. It is considered dysfunctional for social stability as it contributes to the fragmentation of society and undermines social interaction (although it may also create communities on the basis of shared hatred). Contemporary Western culture tries to delegitimize it as improper in its offensiveness. It is not fitting in a civilized society to officially condone violence that is the likely consequence of hatred. It is construed as politically incorrect. But hatred remains a strong emotion with lasting effects, and it does not go away easily for being labeled improper; being subjected to sanctions for its display may simply increase and transfer the anger behind hatred.

But in terms of evolutionism hatred is not an aberration. There are enemies out in the world and hatred mobilizes defense. Hatred as a cool sentiment based on anger, outrage, and indignation may have socially positive functions which are culturally recognized: it mobilizes resistance against oppressors in a lasting fashion, although it is true that it hampers peaceful conflict resolution. Whatever its cultural evaluation, it is very difficult to manage socially: hatred is an emotional fact. It is the accumulation of enormous emotional energy requiring some kind of venting. The problem is that it is a "contagious" emotion.

The expression of hatred toward someone or something in front of a gathering does not, as a rule, make the assembly illegal. The jurisprudence of the ECtHR, for example, assumes that participation in a violent demonstration cannot be punished as long as the participant himself is not violent.[28] Hateful speech can be punished if it incites to violence against identifiable people, and not for the underlying emotion, though in some cases the stirring of hatred is an element that contributes to the dangerousness of speech, because it makes violence more likely.[29] A demonstration where xenophobic sentiments are expressed may remain within the freedom of assembly as long as racist supremacy or discriminatory measures are not advocated.

In the contemporary judicial handling of demonstrations the prevailing assumption is that people will resist hatred. The prevailing social assumption about social order is optimistic. Where worldview-based social tensions run high, the equation changes immediately: where there is religious tension among believers of strong religions, bans on gatherings seem immediately reasonable, even necessary and justified, as the case of India demonstrates. In the case of ethnic strife, demonstrations as a right remain highly contested; at least preventive curtailment is legitimate, and the claim to the right to demonstrate is often described as abusive and intended to provoke. The long history of Orange parades both in New York and in Belfast illustrates this point.[30]

It follows, that assemblies are not necessarily an opportunity to expose one's ideas to a multitude through rational dialogue. Assemblies often serve the exposition of ideas and sentiments of the multitude to others including, paradoxically, members of the same multitude. As a leading contemporary French commentator has put it, demonstrations have the aim of expressing *collective sentiment.* Intellectual debate is not a legal requirement for the protection of the assembly. At times or in circumstances where the assembly does not fit into the rational discourse/free speech paradigm it would follow that only limited protection will apply.[31] However, this is not what happens: in the legal world dominated by the self-confidence of the constitutional regime, it is pretended that the standard "full" protection due to fundamental rights applies. In reality this self-confident constitutional assumption shares the view of His Highness addressing the "Committee for the Drafting of a Guiding Resolution with Reference to the Jubilee Celebrations of the Seventieth Anniversary of His Majesty's Accession to the Throne": "What brings us together in this gathering is our agreement on the question that a mighty demonstration rising out of the midst of the people must not be left to chance, but calls for far-sighted influence from a quarter with a broad general view, in other words, an influence from above."[32]

One of the most important justifications of the robust, speech-like protection granted to the freedom of assembly relies on democratic theory: where disadvantaged and minority groups have no access to the media, or are otherwise marginalized in the communication space, the opportunities of personal gatherings are important for the expression of views. Moreover, assemblies are helpful to express the intensity of a belief.

There are additional functions recognized in constitutional theory and in jurisprudence which justify the extension of speech protection to assemblies. Assemblies have a democratic function as forum and process of generating popular will. In this context freedom of assembly is related to the exercise of popular sovereignty and participation in political life, including the direct influencing of legislation or expressing and—even more important—forging identity. The identity-shaping and affirmation function of assembly extends beyond the political sphere. It serves to build personal identity as well as new social identities and their recognition. "Self-identifying speech does not merely reflect or communicate one's identity; it is a major factor in constructing identity. Identity cannot exist without it. That is even more true when the distinguishing group characteristics are not visible. . . ."[33]

In the context of identity-building assemblies, the emotional dimension is crucial: it is in the interaction of the assembly that people emotionally recognize and shape each other's identity. To have the courage to display one's self is served here by the right to assemble. In this context the mutual acceptance of the participants' shared identity (including specific expressions of that identity) through mass presence is often the most important function of the gathering. In addition, gay pride parades and ethnic group parades indicate an additional message directed to the outside world: they signal the existence of the group and their claim to legitimacy. Although identity politics is a relatively new explicit element of democratic politics, such identity-building is a traditional function and element of assemblies. Assemblies of disenfranchised laborers in France or England in the eighteenth and nineteenth centuries aimed to affirm their common identity by seeing each other and finding reassurance in their great numbers.

Identity-affirming functions of speech may have been recognized, but were never foundational for speech protection. But in many regards demonstration is not about a specific form of speech. It is part of a struggle for inclusion: to be recognized as speaker, as someone capable of speech, and having a voice loud enough to be heard. Through my lawful presence at a legitimate event, even if my speech is uttered from someone else's mouth and my voice comes only as affirmation in the form of background noise, I will raise myself from the status of the barbarian who cannot speak the language of the community. My existence is acknowledged by the recognition of our collective presence, a presence that proves that we have the faculty to express ourselves, even if all we say is that we exist.[34]

Notwithstanding the liberating moment of identity display through communication (where utterance and presence as "message" are the welcome form of communication and the alternative form is communication by destruction), one should keep in mind that this liberation has no bounds: the protection of identity through assemblies is provided to all identities. As it happens, passionate, and (if I may take the liberty of using a term hitherto avoided in these reflections) *irrational* identities are more attracted to formation and affirmation in mass gatherings.

To sum up: the inherent problem of large gatherings is that the people assembled have a riotous potential. The sheer mass of people is capable of forcing political changes outside the recognized pathways of parliamentary democracy. Having such risks in mind, constitutional law authorizes restrictions. When it comes to the constraint monopoly of the state, "emergency" rules may apply. These rules may contain humanitarian elements too, as in the form of restrictive crowd dispersal rules, or preventive rules like curfew or (suspiciously) limiting gatherings to three people (a favorite of military coups). However, with the increasing juridification of democracies, at least the declaration of "emergency" (i.e., that the assembly has to be dispersed by force) has become a matter of judicial review.

Beyond the riot scenario negative cultural values attributed to passions seem to have limited impact on contemporary legal rules applying to the collective display of these emotions, contrary to the effect of fear and the dislike of passions in the Victorian age.[35] Of course the less the prevailing culture finds the expression of anger tolerable, the less interest there will be in the protection of its collective display. The social scripting of the collective display of anger is decisive: it is quite possible that the display of intensive emotions is promoted or accepted by a culture but will be seen as threatening in the context of mass gathering. For example, the culture of an (oppressed) group might encourage the display of anger in threatening forms, but this will not be relevant for its legal treatment. The contemporary legal reaction to gatherings depends on the framing of anticipated events resulting from the gathering, in view of past experiences of assembly. The framing follows assumptions of folk psychology about crowd behavior and reflects assumptions about the capacities and relevant proper role of the police. The less capricious the crowd is seen to be, the less passionate and violent humans are believed to be, and the more that assumptions about human nature reflect a belief in human rationality, the more emphatic is the protection granted to gatherings.

The considerations and ambiguities of freedom of assembly reflect the framing of the event, but all this framing occurs within the archetype of street demonstrations animated by people who could turn (at least in the once-prevailing scenario) into a riotous mob. This underlying frame sustains the possibility for violence and permissible counter-violence, while the legal evaluation of the gathering will depend on the arousal of the archetypal fears, upholding as constitutional the legal regimes of notification.[36] But the positive law of many countries recognizes special regimes for special gatherings where the notification or permit regime of freedom of assembly does not apply. Assemblies present a special problem of emotion management in autonomous, constitutionally privileged organizations. Church gatherings (allegedly private) and religious processions, political rallies at election periods, even sporting events are exempt from ordinary notification or permit regimes. This nearly absolute protection of assembly is granted to eminently passionate activities, namely the free, collective exercise of religion, in the cases of mass gatherings for worship and processions. Of course these mass phenomena are treated under specific constitutional headings, outside freedom of assembly, but the emotional dynamics at such gatherings fits into crowd social psychology, except that there are good grounds not to fear public disturbances.[37] A similar privileged status is often applied in democracies to electoral gatherings and to certain forms of expressing popular will (like the referendum). To a lesser extent picketing is also protected. Moreover, select bodies that provide the venue and organization for the gathering receive special status that guarantees them nearly unchecked power to assemble people. This is the case with churches, as well as parties and trade unions.

Nation, tribe, the religious group, and the family are all constitutionally protected collective phenomena. Some of them might be imaginary communities,[38] but it seems that even imaginary communities need real people to fill physical public space. Shared beliefs generate collective events, and such events become influential facts. Physical togetherness is required to reinforce the constituent beliefs of the community built upon emotional togetherness (what Freud calls "identification").

Many of the gatherings falling under assembly laws are about sharing a common belief approaching faith; the meeting itself aims only to reinforce the belief and the faith-based identity of the participants. One of the problems of passionate gatherings is that, because of the sociopsychological dynamics that governs these situations, the participants may have a tendency to move toward ever-more intolerant positions. Given this cascade of intolerance, the permissive constitutional attitude requires a special sociopsychological explanation.

Freedom of religion and the autonomy of churches are constitutionally protected institutions that create unhindered opportunities for these feasts of emotions. How to explain the permissive constitutional approach, beyond the historical explanation which refers to the past power of churches? In a way, constitutional law protects spheres of emotional display, like family and privacy, together with the emotions that create solidarity, loyalty and community: love, sympathy, and even fear. It is believed that collective emotions of religious assemblies will not carry away the believers. The religious organization itself is believed to safeguard proper control through the *rituals*, traditions, and other means which are managed and manipulated from the top down. In other words, the recognition of the privileged churches involves a recognition of the predictability of the emotions they manage. The church will police its religious events and provide for a certain de-emotionalization. The same logic applies, *mutatis mutandis*, to established political parties, which are perceived constitutionally as responsible emotion managers. In the framing of religion's rights and of church (and party) privileges lies an assumption of respectability. The institution itself is a guarantee that its employees (the clergy) who do the daily passion management can be trusted, because they are socialized or trained in the proper way. It is assumed (mostly correctly) that religious enthusiasts will be isolated and expelled, just as extremist politicians will be marginalized or expelled from a democratic party. Very intense forms of religion, like evangelical movements and so-called "sects," which do not fit well into the above model, challenging the rational social order, cannot be considered guarantors of de-emotionalization. Secularist constitutional orders just like constitutional systems with entrenched mainstream religious organizations remain suspicious of such movements. Constitutional law similarly has difficulties with extremist, passion-raising political parties. However, the normative assumptions of constitutionalism are hardly at ease with reflecting these possibilities. In principle all religions and parties should be equal in a pluralist democracy, and the above distinction, based on folk-psychology assumptions about the different nature of "established" versus "new" religions and churches, and of "democratic" versus "extremist" parties would require *a priori* categorical distinctions. Where equality of similars is the rule, emotionality seems to create differences. Some differences, sometimes.

The matter is even more complicated in mass politics. Traditionally politics was depicted as a setting for reasonable exchange, where will is formed and expressed in reaction to reasonable arguments. For a while—from Sièyes to Guizot—the assumption was that people who do not possess faculties adequate for participation in political decision-making should not be allowed to do so. Under the dictates of economic and political necessities, and in order to reduce the contradiction with promised equality, nineteenth-century liberal regimes grudgingly accepted that people had the right to develop their faculties and as such they can participate in political decision-making, at least via elections. The right (duty) to education was gradually enforced and even construed as a civic obligation; people were granted the potential to become full citizens. But extended electoral participation continued to rely on demonstration for reinvigoration. Consider the British (Second) Reform Act of 1867 which accidentally resulted in modern (that is, expensive) electoral campaigns, the political accountability of MPs, and, in the longer run, in turning elections into a bidding contest of promises of goodies. The original reform initiative reflected a change in the perception of the working class; at least its upper echelons were seen as composed of "respectable" people.[39] But there was too much resistance to reform, until the disenfranchised took the streets. A major planned demonstration in Hyde Park in May 1867 was banned by the government. Nevertheless an enormous crowd gathered, of such size that the well-placed troops did not dare to attack. In this example, demonstration was a corrective to faltering constitutional politics. This corrective function of demonstrations is further legitimized by the right to resist oppression. Even after the full extension of the franchise, a certain inherent rigidity in constitutional systems, a certain bias in favor of the status quo could block the expression of popular will, the correction being when people express themselves directly.

Notwithstanding the positive contribution of demonstrations to the democratic process and the theoretical justification offered for them in theories of republican democracy and popular sovereignty, the emotional ambiguity of demonstrations continues to cloud the picture. The problem is not only the standard one, namely that unleashed passions may undermine public order. The functional justification for the need of direct mass participation in politics is contradicted by experiences of acclamatory politics and plebiscitarianism. The problem with direct decision-making methods is that the politics of emotional manipulation and its momentary considerations prevail at the expense of the more or less rational problem-solving methods of constitutional institutions.[40]

Parties seem to exist to allow cooperation within the rational interest paradigm; they receive constitutional protection on the basis of this assumption. With the performance crisis of parliamentarism and representative government, and with the resulting legitimacy crisis, a new form of mass politics emerged in the 1920s. In this new form of politics, leaders strove to mobilize mass emotions within a democratic electoral scheme which quickly degenerated in a world of emotionalism that valued the "genuine" expression of honest emotions, and was suspicious of reasons that only mask the private interests of corrupt politicians. This is what Loewenstein called in 1937 "emotional politics." In an age of mass production of masses, the orator is replaced by the hypnotist (and later, in the television age, by the brainwasher), "and the act of parliamentary discourse by propaganda." "Indeed propaganda, the epitome of this change of perspective, ceased to be a means of communication . . . and became a technique which made it possible to subject individuals to the power of suggestion."[41]

According to Loewenstein, authoritarian regimes are held together not by violence but by emotionalism. This is what replaces the rule of law. Authoritarian regimes and fascist movements possess an arsenal of techniques for emotional mobilization. Besides nationalist fervor, intimidation, conjured up through the image of physical coercion, is the most common element of political emotionalism. The only genuine goal of such politics and movements is to seize and retain power at all costs. In this, they may succeed even if they operate within the democratic institutional infrastructure. Loewenstein talks explicitly about the perfect adaptation of the politics of emotions to democracy. Following his train of thought, it is plausible that the politics of emotions may, at times, employ democratic techniques and, that in fact, apart from intimidation, democratic populism may be one of the most important means of obtaining power for the enemies of democracy within said democracy. An example of this is when new elections or referenda are extorted by means of emotional mass politics. If constitutional arrangements were intended to safeguard rational political discourse and decision-making, or at least if they were designed as a system that operates under these assumptions, they certainly failed. "Government by suggestion has replaced government by discussion."[42]

In the age of television a different form of emotional politics continued to prevail in virtual space, avoiding the specific emotional dynamics of large crowds. The atomized citizen, turned by now into entertainment consumer, participates in the emotional politics of virtual crowds. Here emotionalism is reinforced in small groups. At this point a new, partly theoretical dilemma emerges for constitutional law. To what extent should constitutional law accommodate and protect procedures and institutions of political will-formation that depart from the rational deliberation model? Is it the duty of constitutional law to limit or bar emotional politics?

While Nazism delegitimized emotional mass politics for posterity, large gatherings continue to play a role for mainstream politics, and much more so for populists and other new entrants. Certain forms of emotionalism remain constitutionally acceptable for the same reasons as nonrational influences at the ballot box: in the last decades, irrational influences seldom drove an unruly mass into the streets in the West and, well, even "rational" players benefited from the techniques of emotional persuasion. Not only is such contained irrationality not an anomaly in politics, but it even seems to be a constituent element of contemporary mass democracies. As far as the rather common situation of nonordinary (non-electoral) politics is concerned, for purposes of nationalistic mobilization in particular, demonstrations remain an important event. Transitions to democracy provide many examples: the mass demonstrations for independence in non-Russian Soviet republics, the velvet and color revolutions that aimed to repair the derailment of elections, the mass rallies in Belgrade *for* Serbia and *later* against Milosevic were all tools to shake up national identity. The politics of emotionalism achieved a new legitimacy. The ambiguity is real: in the face of oppression that employs reason and constraint, emotionalism and mass mobilization promise an alternative.

Theoretical answers regarding the proper place of passionate emotions in people's political participation do not come easily. Constitutionally protected institutions of democracy were never without a strong emotional element. But constitutional design reflects a deep fear and mistrust of passions. It is no accident that many reputable democracies (including the United States and Germany) refrain from having national referenda. Italy allows the negative referendum only. Other democracies have constitutional provisions which limit the subject matter of referenda. The budget, human rights, international treaties, and the dissolution of Parliament are among the excluded topics. These are believed to be the areas where emotionalism could easily undermine more rational approaches (and even fundamental constitutional values) and would squeeze out minorities. Representative democracy is clearly favored as an institution that offers protection against the emotionalism of the crowd.

7

SHAME: ON HIDDEN CONSTITUTIONAL SENTIMENTS

The more things a man is ashamed of, the more respectable he is.
—George Bernard Shaw

Shame, like other moral emotions, enables humans to accept moral arguments, and it generates moral judgments. Further, it creates a predisposition for the social generation of social norms, and as such it contributes to the generation of constitutional institutions. The judicial attitude to shame is one of indifference, mistrust, and reluctance.[1]

Nevertheless, I claim that constitutional law responds to actual social and personal experiences of shame. Any attempt at such showing has to specify what is meant by "shame," as this is a particularly contested notion in psychology. In line with culturally influenced shame research I argue that shame is an emotion or emotion family where the fundamental experience is being exposed to others. Relying on this understanding, first I will consider how constitutional law and the law of torts expressly provide protection against certain socially selected forms of shame in the law of personality and privacy rights. In other contexts constitutional law and judges in particular try to disguise and temper the dictates of social shame, partly because the dictates of shame are morally too burdensome to the majority, partly because professional considerations make judges believe that their role is to counter the arbitrariness that follows from dictates of moral emotions without standards, or because they have other policy priorities. Both trends are visible in constitutional policies that were created to undo the injustice of racial discrimination. But in the rather specific case of Germany a different jurisprudential effort emerged: here the legal and political elite used constitutional law to perpetuate shame, sustaining shame-dictated criminal law.

Irrespective of the specific constitutional policy, shame does play significant role in the shaping of constitutional arrangements. To what extent does the explicit recognition of, and reliance upon shame fit into a liberal constitutional scheme? After all, as participants in the policy debates about the use of shaming in criminal law, in education, and in social control in general have argued, shame generates negative action tendencies, and it causes suffering. Reliance on shame seems to be more than suspect from a humanitarian-liberal perspective. From the psychological perspective such criticism disregards positive action tendencies of shame. Shame can be reconciled with autonomy, but our culture is less and less willing to rely on shame, which will nevertheless play a not fully recognized role in our relations.

1. What Is Shame?

Debates and uncertainties surround the notion of shame in everyday usage—just as with other emotions. Concepts of shame diverge in cultures and scholarly literature, but many psychologists and philosophers agree with Erikson's classic statement: "Shame is early expressed in an impulse to bury one's face, or to sink, right then and there, into the ground. . . . It is essentially rage turned against the self. He who is ashamed would like the world not to look at him."[2] Shame is felt if someone is exposed. Gabriele Taylor relates shame to those aspects of the self that "do not fit the sort of person" one thinks one ought to be. "Revelation of this position . . . will cause him to experience shame. . . . Shame is the emotion of self-protection."[3]

It remains debated whether all societies distinguish between shame and guilt or shame and embarrassment. But even psychoanalytically oriented authors like the late Silvan Tomkins[4] admit that shame has its own physiological foundations (blush). In the following I assume that there is one basic feeling here at play that is called shame (or shame family). Depending on its intensity and its elicitors, it is called differently in different cultures.

The feeling is related to social devaluation and serves the adaptive function of avoiding the social consequences of such devaluation, maintaining acceptance and sustaining self-esteem. It is convincingly argued[5] that the same feeling is present in guilt, but guilt is an affective-cognitive hybrid, and it has other emotional components including fear. In most contemporary Western societies one can distinguish between social devaluation through exposure, which is the fundamental nondifferentiated feeling of shame, and specific cognitive processes related to the feeling and coupled with or generated by other feelings, or feelings and judgments of others. Such differentiation, with undeniably important impacts on social control, resulted in distinguishing social shame (loss of status), humiliation (total denial of being worthy of community membership), mortification, embarrassment and guilt (a complex hybrid). Hereinafter shame stands for social shame, except if otherwise stated.

The cognitive representation of differences and similarities between emotion terms is culture dependent. Cross-cultural similarities about the cognition of emotions do not mean similarities in emotion regulation (that is, what kind of emotional display is required in a culture). Similarity means that members of different cultures describe the antecedents of, and actions that follow, emotions rather similarly.

In Western societies shame and guilt may differ in terms of the typical reaction to the norm-breaking: the anticipation or experience of these different reactions may induce guilt or shame respectively. "What arouses guilt in an agent is an act or omission of a sort that typically elicits from other people anger, resentment, or indignation. What an agent may offer in order to turn this away is reparation; he may also fear punishment or may inflict it on himself. What arouses shame, on the other hand, is something that typically elicits from others contempt or derision or avoidance."[6]

Shame is believed to be more prominent in collectivistic cultures, than in individualistic ones. "Shame evolved from a rank-related emotion and, while motivating prestige competition, cooperation, and conformity, nevertheless continues to play this role in contemporary humans."[7] The boundaries between guilt, embarrassment, and shame are porous even in cultures which distinguish these three emotions, and remain contested.[8] Even if shame is primarily about self-perception (unworthiness), it can be a response to moral violations. In situations that many moral philosophers would qualify as breach of moral rules, the primary feeling is still one of "not living up" to expectations. This can develop into an acknowledgment of guilt, especially if accompanied/triggered by feelings of anger, fear, etc.

The difference between shame and guilt that moral philosophers and everyday language insist upon, is more a matter of cultural construction. Some studies indicate that there is relatively little cognitive difference between shame and guilt within the same culture, for example in Indonesia *both* shame and guilt are somewhat less distant from fear and more distant from anger than in the Netherlands.[9] The differences reflect the emotional-cognitive hybrid nature of the culturally identified emotions.

The salient appraisal of the experience of shame is often defined by the sense of being a bad or improper person, and it may result in long-lasting anger and disgust at the self.[10] Other action tendencies include submissive behavior and withdrawal. The shamed person may assume that his transgression results in disgust or anger in others. Even sadness that is assumed to result from the transgression may result in shame: parents may shame children by expressing sadness that signals disappointment.

At the same time shame has important positive action tendencies capable of behavioral self-control. The disgust that is aroused by shame is not only self-directed; it might generate (signal) the condemnation of others who commit similar transgressions. Likewise, expressions of shame as "authentic" feeling (including simple blushing and facial reactions of shame) may be sufficient to indicate that the person recognizes herself as a member of the community; when victims and third parties accept such showings, that will enable the regeneration of cooperation, trust, etc. Shame is felt for violations of shared, objective ideals of a worthy person.[11] From a regulatory perspective it is important that shame as a feeling emerges when one envisions that her transgression might become known to significant others. In a communitarian society these significant others are significant in the sense that they are in the position to determine communal reactions directed at the exposed person. Even "an imagined gaze [of somebody else] will do"[12] for creating the feeling of being exposed.

What makes shame relevant for law and social control is that it is an instrument of self-control,[13] but as such it can serve as social control instrument. From a constitutionalist perspective shame matters for constitutional institutions, although occasionally embarrassment also contributes in sustaining constitutionally shaped political correctness. The human rights activist may feel embarrassment for realizing that she was partying with racists even if inadvertently (and vice versa). Intuitively it is embarrassing to extend First Amendment protection to racist speech, and it explains why people committed to free speech are at ease creating exceptions in this regard. Of course, all such embarrassment is socially conditioned. Historically, before the condemnation of racism the opposite might have been embarrassing, namely to be seen in the company of an abolitionist or a member of a "lower race."

2. The Presence and Denial of Shame in Constitutional Practices

Public law has both liberating and constraining effects on shaming and shame.[14] It is clear that liberal constitutional law or, for that matter any legal system that is based on a concept of justice, is likely to undo the shame that results from being shamed for "inferiority." A constitutional system will try to undo situations that result in feelings of shame for those who are treated as inferior. But shame remains an ambivalent form of liberation when it comes from shaming the perpetrator.

Constitutional recognition of a contested personal quality, aspiration, or group characteristics contributes to individual shame avoidance. For example, when the freedom to have an abortion is recognized as a dignity concern, or a matter of the right to personal, bodily choice, the shameful aspect of abortion diminishes.[15]

From a constitutionalist perspective various members of the shame family play a role. Shame, and in few contexts guilt, matter for constitutional institutions, including the generation of rights.

While constitutionalism should reflect a program of liberation from undeserved inferiority and exposure, and related shame and humiliation, there are situations where normative arguments support the institutionalization of the dictates of shame as a moral emotion. In other words, shaming may be used constructively in constitutional law. The social use of shame and shaming, as always in the social construction of emotions, is through scripting. Outlawing and, respectively, legitimating conduct, by granting permission, are the legal means of scripting. Behind the scripts of public law, shared (imposed) feelings of shame dictate legal solutions. Contemporary Western culture has diminished the "legitimacy" of public shame and shaming, which limits the legal impact of the relevant moral emotions (in this case shame and a related specific sense of justice); consequently shame as a tool of social control will be less efficient, but still important.

From a legal regulatory perspective shame's conformity-producing functions are of importance. Shamed persons "avoid the shame before it can be completely experienced."[16] Individuals almost continually monitor their thoughts and behaviors from the standpoint of others.[17] The conformity-producing effect of shame is based on shame's relation to dishonor: the shamed (dishonored) person's chance to interact socially diminishes as he is seen as a poor partner. To the extent that the anticipated consequences of norm-breaking result in shame, law-observance will increase. Further, the socially accepted undoing of shame may dictate social and legal institutions that admit shame and limit its negative impacts. Modern constitutional law is particularly concerned about protection against being dishonored, exactly because of the social fear of shame that is related to loss of honor and intimacy. This I call the reputation problem. The reputation problem is dealt with in privacy rights and personality rights, which operate as protection against future shaming, partly by deterrence, partly by setting up a mechanism to diminish shame by legally restoring reputation. Besides, the state that already claims a monopoly over coercion has aspirations to maintain a monopoly of public shaming.

2.a. Reputational Interests and Honor

"Seclusion of thought and sentiments" triggered legal consideration early on. In Britain already in 1769 Justice Yates, dissenting, argued that: "It is certain every man has a right to keep his own sentiments, if he pleases. He has certainly a right to judge whether he will make them public, or commit them only to the sight of his friends."[18]

Privacy (the right of not being exposed) is one of those instances where the role of shame is obvious. Broadly speaking, with the increasing cultural recognition of the private sphere emotions were relegated to the private sphere and became only exceptionally "displayable." The exposure of emotions became a matter of shame and embarrassment, and this was gradually reflected in law. Of course, there are considerable differences among the legal systems reacting to a similar moral emotion; "the sense of what must be kept 'private,' of what must be hidden before the eyes of others, seems to differ strangely from society to society."[19] Privacy (the right to one's sentiments and image as a source of personality rights, contrasted to reputational/status interests in honor) emerged in modern law primarily as a problem of torts in most legal systems. The avoidance of shame was a matter of honor, reputation, dignity—the applicable legal concept differs from system to system. However, privacy found its ways into constitutional law following quite different pathways as public sentiments know little about the public/private law divide. Reinforced by the sociolegal ideology of dignity (which reflects core interests of the self), honor and dignity often find their way in a bundle to modern constitutions in the form of personality rights, while in the United States central aspects of privacy are recognized as part of a strong antigovernmental bias and serve, among other things, legal and psychological needs of personal security.[20]

The desire to be protected from an inquisitive commercial gaze that makes one's image and sentiments public received increased legal attention with the development of photography. The first famous instance where the desire to avoid unwanted exposure prevailed was perhaps the Rachel affair in France in 1858. Sketches were drawn of the celebrated actress at her deathbed on the basis of private photographs owned by a photographer. The family of the actress successfully sued for an injunction. Though later on financial interests of the person were recognized in the name of personality right, it is noteworthy that the early cases were about injunction: middle- and upper-class concerns of honor did not allow for thinking about monetary compensation.[21]

As to the United States in 1890, Warren and Brandeis, two very successful lawyers, published an article in the Harvard Law Review trying to bring into American common law an action for violation of privacy. The Warren-Brandeis paper, this "most influential law review article of all," expresses the impact of strong sentiments. It was perhaps motivated by actual shame and certainly by a general upper-class public sentiment of being shamed by exposition in newspapers catering to the lower classes, a fear of loss of class privilege and supremacy that rests on the mystery of seclusion, being invisible to the masses.[22] It is more than likely that the two socialite authors were angered by continued sensational reports regarding events organized by Mrs. Warren. The anger was caused by exposure (anticipated shame). The arguments of the article concern the emotional impacts of privacy. The crucial personal interest to be protected is the right to be left alone, in the sense of the right *not to be exposed*. This sentiment was justified in terms of a contested legal theory: "[T]he existing law affords a principle from which may be invoked to protect the privacy of the individual from invasion either by the too enterprising press, the photographer, or the possessor of any other modern device for rewording or reproducing scenes or sounds." The concern was similar to that of Henry James, who wrote about "the invasion, the impudence and shamelessness, of the newspaper and the interviewer, the devouring publicity of [modern] life, the extinction of all sense between public and private."[23] Note that here law is about undoing shamelessness, that is, imposing shame by constraint.

Today, in the age of *Facebook* and *Big Brother*, when so many people strive for fame through (self) exposition and exhibition, privacy may be an outdated upper-class concern. Privacy today reflects a partly different legal concern, a different fear of self-exposure, where bodily exposure is of diminished relevance for the self in Western culture. It is likely that it was a "media-driven public sphere and the Victorian ideology of separate spheres" that bothered and influenced the authors, and a male concept "of domestic privacy and its attendant patriarchal ordering of the family also informed their article."[24] But irrespective of what kind of class bias elicits the feelings, without emotional reactions social norms (including rules of emotion display) cannot be scripted and sustained by law.

Technically the Warren-Brandeis argument refers to a liberty doctrine which is reinforced by market interests of the self, and hence it fits easily into law. But it is a fundamental shame concern that makes the argument plausible: it was the resonance of shame that made privacy attractive to legislators and judges, reflecting public sentiment.

Today important economic and political reasons work in favor of privacy protection, but the exposition of the self remains a crucial social concern in an anonymous society. This explains the constitutional interest in protecting the exposition of the self against government intrusion, and this is what animates the constitutional expectations, *viz.* that the state shall take steps to protect the intimate sphere. Ironically such protection may go beyond what prevailing moral emotions and related considerations would dictate. At least Martha Nussbaum argues that "societies need to protect the spaces within which people imagine and explore themselves even when their imaginings are perceived as shameful."[25] Privacy is an efficient institution that provides protection where shame is used for social control: in a way this is the institution that balances shame and shaming.

Beyond the interest in the nonexposure recognized as privacy interest, reputational interests related to honor are recognized, crystallized, and reinforced in law in the institution of defamation. Loss of honor is a shaming event in the sense of loss of status. The sense of honor that once was to be protected because of anticipated shame (you felt shame and were expected to feel it for being shamed in case you lost honor) still dictates laws in many instances. Honor-dictated legislation facilitates access to means to protect honor. What we tend to forget is what made honor such a powerful consideration. It was/is its shaming power.

In many constitutional systems honor seems to be overtaken by dignity-related concerns. Social and legal recognition of dignity reflects a situation where respect is unrelated to what you are: it pertains to all, irrespective of personal merit or status. There are good moral and practical-political reasons for such developments: dignity became poor men's honor, provided to all as a welfare service. The consequence is that dignity cannot be lost, and if it cannot be lost, little (less) shame is to be felt when you are exposed. Simple exposition in a world of exhibitionists is of diminishing concern. Exposition, loss of standing, reputation are of lesser importance in a non-status-based society. Instead of simple exposition of an imperfection, humiliation, that is, the denial of one's fundamentally equal value compared to others, is what matters here. But shame resulting from exposure and resulting higher status loss is less important where competing interests of status equality are at stake. Most people in the public eye enjoy a superficial respect. As public figures they are open to offensive criticism with little legal protection. However, at least in Europe, the image of figures exercising public functions may remain protected. As the German Constitutional Court has formulated it: "Very often the public interest aroused by such figures does not relate exclusively to the exercise of their function in the strict sense. . . . The public has a legitimate interest in being allowed to judge whether the personal behaviour of the individuals in question, who are often regarded as idols or role models, convincingly tallies with their behaviour on their official engagements."[26] But this not apply when it comes to personality rights unrelated to that consideration.

2.b. *Constitutional Design*

In Chapter 3 we discussed the prominent role of fear in constitution-making. Here, in the context of shame and shame-induced secondary emotions like anger, we consider the hidden role of emotion, namely shame in constitutional design. Constitutions and public law legislation handle shame, both sustaining and undoing it. Constitutional law can develop institutional reactions against behavior that is deemed utterly shameful for its denial of humanity, as is the case with racism. Of course, such constitutionalization cannot be described exclusively in terms of shame and shaming. Empathy toward victims and outrage for norm-breaking are contributing too. But not even the interplay of emotions will explain the phenomena; these emotions are used according to political interest considerations within social constructions of understanding emotion.

For a theory of constitutional sentiments it is of equal importance to consider situations where shame would dictate specific societal considerations but this is disregarded, or at least the considerations never refer to shame. It is of importance to see what is the logic and language that buries shame. Shame disappears in the courtroom too. The language of constitutional discussion is that of justice. How emotions, and shame in particular, motivate such concerns of justice remains hidden most of the time. Nevertheless, fundamental findings of justice and injustice are not rational constructs of fairness and merit but moral judgments based on moral emotions like shame.

The importance of shame becomes visible in certain constitutional attempts to create and reinforce the shared national community, sometimes by opening avenues of social inclusion, after the collapse of a previous regime based on shameful, unjust privileges of one group in the society. One of the special techniques of forcing people to accept the constitutional community is via constitutional shaming, while in other instances law liberates people from shame, enabling a community of sentiments.

Until recently no constitution would have referred to shameful past injustice as a foundational ground. Constitutional provisions have long served the undoing of past injustices, but only the pragmatic measures were expressly mentioned, as in the case of the Fourteenth Amendment of the U.S. Constitution. Recently, however, a different pattern seems to have emerged. The Preamble to the Constitution of South Africa reads as follows: "We, the people of South Africa, recognize the injustices of our past; honor those who suffered for justice and freedom in our land. . . ." The Preamble of the "unfinished" European Constitution referred to reunion "after bitter experiences."

This recent shift reflects a change in constitutional identity-building. Revolutionary justifications of constitutional structures referred to a future-oriented grand plan (*Novus Ordo Seclorum*). Traditional nationalism, especially in the process of nation-building through state-formation, justified the state and its national constitution with reference to historical performance that merited constitutional statehood. But in our age victimhood amounts to a claim for compensation, and for this reason there is demand for open recognition of past suffering.[27]

Constitutions are, among other things, about identifying a prefoundational injustice that is to be undone by the constituent act. This is a choice of history—from a set of possible histories. The selection of historical memories is a moral act, a matter of moral responsibility. "Remembrance in this sense is equally important to communities—families, tribes, nations, parties—that is, to human entities that exist often for much longer than individual men and women. To neglect the historical record is to do violence to this identity and thus to the community that it sustains. And since communities help generate a deeper sense of identity for the individuals they comprise, neglecting or expunging the historical record is a way of undermining and insulting individuals as well."[28]

Of course, shaming the adversary is an old constitutional strategy. The American Declaration of Independence begins with a long list of unjust sufferings caused by usurpation. These concerns, however, did not transfer directly into the Constitution except where it was feared that specific injustices would be repeated. But the Supreme Court, at least relatively close in time to the injustices caused by the British, was well aware of their shaming effect: "The constitution had reference to those acts which had palpably caused discontent and shame, and were, unfortunately for us, peculiar to our history. To have inserted them in odious detail, would have disfigured the constitution, and have eternized a disgrace upon the most brilliant page of our history. Against paper money, the convention had provided. They then guarded against the other expedients of wrong."[29] The Revolution was about getting rid of shame.

Contemporary constitutional shaming is to a great extent a matter that emerges in the interaction of the legislature and the judiciary. Both branches of power are inclined to resist public sentiments of shame which are unlikely to become dominant in the culture, and even less to prevail in law for political and psychological reasons. At least in the case of Congressional reparation to the interned Japanese Americans, past injustice was officially recognized and the responsibility of the government was admitted, though without using the language of collective shame. With the presence of past victims and their descendants among the population, or with their ghosts in the minds of the morally sensible members of the community, at least the preconditions for shaming are given at the national level, as victim groups may opt for a policy of shaming in their attempt to shape the public sentiment in their favor. They may rely on exposure of the majority as being beneficiaries of malefactors. But it is relatively easy to resist such complicity by denying causation, and attempts at national shaming involve few of the personal elements that characterize individual shame, namely the exposure of the body, or exposure as not being the moral being one pretends to be.

How the constitution-makers handle shame that might/does originate in past injustice against groups of citizens can be of foundational constitutional importance. Injustices that caused suffering and made the oppressed feel shame for their ill fortune may be singled out as the foundation of the previous regime, and then the new constitutional regime will emerge to undo that injustice. The constitution may attempt to turn the grand injustice of the previous regime that originally shamed its victims, into a source of shame for the beneficiaries of the injustice (hereinafter: foundational shame).

The South African example of undoing apartheid in the new constitutional scheme illustrates this point. Here the social allocation of shame is one where the majority has to be liberated of the shame imposed by former inferiority, while the minority may have moral responsibility emotionally rooted in causing humiliation. But in order to create a new functioning political society, the legislature and the South African Constitutional Court preferred reconciliation instead of continued shaming. In the application of the Constitution the South African Constitutional Court was reluctant to move for a radical positive discrimination and interpreted the antidiscrimination provisions of the Constitution without giving much preference to victims of the apartheid in the name of undoing past injustice. When the Pretoria Municipality charged a consumption-based tariff for electricity and water in former white suburbs and a lower, flat rate in former black townships, the SACC found that the disadvantage to whites is indirect discrimination on the basis of race. The resulting constitutional presumption of unfair discrimination was, however, rebutted because, among other considerations, the complainant was a member of a previously advantaged, though minority group.[30] However, the Court found partly against the policy that was directed against the formerly advantaged. Theunis Roux argued that the Court's position was motivated by prevailing concerns of the rule of law, to the detriment of other consideration of justice, which rely on shame and shaming. "The Court is far more comfortable in the role of enforcing good governance standards than it is in second-guessing the wisdom of policies self-evidently required to redress the legacy of apartheid."[31] The disregard of the emotional was relatively easy for the justices as their declared concern was with the rule of law. This is not a South African peculiarity. In the United States it was the majority that benefited from the injustice of slavery and later on from racial discrimination. But here too judicial considerations of rights and concerns of judicial efficiency unrelated to the injustice, and concerns about the role of the judiciary precluded the consideration of shame and shame-induced responsibility. Of course, in the United States, as in South Africa, the technicalities of antidiscrimination law and affirmative action reflect actual political power relations. In both cases the principal concern was a viable community-building that in reality accommodated the desires of the shameless beneficiaries of discrimination.

However, under specific circumstances, where the majority is embedded in shame, there may be reliance on and deliberate production of shame for foundational injustice, at least a limited one. In Germany the political and intellectual elite successfully imposed shame on the majority for the Holocaust. This was reinforced by the German Constitutional Court.[32] In other countries with different histories such shaming did not occur, at least to the same extent.

Constitutional law that is not animated by empathy toward the victims of humiliating injustice and by public sentiments of shame may contribute to the perpetuation of the feelings of injustice, inferiority, and insecurity. Where racist speech is construed as protected and therefore the harm to racially targeted group members is judicially nonexistent, it is argued that such lack of sensitivity reproduces injustice.[33] The potential victims believe that their fundamental human need for security of life and existence is disregarded shamefully by the state. When authorities tolerate racist attacks and this gesture immediately reminds potential victims of the earlier deprivation of their security, it is a reminder of a shameful status.

Admitting that in all three paradigmatic instances discussed above the handling of shame was politically determined and shame will not flourish for reasons of moral considerations only, I argue that the constitutional handling of shame remains influential even where it is silenced. Further, even where it is not admitted, social shame generated by injustice, together with other feelings that constitute the sense of injustice, do play a role in constitutional decisions about undoing injustice.

Potentially, the above-cited Preamble of the South African Constitution is a program for a radical restorative justice, including reverse discrimination. Indeed, the South African government has programs of corrective action favoring previously disadvantaged groups, and injustices of the past did actually serve to justify remedial action to the detriment of whites. In principle the injustice as recognized in the Constitution and in many statements of courts and government may be a source for lasting shaming of the perpetrators' community. Such impacts are possible even if a court deliberately avoids the language of shame, and limits its analysis to ordinary rule of law considerations. Making the minority accountable for the injustice, partly through shaming, is not the prevailing constitutional strategy. Bishop Desmond Tutu, Chairman of the South African Truth and Reconciliation Commission, described the strategy in these terms: "The perpetrator . . . should be given the opportunity to be reintegrated into the community he has injured by his offense."[34] Of course, shaming is not avoided this way: for the perpetrator his disclosure of human rights violations presupposes exposure and shame. Whether the constitutional recognition of past injustice had the expected impact on the conscience of those who were supposed to be ashamed is a question that is probably highly contentious in South Africa. In a way this is immaterial. In fact, past injustice triggered a different consideration, one that is remarkable in light of the existing bitterness and anger created by apartheid and the gross human rights violations committed in its defense.

Deliberate constitutional and judicial shaming, however, remains accidental. In fact, the interim Constitution of South Africa, which reflected a future-oriented approach, was based on a midnight compromise to avoid large-scale revenge-seeking. The interim Constitution itself understood its role as providing "a historic bridge between the past of a deeply divided society characterised by strife, conflict, untold suffering and injustice, and a future founded on the recognition of human rights, democracy and peaceful co-existence and development opportunities for all South Africans, irrespective of colour, race, class, belief or sex." A Truth and Reconciliation Commission was created: amnesty was offered for disclosure of crimes, diminishing thereby the quest for radical undoing of past injustice. The Constitutional Court seemed to be concerned about institutional solutions that would have contributed to the control of socially divisive public sentiments. As Chief Justice Mahomed stated: "It was realised that much of the unjust consequences of the past could not ever be fully reversed. It might be necessary in crucial areas to close the book on that past." Indeed, the pardon granted under the Truth and Reconciliation scheme was greeted as optimizing "the prospects of facilitating the constitutional journey from the shame of the past to the promise of the future." The pardon was understood to serve national reconciliation that mobilizes the resources of "every person who has directly or indirectly been burdened with the heritage of the shame and the pain of our racist past."[35] In other words, Chief Justice Mahomed envisioned a positive role for shame, one of self-reflection, though he must have been aware of the fact that historically inherited humiliation does not go away without specific action, and that on the other hand those who may be responsible for shameful acts and structures will not necessarily confront the injustice and expose themselves as being morally wrong.

Psychological expediency may, however, support the position of the Court. In a way the social and legal shaming of perpetrators is a most difficult venture. In the South African context perpetrators' shaming was, at least, partly associated with impunity. When it comes to perpetrators' shame, "there is such a degree of terror of shame, such a dread of acknowledging the mess and the flaw that has created the mess, that often all one encounters are many defensive layers against shame which, of course, vary in their degree of sophistication, ingenuity, and effectiveness." In this context one possible emotional and societal strategy is that the "justice that the TRC seeks for South Africa does not attempt to heal the victim at the expense of the perpetrator. Rather, the TRC's goal is to heal the perpetrator alongside the victim, to make the perpetrator a viable part of a new South African society that values both the victim and the perpetrator equally."[36]

The text of the Preamble of the South African Constitution enables policies that would shame the members of the minority white community that benefited from and often contributed to the apartheid regime. But there was much more interest in South Africa in a constitutional and legislative undoing of the shaming effects of the injustice (rights deprivation) of the past that affected the majority. "In victimized communities, where a high value is placed on the ideological understanding of the people's suffering, and how to overcome such suffering, there can be shame associated with not keeping self-control in the face of the oppressor."[37] In shame management healing was the most important. The question is how to achieve that without the liberating force of revenge, or at least sincere, tangible punishment that shames the perpetrators.

Other injustices causing lasting shame to victims were also high on the South African agenda. There was continued shaming from not being able to identify the graves of the disappeared. The role of the law was to undo the shame, for example by providing means to identify the grave, the body, to issue death certificates without further humiliation. One can always describe such activities as justice, but the need for justice arises from a psychological state of the victims.

Shaming will not work if the injustice can be fended off. Defused injustice does not generate enough shame. In the United States the antebellum legislative and judicial policies sustaining the injustice of slavery brought shame on America in the eyes of many people, but as *Plessy v. Ferguson*[38] indicates, this was insufficient to sustain shame given the prevailing prejudice and political interests that were accommodated in the politics of Reconstruction. The remedial element resurfaced in the twentieth century in the Civil Rights Acts legislation. President Kennedy stated in his 1963 message to Congress on Civil Rights that "The venerable code of equity law commands 'for every wrong, a remedy.'"[39] What made public sentiment more favorable to remedy and the Negro in general was, among other things, shame resulting from exposure of the whites as accomplices of cruelty and racist oppression.

Nevertheless, the U.S. Supreme Court never endorsed a judicial policy enforcing shame or undoing shame. This is consistent with the Court's general dislike of empirically nonidentifiable standards. In the context of damages, lasting psychological injury, like shame, might not be compensated at all, though the violation of privacy that causes shame might be the ground for a privacy torts claim.[40]

Around 1968, at the height of exposure of the injustice of racism, there was a moment when there seemed to be enough public sentiment for the judicial acknowledgment of social shame. Some courts were ready to consider race a "suspect" category, "not because [race] is inevitably an impermissible classification, but because it is one which usually, to our national shame, has been drawn for the purpose of maintaining racial inequality."[41] But this attempt was rejected in the name of policy considerations: shame did not seem to offer identifiable standards and clear judicial answers. For the Supreme Court, as for the South African Constitutional Court many years later, rule of law considerations have prevailed in the undoing of past injustice. When it came to affirmative action in *Regents of University of California v. Bakke*, there was no concern about the collective responsibility and resulting shame that would perhaps justify additional burdens imposed on "innocent" present members of society. Even Justice Marshall's passionate language in his partial dissent in *Bakke* which evoked past injustice did stop short of creating a specific duty of restorative justice on the basis of shaming (though the rhetorical effects of his opinion here and in other dissents regarding minority protection do have such impact).[42] But his argument centers on the consequences of discrimination (past and present) on the Negro personality and the needs of a fully integrated society. Emotional consequences of prejudice may be at least a secondary consideration for the Supreme Court, but only in regard to victims.[43]

Again, in the case of the mentally retarded and gays, the recognized history of past discrimination was insufficient for triggering a general constitutional politics of special protection, expressing shame for past injustice.

Even those justices who were sympathetic to a stronger protection of the rights of mentally retarded in granting them middle-level scrutiny would have based this protection on pragmatic considerations, namely, that it was the prejudice of the majority that bothered them and not a moral emotion that *should* develop in their regard. "Most important, lengthy and continuing isolation of the retarded has perpetuated the ignorance, irrational fears, and stereotyping that long have plagued them." For the majority in *Cleburne*, legislation may have relied on sympathy and pity, but that is not the proper ground for the judicial approach.[44]

Likewise, when it comes to gays and lesbians, groups whose members long suffered the emotional consequences of social shaming and discrimination, the legal consideration is that of equality in the sense of nondiscrimination, without emotional considerations. When a Colorado referendum in 1992 restricted the civil rights protection granted to gays, the Supreme Court was interested neither in the psychological impacts the denial of special antidiscrimination protection has on those affected nor in the responsibility of the majority that in principle should feel shame for denying equal membership. The Court was suspicious of animosity against gays and lesbians. but in practical terms it disregarded the emotions behind the animosity just like the emotions of gays: it was sufficient for the decision that the constitutional Amendment to the Colorado Constitution "is so far removed from these particular justifications that we find it impossible to credit them."[45] In this case the Court avoids taking a position regarding the legitimacy of the public sentiments which dictated the criminal legislation. Indirectly, however, such judgments contribute to the cultural setting of display rules; after all, emotions which result in unconstitutional laws will become suspect, or at least it is easier to mobilize against such emotions.

Justice Scalia, dissenting, claimed that the public is entitled to legislate dictates of tradition where traditions solidify specific emotional reactions, in this case disgust elicited by certain sexual practices.[46] However, the appropriateness of legislation dictated by moral emotions remains contested in the contemporary culture, at least when it comes to disgust, partly for pragmatic, partly for moral reasons. For example, Martha Nussbaum finds it unacceptable that antisodomy law relies on disgust, because "when it conduces to the political subordination and marginalization of vulnerable groups and people, disgust is a dangerous social sentiment."[47]

Without special measures, the disadvantageous social position of the shamed victim will persist. The collective victim status creates special social relations and psychological predispositions on both sides resulting in feelings of inferiority, etc. The Canadian Supreme Court concluded that historically created disadvantages, consisting in the deprivation of fundamental human needs, create the likelihood of continued discrimination.[48] Hence, such traditionally discriminated-against groups are to be provided special protection in order to enable them to participate fully in social life. This statement was made in the context of anti-gay discrimination. The consideration is that of vulnerability; that is, the Canadian Court is consequentialist, pragmatic, and remedy-oriented like the U.S. Supreme Court. But one cannot understand in purely consequentialist terms, why special protection is needed, without the hidden work of shame for the creation and survival of such conditions. In addition to these probably partly shame-dictated considerations, the Canadian Court added in *Egan* a consideration based on empathy: "awareness of, and sensitivity to, the realities of those experiencing the distinction is an important task that judges must undertake when evaluating the impact of the distinction on members of the affected group."[49]

3. Moral Sentiments and Collective Shame for Genocide

How to explain that shame, like many other emotions, is judicially nonexistent, at least invisible, in American and Canadian constitutional jurisprudence? Why do the courts rely on proxies like prejudice that are ideological consolidations of the dictates of negative emotions? Why are judges little concerned about the actual emotional consequences of a social situation? In most cases it is the social consequence of the unwanted prejudice that matters for courts. Actual consequences are considered intellectually manageable as they seem factually identifiable, which fits into the rationalistic patterns that prevail in judicial reasoning. Only a few sentiments are expressly admitted, for example, sympathy toward victims or outrage at injustice, but only to deny that this forms a ground for special treatment.[50] Concerns of shame are not even mentioned; perhaps because of an emerging social displacement of shame. Dov Cohen has demonstrated that the term "shame" has been increasingly replaced in ordinary language by "embarrassment" and "humiliation," and to a lesser extent "guilt," in the course of the last 200 years.[51] Perhaps what was once shame is now called embarrassment. But it is also possible that modern society, and the American one in particular moved out of a shame culture, at least in the sense that the prevailing culture (against strong conservative resistance) does not admit that there is much constructive place for shame and, therefore, shaming is wrong, and feeling shame is inappropriate. However, the judiciary had already disregarded shame and shaming as a source of legal considerations, before American public culture turned against the very language of shame.

In "ordinary circumstances" where the issue is the shameful past of the majority, it is unlikely that shame will become part of the constitutional project. However, there are specific historical circumstances where shame is successfully imposed on the majority, perhaps by some external moral or political power, and the constitution may become involved in this process. Even without specific references in the constitution, constitutional law may respond to existing shame-based concerns and reinforce shaming. This happened in postwar Germany with the political understanding of German history under the Third Reich, at least beginning in the sixties. The foundational character of shame is reflected in the famous title of a lecture given by the writer Siegfried Lenz: "Auschwitz Is in Our Custody."[52] The recognition of inhumanity of Germans and Germany resulted in a sense of elite shame that was consolidated in constitutional law and jurisprudence. The legal measures taken against Holocaust denial and racist speech and the related judicial interpretation illustrate how the foundational constitutional injustice of Nazism was turned into a source of social shaming. Such shaming was the result of continuous external pressure, which sometimes insisted on collective guilt.[53]

In other countries with a comparable history of government-enforced genocide as in Hungary or Romania, or perhaps even France, there is less popular and institutionalized shame for the past injustice and for lack of its undoing.[54] There were too many collaborators and collaborating government agents in Hungary, Vichy France, or Romania; not all of them were held accountable in summary proceedings after the war. The books of this past were closed soon enough. De Gaulle has declared that France and Frenchmen had nothing to do with Vichy. In order to glorify *la Grand nation*, one needed amnesia. Thus Vichy simply disappeared from the landscape of French memory. French Jews participated in building the wall of silence in exchange for relative protection. In postwar communist Hungary, where the communist party relied to some extent on the membership of former Hungarian Nazis, the racist nature of the Nazi period was to be forgotten, the atrocities became victimless, and Nazism was purely anticommunist. Soviet anti-Semitism further complicated the matter. Of course, where victims have to be silent, they will be ashamed for that reason.[55]

In Germany in the early postwar years the Allied forces insisted on various forms of collective guilt and punishment and turned the acceptance of moral responsibility for the past into a precondition of political legitimacy. At the end of the 1940s, however, when the collaboration of a stronger Germany was needed, the program of collective guilt and responsibility was abandoned in exchange for a belated self-imposed national shame that in the long run generated genuine soul-searching. At the end of this process, a generation later, a social convention emerged, at least in the public sphere, but perhaps even beyond it: any violation of the "ban on anti-Semitism" convention results in public embarrassment. In the public sphere, embarrassment plays the role political correctness has attained in America.[56]

The international legitimacy of Germany, the credibility of its State and its citizens, depended on the credibility of the sincerity of their disavowal of past injustice.[57] There was a strong suspicion outside Germany and a fear within German society that past injustice might reappear. At least *ex post*, in light of the suffering caused, the Germans were no longer fascinated with the Reich. On the other hand, there was constant fear and suspicion among past victims and their descendants, who continued to perceive themselves as potential victims and hence retained their victim attitudes and reactions, which further increased victimization. Victimhood itself was a constant source of shame among the victims, and to undo it the political elite had to be particularly sensitive. As long as the community does not feel and, more important, does not express shame, both through the acts of its individual members and as a collective, through its public institutions, the shameful conditions are not undone. Expressions of shame may/should include searching, even begging, for reconciliation and leniency through legislation—at a minimum, for some symbolic compensation to victims.

Under such circumstances and considerations the reappearance of some component elements of the foundational injustice is enough to generate insecurity and mobilize shame among the majority.[58] One may disagree with the strictly punitive and interventionist German legal attitude regarding hate speech, but the moral foundations dictated by shame and identified by the German authorities for such active prevention remain of relevance here. After World War II Karl Jaspers wrote about the political "guilt" (*Schuld*) of Germans and stated that a people is responsible for its statehood—not to be confused with moral or legal guilt.[59] Forty years after the end of World War II the German Supreme Court wrote about the specific duties of Germans toward Jews:

> The historical fact itself, that human beings were singled out according to the criteria of the so-called Nuremberg laws and robbed of their individuality for the purpose of extermination, puts Jews living in the Federal Republic in a special, personal relationship vis-à-vis their fellow citizens; what happened [then] is also present in this relationship today. It is part of their personal self-perception to be understood as part of a group of people who stand out by virtue of their fate and in relation to whom there is a special moral responsibility on the part of all others, and that this is part of their dignity. Respect for this self-perception, for each individual, is one of the guarantees against repetition of this kind of discrimination and forms a basic condition of their lives in the Federal Republic. Whoever seeks to deny these events denies vis-à-vis each individual the personal worth of [Jewish persons]. For the person concerned, this is continuing discrimination against the group to which he belongs and, as part of the group, against him.[60]

"The juridification of 'working through the past' remained a distinctive feature of German political and legal culture."[61] Compare this with the consequences of a victim compensation jurisprudence that denies shame and sensitivity. After the collapse of communism the first freely elected Hungarian government decided to undo past injustice by paying partial compensation to victims who were dispossessed after 1949. The statute did not list confiscation on grounds of Nazi race laws among the grounds for compensation. The Hungarian Constitutional Court considered the statute unconstitutional but failed to undo the material damage resulting from delayed compensation.[62] Further, another law offered compensation to those who on grounds of racial or political (social class-based) discrimination suffered injury or lost immediate family members. In a resulting case regarding compensation for personal injury and loss of life the Constitutional Court ruled in 1995 that after the transition period the democratic Hungarian state was under no obligation to compensate victims for personal injuries caused by the conduct of state officials in previous regimes. Compensation for personal injuries, loss of life, and suffering is based mostly on an *ex gratia* gesture of the democratic government; however, denial of compensation in the *ex gratia* scheme to victims of past race-based discrimination constitutes impermissible discrimination. Therefore it was held unconstitutional that Jews who were deported to Germany are ineligible for compensation; the law that considered their suffering a matter not caused by Hungarian authorities was discriminatory. However, when a new law offered much less for loss of life for people exterminated by the Nazis than to the descendants of those who perished in Soviet camps as prisoners of war, the Hungarian Constitutional Court found these "differentiated" measures of compensation reasonable, given the limited financial possibilities of the state acting *ex gratia*.[63]

While postwar Germany built up its shame politically and judicially, in Hungary it was never made clear who committed the crime, except that the Stalinist leadership for a brief moment referred to the Hungarian nation as "guilty." It was, of course, officially admitted that what was done to Jews was outrageous, but when an unofficial assembly of pastors asked the Jews for forgiveness in 1945 this was rejected with "a very noticeable" irritation by public opinion.[64] The idea that the Hungarian people might be responsible or should assume moral and material responsibility was rejected by the majority of Hungarians as self-debasement. The case illustrates perfectly well the sociopsychological difficulties of feeling shame for past collective action and for membership in a morally highly problematic community even if the specific acts committed by, and in the name of, such a group are felt to be repulsive.

Postgenocidal constitutional regimes exist under the assumption that their institutions and citizens do not in any regard allow for the characteristics of the genocidal regime and its supporters to resurface. Shame can be instrumental here. The anticipation of the shame helps the person to avoid awkward situations by preventive distancing. The observer is within me. But the stronger the feeling of collective shame is institutionally recognized, the less the individual must feel ashamed. The individual may rely on the fixed institutions of the community, as (and as soon as) these institutions collectivize shame by addressing the issue of never settled past injustices.

We are ashamed because we are seen as something different from what we pretend to be or what our social status would require. If seen in the company of "deviants," I am ashamed because I assume that being seen in the company of despicable people will lead others to the conclusion that I am one of "them." As a decent citizen of a constitutional democracy I feel uncomfortable in the company of racists. I am afraid people will consider me a racist. I am concerned because I might be in their company, because we have things in common. One feels disgust and shame listening to a racist cab driver and shame for not shutting up the guy. A decent member of a community with a genocidal past is ashamed that there are active racists in her society. I am ashamed of being classified as their tacit accomplice, a member of a society where racism is possible, even legitimate. I am seen as "one of them," even in the absence of the disapproving glances of observers. One does not need actual observers (like the official shaming forum of the EU or the UN) for such a moral feeling to occur in a nation. But this mechanism, which already presupposes a personal commitment to a specific kind of decency, a commitment that pertains to the moral high ground, is less likely to occur where membership is not actual, only virtual, as is the case with membership in the *past* of a nation.

The absence or presence of shame must be interpreted in the context of historical experience. In a number of countries victims and potential victims perceive today that the majority of the population shows no sign of outrage when victim groups of past atrocities are threatened. The growing visibility of recurrent anti-Semitic atrocities in postcommunist countries is reinforced by the insufficiency of collective responses to such actions. The lack of any firm collective and credible governmental condemnation of, and sanctions against, racism, allows anti-Semitism to become increasingly and openly admissible. At the level of emotions all this can be accounted to lack of shame. As there is no shame to mobilize against the transgression, the normalization of racism goes ever further. For victims and their descendants the public silence about racism and the absence of shame are interpreted in the context of the unfinished business of restoration and reparative justice. A constitutional position, like the one in Germany, changes the context.

A constitutionally endorsed moral obligation of shame for the Holocaust and genocide in general is understood here as a kind of collective moral obligation, which is satisfied by institutional and collective action. But such "collectivistic" morality has its practical problems, as it may operate in an emotional vacuum, and public sentiments will not endorse it. Most moral theories posit the autonomy of the individual's conscience, and I have no reason to consider it otherwise. In applying this approach, a community or group cannot be a moral entity and cannot be the subject of moral obligations. Hence the above assumption regarding the moral obligation of the collective makes sense only as shorthand. This means that all members of a community must have the obligation specifically because of their belonging to the community, as an individual act or choice, even if the belonging is a happenstance. Morality remains a matter of individuality, even if the source of the moral obligation resides in community membership. But the dividing line between individual responsibility and moral obligations of the collective are not as neatly separate as it is stated by those who (rightly) refuse collective responsibility in the context of collective punishment.

Let us take the example of the genocidal massacres in the Balkan in the nineties. The government of Yugoslavia instigated the atrocities. The majority of Serbs elected that very government. They were aware of its aspirations, though not the means. Governmental policies were popularly endorsed to the extent that Milosevic was reelected even after the atrocities. Are citizens in a quasi-democratic system not responsible for the government they elect, particularly where it is really the promise of extremist measures that may entail atrocities that makes the policy publicly attractive? Can't one expect a new popular policy that is dictated by shame for what happened, shame for being seen as a moral contributor to the atrocities?[65] I am not claiming that normative considerations will be drawn from lack of feelings of collective shame or guilt. But the injustice of genocide creates moral emotions in bystanders who would expect something similar among those who contributed politically to such developments. One should feel shame if he is exposed as a part and member of a collective, if atrocities were committed on behalf of, or in the name of that collective. These were committed in his name, on his behalf.

There are, however, formidable cognitive obstacles in the way of forming such feelings. People sustain and even reinforce pre-existing categories and frames which make them exempt from participating in the chain of past events. Only traumatic collapse of the personal life world and the community that reinforced one's belief and identity gives a chance for breaking the cognitive frames. There are a number of coping techniques for dispositional forgiveness, that is, a general tendency to forgive. Strelan indicates that "individuals may blame an actual situation, for example, the circumstances surrounding a debilitating illness or accident. More likely, however, they may react to the perceived abstract source of the circumstances that led to the situation, by blaming what happened on 'life,' or 'an unjust world,' or 'fate,' . . . and also 'the cruel world' that brought about the circumstances which caused the accident." Self-forgiveness is another important mechanism that applies even where framing of one's act is of no help in denying transgression. Self-forgiveness does not necessarily mean denial of the appropriateness of shame and that harm was caused to others. "Taking responsibility is a key aspect of self-forgiveness, . . . in forgiving the self, individuals do not abdicate responsibility for their part in a negative outcome, nor do they transfer blame to circumstances or another."[66]

Ironically, those members of the community who took a stand against the majority policy feel more shame than others. They are troubled because of lack of self-condemnation by the majority. Bystanders who are in the position of imposing their perspective on regime formation may find it appropriate to impose shame on all members of the society. Once again, this is not a matter of collective punishment, though a collective duty to pay, for example, compensation as part of state responsibility (resulting in a higher tax rate) is quite legitimate. Such measures will affect all the citizens of the country, even if they never supported the actual genocidal policies. The amorality of those who participated in genocide is partly the result of their lack of shame; if one does not feel shame for what they did, one runs the risk of opening oneself up to being or becoming what they were. Those who are for racial discrimination voluntarily exclude themselves from the community of those who feel shame for such positions. *Vice versa*, those who feel shame in a way distinguish themselves from the perpetration, but remain, painfully, part of the larger community. The conditions for a decent society cannot be met in a "successor state" without the condemnation of the Holocaust or other genocide by the overwhelming majority and their government. Condemnation is authentic if it is accompanied by the moral sentiment (emotion) of shame. Decency is not satisfied when social institutions force members of a legitimate social group of victims to feel ashamed and live in fear just for having a given personal identity.[67]

The social-decency argument is based on moral claims of the community. Here, the members of the community feel they have an obligation to themselves to remedy injustice. The need to undo injustice is related to the actors' dignity. The individual has an obligation to him- or herself. Shame is to be felt if people would like to live in decent society. According to the German proverb, so long as there is shame there is hope for virtue: a person who is ashamed for an act (not necessarily for her own act) is most likely a moral being. Isn't the expected shaming of younger generations of Germans, Slovaks, and Hungarians, who had nothing to do with the Holocaust, an excess of decency? Can one expect feelings of shame for events resulting from conflicts among members of past generations? Members of a society where genocide occurred are not required to be moral virtuosi or acrobats in order to admit that a terrible crime was committed in and by the society that they inherited from their ancestors.

Moral philosopher Patricia Greenspan argues in favor of the possibility of "liberal guilt" that we have for misdeeds of fellow citizens, but as Gabriele Taylor reminds us, "Guilt cannot arise from the deeds or omissions of others."[68] Feelings of guilt, that is, actual emotions, are not out of question but it is more an emotion of shame that is at play here, in a role that liberal moral theory finds legitimate. The person sees herself exposed as associated with people who are in breach of moral norms. "It is the narcissistic wound inflicted by shame that causes the greatest suffering, the greatest self-punishment, that we associate with a bad conscience. In short: shame creeps through guilt and feels like retribution."[69]

Is it reasonable for the generation of descendants to be demanded to step on the snow of yesteryears? There is nothing absurd in shame about the past. Peter de Marneffe has put the point this way: "If being a morally inadequate person is a good reason to feel ashamed, why isn't having been a morally inadequate person also a good reason, since one is, in many important respects, the same person?"[70] As long as the descendants of perpetrators are the inheritors of the "forms of life" that enabled mass atrocities, this legacy dictates vigilance: shame is patrolling our moral borders. "Our own life is linked to the life context in which Auschwitz was possible . . . intrinsically."[71]

As the Hassidic teacher, the Baal Shem Tov stated: "Remembrance Is the Secret of Redemption." Collective shame, once institutionalized, will quickly make the potential victims feel more secure and integrated. It improves the moral qualities of society by opening up a learning process. It is only through collective learning that the past can be intellectually processed and neutralized and finally turned into simple history. Accepting shame means taking responsibility for past crimes committed by the state and other social institutions. Such a responsibility dictates that a society must dispose of the falsifications present in its history. When a society ignores this responsibility, it enables falsification of patterns of behavior that resulted in gross injustice in the past. There will be no moral sentiment guiding us at the reoccurrence of those patterns.

Shame, as defined above, is the emotion generated by exposure. Denial of shame implies that there is nothing to be exposed. Where negation, silence, and indifference surround foundational genocide in a community, its members and past members are left with nothing to prevent identification with and repetition of evil. Shame would prevent identification with what one feels ashamed about. With silence there is nothing acting preventively. Institutionalized shame as a mechanism of anticipation is by no means a serious burden on the collective moral consciousness, and the collective responsibility accepted in historical memory is even less of a burden on the psyche of the individual. In normal times the obligations of the individual are satisfied by the proper functioning of institutionalized public consciousness, acting out, among other places, in law.

4. Is Shaming a Proper Constitutional Strategy?

The above analysis indicates that on the one hand constitutional law shields against shaming, while in other contexts shame may dictate constitutional arrangements. While the first approach raises issues as to the propriety of overprotection, constitutional policies formed by shame-

"based" moral emotions raise other concerns. Is it conducive to constitutionalism, is it healthy for the human psyche, is it reasonable at all to perpetuate and strengthen feelings of shame among citizens?[72]

Shame and guilt are often considered negative emotions that are to be avoided, partly because of the suffering caused by the feeling, partly because of the reactions generated by it. Normative systems are inevitably guilt- and shame-inducing. Noticing the violation of the moral code triggers guilt and shame: shame to the extent that one envisions that she will be exposed as different and unworthy on account of the violation. "Feeling ashamed" is shaping law observance. Further it may generate conduct that will have an impact on other people's behavior. Contrary to guilt, shame is capable of *ex ante* behavior motivation because it anticipates emotionally forceful reactions of important others.

Social critics of shame distrust shame-based social control. Relying on the negative functions of shame they emphasize that shame is typically used as a strategy of social submission: the shaming gaze induces inferiority. This is true in matters of race and gender: "A woman must continually watch herself. . . . Women watch themselves being looked at."[73]

The shaming presentation of subordinate, discriminated groups (blacks, migrants, Jews, women, apostates, etc.) certainly helps to sustain the representations of negative moral character attributed to these groups both within the group and among bystanders. But one should not blame a feeling for being used and abused in a society of unjust domination. Denying that it can have a more proper social control function is unwarranted. Shame may have been seized for psychological domination, but as the history of feminism indicates, liberation means learning how to liberate oneself from such a gaze once actual social conditions and emotional support exist for such emancipation. Shaming is not a unidirectional process, and in an open society one can liberate herself from it to a great extent where the culture allows it.

Martha Nussbaum raised prudential objections to reliance on shame. She attributes anticipatory functions to guilt and not to shame. In her peculiar psychology, guilt recognizes the rights of others, hence it makes norm violation recognition possible, and hence the desire for reparation. She argued within the context of shaming punishments that "shame is likely to be normatively unreliable in public life, despite its potential for good."[74] For this reason she finds no place for shaming in a liberal society. Further, there is no place in law for shaming group members on grounds of their immutable characteristics. From a liberal perspective it is hard to disagree with the assumption that law should not contribute to the survival of prejudice that results in shame but Nussbaum's criticism is directed to the failure of liberal society to inhibit infantile social narcissism.

The suspicion about the intimidating power of shame originates in developmental and child psychopathology.[75] The assumptions about the negative impacts of shame draw on specific experiences in child rearing (abusive parental reliance on shaming, negative developmental consequences of shame generated by trauma, etc.). While such consequences are likely, the criticism itself is misplaced because it generalizes personality disorders associated with shame in situations such as depression, aggression, and social anxiety. In many instances it is the negative pathological self-attribution that generates shame and not the other way round. One should not confuse global self-attribution of failure with ordinary shame. *Unacknowledged* shame takes the direction of compulsive assaults. Continuing, lasting pervasive embarrassment, indignation, resentment, and hatred are always pathological—but this is not the typical operation of shame. Tomkins was concerned about the destruction of the child's self-confidence in the "crucible of compounded humiliation." Shame is a mediator between insult, anger, and aggression. In cultural terms, if one feels shame for being dishonored, that might push him to violent defense of honor. However, when it comes to terrorism and war in most instances it is humiliation and resulting desperateness and not shame that causes the violent reaction.[76]

Being seen as "an object of scrutiny, as the focus of another's attention, brings one to a new consciousness of oneself, as something seen through another's eyes," so that the observed person "is fixed as something—with limited probabilities rather than infinite, indeterminate possibilities."[77] Certainly, shame as an instrument of social control has negative potentials and ambiguous social and psychological consequences. However, a normative conclusion that shaming as a policy tool generates violence through anger and, therefore, is an inadequate tool for social control is misplaced. It is humiliation through law that is to be avoided, and perhaps law should stand up against humiliation. A constitutional policy should liberate people from humiliating shame. But there are no psychological reasons that would require constitutional law of a liberal democracy to renounce social control through shaming, and neither the social nor the psychological consequences envisioned by developmental psychology offer compelling objections to constitutional and social policies that admit the positive role of shame. After all, shame may generate recognition of *responsibility and it contributes to maturity.*[78] People can handle shame constructively if they are able to acknowledge it and work out a way of "making their peace" with those who have harmed them.[79] One can rely on shame-induced self-improvement. The external signs of shame signal, in many cases, that a moral violation has occurred and the actor feels that he is exposed as not being up to the moral expectations, that is, it expresses respect for the transgressed norm or related moral or other quality. Shame mobilizes attempts at reparation. The shame-induced need to apologize contributes to mending social relations. Apology contributes to forgiving, and forgiving can improve the psychological functioning of people. Admission of wrongdoing is not enough. What matters is that the apology has to be credible; the perpetrator has to be (has to be seen) truly sorry.[80] Shame makes the apology credible.

What we envision here for legal institutionalization is a nonperpetual emotion of shame, one with a short life span that does not result in hatred or self-hatred; on the contrary, it reduces hatred. As Lynd stated: "The very fact that shame is an isolating experience also means that if one can find ways of sharing and communicating it, this communication can bring about particular closeness with others. . . ."[81] Normal shame and embarrassment are an almost continuous part of all human relations.[82] The presence of shame in the emotional repertoire and the existence of social techniques of shaming and expectations of shame do not equal continual exposure to a shame environment that develops a disposition to acute shame.

Constitutionally endorsed shame is necessary and often sufficient in mobilizing against lies, but it will not generate feelings of guilt because it is mediated through public institutions. There is no need for living in permanent individual (psychic) shame as long as shame functions are taken over by the collective memory. Hence there will be no aggression, and shame will not have paralyzing or self-destructive effects. Collective actions dictated by shame should send reinforcing messages to actual and potential victims.

Messages generated by shame and outrage should make clear for both potential victims and ready-to-act perpetrators that any attempt to assert racial discrimination will be met with firm social condemnation. Shame—even collective shaming—is not humiliating. Rather, shame for genocide—mere recognition in the collective consciousness—enables people to recognize themselves as moral beings. Shame is indispensable for the moral rehabilitation of the society.

Writing from a communitarian perspective Amitai Etzioni is also ready to rely on shame as a tool of social control. Shame is instrumental to the behavioral improvement of equal and autonomous individuals.[83] But a communitarian endorsement might be quite inconvenient for a liberal constitutionalist theory, and moral philosophers of Kantian pedigree have their own objections to reliance on shame as a strategy of social control. "In the scheme of Kantian oppositions, shame is on the bad side of all the lines. This is well brought out in its notorious association with the notion of losing or saving face. 'Face' stands for appearance against reality and the outer versus the inner, so its values are superficial; I lose or save it only in the eyes of others, so the values are heteronymous. . . ."[84] In this tradition, which includes John Rawls, shame is a feeling resulting from a shock to one's self-esteem, and therefore it is unrelated to morality that is concerned with *moral* wrong-doing.[85] Morality presupposes autonomous decisions while with shame we are concerned about the moral standards of others. To save autonomy as the basis of morality in a world where actual shaming is a tool of social control, John Kekes argues that the moral agent feels shame in his own eyes.[86] Bernard Williams claims that there are positive uses of shame; autonomy is saved by claiming that mature agents feel shame only for shaming (being exposed to) by those whom they respect.[87] This position has sociological attractiveness: imposition of shame, especially in open societies, is *partly* a matter of the preliminary choice of reference of the shamed person. In individualistic open societies the person has some choice as to *who* will have the power to shame him—whose gaze matters. In certain basic regards, like nakedness, there is little choice, but even here with changing social conventions, as in the context of nudism, there can be alternatives for respect and identification. There is no guarantee that those who will be respected are respected for their moral autonomy, but this, again, does not rule out that shame fits into autonomy-based morality.

Cheshire Calhoun admits that shame is a fact of social life, but he claims that morality is practiced with others in a social world and by accepting the power of shame one respects the other, which is the foundation of social morality.[88] In Bernard Williams's perspective it is the indeterminacy of moral truth that necessitates reliance on external judgment, hence the justification for shame-induced heterogeneity. "Without it, the convictions of autonomous self-legislation may become hard to distinguish from an insensate degree of moral egoism."[89]

A constitutional policy that relies on the ways society and the mind operate does not necessarily betray Kantian autonomy. The moral judgments are still made on the basis of full commitment to individual agency (autonomy): the constitutional policy that allows the operations of shame may be (for some people: must be) justified in that mirror. In a real world the Kantian assumptions of agency are simply unsustainable, and with the fallibility of our autonomous choices and with many, conflicting, ethical standards we have to respect other people's judgment.

Notwithstanding the limited but undeniable psychological shortcomings (at least for the majority of social situations and actors) of the above normative theories, shame as a source of morality remains relevant for liberal constitutionalism; the moral legitimacy of shame in a constitutional strategy has been sustained. A community of honestly ashamed citizens does not tolerate the humiliation of any minority. (I hope.) If shame is activated it will direct the individual to report racism and to testify against racists. As a minimum the sense of shame (*pudeur*) bars the hidden glorification of the shameful.

Expectations of shame dictate symbolic actions like a formal attempt to name and find the living perpetrators of genocide. Symbolic gestures, if applied honestly, are sufficient to break the image of continuity of shameful activities. The simplest legal act of discontinuity with the shameful past is the institutionalized expression of shame both at the governmental (public) level and in social action. As Christopher Lasch would put it, where society is the patient, politics and therapy are indistinguishable. In this logic shame should be made part of official politics.

While the objections based on psychopathology and moral theory may be insufficient to deny the propriety of a constitutional policy that grants a place to shame-based moral emotions, an empirical difficulty originating in the culture of contemporary Western societies limits the relevance of normative considerations. Before advocating reliance on shame we have to answer the question: Is there still a place for efficient shaming as a constitutionally endorsed and induced policy in the emotional culture of a postmodern society? If shame does not matter any more, it is of little use to refer to it.

According to a popular but contested view, whole societies operate on fundamental assumptions of shame. Ruth Benedict suggested that Japan has a shame culture, and entire European cultures are based on guilt.[90] Genocide (against other ethnicities) did not result in overwhelming shame in Japan; it did not result in guilt in most other countries either. It seems that the nature of social culture does not fully determine constitutional strategies. Under specific historical circumstances sympathy with victims and the acceptance of parts of a history tainted with shameful injustices may induce constitutional strategies, including the recognition (scripting) of shame.

However, from a cultural perspective shame as a tool of contemporary social control is in bad shape. Too many critical arguments were made against it, often out of context, as the psychopathology-based criticism of shame (cited above) indicates. The efforts to liberate the individual from the personality-distorting effects of shame helped to delegitimize and disregard the language of shame. "Shame is subject to extensive repression in modern societies. This repression is both caused by and gives rise to rampant individualism."[91] Shame is considered both problematic and less and less capable of efficient social control in the West. Different societies move away from relying in their culture of social control on concepts of shame. Whether this is a good, efficient, or reasonable strategy is irrelevant. It just happens due to changes in the culture and/or because those groups that relied on shame are losing cultural and political battles. Americans, as Dov Cohen observed, are losing the vocabulary of shame,[92] partly because of the attacks on shame coming from all corners of academia. It is felt to be archaic, something left behind. Psychotherapy, which is concerned with self-esteem, has pathologized shame.[93] Other languages crowded out shame. The rationality of legalism also denies shame (like, *prima facie* most other emotions): it finds it irrelevant. Of course, antidiscrimination law had liberating effects and removed, at least partly, the badge of inferiority and the resulting shame. But in terms of language this had a peculiar consequence. Once liberated from shame, victim groups started to argue for improvement and reparation. In this process victim status as such became a legitimate argument for compensation; self-conscious victims working on public sentiments feel much less shame. Hence many other positions of inferiority are perceived as the result of victimization. Victimhood becomes the key to denying responsibility. No shame is felt even where the failure to live up to expectations is due to one's own failure; the unpleasant situation is explained as one of victimization (fault of others). The language of victimhood attempts to impose guilt on those who are blamed for the real or alleged suffering of the victims.

However, the diminished reliance on shame is not only a consequence of socially and culturally shaped language uses. Moving out of shame means that social relations and phenomena are not talked about in terms of shame. In the prevailing social construction of the ego self-esteem becomes crucial, and therefore liberation from humiliation and the restoration of pride become central in public discussion. This is not to say that emotions of shame (in the sense of feeling oneself blush, etc.) are not common, but their elicitors might be different and, particularly in a consumer society, unrelated to morality: for example, with the present level of individualistic self-esteem it is of lesser concern if one is exposed to peers. The consequences of exposure are believed less important for the self, and the shaming power of the community is lesser anyway. In a society where dependence on one's group is not crucial anymore, for example because anonymous welfare services are available for fallback, shame will be less relevant than when negative evaluation by one's own social group was more threatening because of the dependence on the group. It is increasingly the case that only humiliation mobilizes mechanisms of shame. In a narcissist culture the self becomes the point of reference, and why would one feel shame if she is exposed to herself, except for being an imperfect consumer?

Of course, such disregard and social loss of shame is not simply the result of lasting libertarian liberation. American individualism flourishes by allowing people to believe that they are appropriate in accordance with what their own definition suggests. Here it is less likely that one gets into situations where one does not fit the sort of person one thinks one ought to be. What you ought to be is not other people's business. Partly thanks to changes in law, you can be exposed as a homosexual without feeling shame, you can be exposed as a school dropout, and even as a collector of Nazi memorabilia, without shameful consequences. It is not other people's business; therefore you don't lose face.

The demise of shame in contemporary culture is partly countered by an increased legal recognition of certain victim claims. Contemporary culture became receptive to victims' claims. Cultures of complaint have become popular, even irresistible, in affluent Western societies. Culture has become narcissistic. This is partly due to the demise of the masculine and destructive war heroism and the emergence of a troubled conscience among citizens of former colonizing countries. The change in public mood has created an opportunity for victims. With endless picturing of the horror coming from Auschwitz & Co., the moral supremacy of victim-martyrs has become difficult to resist. At least victims have been liberated from the stigma of being losers; they can claim moral superiority as innocent victims of the unjust "other." While the primary targets of such tactics are those on whom responsibility and guilt are to be imposed, such exposure may generate shame (see above, in the context of genocide).

While the discrediting of masculine heroism created the proper intellectual atmosphere for a culture of complaint, this latter owes its political success to the advance of democracy, democratic egalitarianism, and welfarism. It pays to be a victim where there is insurance. Interest assertion increases the chances of single-agenda victim groups in egalitarian-democratic regimes. It is much less risky, and it is more legitimate, to organize around victimization in a sensitive social and political environment. The strategy of victimhood-based politics is to generate feelings of guilt instead of inconveniently feeling ashamed.

Contrary to what follows from a sense of guilt (namely acceptance of punishment and restoration) the outcome of constitutional debates regarding victimhood as a source of rights (at least a right to enhanced special protection) depends very much on shame-induced mobilization and generation of emotions of compassion and shame among former oppressors and beneficiaries of injustice. In fact, shaming is an important strategy in the process of claiming rights. This is often disguised by language that refers to injustice: most political and legal arguments are about justice. But the references to and images of injustice are about generating emotions, namely outrage (if the injustice can be seen as norm violation, which is not always the case as the relevant norm is often debated), or at least sympathy (with suffering), or shame that is intended to immobilize the opponents of the norm. Disgust and outrage are to mobilize sympathizers for new rights, shame is applied to adversaries to disarm them.[94]

Victims' concerns are turned into rights. Victimhood pervades not only domestic argumentation but international relations too. In our international system, which finds pleasure in calling itself global, sympathy toward victims—and their rescue—has become a new legitimization for international intervention. Its limited and ambiguous status is exemplified in Somalia and Kosovo. In a postcolonial world, interventionism and penetration cannot be justified by any self-declared "*mission civilisatrice*" as they were in the first half of the twentieth century. The intervention must serve the protection of victims, and is dictated more by guilt than shame for what the community did allow to happen elsewhere (see the Rwanda argument in the Darfur context: powerful nations are guilty for the Rwanda massacres because they moved their troops out, instead of sending reinforcements; therefore they should intervene in Darfur). One of the feelings that animate such humanitarian demands is the sense of shame in the bystander, a shame that results from his sense of helplessness and impotence. He exposed himself at the time of the Rwanda massacres as impotent, and this is going to happen again.

We have seen in the South African context that the constituent moment is understood as a moment of admitting victimhood. Whatever the expression used, feelings of shame and humiliation were the formative emotions among the oppressed majority, though the emotion itself did not determine the way the unjust situation was to be overcome in the rationalistic structures of the constitution. These emotions may serve, among other ends, as a drive toward a constitutional policy of redressing the injustice. They may also shape the collective mentality to avoid the repetition of the past. Humiliation in particular may force acceptance of specific, otherwise problematic legal measures intended to undo the injustice. The redress of the injustice through institutionalized shame is separate from material reparation or continued revenge: it is based on a demand for apology. It reminds the person to suppress inside herself certain tendencies. Others (the bystanders) who express contempt at the recurrence of the injustice will reinforce the grounds for shame.

Such shaming based on past injustice does not wholly work if the law or bystanders have to shame the majority identity, especially if the identity is based on the assumption that other people's suffering originates in a trait of that identity, for example, where racial supremacy is a constituent element of the majority identity. One cannot construe the constitutional affirmative protection of the *Dalit* and scheduled castes in India expecting shame-induced compliance from higher-caste Hindus who continue to build their superiority-centered identity around their religious, purity-based gut feelings, like disgust. Likewise, in the majority of postcommunist countries, where the oppressive regime relied on a relatively large social basis of collaborationists, there is little chance that the accomplices of the past regime will feel shame for their collaboration. In the absence of strong emotional mobilization and without the pressure of constitutional sentiments, they are successful in collective denial.

NOTES

Introduction

1. Abraham Lincoln, "Address to the Young Men's Lyceum," in *Abraham Lincoln: Speeches and Writings, 1832–1858*, ed. Don E. Fehrenbacher (New York: Library of America, 1989), 28; Robert C. Solomon, *The Passions* (New York: Anchor, Doubleday, 1976), 11.

2. Joseph LeDoux, *The Emotional Brain* (New York: Simon & Schuster, 1996), 19.

3. Except where I state otherwise, fundamental rights and human rights are used interchangeably.

4. Jérôme Mavidal and Emile Laurent, eds., *Archives parlementaires de 1787 à 1860: Recueil complet des débats législatifs et politiques des Chambres françaises, imprimé par ordre du Corps législatif. 1e série, 1787–1799*, VIII (Paris: P. Dupont, 1875–89) (henceforth *AP*), 222. <www.gallica.fr> (1 March 2009).

5. See, e.g., John Forgas, "Mood and Judgment: The Affect Infusion Model," *Psychological Bulletin* 117, no. 1 (January 1995): 39–66.

6. For the belief that reason and emotion can be separated, see the jury instruction quoted in *California v. Brown*, 475 U.S. 1301 (1986), where the jury was told that it "must not be swayed by mere sentiment, conjecture, sympathy, passion, prejudice, public opinion or public feeling." The jury decision is rebaptized from emotional response to "moral inquiry," *California v. Brown*, 479 U.S. 538, 545 (1987) (Justice O'Connor concurring). See Susan A. Bandes, "The Heart Has Its Reasons: Examining the Strange Persistence of the American Death Penalty," *Special Issue: Is the Death Penalty Dying? Studies in Law, Politics, and Society* 42, no. 1 (2008): 21–52, 42, referring to *Saffle v. Parks*, 494 U.S. 1257, 1272–1273, n. 13 (1990).

7. Joshua Greene and Jonathan Cohen, "For the Law, Neuroscience Changes Nothing and Everything," *Philosophical Transactions of the Royal Society of London, Series B, Biological Sciences* 359, no. 1451 (29 November 2004): 1775–1785.

Richard Rorty was skeptical about the impact: "The prodigious achievement of natural science in the direction of the knowledge of things contrasts brutally with the collapse of this same natural science when faced with the strictly human element. Ortega insisted that increasing knowledge of how things such as the human brain and the human genome work will never help us figure out how to envisage ourselves and what to do with ourselves." Richard Rorty, "Philosophy-Envy," *Daedalus* 133, no. 4 (Fall 2004): 18–24, 22–23. See further Richard Rorty, "The Brain as Hardware, Culture as Software," *Inquiry* 47, no. 3 (June 2004): 219–235.

8. Susan A. Bandes, "Introduction," in *The Passions of Law*, ed. Susan A. Bandes (New York: New York University Press, 1999), 1–15, 7. For a critical survey of "Law and Emotions" see, e.g., Terry Maroney, "Law and Emotion: A Proposed Taxonomy of an Emerging Field," *Law and Human Behavior* 30, no. 2 (April 2006): 119–142; Matthias Mahlmann, "Ethics, Law, and the Challenge of Cognitive Science," *German Law Journal* 8, no. 6 (June 2007): 577–615.

9. John Stuart Mill, *On Liberty*, ed. Gertrude Himmelfarb (London: Penguin Books, 1985), 152.

10. Jesse Prinz, "The Emotional Basis of Moral Judgments," *Philosophical Explorations* 9, no. 1 (March 2006): 29–43, 30.

11. See, e.g., Jon Elster's discussion of the measures of transitional justice. Elster first lists emotions with their relevant action tendency and then (adding many factors to the calculus) explains/predicts in terms of these action tendencies the applied sanctions. Jon Elster, *Closing the Books: Transitional Justice in Historical Perspective* (New York: Cambridge University Press, 2004). Martha Nussbaum and Dan Kahan, in a more prescriptive way, discuss how disgust shapes/should shape criminal law and punishment.

I will refer to public sentiments as I find it difficult, at least in the constitutional law context, to establish correspondence between specific emotions and specific legal solutions. Instead of attributing specific legal solutions to specific emotions, I will only show how emotional reactions (e.g., shame) are taken into consideration or disregarded in a *set* of legal measures.

12. Theme Issue "Law and the Brain," *Philosophical Transactions of the Royal Society of London, Series B, Biological Sciences* 359, no. 1451 (29 November 2004); Henry T. Greely, "The Social Effects of Advances in Neuroscience: Legal Problems, Legal Perspectives," in *Neuroethics: Defining the Issues in Theory, Practice, and Policy*, ed. Judy Illes (Oxford: Oxford University Press, 2005), 245–250.

I am less sanguine and would like to follow Tanina Rostain's advice: "Legal policies and initiatives need to be informed by a modest conception of social science. Such a conception acknowledges the limitation of social science knowledge and recognizes that string causal explanations of human behavior cannot be permitted to supplant normative debate." Tanina Rostain, "Educating Homo Economicus: Cautionary Notes on the New Behavioral Law and Economics Movement," *Law and Society Review* 34, no. 4 (December 2000): 973–1006, 973.

13. Bandes, "The Heart Has Its Reasons," 43 (with additional examples of passion in the legal debate on the death penalty).

14. Obviously, constitutional law is not limited to the constitution, and the constitution's meaning is changed today to a great extent through the decisions of high courts. I look into this problem only where it's inevitable, partly because the matter deserves a full monograph, and partly because I don't find it appropriate to discuss specifics of judicial decision-making. Firsthand personal experience can be misleading for a descriptive theory.

1. From Emotions to Constitutional Institutions

1. Frans de Waal, *Primates and Philosophers: How Morality Evolved* (Princeton: Princeton University Press, 2006), 4.

2. David A. Pizarro and Paul Bloom, "The Intelligence of the Moral Institutions: Comment on Haidt (2001)," *Psychological Review* 110, no. 1 (January 2003): 193–196, 194.

3. David Hume, *A Treatise of Human Nature*, ed. Lewis Amherst Selby-Bigge (Oxford: Oxford University Press, 1975). The alternative strategy is that of Spinoza, who advocates the domination of passions by intellect.

4. For example, "[the decisions] appear to be, based on reason rather than caprice or emotion." *Gardner v. Florida*, 430 U.S. 349, 358 (1977).

5. Michael Joseph Oakeshott, *Rationalism in Politics and Other Essays* (Indianapolis: Liberty Press, 1991), 99; Isaiah Berlin, "Two Concepts of Liberty," in *The Proper Study of Mankind: An Anthology of Essays*, ed. Henry Hardy and Roger Hausheer (New York: Farrar, Straus and Giroux, 1997), 191–242, 235.

6. Barbara H. Rosenwein, "Worrying about Emotions in History," *American Historical Review* 107, no. 3 (June 2002): 821–845, 827.

7. As Daniel Kahneman has stated in his Nobel lecture, "the perceptual system and the intuitive operations of System 1 generate impressions of the attributes of objects of perception and thought. These impressions are not voluntary and need not be verbally explicit. . . . The label 'intuitive' is applied to judgments that directly reflect impressions." Daniel Kahneman, "Maps of Bounded Rationality: A Perspective on Intuitive Judgment and Choice," in *Les Prix Nobel. The Nobel Prizes 2002*, ed. Tore Frängsmyr (Stockholm: Nobel Foundation, 2003), 449–489, 450–451; John A. Bargh and Tanya L. Chartrand, "The Unbearable Automaticity of Being," *American Psychologist* 54, no. 7 (July 1999): 462–479.

8. Cf. Ronald de Sousa, *The Rationality of Emotion* (Cambridge, Mass.: MIT Press, 1987), xv; Antonio R. Damasio, *Descartes' Error: Emotion, Reason, and the Human Brain* (New York: G. P. Putnam, 1994).

9. Feeling is often defined as cognition about one's emotional status: "I feel sad."

10. Robert H. Frank, *Passions within Reason: The Strategic Role of the Emotions* (New York: W. W. Norton, 1988).

11. "The emotion need not be the product of a cultural model in the synchronic sense that the individual produces it in order to conform to the model. The emotion may depend on the model in the diachronic sense that the existence of the model in the culture helped shape what is now a relatively automatic reaction to certain situations."

Paul E. Griffiths, *What Emotions Really Are: The Problem of Psychological Categories* (Chicago: University of Chicago Press, 1997), 142.

12. Arlie Russell Hochschild, "Emotion Work, Feeling Rules, and Social Structure," *American Journal of Sociology* 85, no. 3 (November 1979): 551–575; Arlie Russell Hochschild, *The Managed Heart: Commercialization of Human Feeling* (Berkeley: University of California Press, 1983).

13. James R. Averill, "Emotion and Anxiety: Sociocultural, Biological, and Psychological Determinants," in *Explaining Emotions*, ed. Amelie Oksenberg Rorty (Berkeley: University of California Press, 1980).

14. On intuition being reasoning from unconscious premises, not involving working memory, see Monica Bucciarelli, Sangeet Khemlani, and Philip N. Johnson Laird, "The Psychology of Moral Reasoning," *Judgment and Decision Making* 3, no. 2 (February 2008): 121–139.

15. As a matter of fact, the relationship is partly regulated by constitutional law: modern constitutions consolidated the public/private divide and tried to push emotions into the private sphere. This was the (in)famous act that deprived most emotions of social respectability in exchange for governmental nonintervention. But in constitutional law, the word "emotion" is not mentioned, only the place that is thought to be proper for their display is protected: constitutions talk about the inviolability of correspondence and of the home, which are the (private) places for emotions.

16. See Chapter 2.

17. See Guy Elcheroth, "Les expériences de vulnérabilité collective. Thèse" (Lausanne: Université de Lausanne, 2007) (manuscript). Elcheroth found that while victims of gross human rights violations were less interested in supporting a legalistic defense of human rights, members of the vulnerable community the victims belonged to were much more supportive. The individual emotions of the actual victims were reflected in the sentiments of the greater community whose members felt threatened and humiliated because of what happened to other members of the group. The collective sentiment reinterpreted even the strongest personal sentiments. Elcheroth's study concerned ethnic groups which were brutalized in the Yugoslav wars of the nineties.

18. See Jon Elster, *Alchemies of the Mind: Rationality and the Emotions* (Cambridge: Cambridge University Press, 1999), 87.

19. People use "simple heuristics that make us good." Cass R. Sunstein, "Moral Heuristics," *Behavioral and Brain Sciences* 28, no. 4 (August 2005): 531–542.

20. William Pitt, *The Speeches of William Pitt in the House of Commons, Volume I.* (London: Longman, Hurst, Rees & Orme, 1808), 394, quoted after Boyd Hilton, *A Mad, Bad, and Dangerous People? England 1783–1846* (Oxford: Oxford University Press, 2008), 194. By claiming the moral high ground for the constitutional status quo, Pitt managed to corner Fox into the position of radical internationalist as he was betting on nationalist liberty to catch the public sentiment. Hilton states that until the 1850s "feelings of Englishness, in so far as they existed, were far more bound up with institutions like the monarchy, Parliament and the common law than with ethnicity" (247).

21. Where possibilities for social action are limited, the appropriateness of sentiments becomes a program of its own, approaching a private virtue program. Proper affection becomes a moral imperative. "But what can any individual do?" (to end slavery) asks Harriet Beecher Stowe at the end of *Uncle Tom's Cabin*. Her answer is: "They can see to it that they feel right." Quoted in Glenn Hendler, *Public Sentiments: Structures of Feeling in Nineteenth-Century American Literature* (Chapel Hill: University of North Carolina Press, 2001), 2. I am indebted to Hendler's concept of public sentiment.

22. Charles de Secondat, Baron de Montesquieu, *The Spirit of Laws* (Amherst, N.Y.: Prometheus Books, 2002), 19. For contemporary uses of the public sentiment tradition, see Tzvetan Todorov, *La peur des barbares. Au-delà du choc des civilisations* (Paris: Robert Laffont, 2008); Dominique Moïsi, *La géopolitique de l' émotion* (Paris: Flammarion, 2008).

23. See, e.g., Hillel Sterner, "Moral Rights," in *The Oxford Handbook of Ethical Theory*, ed. David Copp (New York: Oxford University Press, 2005), 459–479.

24. John R. Searle, *The Construction of Social Reality* (London: Allen Lane, 1995), 23.

25. Elcheroth provides an excellent example of the unfinished and creative nature of public sentiment. When Luxembourg was occupied by the Germans during World War II, the German authorities requested the population to indicate their nationality, language, and citizenship. The overwhelming majority answered to all three questions: "Luxemburgeoise," an identity that did not exist earlier and could not be considered to result from the workings of public opinion controlled by the occupying forces. See Elcheroth, "Les expériences," 40–41.

26. Roberto Mangabeira Unger, *Knowledge and Politics* (New York: Free Press, 1975), 24.

27. By the seventeenth century "sentiment" and "sentimental" were used to denote "both opinion and emotion." Raymond Williams, *Keywords: A Vocabulary of Culture and Society* (New York: Oxford University Press, 1983), 281.

28. Jürgen Habermas, *The Structural Transformation of the Public Sphere: An Inquiry into a Category of Bourgeois Society*, trans. Thomas Burger and Frederick Lawrence (Cambridge, Mass.: Polity Press, 1989).

29. Images are the key to conveying affect, and faces of individual victims are crucial to generating compassion. See Paul Slovic, "'If I Look at the Mass I Will Never Act': Psychic Numbing and Genocide," *Judgment and Decision Making* 2, no. 2 (April 2007): 79–95; Barbie Zelizer, *Remembering to Forget: Holocaust Memory through the Camera's Eye* (Chicago: University of Chicago Press, 1998).

30. Eldar Shafir and Robyn A. LeBoeuf, "Rationality," *Annual Review of Psychology* 53, no. 1 (February 2002): 491–517, 499.

31. The influence can be demonstrated through the effect of images of war and differences in public sentiment between cases where photographers have direct access to the theater of war as in Vietnam, and other situations where they don't have such access.

32. Evolutionary biology "predicts" retrospectively that activities that reflect moral judgments originate in evolutionary needs satisfied by emotions and morality, as social

co-operation was based on the operation of social emotions. Moral choices would reflect increased reproductive success, by enhancing direct and indirect fitness. Moral judgment will be nepotistic (favoring one's offspring against all other people, and favoring kin against all nonkin, etc.), where priorities are given in relation to personal closeness, with little concern for injury (life saving) to enemies and other people considered to belong to unworthy social groups. Lewis Petrinovich, *The Cannibal Within* (New York: Aldine de Gruyter, 2000), 8–9.

33. David Hume, *An Enquiry Concerning Human Understanding and Concerning the Principles of Morals*, ed. Lewis Amherst Selby-Bigge and Peter H. Nidditch (Oxford: Clarendon Press, 1975, 3rd ed.), 172–173.

34. Cf. Darcia Narvaez, Irene Getz, James R. Rest, and Stephen J. Thoma, "Individual Moral Judgment and Cultural Ideologies," *Developmental Psychology* 35, no. 2 (March 1999): 478–488.

35. Matthias Mahlmann, "Ethics, Law and the Challenge of Cognitive Science," *German Law Journal* 8, no. 6 (June 2007): 577–615, 602. One can agree with Mahlmann without claiming, as he does, that the motivational force originates in moral reasoning.

36. Hume, *Enquiry*, 172–173.

37. Joshua D. Greene, R. Brian Sommerville, Leigh E. Nystrom, John M. Darley, and Jonathan D. Cohen, "An fMRI Investigation of Emotional Engagement in Moral Judgment," *Science* 293, no. 5537 (14 September 2001): 2105–2108.

38. Daniel M. Bartels, "Principled Moral Sentiment and the Flexibility of Moral Judgment and Decision Making," *Cognition* 108, no. 2 (August 2008): 381–417, 405.

39. Of course, the feeling of anger may be enough to attribute agency and causation to the most visible or least beloved person in sight. It is the construction of harming, and the attribution of harm's cause that turns the event into a moral one. But it will be the emotion (the fear or anger) that forces us to construe the attribution. In problems related to fairness and altruism, which are not apt to be construed in terms of harm, social (survival- and cooperation-related) concerns will provide the background knowledge, and attribution remains important. In order to be angry at the norm-breaker you have to feel that he caused the breach.

40. Shaun Nichols and Ron Mallon, "Moral Dilemmas and Moral Rules," *Cognition* 100, no. 3 (July 2006): 530–542. Morality is probably not a "natural kind." Joshua Greene and Jonathan Haidt, "How (and Where) Does Moral Judgment Work?" *Trends in Cognitive Sciences* 6, no. 12 (1 December 2002): 517–523, 522.

41. Richard A. Schweder, "When Cultures Collide: Which Rights? Whose Tradition of Values? A Critique of the Global Anti-FGM Campaign," in *Global Justice and the Bulwarks of Localism: Human Rights in Context*, ed. Christopher Eisgruber and András Sajó (Leiden, Netherlands: Martinus Nijhoff, 2005).

42. Friedrich Nietzsche, *On the Genealogy of Morals; Ecce Homo*, trans. Walter Kaufmann and R. J. Hollingdale (New York: Vintage Books, 1967), 76.

43. In reality, bottom-up and (near) top-down sentiments interact in the making of fundamental rights. For example, slavery was despised by British prime ministers as well as by many laborers.

44. What requires explanation is how we overcome conformism and how new norms can emerge at all.

45. "Unless and until we can offer the injured and insulted victims of most of the world's traditional as well as revolutionary governments a genuine and practicable alternative to their present condition, we have no way of knowing whether they really enjoy their chains." Judith Shklar, "The Liberalism of Fear," in *Liberalism and the Moral Life*, ed. Nancy L. Rosenblum (Cambridge, Mass.: Harvard University Press, 1989), 34.

On changes of attitude regarding FGM see <http://www.nytimes.com/2004/06/08/international/africa/08cutt.html?ei=5007&en=fbe3b906545643a1&ex=1402027200&partner=USERLAND&pagewanted=all> (May 27, 2009).

46. Other candidates that may serve as natural stimuli for moral emotions with a pedigree of evolutionary fitness include: penetration into the territory (the environmental concern), which can result in anger; a sense of injustice; endowment expectations; and contamination, which can result in disgust and perhaps fear, leading to divinity rules, which may or may not count as morality. These instances represent distant, potential bodily harm, and for this reason, in the present context where I consider the moral regulatory power of natural moral sentiments, I don't discuss them as separate from harm.

47. "We reconfirm today that a court's default position must favor life." *In re guardianship of Theresa Marie Schiavo Incapacitated. Robert Schindler and Mary Schindler v. Michael Schiavo*, No. 2D00–1269. January 24, 2001. In the District Court of Appeal of Florida, Second District.

48. By "human rights," I mean fundamental legal claims to a faculty of action. These claims are often made in reference to (open) constitutional and supra-legal sources. In the present context, fundamental constitutional rights and human rights are used interchangeably, unless I state otherwise. Human rights are understood here as legal rights, at least in the sense that they are capable of defining legal decisions, even if there is no specific legal remedy available for a specific human rights claim at a given moment. Finally, the present discussion assumes that human rights are state-oriented, that is, intended to regulate governmental behavior. This is not to say that the same moral principles or emotions which shape human rights are not at play in private relations.

49. Adam Smith, *The Wealth of Nations* (New York: Bantam Classic, 2003), 194.

Chapter 4 offers a case study of the conditions of recognizing a claim as fundamental right.

50. Cf. Thomas L. Haskell, "The Curious Persistence of Rights Talk in the 'Age of Interpretation,'" *Journal of American History* 74, no. 3 (December 1987): 984–1012, 990.

51. For a practical example in the context of abolitionism, see Chapter 4.

52. The difficulty of transition justice, that is, the calling to account of perpetrators of mass atrocities and compensation to victims of human rights abuses, consists in the fading away of social interest in the matter once the past becomes another continent.

53. Hannah Arendt, *On Revolution* (London: Penguin Classics, 1990), 82; Jean-Jacques Rousseau, *Discourse on the Origin of Inequality of Mankind* (Mineola,

N.Y.: Dover, 2004), 21; Jean-Jacques Rousseau, *Émile*, trans. Allan Bloom (New York: Basic Books, 1979), 221.

For Rousseau "it is our common miseries that turn our hearts to humanity." *Discourse*, 106–107. "In *this* weeping child, *this* grieving mother . . . we are encouraged to read the sufferings of *humanity* as a whole." David J. Denby, *Sentimental Narrative and the Social Order in France, 1760–1820* (New York: Cambridge University Press, 1994), 139.

54. See Tzvetan Todorov, *A Passion for Democracy: Benjamin Constant*, trans. Alice Seberry (New York: Algora, 1999).

55. "Ordinary legislation" may be part of the decentralized constitution, where there is public and institutional identification with the specific legislative solution as in France, where long-standing "ordinary" legislative solutions, mostly born of specific historical choices and commitments, became recognized *ex post* as embodiments of constitutional principles, or in Britain where select pieces of legislation were recognized *ex post* as part of the unwritten constitution.

56. I am grateful to Michael W. Dowdle who called my attention to these processes. He perceives judicial process as a dramatic constitutional transformation process that establishes metaphors. Michael W. Dowdle, "Constitutional Poiesis: The Courts and Constitutional Transformation" (manuscript). For the role of public sentiment in the rejection of slavery in *Somerset* and in the abolitionist petitions, see Chapter 4.

57. Hilton, *A Mad, Bad, and Dangerous People?*, 31. Of course, as Hilton explains, the "the sudden surge of feeling" worked hand in hand with, and in reaction to, other "spiritual" and economic influences.

On the contribution of constitutional sentiments, see also Chapter 4.

58. For details see Chapter 3.

59. *New Testament*, Mark 5:12.

Martha Nussbaum is representative of those who deny that *vicious* emotions can represent values. She took this position in the context of the debate regarding the acceptability of disgust as a regulator. For Nussbaum, entire classes of basic emotions like disgust and even shame are too problematic to serve as foundations/expressions of values in a liberal society. Martha Nussbaum, *Hiding from Humanity: Disgust, Shame, and the Law* (Princeton: Princeton University Press, 2004).

60. James Fitzjames Stephen, *Liberty, Equality, Fraternity: And Three Brief Essays* (Chicago: University of Chicago Press, 1991), 126.

61. Richard Posner, "Emotion versus Emotionalism in Law," in *The Passions of Law*, ed. Susan A. Bandes (New York: New York University Press, 1999), 309–329, 318.

Unusually for international human rights law, Art. 5(a) of the Convention on the Elimination of All Forms of Discrimination Against Women mandates the enforcement of moral intuitions that prevail in certain societies only, going as far as openly accepting that emotionally opposite customary practices are to be changed.

62. Oliver Wendell Holmes, *The Common Law* (Cambridge, Mass.: Harvard University Press, 1963), 35.

63. "We can always ask whether a given act or set of social practices, occurring as it does in a particular socio-ecological context, is *genuinely* functional with respect to meeting basic needs and so on." Peter Railton, "Naturalism Relativized?" in *Moral Psychology*, Vol. 1, *The Evolution of Morality: Adaptations and Innateness*, ed. Walter Sinnott-Armstrong (Cambridge, Mass.: MIT Press, 2008), 37–44, 43–44. See further, Owen Flanagan, Hagop Sarkissian, and David Wong, "Naturalizing Ethics," in the same volume, 1–25.

64. Christine McKinnon, *Character, Virtue Theories, and the Vices* (Peterborough, Ont.: Broadview Press, 1999), 6.

65. Ibid., 13.

66. John Stuart Mill, *On Liberty* (London: Penguin Books, 1985), 152.

67. Cf. Jonathan Baron and Mark Spranca, "Protected Values," *Organizational Behavior and Human Decision Processes* 70, no. 1 (April 1997): 1–16.

68. Philip E. Tetlock, Orie V. Kristel, S. Beth Elson, Melanie C. Green, and Jennifer S. Lerner, "The Psychology of the Unthinkable: Taboo Trade-Offs, Forbidden Base Rates, and Heretical Counterfactuals," *Journal of Personality and Social Psychology* 78, no. 5 (November 2000): 853–870.

69. John Lansing, in Max Farrand, *Records of the Federal Convention of 1787, Volume I.* (New Haven: Yale University Press, 1911), 250.

70. Eric Posner, "Law and Emotions," *Georgetown Law Journal* 89, no. 5 (June 2001): 1977–2012.

71. In fact it was not enough to abolish the caste system in the Indian Constitution. Indian law had to criminalize acts of public humiliation, including the denial to a member of a Scheduled Caste or a Scheduled Tribe of any customary right of passage to a place of public resort. See The Scheduled Castes and The Scheduled Tribes (Prevention Of Atrocities) Act, 1989, Art. 3(1). According to Art. 3(1)(x) it is an offense of atrocity whoever "intentionally insults or intimidates with intent to humiliate a member of a Scheduled Caste or a Scheduled Tribe in any place within public view."

72. Otto Bauer, *The Question of Nationalities and Social Democracy* (Minneapolis: University of Minnesota Press, 2000). According to Bauer, in class-differentiated societies, the cultural identity of the ruling classes holds the nation together.

73. Judith N. Shklar, *Political Thought and Political Thinkers* (Chicago: University of Chicago Press, 1998), 385.

74. The increased heterogeneity may result from the artificial setting of state boundaries or from increased migration in a global world. In both instances, very heterogeneous groups with conflicting values have to live together. For example, intensive religiosity (fundamentalism) in well-organized communities increases adherence to moral conventionalism: it counts intuitively as morally proper what the community believes to be true, except where the "truth" or its consequences generate visceral reactions like disgust. Nevertheless, studies have found considerable within-group variation, showing the power of the self, cognitive development, and differences in personal learning history. Narvaez, Getz, Rest, and Thoma, "Individual Moral Judgment,"482.

75. Mill, *On Liberty*, 65.

76. For a stronger formulation see William M. Reddy, "Against Constructionism: The Historical Ethnography of Emotions," *Current Anthropology* 38, no. 3 (June 1997): 327–351, 335. "Emotional control is the real site of the exercise of power: politics is just a process of determining who must repress as illegitimate, who must foreground as valuable, the feelings and desires that come up for them in given contexts and relationships."

77. On display rule support (and social emotion regulation in general) in criminal law see Terry A. Maroney, "Law and Emotion: A Proposed Taxonomy of an Emerging Field," *Law and Human Behavior* 30, no. 2 (April 2006): 119–142, 130, with additional literature.

78. Toni M. Massaro, "Show (Some) Emotions," in *The Passions*, ed. Bandes, 80–120, 93.

79. Mill, *On Liberty*, 152.

80. It would be wrong to limit the constitutional law–emotions relationship to moral sentiments. In many instances, basic emotions shape and sustain constitutional institutions, and constitutional law contributes to their sociocultural management.

81. David A. J. Richards, *Conscience and the Constitution: History, Theory, and Law of the Reconstruction Amendments* (Princeton: Princeton University Press, 1993).

82. Michael Walzer, *Thick and Thin: Moral Argument at Home and Abroad* (Notre Dame, Ind.: University of Notre Dame Press, 1994), 69.

83. Georg Jellinek, *Die sozialethische Bedeutung von Recht, Unrecht und Strafe* (Berlin: O. Häring, 1908), 45.

84. Walzer, *Thick and Thin*, 7.

85. Joel Feinberg and Jan Narveson, "The Nature and Value of Rights," *Journal of Value Inquiry* 4, no. 4 (December 1970): 243–257, 243. For the identity-boosting effects of being a rights holder, see the following remark: "'Rights' feels so new in the mouths of most Black people. It is still so deliciously empowering to say. It is a sign for and gift of selfhood." Patricia J. Williams, *The Alchemy of Race and Rights* (Cambridge, Mass.: Harvard University Press, 1991), 164.

86. For a social representation-based model of human rights, see Willem Doise, "Les représentations sociales," in *Psychologie sociale de la cognition*, ed. Nicole Dubois (Paris: Dunod, 2005), 153–207; Willem Doise and Monica Herrera, "Social Representations of Human and Collective Rights: A Case Study in Quebec," in *Global Justice*, ed. Eisgruber and Sajó, 85–97.

87. For a summary of the role of humiliation-based claims see, e.g., Moïsi, *La géopolitique de l'emotion*, chapter IV.

88. *O'Connor v. Donaldson*, 422 U.S. 563, 575 (1975).

89. Ejan Mackaay, "The Emergence of Constitutional Rights," *Constitutional Political Economy* 8, no. 1 (March 1997): 15–36. I follow Mackaay's reconstruction of the economic and political contingencies that led to self-limiting government. On some details of the American process see Chapter 3.

90. Mancur Olson, *The Rise and Decline of Nations: Economic Growth, Stagflation, and Social Rigidities* (New Haven: Yale University Press, 1982), 48.

91. The concern with abuse of power is unrelated to the absolute level of oppression. The *lettre de cachet* was much less used on the eve of the French Revolution than earlier, but it was more in conflict with the emerging standards of political decency than earlier when its use was more habitual and the royal power was more respected. The Americans became more sensitive to what constitutes birthright, and the French commoners felt more envy as privileges were felt less appropriate.

92. This model is used as a general explanatory model for the acceptance of humanitarian norms and human rights in the presence of collective vulnerability. See Elcheroth, "Les expériences," 52. The constitution provides protection against fundamental collective vulnerabilities, but it remains irrelevant or unacceptable for those who did not feel/were not vulnerable, and in particular benefited from other people's vulnerability.

93. Edna Ullmann-Margalit and Cass R. Sunstein, "Inequality and Indignation," *Philosophy & Public Affairs* 30, no. 4 (Fall 2001): 337–362.

94. Elias Canetti, *Crowds and Power*, trans. Carol Stewart (New York: Viking Penguin, 1984), 24.

95. Martha Nussbaum argued that "the relationship between compassion [the sentiment she was studying] and social institutions is and should be a two-way street: compassionate individuals construct institutions that embody what they imagine; and institutions, in turn influence the development of compassion in individuals." Martha Nussbaum, *Upheavals of Thought: The Intelligence of Emotions* (Cambridge: Cambridge University Press, 2001), 405.

96. *Furman v. Georgia*, 408 U.S. 238, 308 (1972) (Justice Potter Stewart, concurring). Stewart's position was that because of the desire for retribution capital punishment cannot be unconstitutional. He describes the result of frustrated emotions when sentiment is not allowed to operate in criminal law, in the following terms: "When people begin to believe that organized society is unwilling or unable to impose upon criminal offenders the punishment they 'deserve,' then there are sown the seeds of anarchy—of self-help, vigilante justice, and lynch law." See further Justice Blackmun's admittedly emotional dissent, where he found that notwithstanding his "abhorrence for the death penalty" he found himself bound by precedent. Ibid., 405.

97. William M. Reddy, *The Navigation of Feeling: A Framework for the History of Emotions* (Cambridge: Cambridge University Press, 2001), 124.

98. For details on the history of the regulation of display of passions at mass gatherings see Chapter 6.

99. Peter N. Stearns and Carol Z. Stearns, "Emotionology: Clarifying the History of Emotions and Emotional Standards," *American Historical Review* 90, no. 4 (October 1985): 813–836. In the Stearns' usage "emotionology" concerns social standards of emotion expression and management.

100. Susan A. Bandes, "The Heart Has Its Reasons: Examining the Strange Persistence of the American Death Penalty," Special Issue: Is the Death Penalty Dying? *Studies in Law, Politics and Society* 42, no. 1 (2008): 21–52, 43.

101. On the emotional aspects of mercy and pardon see Dan Markel, "Against Mercy," *Minnesota Law Review* 88, no. 6 (June 2004): 1421–1480; Stephanos

Bibas and Richard A. Bierschbach, "Integrating Remorse and Apology into Criminal Procedure," *Yale Law Journal* 114, no. 1 (October 2004): 85–148.

102. After World War II, constitutions were more concerned about putting pre-constitutional punishment beyond the reach of the constitution, and constitutional law was mobilized to enable the prosecution of malefactors beyond the ordinary statute of limitations. See, e.g., Germany. Lack of prosecution of war criminals or denial of compensation to certain social groups is often interpreted as the reiteration of the original humiliation and injustice.

103. Empirical findings raise serious doubts about the therapeutic value of trials in the case of mass atrocities. For additional difficulties of the treatment of past injustice, see Chapter 7 on shaming for mass atrocities.

104. Lucinda Aberdeen, "Positioning and Postcolonial Apologizing in Australia," in *The Self and Others: Positioning Individuals and Groups in Personal, Political, and Cultural Contexts*, ed. Rom Harré and Fathali Moghaddam (Westport, Conn.: Praeger, 2003), 189–198.

105. See the emotional reactions to the various and partly constitutionally mandated or supported justice and reparation programs after the collapse of totalitarian regimes following the end of World War II and of communism. Jon Elster, *Closing the Books: Transitional Justice in Historical Perspective* (New York: Cambridge University Press, 2004).

106. See the difficulties of the recognition of symbolic responsibility in Japan.

107. Beginning with the last third of the eighteenth century, certain rights (though at the level of generality) were taken to exist without specific reference to their location. What mattered was that reason had access to them.

108. Abraham Harold Maslow, *Motivation and Personality* (New York: Harper and Row, 1970), 129. "A basic human need logically gives rise to a right"—though Bay excluded desires from needs. Christian Bay, "Self-respect as a Human Right: Thoughts on the Dialectics of Wants and Needs in the Struggle for Human Community," *Human Rights Quarterly* 4, no. 1 (February 1982): 53–75, 67. See further Johan Galtung, *Human Rights in Another Key* (Oxford: Polity Press, 1994).

109. The legitimacy of rational theories in morals is not affected by the relative importance of the influence of reason on the acceptance and structuring of rights. Such intellectual endeavors of moral philosophers interested in the good life are, however, separate from the actual processes of rights structuring, although they are not without consequences for social selection of rights.

110. Ernst Cassirer, *The Philosophy of Enlightenment*, trans. James P. Pettegrove and Fritz C. A. Koelin (Princeton: Princeton University Press, 1951), 5–6. Hume too thought that the moral sense is common to all men. Gertrude Himmelfarb, *The Roads to Modernity* (New York: Knopf, 2005), 32–34.

111. Hume, *Enquiry*, 173. For a discussion of human nature-based human rights see Raimundo Panikkar, "Is the Notion of Human Rights a Western Concept?" *Diogenes* 120 (Winter 1982): 75–102. On anthropological universality see Donald Brown, *Human Universals* (San Francisco: McGraw-Hill, 1991). The taxonomy of common human characteristics remains controversial.

112. Ara Norenzayan and Steven J. Heine, "Psychological Universals: What Are They and How Can We Know?" *Psychological Bulletin* 131, no. 5 (September 2005): 763–784, 763.

113. It seems that there is a universal difference in the emotions according to gender that makes generalizations about the shared ground of morality and human rights even more complicated. Generally speaking, women are not interested in some of the moral emotions man are. In particular women are much less interested in revenge. For the biological differences see Louann Brizendine, *The Female Brain* (London: Bantam Books, 2007).

114. For the important cognitive mechanisms preventing the development of such emotions see Chapter 4.

115. John Locke, *An Essay Concerning Human Understanding* (London: Hackett, 1996), 15–16.

116. Rom Harré, ed., *The Social Construction of Emotions* (Oxford: Basil Blackwell, 1986), 12.

117. Dario Spini and Willem Doise, "Universal Rights and Duties as Normative Social Representations," in *The Psychology of Rights and Duties: Empirical Contributions and Normative Commentaries*, ed. Norman J. Finkel and Fathali M. Moghaddam (Washington, D.C.: American Psychological Association, 2005), 22.

118. See Michael Crowson, "Human Rights Attitudes: Dimensionality and Psychological Correlates," *Ethics and Behavior* 14, no. 3 (July 2004): 235–253.

119. Not all innate emotions have corresponding universal facial expression. Paul Ekman, "Basic Emotions," in *Handbook of Cognition and Emotion*, ed. Tim Dalgleish and Michael J. Power (New York: John Wiley & Sons, 1999), 45–60. For a criticism of basic emotions see Andrew Ortony and Terence J. Turner, "What's Basic about Basic Emotions?," *Psychological Review* 97, no. 3 (July 1990): 315–331.

120. Griffiths, *What Emotions Really Are;* Abigail A. Marsh, Nalini Ambady, and Robert E. Kleck, "The Effects of Fear and Anger Expressions of Approach- and Avoidance-Related Behaviours," *Emotion* 5, no. 1 (March 2005): 119–124; Hillary Anger Elfenbein and Nalini Ambady, "Is There an In-Group Advantage in Emotion Recognition?," *Psychological Bulletin* 128, no. 2 (March 2002): 243–249.

121. Boaventura De Sousa Santos, *Toward a New Common Sense: Law, Science, and Politics in the Paradigmatic Transition* (New York: Routledge, 1995); Will Kymlicka, *Liberalism, Community, and Culture* (Oxford: Clarendon Press, 1989).

122. Jerome Bruner, "Homo Sapiens, a Localized Species," *Behavioral and Brain Sciences* 28, no. 5 (October 2005): 694–695.

123. Sam McFarland and Melissa Mathews, "Do Americans Care about Human Rights?," *Journal of Human Rights* 4, no. 3 (July–September 2005): 305–319. (Americans steadily support the rights of their own minorities, women, and homosexual persons, but promoting and defending human rights abroad is attractive to only half of Americans (on average).

Where concerns of collective vulnerability guide public sentiment, the support for protective human rights increases. See Elcheroth, "Les expériences," 346.

124. Winnifred R. Louis and Donald M. Taylor, "Rights and Duties as Group Norms: Implications of Intergroup Research for the Study of Rights and Responsibilities," in *The Psychology of Rights*, ed. Finkel and Moghaddam, 105–134, 106. Louis and Taylor criticize universalism because in their belief "universal motivational and cognitive aspects of human psychology are behaviourally expressed in interaction with social norms that vary importantly by group membership within and across societies" (106). However, a survey of cross-national studies indicates some commonality in the endorsement of human rights. The majority view in most countries condemns human rights violations, at least on most fundamental issues of human rights. But this is far from a consensus, and intracultural differences are sometimes more important than intercultural ones; differences in personal value orientations explain to a considerable extent the intracultural variance. For a summary see Spini and Doise, "Universal Rights and Duties," 21–48.

125. Searle, *The Construction*, 45. According to a constitutive rule, certain pieces of paper (an object) issued by the Bureau of Engraving and Printing count as money as long as it is accepted in acts of collective intentionality. The difficulty with human rights is that they remain somewhat metaphysical: there is no object or observable conduct that will be handled by the constitutive rule. On the self-referentialism of human rights see András Sajó, "Ambiguities and Boundaries in Human Rights Knowledge Systems," in *Global Justice*, ed. Eisgruber and Sajó, 17–41.

126. Racial difference and inferiority as proto-scientific concepts were already advanced by Jefferson, and his position was taken up as uncontested truth by those who stood for sustaining slavery. On the impact of sociological crowd theories on the freedom of demonstration, see Chapter 6.

127. *Buck v. Bell*, 274 U.S. 200 (1927). "It is better for all the world, if instead of waiting to execute degenerate offspring for crime, or to let them starve for their imbecility, society can prevent those who are manifestly unfit from continuing their kind. The principle that sustains compulsory vaccination is broad enough to cover cutting the Fallopian tubes. . . . Three generations of imbeciles are enough." Cf. Paul A. Lombardo, "Three Generations, No Imbeciles: New Light on *Buck v. Bell*," *New York University Law Review* 60, no. 1 (April 1985): 50–62, arguing that Carrie Buck was a rape victim and not feeble-minded.

128. Dario Spini, Guy Elcheroth, and Rachel Fasel, "The Impact of Group Norms and Generalization of Risks across Groups on Judgments of War Behavior," *Political Psychology* 29, no. 6 (December 2008): 919–941. "Identification with all humanity positively predicts concern for universal human rights, contributions to international charities, activism in a human rights organization, and greater global knowledge." Derek Brown and Sam McFarland, "Identification with All Humanity and Selective Exposure to Humanitarian Concerns," Paper presented at the International Society of Political Psychology Annual Convention, Portland, Ore., 15 July 2007. <http://www.allacademic.com//meta/p_mla_apa_research_citation/2/0/4/7/1/pages204718/p204718-1.php> (3 May 2009).

129. Peter L. Berger, Brigitte Berger, and Hansfried Kellner, *The Homeless Mind: Modernization and Consciousness* (New York: Random House, 1973), 83.

130. Shklar, "The Liberalism of Fear," 34.

131. A troubling new development is that the increased interaction, the possibility of stronger interconnectedness with faraway non-human rights cultures, and ideologies of multicultural tolerance enable local ethnic communities of tolerant societies to disregard the universalistic human rights system of their country of residence, and reinstate the differing standards of the distant original community they had once physically abandoned, but have now emotionally recaptured.

132. Oakeshott, *Rationalism*, 61–69, 119–129. The counterargument is that there is a strong emotional difference between moral judgments of norm violation and conventional judgments on norm violation. James R. Blair, "A Cognitive Developmental Approach to Morality: Investigating the Psychopath," *Cognition* 57, no. 1 (October 1995): 1–29; Shaun Nichols, "Norms with Feeling: Towards a Psychological Account of Moral Judgment," *Cognition* 84, no. 2 (June 2002): 221–236.

133. Cf. John T. Jost and Orsolya Hunyadi, "The Psychology of System Justification and the Palliative Function of Ideology," *European Review of Social Psychology* 13, no. 1 (January 2003): 111–153.

134. Jerome Seymour Bruner, *Acts of Meaning* (Cambridge, Mass.: Harvard University Press, 1990), 47. "G. W. Allport . . . proposed that habits, once established, take on the role of motives: the seasoned sailor develops a desire to go to sea. . . ." (149).

135. Ibid., 47.

136. In order to avoid indignation and condemnation, a preferred strategy of legal change is category (classification) change. It is easier to sell the idea that pension rights should be granted to all couples including homosexual ones if this is presented in terms of the equality of all humans, while arguing that homosexual couples are not different from traditionally married couples generates, at least for a while, gut reactions of indignation and rejection.

137. Gerd Gigerenzer, "Moral Intuition = Fast and Frugal Heuristics?" in *Moral Psychology*, Vol. 2. *The Cognitive Science of Morality: Intuition and Diversity*, ed. Walter Sinnott-Armstrong (Cambridge, Mass.: MIT Press, 2008), 1–26.

138. Following Montaigne and Pascal, Derrida talks about the "mystical foundation of authority." "Custom creates the whole of equity, for the simple reason that it is accepted. It is the mystical foundation of its authority; whoever carries it back to first principles destroys it." Jacques Derrida, "Force of Law: The 'Mystical Foundation of Authority,'" in *Deconstruction and the Possibility of Justice*, ed. Drucilla Cornell, Michel Rosenfeld, and David Gray Carlson (New York: Routledge, 1992), 12–13; Blaise Pascal, *Thoughts, Letters, and Minor Works* (New York: Kessinger, 2004), 105.

139. Ullmann-Margalit and Sunstein, "Inequality," 356.

140. Jürgen Habermas, *Time of Transitions*, trans. Max Pensky (Oxford: Polity Press, 2006), 26–27.

141. Jana Schaich Borg, Debra Lieberman, and Kent A. Kiehl, "Infection, Incest, and Iniquity: Investigating the Neural Correlates of Disgust and Morality," *Journal of Cognitive Neuroscience* 20, no. 9 (September 2008): 1529–1546, 1530.

142. Symbols are particularly successful in triggering habitual responses. David O. Sears, Carl P. Hensler, and Leslie K. Speer, "Whites' Opposition to 'Busing': Self-Interest or Symbolic Politics," *American Political Science Review* 73, no. 2 (June 1979): 369–384, 371.

143. Some scholars claim that the emotion felt is described as anger and the reason offered by the subject is based on some presumption of symbolic harm, in the national symbol context harming the (imaginary) community. Roberto Gutierrez and Roger Giner-Sorolla, "Anger, Disgust, and Presumption of Harm as Reactions to Taboo-Breaking Behaviors," *Emotion* 7, no. 4 (November 2007): 853–868, 865.

144. Shaun Nichols, *Sentimental Rules: On the Natural Foundations of Moral Judgment* (Oxford: Oxford University Press, 2004), 132.

145. Many American citizens were ready to trade off civil liberties for the promise of greater security. Darren W. Davis and Brian D. Silver, "Civil Liberties vs. Security: Public Opinion in the Context of the Terrorist Attacks on America," *American Journal of Political Science* 48, no. 1 (January 2004): 28–46.

146. See *Cohen v. California*, 403 U.S. 15 (1971), *Texas v. Johnson*, 491 U.S. 397 (1989), *Tinker v. Des Moines School District*, 393 U.S. 503 (1969).

147. Leon R. Kass, "The Wisdom of Repugnance," *New Republic* 216, no. 22 (June 1997): 17–26.

148. Cheshire Calhoun, "Making Up Emotional People: The Case of Romantic Love," in *The Passions*, ed. Bandes, 217–239, 223; Alison M. Jaggar, "Love and Knowledge: Emotions in Feminist Epistemology," in *Gender/Body/Knowledge: Feminist Reconstructions of Being and Knowing*, ed. Alison M. Jaggar and Susan R. Bordo (New Brunswick: Rutgers University Press, 1989), 145–171, 160.

149. Bruner, *Acts*, 47.

150. Mr. Justice Frankfurter's concurring opinion in *Louisiana ex rel. Francis v. Resweber*, 329 U.S. 459, 471 (1947). (Sending Francis a second time to the electric chair, when the machine failed the first time, is not cruel and unusual punishment.)

151. A 2005 Westlaw search found the word "sentiment" in 583 judgments of the Supreme Court (from the beginning); out of this, 395 were from the period after 1900. "Emotion" is mentioned in 180 documents, 174 of them after 1900, but only 12 after 1995.

152. *DeShaney v. Winnebago Cty. DSS*, 489 U.S. 189, 212, 202–203 (1989).

For a sympathetic reading see Benjamin Zipursky, "DeShaney and the Jurisprudence of Compassion," *New York University Law Review* 65, no. 4 (October 1990): 1101–1149 (arguing that compassion enables the understanding of the parties' perspective, in this case what amounts to deprivation).

Justice Blackmun, relying on Robert M. Cover, *Justice Accused: Antislavery and the Judicial Process* (New Haven: Yale University Press, 1975), referred to antebellum judges who were morally outraged by slavery but believed that they had to be guided by formalism in fugitive slave cases. The tragedy of formalism indicates that law should have a non-negationist strategy for the appropriate use of emotions in decision.

153. Laurence Tribe, "Revisiting the Rule of Law," *New York University Law Review* 64, no. 3 (June 1989): 729–730. This was the position of Justice Blackmun's passionate dissent: "compassion need not be exiled from the province of judging." Zipursky, "DeShaney," 203.

154. *In re guardianship of Theresa Marie Schiavo Incapacitated. Robert Schindler and Mary Schindler v. Michael Schiavo*, No. 2D00–1269. January 24, 2001. In the District Court of Appeal of Florida, Second District.

155. *California v. Brown*, 479 U.S. 538, 545 (1986). See further with additional literature Bandes, "The Heart Has Its Reasons."

156. Heidi Kitrosser, "Containing Unprotected Speech," *Florida Law Review* 57, no. 4 (September 2005): 843–905, 893.

157. *Louisiana ex rel. Francis v. Resweber*, 329 U.S. 459, 471–472 (1947) (Justice Frankfurter concurring).

158. "The [Eighth] Amendment must draw its meaning from the evolving standards of decency that mark the progress of a maturing society." *Trop v. Dulles*, 356 U.S. 86, 101 (1958); *Coker v. Georgia*, 433 U.S. 584, 592 (1977).

159. *Furman v. Georgia*, 408 U.S. 238, 332 (1972) (Justice Marshall concurring). *Atkins v. Virginia*, 536 U.S. 304, 316 (2002).

160. See *Lawrence v. Texas*, 539 U.S. 558 (2003).

161. *Texas v. Johnson*, 755 S. W. 2d. 97, quoted affirmatively *Texas v. Johnson*, 491 U.S. 397, 401 (1989).

162. Elizabeth Anderson, "Moral Heuristics: Rigid Rules or Flexible Inputs in Moral Deliberation?," *Behavioral and Brain Sciences* 28, no. 4 (August 2005): 544–545, 545. ("our task is to design decision-making institutions so that our heuristics function.")

163. Mill, *On Liberty*, 64, 67.

164. The obligations-based legal system is not a late totalitarian invention. Note that in 1789 the French Assembly was short a hundred votes to opt for a Declaration of Duties as suggested by delegates influenced by Church teachings.

165. Joshua Dressler, "Hating Criminals: How Can Something That Feels So Good Be Wrong?" *Michigan Law Review* 88, no. 6 (May 1990): 1448–1473 ("assaultive retribution . . . treats the criminal as a hated person without rights"), 1453. See further Jeffrie G. Murphy and Jean Hampton, *Forgiveness and Mercy* (New York: Cambridge University Press, 1988).

166. Robert Solomon, "Justice v. Vengeance: On Law and the Satisfaction of Emotion," in *The Passions*, ed. Bandes, 123–148, 131.

167. Evil grows in our human interaction from our ordinary emotions. "Aurel Kolnai . . . showed how Nazi ideals and the prodigious evils into which they led represented not so much the inexplicable efflorescence of other-worldly Evil as an unmysterious product of the exaggerated emphasis on certain positive human values—values of patriotism, of national and cultural unity. . . . These were real values, . . . even when they were relentlessly pursued and promoted at the expense of ordinary pedestrian values such as justice, humanity, charity. . . ." David Wiggins, *Ethics. Twelve Lectures on the Philosophy of Morality* (London: Penguin Books, 2006), 61.

2. A Sentimental *Déclaration* of the Rights of Man

1. Beyond positive law (that is, beyond that to which one may refer before a court), the Declaration remained an inevitable point of departure in France (and outside it as well). For this very reason, it soon came to influence the operations of the French Conseil d'État (Council of State)—without binding positive legal force—until ultimately becoming, in 1958, an official component of the French Constitution, and, beginning in 1971, of more or less direct applicability in constitutional review.

2. *AP*, VIII 284 <www.gallica.fr> (1 March 2009).

3. Edmund Burke, *Reflections on the Revolution in France* (Harmondsworth, Middlesex: Penguin Books, 1969), 175. Himmelfarb claims that for Burke the whole French Revolution "was nothing less than a moral revolution, a total revolution, a revolution of sentiment and sensibility penetrating into every aspect of life." Gertrude Himmelfarb, *The Roads to Modernity* (New York: Knopf, 2005), 91.

4. The decree of January 24, 1789, was drawn up by Necker. It calls for the convening of a consultative body and distinguishes the Estates. It also puts forth the principle of numerical proportionality between representatives and those represented: it would establish "an assembly representative of the entire nation." See François Furet, *Revolutionary France 1770–1880*, trans. Antonia Nevill (Oxford: Blackwell, 1992), 55.

Emmanuel Joseph Sieyès's pamphlets of 1788–1789 militate for popular representation: "Essai sur les privilèges," November 1788; "Vues sur les moyens d'exécution dont les représentants de la France pourront disposer en 1789"; "Qu'est-ce que le Tiers État?" January 1789.

The King too greets the participants at the opening of the assembly of the Estates-General as representatives of "the Nation". It is noticeable that the King speaks the language of the emotions in his opening address. He talks of an "exalted public mood" and praises the sensitivity—*sensibilité*—of the first two Orders, which led them to renounce their fiscal privileges.

5. The words of Clermont-Tonnerre in the statement of the Constitution Committee, 27 July, 1789, *AP*, VIII 283–284, cited after Keith M. Baker, "Constitution," in *A Critical Dictionary of the French Revolution*, ed. François Furet and Mona Ozouf, trans. Arthur Goldhammer (Cambridge, Mass.: Belknap Press of Harvard University Press, 1989), 479–493, 483.

6. Barentin presents the King's program, *AP*, VIII 3. I cite the debates according to the *AP*.

7. For Pitkin, the constitution is a function of actual societal identity, having an unambiguously psychological dimension. Hanna Fenichel Pitkin, "The Idea of a Constitution," *Journal of Legal Education* 37, no. 2 (1987): 167–169, 167. Pitkin admits that the American Constitution is something that is enacted, however; "how we are able to constitute ourselves is profoundly tied to how we are already constituted by our own distinctive history" (169). "Thus," she concludes, "there is a sense . . . in which our constitution is sacred and demands our respectful acknowledgement. If we mistake who we are, our efforts at constitutive action will fail" (169).

8. Furet, *Revolutionary France*, 50–51. (italics mine).

9. Jacques Necker, *De l'administration des finances de la France* (Paris: Panckouke, 1784), quoted ibid., 53–54.

10. Even so, the makers of the Constitution refer to themselves as the representatives of the French people in the Preamble to the Declaration.

11. In Taine's view, the representatives accepted Rousseau's teaching out of weakness, and led by a sense of faith. They considered themselves responsible to their constituents, to the people, whom they felt they saw in the agitators in the gallery and the coffeehouse leaders. Hippolyte Taine, *Les origines de la France contemporaine. La révolution*, Volume I (Paris: Hachette, 1904), 57, 145, 150; for the Camille Desmoulins citation see ibid., 146.

12. *AP*, VIII 146.

13. Simon Schama, *Citizens: A Chronicle of the French Revolution* (New York: Knopf, 1989), 367–368.

14. *AP*, VIII 124, 16 June 1789.

15. Neither the King himself nor Sieyès considered the mandates formulated in the *cahiers* to have binding force, but the Assembly's position was that representatives must request release from their mandates individually. In Sieyès's view, the representational mandate came from the nation as a whole.

16. The dispatch of officers was ordered, for example, to manage the dissatisfaction arising from high grain prices, see *AP*, VIII 136; at Mirabeau's recommendation, they protest the troop concentrations in a message to the King of July 9. *AP*, VIII 212, 9 July, 1789.

17. *AP*, VIII 214. In light of two centuries of constitutional legal debate, such doubts and uncertainty are entirely justified.

18. *AP*, VIII 222.

19. Lafayette, *AP*, VIII 221.

20. E.g., *AP*, VIII 224. The exercise of constituent power meant the exercise of sovereignty, though this was to be exercised by distributing it. But a constituent power as sovereign power may exercise the not yet allocated power. See Arnaud Le Pillouer, *Les pouvoirs non-constituants des assemblées constituantes: Essai sur le pouvoir instituant* (Paris: Dalloz, 2005).

21. Cf. Schama, *Citizens*, 448.

22. *AP*, VIII 235.

23. Quoted by Schama, *Citizens*, 446–447.

24. *AP*, VIII 252, 266.

25. Mirabeau, *AP*, VIII 274, 294.

According to Taine, at least 120 representatives had fled by October 1789, about half of them carrying passports. When votes were recast soon thereafter—a matter of days—the minority opposition votes had disappeared, clearing the way for unified national enthusiasm and common will.

26. Gouverneur Morris's letter to George Washington, Paris, 24 January 1790. <http://www.familytales.org/dbDisplay.php?id=ltr_gom4582&person=gom> (4 May 2009).

27. Jeremy Jennings: "The Déclaration des droits de l'homme et du citoyen and Its Critics in France: Reactions and Idéologie," *Historical Journal* 35, no. 4 (1992): 839–859, 846.

28. *AP*, VIII 333, 3 August. Already on July 28 there was a feeling that "France is writhing in anarchy," *AP*, VIII 292.

29. *AP*, VIII 336–339.

30. *AP*, VIII 343.

31. Before dawn of the previous morning, on August 4, some 100–120 representatives at their regular coffeehouse tables decided to propose a nullification of feudal privileges. This was in line with the instructions given in the original Breton *cahiers.*

The Club Breton was the first party-like organization in the Constituent Assembly, and was the first to demand a unification of the Three Estates.

32. Quoted in Archibald Alison, *History of Europe from the Commencement of the French Revolution in MDCCLXXXIX to the Restoration of the Bourbons in MDCCCXV*, Volume I (Edinburgh: William Blackwood and Sons, 1899), 590.

33. See John Emerich Edward Dalberg-Acton, *Lectures on the French Revolution* (Kitchener: Batoche Books, 1999), 94.

34. Robert de Crèvecoeur, ed., *Le journal d'Adrien Duquesnoy*, Volume I (Paris: A. Picard, 1894), 269. Cf. Fred Morrow Fling, "The Authorship of the Journal of Adrien Duquesnoy," *American Historical Review* 8, no. 1 (October 1902): 70–77.

35. Comte de Mirabeau, *Le Courrier de Provence*, no. 24 (1789). At the sight of collective frenzy Lally Tollendal suggests that the president close the session, in vain.

Among contemporaries perhaps the most frequently used term to describe these events is "enthusiasm." According to Assembly minutes, after delegate Le Guen, dressed in peasant garb, read his speech "all were swept up with the enthusiasm." *AP*, VIII 346. The reading—and the outfit—do not exactly suggest spontaneity on the part of the speaker. As for the enthusiasm, see also the Marquis de Ferrières's letter of August 7, in which he recalls this session as the most memorable of all, "an exemplar of France's noble enthusiasm":

"The unfortunate circumstances in which the nobility find themselves, the insurrection raised in all parts against them, the provinces of Franche-Comté, Dauphiné, Burgundy, Alsace, Normandy, and Limousin, agitated by the most violent convulsions, and partly devastated, more than one hundred and fifty castles burned, seigniorial titles sought out furiously, and burned, the impossibility of opposing the torrent of the Revolution, the misfortunes that would result from even a futile resistance, the ruin of the most beautiful kingdom of Europe, in the prey of anarchy and devastation, and above all, the love of country innate in the hearts of the French, a love which is an imperative duty for the nobility, obliged by state and honor, to sacrifice their wealth and their very lives, for the King and the Nation, all prescribed for us the conduct we must follow." A letter from the Marquis de Ferrières (a delegate of Samur's noblemen), in Marquis de Ferrières, *Correspondance inédite, 1789, 1790, 1791*, trans. Lloyd Benson (Paris: Armand Colin, 1932), 113–119. <http://facweb.furman.edu/~bensonlloyd/FerriersLetter7August1789.htm> (9 February, 2009).

The King himself, when rejecting the injustice of this deprivation of rights, writes thus to the Archbishop of Arles: "I think my concession to providence shall be that I do not give in to the enthusiasm that has overcome all order." <http://www.royet.org/nea1789–1794/archives/documents_divers/louis16_lettre_archeveque_arles_4aout_xx_08_89.htm> (9 February 2009).

36. "Ivresse" means drunkenness, and the contemporary notes of antirevolutionary authors refer to high levels of alcohol consumption. See Patrick Kessel, *La nuit du 4 août 1789* (Paris: Arthaud, 1969), 192–195.

The panic and exaltation do not rule out that some people, and the Club Breton members in particular, felt genuine sympathy for the suffering of the poor. Given that the prevailing culture favored sentimentalism, people described their acts in sentimental terms and believed, at least to some extent, their own description. It is not surprising that both Arendt and Reddy describe August 4 in terms of compassion and find that August 4 is the consequence of sentimentalism. Hannah Arendt, *On Revolution* (London: Penguin Classics, 1990); William M. Reddy, *The Navigation of Feeling: A Framework for the History of Emotions* (New York: Cambridge University Press, 2001).

37. François Furet, "Night of August 4," in *Critical Dictionary*, 107–114, 108.

38. Acton, *French Revolution*, 84. Lord Acton quotes Henri comte de Virieu: "There are only two means of calming an excited populace, kindness and force. We have no force; we hope to succeed by kindness."

39. Maillot, July 18, 1789, in reference to the Foulon lynching. Quoted in Timothy Tackett, "Nobles and Third Estate in the Revolutionary Dynamic of the National Assembly: 1789–1790," *American Historical Review* 94, no. 2 (1989): 271–301, 280. On the omnipresence of fear see Kessel, *La nuit*, 195.

40. Mirabeau, *Le Courrier de Provence*, no. 24, 2–3.

41. Jules Michelet, *History of the French Revolution*, trans. Charles Cook (Chicago: University of Chicago Press, 1967), 243. Elster in particular emphasizes the importance of envy. Jon Elster, "The Making of the Declaration of 1789" (manuscript). As to the feudal privileges: "Whereas the vertical relations generated hatred [in the Third Estate representatives], the horizontal ones caused envy." Cf. Tackett, "Nobles," 282.

Consider also the view of the Marquis de Ferrières: "The cities imitate the provinces: the deputies are bursting from the promptings that tyrannize them. It seems that a sentiment of hatred, and a blind drive for vengeance, rather than a love of the good, are driving spirits." Marquis de Ferrières, *Mémoires du Marquis de Ferrières, avec une notice sur sa vie, des notes et des éclaircissemens historiques*, Volume I (Paris: Baudouin, 1822), 186.

42. *AP*, VIII 347. The delegates from Provence wish to return to their constituents for instruction. Dijon wants territorial and representational autonomy. In this regard, all insist that one unified set of regulations—the Constitution—applies throughout France.

43. This would naturally require the commitment of those involved, and opportunities bestowed by institutions. In some cases, the session president, pointing to procedural rules, disallows any fresh debate on already published—but far from unambiguous—decisions.

44. Not even the priesthood wanted this state-provided solution any longer, because if the state were to pay the priests, it would obviously cover only bare necessities. This explains why they attempted to classify the tithe as a right of property.

45. According to the French tradition of Gallicanism, the ruler (and later the state, as his legal successor) holds power over the Church, to the detriment of the Pope at Rome.

46. Furet, *Revolutionary France*, 72.

47. Louis Adolphe Thiers, *Histoire de la Révolution Française*, Volume I (Paris: Furne & Cie, 1839), 149. See further Mirabeau, *AP*, VIII 639. It was common knowledge among contemporaries in the first days of August that the vote on August 4 was about the Declaration. Kessel, *La nuit*, 230.

48. Within the Constituent Assembly, many members considered the Declaration to be dangerous, or at least superfluous; outside the Assembly, the significance of the Declaration was far from obvious. Public opinion was partly critical: the pamphlets of Paris make all metaphysical efforts ridiculous. Many also oppose the Declaration because they fear the anarchy of freedom. See Antoine de Baecque, "Le choc des opinions: Le dèbat des droits de l'homme, juillet-août 1789," in *L'an 1 des droits de l'homme*, ed. Antoine de Baecque, Wolfgang Schmale, and Michel Vovelle (Paris: Presses du CRNS, 1988), 17.

49. According to Baecque, this text was chosen because the thirty-man committee's proposals (as a result of its composition) were, in contrast to the proposals of individuals, a fit for the relations of power and inclinations within the Assembly, and for the compromises to which it was inclined.

50. For example, Art. 3 of Target's Draft mentioned honor together with life, liberty, and property, and it is mentioned again separately to emphasize that all men have equal right to honor (Art. 14). Baecque, "Le choc des opinions," 81.

51. *AP*, VIII 407–408, 12 August, 1789.

52. *AP*, VIII 476, 23 August, 1789.

53. *AP*, VIII 472, de Laborde, 22 August, 1789.

54. *AP*, VIII 480. To this, the bishop of Lydda proposes that these truths find a place in the Constitution (which is where every issue finding no consensus is temporarily shunted), but that nonetheless the principle ensuring religions freedom should be qualified by the proviso that religious practice shall not disturb public order. It went without saying that the Catholic religion posed no such threat.

55. *L'an 1 des droits de l'homme*, ed. Baecque, Schmale, and Vovelle, 159.

56. Ibid., 30.

57. *AP*, VIII 427. "Projet de Gouges-Cartou, 12 August, 1789." Sieyès finds the basis for these principles in human nature.

58. Here is one typical example from the commission of Sénéchausée, the district of D'Agenois, to the Third Estate: "Finally the fortunate day has arrived when reason, philosophy, and humanity recover their long-neglected rights with the restoration of liberty. . . ." *AP*, I 686. Demands are justified by experience of past injustice.

59. Jennings, "The Déclaration des droits," 840.

60. Jean-Paul-Rabaut Saint-Etienne, *Précis historique de la Révolution Française* (Paris: Treuttel et Wuertz, 1792), 200. Quoted ibid.

61. "They had to descend from the most abstract principles to the most materialistic application of equality. . . ." Rivarol, *Journal Politique National*, no. 1, 9, quoted in Kessel, *La nuit*, 131.

62. Ernst Cassirer, *The Philosophy of Enlightenment* (Princeton: Princeton University Press, 1951), 5–6.

63. In the words of Thouret's draft of August 1, "the ineluctable need and desire for happiness has been placed in the hearts of men," and the political society is a means to achieving this goal of the heart. *AP*, VIII 323.

Mention of emotion (*sensibilité*), the testimony of feeling, is at least as frequent in the 1789 debates as references to reason.

64. Roland Mortier, "Unité ou scission du siècle des Lumiéres?," in Roland Mortier, *Clartés et ombres du siècle des Lumières: Etudes sur le XVIII siècle littéraire* (Geneva: Droz, 1969), 114–124. David J. Denby, *Sentimental Narrative and the Social Order in France, 1760–1820* (New York: Cambridge University Press, 1994).

65. See Reddy, *Navigation of Feeling*. Feelings that slowly consolidate in a community become manifested in the longer term through abstract, conceptual modes of expression.

66. Roger Barny, *Les contradictions de l'idéologie révolutionnaire des droits de l'homme 1789–1796: Droit naturel et histoire* (Annales Littéraires de l'Université de Besançon, no. 493) (Paris: Diffusion, Les Belles Lettres, 1993), 17.

67. Cf. ibid., 14.

68. Susan Maslan, "The Anti-Human: Man and Citizen before the Declaration of the Rights of Man and of the Citizen," *South-Atlantic Quarterly* 103, no. 2–3 (2004): 357–374, 362.

69. Cf. Schama, *Citizens*, 203–247.

70. Jean-Antoine-Nicolas de Caritat Condorcet, *Lettres d'un bourgeois de New-Haven* (Paris: Collé, 1788); Jean-Antoine-Nicolas de Caritat Condorcet, ed. Arthur O'Connor and François Arago, *Œuvres de Condorcet*, Volume XIII (Paris: Firmin Didot frères, 1847), 14. Jean-Antoine-Nicolas de Caritat Condorcet, *Condorcet: Foundations of Social Choice and Political Theory*, trans. Iain McLean and Fiona Hewitt (Aldershot: E. Elgar, 1994), 294.

71. The nation as an abstract entity cannot express itself without its representatives. The idea that the representatives could be bound by the nation is an impossible paradox. (Michel Troper, personal communication).

72. Jean-Antoine-Nicolas de Caritat Condorcet, "Essai sur la constitution et les fonctions des Assemblées provinciales," in *Œuvres de Condorcet*, XIII, ed. O'Connor and Arago, 47. This view is countered by that of Sieyès, which furthers national sentiment instead; its nation-oriented concepts of mandate and sovereignty found easy success.

73. *AP*, VIII 221, 11 July.

74. *AP*, VIII 422, Article 7 of Sieyès's draft of the Declaration (12 August). Several other drafts provide that sentiments are protected together with thoughts in the freedom of expression and/or freedom of religion articles. See *L'an 1 des droits de l'homme*, ed. Baecque, Schmale, and Vovelle, 240, 243, 262.

75. See Robespierre's speech of September 12, 1789: "the people cannot completely exercise its rights/power in any way other than the appointment of representatives; . . . nothing is more natural than the desire to practice these rights and to make its feelings known." *AP*, VIII 617.

76. On May 7, Mirabeau begins publishing the *Journal des Estates-Genereaux.* The government bans it immediately. "The next day [Mirabeau] started a newspaper [*The Letters of M. Mirabeau to His Constituents*], in the shape of a report to his constituents, and when the Government attempted to suppress it, he succeeded, on May 19, in establishing the liberty of the press." Acton, *French Revolution*, 55. Mirabeau simply disregarded the government order, and the government was too weak to take action against him.

77. Schama, *Citizens*, 363. Mirabeau was the one who emphasized the theatrical feel of the Assembly in his *Aperçu* addressed to Montmorin of December 23, 1790. Already Necker had planned the assembly of Estates to be a pleasing, dignified spectacle. Cf. Taine, *Les origines*, 176.

3. "The Greatest of All Reflections on Human Nature"

1. Beyond the emotions management function that is emphasized here, constitutions have social conflict management functions, where rational considerations do play their role. Constitutions also are (may be) reasonable (efficient) answers to irrational (inefficient) public and political behavior.

2. Bernard Bailyn, *The Ideological Origins of the American Revolution* (Cambridge, Mass.: Harvard University Press, 1967), 120. See further William N. Eskridge and John Ferejohn, "Structuring Lawmaking to Reduce Cognitive Bias: A Critical View," *Cornell Law Review* 87, no. 2 (January 2002): 616–647, 638. "The Framers . . . wanted energetic governance but were *fearful* of an overbearing government and of radical, year-to-year shifts in state policies and rules" [emphasis added].

3. Max Farrand, *The Framing of the Constitution of the United States*, Volume I (New Haven: Yale University Press, 1913), 94.

Randolph argued that "some check therefore was to be sought for against this tendency of our Governments [to be ruled by passionate proceedings]." Randolph, in Max Farrand, *Records of the Federal Convention of 1787*, Volume I–II (New Haven: Yale University Press, 1911), 51.

4. James Madison, *Debates*, June 1. <http://www.yale.edu/lawweb/avalon/debates/601.asp> (19 April 2009) [emphasis added]; Farrand, *Framing*, I, 19 [emphasis added]; Farrand, *Framing*, II, 646–647 [emphasis added].

5. Martin H. Redish and Elizabeth J. Cisar, "'If Angels Were to Govern': The Need for Pragmatic Formalism in Separation of Powers Theory," *Duke Law Journal* 41, no. 3 (December 1991): 449, 451.

6. U.S. Constitution, Article 1, section 10, clause 1, 12, 15, 16. See Leonard L. Richards, *Shays's Rebellion. The American Revolution's Final Battle* (Philadelphia: University of Pennsylvania Press, 2001), 135.

7. ". . . human rights were the chief knowledge of the times when it [the Articles of Confederation] was framed so far as they applied to oppose Great Britain." Randolph, in Max Farrand, *Records*, I, 26.

8. John Phillip Reid, *Constitutional History of the American Revolution*, Volume I, *The Authority of Rights* (Madison: University of Wisconsin Press, 1986), 25.

9. Lansing in Farrand, *Records*, I, 250.

In later periods constitution-making was increasingly viewed as professional legal or political work, in the sense of creating viable compromise among power-holding groups, but psychological assumptions continued to play an important role, as in the case of excluding referenda and insisting on the supremacy of dignity in the making of the Federal Constitution of Germany.

10. John Adams, "Thoughts on Government, and Letter to John Penn" (1776), in *Papers of John Adams*, Volume IV, ed. Robert J. Taylor, et al. (Cambridge, Mass.: Belknap Press of Harvard University Press, 1977), 86–93, 90. As to Paine see Thomas Paine, *Rights of Man. Common Sense and Other Political Writings* (Oxford: Oxford University Press, 1995).

11. David Hume, *Essays: Moral, Political and Literary*, ed. Eugene F. Miller (Indianapolis: Liberty Classics, 1987), 42 (first published 1742). See further Morton Gabriel White, *Philosophy, The Federalist, and the Constitution* (New York: Oxford University Press, 1987), 98.

12. James Madison, "The Utility of the Union as a Safeguard against Domestic Faction and Insurrection (continued)," *Federalist Papers*, No. 10 (New York: Penguin, Mentor, 1961), 77–78. (Factions bring instability, injustice, and confusion.)

Elbridge Gerry, referring to the troubles of Shays's Rebellion: "The evils we experience flow from the excess of democracy." Farrand, *Records*, I, 48.

13. See, for example Wilson in Farrand, *Records*, I, 74; Hamilton in Farrand, *Records*, I, 285, 376; Lansing in Farrand, *Records*, I, 250; Morris in Farrand, *Records*, I, 74, 514. Franklin, too, argued based on a theory of passions though his understanding was closer to a traditional virtue theory. He too singled out negative features, namely ambition and avarice, as constitutional cornerstones. Farrand, *Records*, I, 82.

In the folk psychology of the French Revolution, fear was stamped as a very negative sentiment, one not to be manipulated but expelled. Bergasse, charged to present the draft of the Constitution's chapter on the judiciary, begins his structural arguments by calling fear the most corrupting human sentiment. *AP*, VIII 440 (August 17, 1789). Dumont considered unsustainable the abolition of feudalism because it was only a dictate of fear. Mirabeau warns against writing a "declaration of war against tyranny . . . guided by resentments created by the abuses of despotism." *AP*, VIII 438 (August 17, 1789).

14. *Notes of Major William Pierce (Georgia) in the Federal Convention of 1787.* <http://www.yale.edu/lawweb/avalon/const/pierce.htm> (19 April 2009).

Constitutions are perceived as tools of emotion management in France as well. When in 1789 Mirabeau reports on behalf of the drafting committee (committee of five) charged to present the draft of the Declaration, he says that the Declaration has to be of use to a people unprepared for liberty because of the "impression of facts" and not because of lack of reasoning. In conformity with the tenor of the day, Mirabeau set the constitution-makers the task of defining what pertains to human nature generally, not to local variations. This is not the only strategy for handling public sentiments. The alternative is to deny and exile them, perhaps together with those who share such sentiments: this became the prevalent approach in the French Revolution.

15. James Madison, "The Utility of the Union as a Safeguard against Domestic Faction and Insurrection (continued)," *The Federalist*, November 22, 1787, No. 10 [emphasis added].

16. James Madison, "The Structure of the Government Must Furnish the Proper Checks and Balances between the Different Departments," *The Federalist*, February 6, 1788, No. 51, 322.

17. In many regards the founding fathers could rely on the states' experiences; in other respects though, the Constitution was denying solutions developed at the state level, especially in regard to popular-revolutionary solutions. See Robert F. Williams, "The State Constitutions of the Founding Decade: Pennsylvania's Radical 1776 Constitution and Its Influences on American Constitutionalism," *Temple Law Review* 62, no. 2 (Summer 1989): 541–574; Christian G. Fritz, "Recovering the Lost Worlds of America's Written Constitutions," *Albany Law Review* 68, no. 2 (2005): 261–293.

18. Carl Schmitt, *The Crisis of Parliamentary Democracy*, trans. Ellen Kennedy (London: MIT Press, 1985), 16–17.

19. See, e.g., Governeur Morris, July 17, Farrand, *Records*, II, 25. For the use of the term in France, see Chapter 2.

20. "Of all the suggested constitutional innovations in Pennsylvania, possibly the most sobering was *rejected* in the constitutional convention: 'That an enormous Proportion of Property vested in a few individuals is dangerous to the Rights, and destructive of the Common Happiness of Mankind; and therefore every free State hath a Right by its Laws to discourage the Possession of such Property.' " Williams, "The State Constitutions," 557.

Rhode Island and Vermont offered "dangerous examples" tempting to many, even in Massachusetts, which finally opted (in a controversial ratification process) for a quite aristocratic bicameral system. Many town hall democracies disregarded the Massachusetts Constitution, finding it completely irrelevant. Egalitarian ambitions and sentiments played a similarly destabilizing role in French constitution-making. The 1791 French Constitution restricted the franchise at the price of great logical inconsistency, but in the revolutionary enthusiasm of 1793 egalitarianism prevailed. Universal male suffrage followed (though the Constitution itself was adopted in open ballot).

21. Rufus King to James Madison, January 22, 1788. Quoted in Richards, *Shays's Rebellion*, 143.

22. See Chapter 2.

23. Shaun Nichols, *Sentimental Rules: On the Natural Foundations of Moral Judgment* (New York: Oxford University Press, 2004), 125.

24. Shared experiences of fear create a common point of reference, one of nearly irresistible force. Such shared fear generates a common understanding that sometimes

develops into quasi-taboo. Such taboo may be constitutionalized which, if invoked, has the power of a conversation stopper, as happened during Nazi terror.

25. Robert Solomon, "Emotions, Thoughts, and Feelings: What Is a 'Cognitive Theory' of the Emotions and Does It Neglect Affectivity?," in *Philosophy and the Emotions*, ed. Anthony Hatzimoysis (Cambridge.: Cambridge University Press, 2003), 1–18, 2; Nico Frijda, *The Emotions* (Cambridge: Cambridge University Press, 1986), 173 (quoted approvingly in Jon Elster, *Strong Feelings: Emotion, Addiction, and Human Behavior* [Cambridge, Mass.: MIT Press, 1999], 37).

Other people's fear is not the only emotion that serves as information. Anger, resentment, and hatred can also serve common orientation. In the early days of the French Revolution it was resentment that created at least a limited shared understanding of what *equal* fundamental rights should be.

26. On empathy, see Chapter 4.

27. Jesse Prinz, *Gut Reactions: A Perceptual Theory of Emotion* (Oxford: Oxford University Press, 2004), 49.

28. ". . . The amygdala is involved when there is a cognitive awareness of the aversive properties of events acquired without direct aversive experience. . . ." Elizabeth A. Phelps, "The Interaction of Emotion and Cognition: The Relation between the Human Amygdala and Cognitive Awareness," in *The New Unconscious*, ed. Ran R. Hassin, James S. Uleman, and John A. Bargh (Oxford: Oxford University Press, 2005), 61–76, 67. On learned emotional reactions see Antonio R. Damasio, *The Feeling of What Happens: Body and Emotion in the Making of Consciousness* (New York: Harcourt Brace, 1999).

29. Many delegates to the French Assembly shared past fears generated by the dreaded *lettre de cachet* (royal arrest warrant), actual persecution, and humiliation; outrage and fear were generated by judicial murder dictated by bigotry.

30. "This emotional response to the fear and disgust of others has obvious advantages for survival. If someone looks afraid, then we should be vigilant since there is probably something nearby that we too should avoid." Chris D. Frith and Tania Singer, "The Role of Social Cognition in Decision Making," *Philosophical Transactions of the Royal Society B* 363, no. 1511 (12 December 2008): 3875–3886, 3877.

31. Robert Solomon, *Not Passion's Slave: Emotions and Choice* (Oxford: Oxford University Press, 2003), 206.

32. Social panic played a crucial rule on the fateful night of August 4, 1789 in Paris; it may be of relevance in less dramatic contexts as well.

33. Paul Slovic attributes human distortion of risky events to "intuitive judgments, emotional responses, and other subtle, nonconscious reactions to external stimuli." Paul Slovic and Sarah Lichtenstein, "Comparison of Bayesian and Regression Approaches to the Study of Information Processing in Judgment," *Organizational Behavior and Human Performance* 6, no. 6 (November 1971): 649–744, 712–716.

34. *Whitney v. California*, 274 U.S. 357, 375–376 (1927) (Justice Brandeis concurring). Consider for example what Richard Henry Lee had to say about liberty: "May the cause of liberty be ever conducted with prudence, but never benumbed by too frigid estimates of difficulty or danger." Richard Henry Lee to the Virginia Convention

1775. Quoted in Jack P. Greene, *Understanding the American Revolution* (Charlottesville: University Press of Virginia, 1995), 212; further: "I too love Liberty, but it is a regulated Liberty, so that ends & principles of society may not be disturbed by the fury of a Mob. . . ." ibid., 218.

35. See Chapter 5.

36. The present theory of constitutional sentiments is not one that denies the presence and importance of "positive" (rewarding) emotions, even if the constitution itself is primarily about preventing evil and not about feeling good. Those who make and ratify constitutions are humans with a full set of emotional dispositions. Humans are not only pain avoiders but also seekers of mental reward (i.e., rewarded chemically in the brain). The Declaration of Independence recognizes the pursuit of happiness as fundamental, and the Constitution was intended to "promote general Welfare." But there are constitutional limits to the constitutional manufacturing of happiness. Government cannot be a successful provider of happiness; in fact this is one of the dangers classic liberal constitutionalism tries to prevent.

37. Judith Shklar, "The Liberalism of Fear," in *Liberalism and the Moral Life*, ed. Nancy L. Rosenblum (Cambridge, Mass.: Harvard University Press, 1989), 21–39, 21.

38. Ibid., 31–32. "To call the liberalism of fear a lowering of one's sights implies that emotions are inferior to ideas and especially to political causes."

39. Jean Decety, Kalina J. Michalska, and Yuko Akitsuki, "Who Caused the Pain? A Functional MRI Investigation of Empathy and Intentionality in Children," *Neuropsychologia* 46, no. 11 (September 2008): 2607–2614.

40. Judith N. Shklar, *Ordinary Vices* (Cambridge, Mass.: Belknap Press of Harvard University Press, 1984), 29. Even in the abolition of slavery that was concerned primarily with the suffering of slaves and salvation., fear of cruelty, expressed sometimes as outrage, played an important role in the British and American antislavery sentiment animating the abolitionist movement. This concern was slowly translated into the language of *rights of slaves.*

41. Without evolutionary advantages cruelty should have been eliminated in the course of evolution. The treatment of other humans as indifferent objects reflects a total disregard. Such disregard serves the reinforcement of domination and/or other positions that are important for reproductive success. For the contemporary debate see Victor Nell, "Cruelty's Rewards: The Gratifications of Perpetrators and Spectators," *Behavioral and Brain Sciences* 29, no. 3 (June 2006): 211–257.

42. Shklar, *Ordinary Vices*, 8. Shklar rightly extends her definition to include "deliberate and persistent humiliation, so that the victim can eventually trust neither himself not anyone else" (37). The citizen is by definition weaker.

43. Alain Badiou, *The Century* (Cambridge, Mass.: Polity Press, 2007), 115.

44. Ervin Staub, "Moral Exclusion, Personal Goal Theory, and Extreme Destructiveness," *Journal of Social Issues* 46, no. 1 (Spring 1990): 47–65.

45. Immanuel Kant, *Critique of Practical Reason*, trans. Lewis White Beck (New York: Maxwell Macmillan International, 1993), 51.

46. It remains a matter of contention whether the willful use of painful treatment for the direct protection of socially uncontested highest values falls within the category of torture. This comes up most dramatically in "ticking bomb" and similar life-threatening situations. See further Michel Terestchenko, *Du bon usage de la torture, ou comment les démocraties justifient l'injustifiable* (Paris: La Découverte, 2008).

47. Mika Haritos-Fatouros, "Cruelty: A Dispositional or a Situational Behavior in Man?" in Nell, *Cruelty*, 230.

48. If cruelty were a personality disorder, the public law strategy would rely on psychological tests for screening members of the forces of order.

49. While the Cadiz Constitution of 1812 (Spain) contained no provisions on fundamental rights, it did have detailed rules on the administration of criminal law, and among the procedural rules it expressly singled out the prohibition of torture (Art. 303). As to the French Declaration, its Article 5 states that law "can only prohibit such actions as are hurtful to society. Nothing may be prevented which is not forbidden by law, and no one may be forced to do anything not provided for by law" while, according to Article 8, the law "shall provide for such punishments only as are strictly and obviously necessary, and no one shall suffer punishment except it be legally inflicted in virtue of a law passed and promulgated before the commission of the offense."

50. Shklar, *Ordinary Vices*, 43.

51. Farrand, *Framing*, II, 642.

52. The term "committee" applies to decision-making bodies which are agents to some principal. The founding fathers were agents of their respective states, and a national parliament is the agent of the people as principal. Eskridge and Ferejohn discuss constitution-making as decision-making in committee, where constitutional choices reflect cognitive bias. They claim that officeholders have "public-regarding self-images" as they fool themselves. The officeholders' deliberations will not yield efficient or optimal results "even if all participants are public-regarding." Committee decision has built-in tendencies to mental mistake. Eskridge and Ferejohn, "Structuring Lawmaking," 623. The classic source on bias is Daniel Kahnemann, Paul Slovic, and Amos Tversky, *Judgment under Uncertainty: Heuristics and Biases* (Cambridge: Cambridge University Press, 1982).

53. "People testing a hypothesis tend to search (in memory and the world) more often for confirming than for disconfirming instances and to recognize the former more readily." Alfred R. Mele, "Emotion and Desire in Self-Deception," in *Philosophy and the Emotions*, ed. Anthony Hatzimoysis (Cambridge: Cambridge University Press, 2003), 163–179, 164.

54. Eskridge and Ferejohn, "Structuring Lawmaking," 621–623.

55. Benedetto De Martino, Dharshan Kumaran, Ben Seymour, and Raymond J. Dolan, "Frames, Biases, and Rational Decision-Making in the Human Brain," *Science* 313, no. 4 (August 2006): 684–687, 684.

56. Ibid., 687, referring to Keith E. Stanovich and Richard F. West, "Individual Differences in Reasoning for the Rationality Debate?," in *Heuristics and Biases: The Psychology of Intuitive Judgment*, ed. Thomas Gilovich, Dale W. Griffin, and Daniel

Kahneman (New York: Cambridge University Press, 2002), 421–440. De Martino et al., "However, in modern society, which contains many symbolic artifacts and where optimal decision-making often requires skills of abstraction and decontextualization, such mechanisms may render human choices irrational" (687).

The framing bias can be described as the glass is half full/half empty problem. An identical problem is solved differently if differently framed, for example as a problem of saving lives or allowing death. Amos Tversky and Daniel Kahneman, "The Framing of Decisions and the Psychology of Choice," *Science* 211, no. 4481 (30 January, 1981): 453–458. The trolley problem shows similarities with this framing phenomenon.

57. Mele, "Emotion and Desire," 165.

58. This long-awaited public fear animated the nationalists, allowing them to have a national constitution. See Richards, *Shays's Rebellion*, 187, n.17.

59. There is increasing evidence that cognitive bias is emotion-based. Drew Westen, Pavel S. Blagov, Keith Harenski, Clint Kilts, and Stephan Hamann, "The Neural Basis of Motivated Reasoning: An MRI Study of Emotional Constraints on Partisan Political Judgment during the U.S. Presidential Election of 2004," *Journal of Cognitive Neuroscience* 18, no. 11 (November 2006): 1947–1958; Michael Shermer, "The Political Brain," *Scientific American* (July 2006). <http://www.sciam.com/article.cfm?id=the-political-brain> (28 April 2009).

60. Eskridge and Ferejohn, "Structuring Lawmaking," 640. "Heuristics" in the quote refers to bias. The power to resist bias in emergencies is limited. In law it is quite common that the need to resist bias in emergencies is recognized only *ex post facto*. For the American Civil War, see *Ex parte Milligan*, 71 U.S. (4. Wall.) 2 (1866), for World War II see *Korematsu v. United States*, 323 U.S. 214 (1944).

61. In the availability heuristics "one judges the probability of an event . . . by the ease with which relevant instances are imagined or by the number of such instances that are readily retrieved from memory." The availability of an event is determined in part by "emotional saliency." Paul Slovic, Howard Kunreuther, and Gilbert White, "Decision Processes, Rationality and Adjustment to Natural Hazards," in Paul Slovic, *The Perception of Risk* (London: Earthscan Publication, 2000), 1–31, 13.

On the relation between fear and liberty in the Constitution, see *Whitney v. California*, 274 U.S. 357, 376–378 (1927) (Justice Brandeis concurring). Consider also the impact on risk-taking of low-probability events with catastrophic consequences (which are a typical concern of constitutions). A few high-profile terrorist attacks suffice to trigger representativeness bias.

62. See for example Gerd Gigerenzer, "Dread Risk, September 11, and Fatal Traffic Accidents," *Psychological Science* 15, no. 4 (April 2004): 286–287. Fear of terrorist attacks after 9/11 forced people to drive instead of flying, resulting in a higher death toll than what the four airplane crashes produced.

63. The President can be removed only if high crime is committed; his mischiefs must be seen in this frame only.

64. In fact, in view of the relatively high occurrence of the conviction of innocents, even these frames are insufficient. According to the results of the Innocence Project

there have been so far 232 post-conviction DNA exonerations in U.S. history. <www. innocenhttp://www.innocenteproject.org/know/ceproject.org/know/> (19 April 2009).

65. Jerome Seymour Bruner, *Acts of Meaning* (Cambridge, Mass.: Harvard University Press, 1990), 23. The problem is partly related to the ambiguity of "we." At least from a sociological perspective societies are divided: what is presented as our design that serves "our" ends is a device for the ends of some, but not the design for the pleasure of "all."

66. Elizabeth Anderson, "Moral Heuristics: Rigid Rules or Flexible Inputs in Moral Deliberation?" [Commentary on Cass Sunstein, "Moral Heuristics,"] *Behavioral and Brain Sciences* 28, no. 4 (August 2005): 544–545.

67. Frith and Singer, "Social Cognition," 3884.

68. Eskridge and Ferejohn, "Structuring Lawmaking," 621–623.

69. The Constitution of the Fifth Republic in France offers a good example. It is a system of dual executive but does not regulate the situation where the parliamentary majority and the President are of different political orientations. The President has the power to appoint the Council of Ministers. The Constitution is silent regarding the duty to respect the will of the parliamentary majority.

70. Leonard W. Levy, *Original Intent and the Framers' Constitution* (New York: Macmillan, 1988), 349. On open texture see Chapter 2.

71. Gerd Gigerenzer, "Moral Intuition = Fast and Frugal Heuristics?" in *Moral Psychology*, Vol. 2, *The Cognitive Science of Morality: Intuition and Diversity*, ed. Walter Sinnott-Armstrong (Cambridge, Mass.: MIT Press, 2008), 1–26.

72. Ibid., 2–3. The number of formal rejections is far below 1 percent of the total population. Agence de la biomédecine—Bilan d'application de la loi de bioéthique—octobre 2008, 5.

73. Alain Tesniere, *Les yeux de Christophe: L'affaire d'Amiens* (Paris: Editions du Rocher, 1993).

The constitutional concept of dignity is often a nonspecific answer to a diffuse emotional concern, such as humiliation seeking to generate outrage. With an increased penetration of constitutional review into policy choices, the heuristics endorsed by the prevailing culture or professional ethics may be reviewed judicially where the moral intuitions of judges will reexamine, reinforce, or shape the original cultural or professional choice.

74. Randall Collins, "Social Movements and the Focus of Emotional Attention," in *Passionate Politics: Emotions and Social Movements*, ed. Jeff Goodwin, James M. Jasper, and Francesca Polletta (Chicago: University of Chicago Press, 2001), 27–44, 42.

75. Jacques Derrida, "Force of Law: The 'Mystical Foundation of Authority,'" in *Deconstruction and the Possibility of Justice*, ed. Drucilla Cornell, Michel Rosenfeld' and David Gray Carlson (New York: Routledge, 1992), 13.

76. In the 1814 Constitution, the king was elected and had no absolute veto power, and the franchise was much more extended than in the model.

77. Nation-state building after a war of independence falls under this heading, as in the case of Israel in 1948.

78. Jon Elster, "Forces and Mechanisms in the Constitution-Making Process," *Duke Law Journal* 45, no. 2 (November 1995): 364–396, 370–371.

79. One way to read the Japanese Constitution is that it expresses fear, mistrust, and contempt that the Americans felt in 1945.

80. Concessions to the emerging revolutionary power were also an important consideration. These concerns were consolidated in the constitutional amendments of the *Oktober reform* of 1918, which contained some of the fundamental choices that became a given for the 1919 Weimar Constitution.

81. Presidentialism was ruled out in Hungary in 1989–90 because it was seen as a way to sustain communist power. To what extent such sentiments are to be considered decisive is hard to say in divided societies: in Hungary in a 1990 referendum a majority of 5000 decided that there should be no popularly elected president.

82. It corresponded to De Gaulle's vision of running France, which was perhaps less fear-driven. Efficiency, contempt of parliamentarism, grandeur, and popular legitimacy were his crucial considerations.

83. Cf. Clifford Geertz, "The Integrative Revolution: Primordial Sentiments and Civil Politics in the New States," in *The Interpretation of Cultures: Selected Essays* (New York: Basic Books, 1973), 255–310. He refers to Nehru, who considered such grounds of state-building concessions "to narrow loyalties, petty jealousies, and ignorant prejudices." He also refers to Isaiah Berlin, who emphasized that in some of these efforts in modern state-building there is an element of "social assertion of the self as 'being somebody in the world.' "

84. Elster, "Forces and Mechanisms," 380.

85. As to New States: their constitutions hardly ever challenge "the givenness that stems from being born into a particular religious community, speaking a particular language." Geertz, "The Integrative Revolution," 259.

86. Even communist states, at any rate once state consolidation had been achieved, considered the constitution a necessary attribute of state organization, even if fear of cruelty did not apply in this case. This is certainly true of the Stalinist period. Later, when former communist victims of Stalin's cruelty came to power, an element of fear-based concern animated the law. It was a limited concept, expressed as "socialist legality." More important, crucial provisions against the cruel treatment of communist leaders were incorporated into important secret Party documents on nomenclature privileges.

87. Ian Buruma, "The Lessons of the Master," [review of Patrick French, *The World Is What It Is: The Authorized Biography of V.S. Naipaul*] *New York Review of Books* 55, no. 18 (20 November 2008): 22, 24.

4. Empathy and Human Rights

1. Empathy sometimes extends to mind reading, "theory of mind," and the like. In the present context it is limited to emotions, though in the context of the perception-action model these considerations do not conflict. Emotions of others do trigger mirror

neurons, though in slightly different brain areas than when one observes other people performing an action.

2. Martin Hoffman, *Empathy and Moral Development: Implications of Caring and Justice* (Cambridge: Cambridge University Press, 2000), 30. In Preston and de Waal's Perception-Action Model the definition of empathy focuses on the process: the "attended perception of the object's state automatically activates the subject's representation of the state, situation, and object, and that activation of these representations automatically primes or generates the associated automatic and somatic responses, unless inhibited." Stephanie D. Preston and Frans B. M. de Waal, "Empathy: Its Ultimate and Proximate Bases," *Behavioral and Brain Sciences* 25, no. 1 (February 2002): 1–20, 3.

3. Alvin Goldman, "Ethics and Cognitive Science," *Ethics* 103, no. 2 (January 1993): 337–360, 355. For the emotionalist position see Shaun Nichols, *Sentimental Rules: On the Natural Foundations of Moral Judgment* (New York: Oxford University Press, 2004), 43. (A minimal mind-reading capacity is sufficient, and one does not have to imagine oneself in the position of another. It is enough to attribute motivation.)

4. William D. Casebeer, "Moral Cognition and Its Neural Constituents," *Nature Reviews Neuroscience* 4, no. 10 (October 2003): 840–847, 844.

5. Jean Decety, Kalina J. Michalska, and Yuko Akitsuki, "Who Caused the Pain? An fMRI Investigation of Empathy and Intentionality in Children," *Neuropsychologia* 46, no. 11 (September 2008): 2607–2614, 2611.

The relevance of empathy for social bonds is revealed by empathy deficit, which is likely to increase antisocial behavior. Lack of empathy in psychopaths results in a moral competence deficit. James R. Blair, "A Cognitive Developmental Approach to Morality: Investigating the Psychopath," *Cognition* 57, no. 1 (January 1995): 1–29. For a corroboration at the level of fMRI studies see Shirley Fecteau, Alvaro Pascual-Leone, and Hugo Theoret, "Psychopathy and the Mirror Neuron System: Preliminary Findings from a Non-psychiatric Sample," *Psychiatry Research* 160, no. 2 (15 August 2008): 137–144.

6. Hoffman, *Moral Development*, considers the feelings of injustice both separately from and related to situations where others don't receive their due.

7. Frederique de Vignemont and Tania Singer, "The Empathic Brain: How, When and Why?" *Trends in Cognitive Sciences* 10, no. 10 (1 October 2006): 435–441, 435; Preston and de Waal, "Empathy," 55; Alessio Avenanti, Ilaria Minio-Paluello, Ilaria Bufalari, and Salvatore M. Aglioti, "The Pain of a Model in the Personality of an Onlooker: Influence of State-reactivity and Personality Traits on Embodied Empathy for Pain," *NeuroImage* 44, no. 1 (1 January 2009): 275–283, 276.

8. Yan Fan and Shihui Han, "Temporal Dynamic of Neural Mechanisms Involved in Empathy for Pain: An Event-related Brain Potential Study," *Neuropsychologia* 46, no. 1 (January 2008): 160–173. On the basis of event-related brain potential studies, the authors report that empathy for pain consists of early emotional sharing and late cognitive evaluation.

On gender differences in empathy see de Vignemont and Singer, "The Empathic Brain," 437. The difference could be attributed to problem-framing due to differences in gender role and related concepts of the self, but the neural differences between male and female brains could also be involved. See Louann Brizendine, *The Female Brain* (London: Bantam Books, 2007).

9. Hoffman, *Empathy.* Such behavior may have evolutionary advantages, as through reciprocation or other factors.

10. Preston and de Waal, "Empathy," 6. For empathy blockers see below at 4.b.

11. Ibid., 5; Claus Lamm, C. Daniel Batson, and Jean Decety, "The Neural Substrate of Human Empathy: Effects of Perspective-taking and Cognitive Appraisal," *Journal of Cognitive Neuroscience* 19, no. 1 (January 2007): 42–58; Claus Lamm, Eric C. Porges, John T. Cacioppo, and Jean Decety, "Perspective Taking Is Associated with Specific Facial Responses during Empathy for Pain," *Brain Research* 1227 (28 August 2008): 153–161, indicating that top-down processes of deliberate choice of perspective ("putting oneself in the shoes of the person in pain") result in higher distress and specific physiological processes. See also Adam Smith: "The compassion of the spectator must arise altogether from the consideration of what he himself would feel if he was reduced to the same unhappy situation, and, what perhaps is impossible, was at the same time able to regard it with his present reason and judgment." Adam Smith, *The Theory of Moral Sentiments* (Amherst: Prometheus Books, 2000), 8.

Professional training may result in blocking empathy completely. Yawei Cheng, Ching-Po Lin, Ho-Ling Liu, Yuan-Yu Hsu, Kun-Eng Lim, Daisy Hung, and Jean Decety, "Expertise Modulates the Perception of Pain in Others," *Current Biology* 17, no. 19 (9 October 2007): 1708–1713.

12. Justin H. Park, Mark Schaller, and Mark Van Vugt, "Psychology of Human Kin Recognition: Heuristic Cues, Erroneous Inferences, and Their Implications," *Review of General Psychology* 12, no. 3 (September 2008): 215–235. See further Jesse J. Prinz, "Is Empathy Necessary for Morality?," in *Empathy: Philosophical and Psychological Perspectives*, ed. Peter Goldie and Amy Coplan (Oxford: Oxford University Press, forthcoming).

13. Lamm, Porges, Cacioppo, and Decety, "Perspective," 153–161. (Empathy does not only rely on automatic processes, but is also strongly influenced by top-down control and cognitive processes.)

14. Nancy Eisenberg and Amanda Sheffield Morris, "The Origins and Social Significance of Empathy-related Responding. A Review of Empathy and Moral Development: Implications for Caring and Justice by M. L. Hoffman," *Social Justice Research* 14, no. 1 (March 2001): 95–120.

15. Lawrence Stone, *The Family, Sex, and Marriage in England, 1500–1800* (New York: Harper and Row, 1977). On the centrality of sentimentalism in the eighteenth century as a result of social and cultural changes see Chapter 2.

16. Thomas L. Haskell, "Capitalism and the Origins of Humanitarian Sensibility," Parts 1 and 2, in *The Antislavery Debate: Capitalism and Abolitionism as a Problem of Historical Interpretation*, ed. Thomas Bender (Berkeley: University of California Press, 1992), 107–160, 107. Many historians claim that the humanitarian sentiment was selfish although the selfishness may have not been conscious. But even Foucault has admitted that a new sensitivity to suffering did play a role, although the humanitarian approach

to the severity of punishment was purely instrumental; humanitarianism intended to punish more efficiently. Michel Foucault, *Discipline and Punish: The Birth of the Prison*, trans. Alan Sheridan (New York: Vintage Books, 1977), 82.

17. Stone, *The Family, Sex*, 238; Adam Hochschild, *Bury the Chains: Prophets and Rebels in the Fight to Free an Empire's Slaves* (Boston: Houghton Mifflin Harcourt, 2005), 323–324. In the discussion of the history of British abolitionism I rely to a great extent on Hochschild.

18. After the Romantic period sentimentalism was of lesser legitimating power. However, if one considers nineteenth-century popular publications in the United States, sentimentalism was still quite influential. Public sentiments were played out in a sentimental key. Cf. Glenn Hendler, ed., *Public Sentiments: Structures of Feeling in Nineteenth-Century American Literature* (Chapel Hill: University of North Carolina Press, 2001).

19. Herbert McCloskey and Alida Brill, *Dimensions of Tolerance* (New York: Sage, 1983), 13.

20. Hochschild, *Bury the Chains*, 87.

21. Charles de Secondat and Baron de Montesquieu, *Spirit of the Laws*, trans. Thomas Nugent, rev. J. V. Prichard (London: G. Bell & Sons, 1914), Book XV.

22. *R. v. Knowles, ex parte Somerset[t]*, (1772) Lofft 1, 98 E.R. 499, 20 S.T. 1., as quoted in George Van Cleve, "*Somerset's Case* and Its Antecedents in Imperial Perspective," *Law and History Review* 24, no. 3 (Fall 2006), 601–646, 630.

23. Alan Watson, "Lord Mansfield: Judicial Integrity or Its Lack: Somerset's Case," *Journal of Comparative Law* 1, no. 2 (2006): 225–234, 227. <http://www.alanwatson.org/somersets_case.pdf> (25 Febr. 2009).

24. David Brion Davis, "Preservation of English Liberty," in *The Antislavery Debate*, ed. Bender, 65–104, 67. Cf. Van Cleve, "Somerset's Case," 631.

25. Hochschild, *Bury the Chains*, 134.

26. Ibid., 87.

27. Diderot in Abbé Raynal, *Philosophical and Political History of the Settlements and Trade of the Europeans in the East and West Indies* (1770). Quoted in De Paul Hyland, Olga Gomez, and Francesca Greensides, eds., *The Enlightenment: A Sourcebook and Reader* (New York: Routledge, 2003), 26.

28. Davis, "Preservation," 66.

29. Bernard Bailyn, *Faces of Revolution* (New York: Knopf, 1990), 222.

30. The *Amistad* case, in which John Quincy Adams's injustice-based arguments were surprisingly effective, is a somewhat exceptional one.

31. True, Garrison referred to the Declaration of Independence as a reason for abolitionism, but he added that for this reason all forms of oppression that turn a man into a thing create indignation and abhorrence, feelings he finds commanding. Emotions based on personal disgust did play a comparable role in the movement to abolish the death penalty.

32. Cf. with John Wesley's position in John Wesley, *Thoughts upon Slavery*, in John Wesley, *The Works of the Reverend John Wesley, A.M.*, Volume VI (New York: T. Mason, 1839) (1774), 278–293. What we see here in action is not a generic religious

benevolence or religion-enhanced compassion. Empathy is not "systematically implicated in religious prosociality." Ara Norenzayan and Azom F. Shariff, "The Origin and Evolution of Religious Prosociality," *Science* 322 (3 October 2008): 58–62, 62.

33. The sudden outburst of public sentiment and its quick transposition into public opinion is remarkable. Already in 1787 in Manchester the abolitionist petition was signed by one-fifth of the local population. This was "the first mass petition on any subject." Boyd Hilton, *A Mad, Bad, and Dangerous People? England 1783–1846* (Oxford: Clarendon Press, 2006), 184.

34. Sir John Doyle, quoted in Hochschild, *Bury the Chains*, 306; Hilton, *Dangerous People?*, 193.

35. For a while British and American abolitionists tried to use similar legal techniques, especially mass petitioning. This became, however, impractical in the United States, because at the end Southerners in Congress passed the "gag resolution" to table all petitions related in any way to slavery.

Neither in Britain nor in the United States was it obvious that the electoral process could be used for humanitarian purposes. Using electoral politics for abolitionist goals was a divisive issue among radical American abolitionists. For example, Garrison rejected the political methods offered by democracy, like voting exclusively for abolitionist candidates in elections. This position is the opposite of that of the British abolitionists, whose strategy was centered on parliamentary political action.

36. Thomas Paine, "African Slavery in America." Paine wrote the pamphlet in 1774 and published it March 8, 1775, a few weeks before the founding of the first antislavery society in Philadelphia.

37. Article I, Section 9, had provided in regard to slaves that "the importation of such persons as any of the States shall think proper to admit, shall not be prohibited by the Congress prior to the year 1808. . . ."

38. Quoted in W.E.B. Du Bois, *The Suppression of the African Slave-Trade to the United States of America 1638–1870* (New York: Longmans, Green, 1896), 100. For humanitarian and religious arguments see, for example, the January 1794 address of the Delegates from the several [abolitionist] Societies to the Citizens of the United States, or the December 11, 1829, Memorial of the [abolitionist] Convention, advocating colonization. *Journal of Negro History* 6, no. 3 (July 1921): 310–375, 349, 357.

39. Charles Francis Adams, *Richard Henry Dana*, Volume I (Boston: Houghton Mifflin, 1891), 127. Quoted in Leonard W. Levy, "Sims' Case: The Fugitive Slave Law in Boston in 1851," *Journal of Negro History* 35, no. 1 (January 1950): 39–74, 39–40.

40. Quoted after James M. McPherson, *Battle Cry of Freedom* (New York: Oxford University Press, 1988), 82.

41. Eric Foner, *Free Soil, Free Labor, Free Men: The Ideology of the Republican Party before the Civil War* (New York: Oxford University Press, 1970), 9.

42. McPherson, *Battle Cry*, 497. "[T]he moderates, led by Lincoln, . . . shared the radicals' moral aversion to slavery but feared the racial consequences of wholesale emancipation. Events during the first half of 1862 pushed moderates toward the radical position" (494).

43. Aileen S. Kraditor, *Means and Ends in American Abolitionism: Garrison and His Critics on Strategy and Tactics, 1834–1850* (Chicago: I. R. Dee, 1989), 241. American abolitionists made references to equality, given the promise of equal liberty in the Declaration of Independence, but the constitutional debate was framed in terms of state rights, which successfully barred pro-slavery arguments, and radical abolitionists were skeptical about constitutional arguments. Garrison and Phillips remain on record as saying that the "US Constitution [is] a covenant with death and an agreement with hell." See David A. J. Richards, *Conscience and the Constitution: History, Theory, and Law of the Reconstruction Amendments* (Princeton: Princeton University Press, 1993), 53. However, equality was important in a non-legal sense. Most abolitionists honestly believed in racial equality, a conviction important both for them and for the audience they wanted to convince. The stronger the community between the White and the Negro, the more difficult it was to resist compassion through categorization.

44. Jonathan Haidt-Fredrik Bjorklund, "Social Intuitionists Answer Six Questions about Moral Psychology," in *Moral Psychology*, Vol. 2, *The Cognitive Science of Morality: Intuition and Diversity*, ed. Walter Sinnott-Armstrong (Cambridge, Mass.: MIT Press, 2008), 181–217, 211.

45. Elizabeth B. Clark, " 'The Sacred Rights of the Weak': Pain, Sympathy, and the Culture of Individual Rights in Antebellum America," *Journal of American History* 82, no. 2 (September 1995): 463–493.

46. Thomas Clarkson, *The History of the Rise, Progress, and Accomplishment of the Abolition of the African Slave-Trade by the British Parliament*, Volume II (London: Longman, Hurst, Rees, and Orme, 1808), 111. Quoted in Hochschild, *Bury the Chains*, 156. Cf. Hilton, *Dangerous People?*, 184.

The American abolitionist movement relied on British techniques of deliberate emotional persuasion and mobilization. Garrison went to England to learn from Thomas Clarkson. Many years earlier Clarkson went to revolutionary Paris to give advice, and Mirabeau used a slave ship model in the Assembly to visually represent the sufferings of the middle passage.

Suffering made visible remains a major tool in contemporary politics, including human rights politics. See Arthur Kleinman and Joan Kleinman, "The Appeal of Experience: The Dismay of Images: Cultural Appropriations of Suffering in Our Times," in *Social Suffering*, ed. Arthur Kleinman, Veena Das, and Margaret Lock (Berkeley: University of California Press, 1997), 1–23.

47. Kraditor, *Means and Ends*, 242. "You can act as if you felt that you were bound with those who are in bonds; . . . as if every blow that cuts their flesh, lacerated yours." Abolitionist educator Beriah Green, quoted in Kraditor, *Means and Ends*, 238; for Chandler see Clark, "Sacred," 482. Chandler invented the "Am I not a Woman and a Sister?" slogan.

48. Kraditor, *Means and Ends*, 241; Richards, *Conscience*, 39; see also 242.

49. Cf. Hochschild, *Bury the Chains*, 222. "People are more likely to care about the suffering of others in a distant place if that misfortune evokes a fear of their own."

50. Bernard Williams, *Shame and Necessity* (Berkeley: University of California Press, 1993), 124.

51. Ibid., 124–125.

52. Mark Twain, *The Autobiography of Mark Twain*, ed. Charles Neider (New York: Harper and Row, 1959), 6. Mark Twain tells a story about his mother that indicates how the compassion of people with a strong sense of justice and sensibility could resist the perceptional blinders of the environment:

> We had a little slave . . . [he] had been brought away from his family and his friends, half-way across the American continent, and sold. . . . [O]ne day, I lost all my temper, and went raging to my mother, and said . . . wouldn't she please shut him up. The tears came into her eyes, and her lip trembled, and she said something like this:
> "Poor thing, when he sings, it shows that he is not remembering, and that comforts me. . . ."
> . . . She . . . was capable with her tongue to the last—especially when a meanness or an injustice roused her spirit. (6–7)

53. Repressive regimes devote particular attention to hiding pictures and stories of suffering that might have a mobilizing effect among their citizens and abroad. For example, in the United States there were certain censorial restrictions on abolitionist literature in the South.

54. James G. Birney, "A Letter on the Political Obligations of Abolitionists, (1839)," in *Antislavery Political Writings, 1833–1860, A Reader*, ed. C. Bradley Thompson (New York: M. E. Sharpe, 2004), 75–97, 76. Garrison himself always insisted on the need for the repentance of slave-holder sinners, and on moral suasion. See further Davis, "Preservation," 87.

55. Clark, "Sacred," 464, quoting James Freeman Clarke's sermon, published in 1842.

56. Ibid., 467.

57. There are other, more gradual processes of change in emotion display and moral sentiment, albeit less spectacular than the outburst of humanitarian sensibility that contributed to the spread of human rights. For a concise history of the shifting of "thresholds of embarrassment," see Norbert Elias, *Power and Civility: The Civilizing Process*, trans. Edmund Jephcott (New York: Pantheon, 1982).

58. Ibid., 473. Thomas Laqueur, "Bodies, Details, and the Humanitarian Narrative," in *The New Cultural History*, ed. Lynn Hunt (Berkeley: University of California Press, 1989), 176–204, describes how the body and pain were liberated as topics in eighteenth-century humanitarianism, which was intimately related to abolitionism.

59. Clark, "Sacred," 474.

60. Hochschild, *Bury the Chains*, 91. Among the 12 founding members of the Society for Effecting the Abolition of the Slave Trade, the three non-Quakers were Evangelicals. Two of them were ridden with nearly pathological personal guilt. Thomas Clarkson, the third non-Quaker founder, became interested in abolition by accident, through scholarly ambition but visions of suffering and cruelty influenced his thought and imagination all his life.

61. Kraditor, *Means and Ends*, 236.

62. With the rapid carriage service introduced from 1782, "a journey that had taken up to 38 hours now took just 16." <http://postalheritage.org.uk/history/downloads/BPMA_Info_Sheet_MailCoaches_web.pdf> (25 Febr. 2009).

63. Eric Foner, "Rights and the Constitution in Black Life during the Civil War and Reconstruction," *Journal of American History* 74, no. 3 (December 1987): 863–888, 863.

64. "To compassionate, i.e., to join in passion. . . . To commiserate, that is, to join in misery. . . . This in one order of life is right and good; nothing more harmonious; and to be without this, or not to feel this, is unnatural, horrid, immane." The Earl of Shaftesbury, quoted in Gertrude Himmelfarb, *Poverty and Compassion* (New York: Vintage Books, 1992), 3.

65. Hannah Arendt, *On Revolution* (New York: Viking Press, 1963), 76.

66. Smith, *Moral Sentiment*, 4.

67. Catharine Esther Beecher, *A Treatise on Domestic Economy* (Boston: Marsh, Capen, Lyon, & Webb, 1841). Quoted in Susan M. Ryan, *The Grammar of Good Intentions: Race and the Antebellum Culture of Benevolence* (New York: Cornell University Press, 2005), 1.

68. "It is not from the benevolence of the butcher, the brewer, or the baker, that we expect our dinner, but from their regard to their own interest. We address ourselves, not to their humanity but to their self-love, . . ." Adam Smith, *The Wealth of Nations* (New York: Bantam Classics, 2003), 23–24.

69. Smith, *Moral Sentiment*, 191–192. Smith added that "it is not the soft power of humanity" nor benevolence but reason and conscience, the little "man within" that will remind us of the shame of self-love. The mechanism he describes has little to do with reason: the correction comes from self-restraining emotions of resentment and shame.

70. Smith, *Wealth*, 493.

71. Davis, "Preservation," 74–75.

72. Child labor got some regulatory attention (after 50 years of neglect) beginning with the protection of pauper apprentices in textile mills (see The Health and Morals of Apprentices Act of 1802). The fact that the children were forced into work by Poor Law guardians did not raise an eyebrow.

73. Similar contemporary developments were noticed by Kleinman and Kleinman, *Appeal*, 14. They claim that individualistic representation of contemporary suffering that is part of humanitarian strategies "may in time also thin out the social experience of suffering. It can do this by becoming part of the apparatus of cultural representation that creates societal norms, which in turn shapes the social role and social behavior of the ill, and what should be the practices of families and health-care providers. The American cultural rhetoric, for example, is *changing from the language of caring to the language of efficiency and cost*; it is not surprising to hear patients themselves use this rhetoric to describe their problems" (emphasis added).

74. Davis, "Preservation," 85; Edward Palmer Thompson, *The Making of the English Working Class* (New York: Random House, 1963), 342.

75. Hochschild, *Bury the Chains*, 349–350. Wilberforce was of the opinion that the poor should know "that their more lowly path has been allotted to them by the hand of God; that it is their part . . . contentedly to bear its inconveniences" (ibid., 314), but at the sight of starving workers he contributed a considerable percentage of his personal income to them.

76. Preston and de Waal, "Empathy," 1.

77. Maximilien Robespierre, "Sur les principes de morale politique," speech to the National Convention, February 5, 1794. http://www.royet.org/nea1789-1794/archives/discours/robespierre_principes_morale_politique_05_02_94.htm (May 27, 2009).

78. See for example, the paralysis of a sense of compassion and responsibility in the Kitty Genovese murder. John M. Darley and Bibb Latané, "Bystander Intervention in Emergencies: Diffusion of Responsibility," *Journal of Personality and Social Psychology* 8, no. 1 (January 1968): 377–383; Bibb Latané and John M. Darley, "Group Inhibition of Bystander Intervention in Emergencies," *Journal of Personality and Social Psychology* 10, no. 3 (November 1968): 215–221.

79. For a discussion of emotional resonance blockers see Douglas F. Watt, "Social Bonds and the Nature of Empathy," *Journal of Consciousness Studies* 12, no. 8–10 (August–October 2005): 185–209, 198–199. Adam Smith mentions that distance diminishes the intensity of fellow feeling. Smith, *Moral Sentiment*, 191–192.

On numbing see Paul Slovic, "'If I Look at the Mass I Will Never Act': Psychic Numbing and Genocide," *Judgment and Decision Making* 2, no. 2 (April 2007): 79–95, 90–92. The problem of numbing is this: In order for a change in a stimulus to be noticeable a fixed percentage must be added; sensations grow in a non-linear way. The death of one person alone is more noticeable than the death of a hundred in the daily routine of a war. Without identifiable victims, compassion collapses, or at least there is less altruistic contribution that would favor a victim group than individual victims. "Our capacity to feel is limited." Beyond political realities that bank intuitively on psychic numbing tendencies, this mechanism explains why genocide elicits relatively little compassion, or at least action-prone compassion even in people who are very altruistic and sensitive.

80. For moral entrepreneurs distant events may be sufficient to counter rational objections. Distant distressing events, once they become known, generate at least minimal empathy, and opponents of humanitarian intervention cannot simply say unconditionally that the event is irrelevant.

81. Linda L. Putnam and Dennis K. Mumby, "Organisations, Emotion, and the Myth of Rationality," in *Emotion in Organisations*, ed. Stephen Fineman (London: Sage, 1993), 36–57, 37. This approach follows Arlie Russell Hochschild, *The Managed Heart: Commercialization of Human Feeling* (Berkeley: University of California Press, 1983).

82. Martin L. Hoffman, "How Automatic and Representational Is Empathy, and Why?" *Behavioral and Brain Sciences* 25, no. 1 (February 2002): 38–39, 39.

83. "[O]ne means of lessening feelings of collective guilt for current harm to another group is by referencing the ingroup's own past victimization." Michael J. A. Wohl

and Nyla R. Branscombe, "Remembering Historical Victimization: Collective Guilt for Current Ingroup Transgressions," *Journal of Personality and Social Psychology* 94, no. 6 (December 2008): 988–1006, 988. (Reminders of the 9/11 victimization of Americans reduce their collective guilt for the suffering of the Iraqis linked to America's involvement in Iraq.)

84. See Bernard Williams, *Shame and Necessity* (Berkeley: University of California Press, 1993), 125.

85. Shaun Nichols, "Folk Intuitions on Free Will," *Journal of Cognition and Culture* 6, no. 1–2 (2006): 57–86, 80.

86. Haskell, "Capitalism," 124. Here I follow Thomas Haskell's concept of transformation of cognitive structures, putting the emphasis on the emotional part of such cognitive structures. "[T]hese cognitive structures underlay *both* the reformers' novel sense of responsibility for others and their definition of their own interest" (111). Strong emotions of particularly sensitive people might overcome the conventions.

87. Ibid., 131. Abolitionists deliberately tried "to extend our sympathies beyond 'the little limits of our own State and neighborhood.'" Clark, "Sacred," 464.

88. Quoted after David J. Denby, *Sentimental Narrative and the Social Order in France, 1760–1820* (New York: Cambridge University Press, 1994), 147.

89. Thomas Paine, *Rights of Man*, ed. Mark Philip (Oxford: Oxford University Press, 1995), 300, 275. Paine switches to a sentimentalist argument in his justification of relief rights. Beyond the equal respect toward all citizens, it is compassion again that makes the welfare rights claims justified. Once welfare measures are applied as a right, "the hearts of the humane will not be shocked by ragged and hungry children, and persons of seventy and eighty years of age begging for bread" (301).

90. For these distinctions and further literature see Kleinman and Kleinman, *Appeal*, 2.

91. For the history of slavery and its abolition in France see, for example Olivier Pétré-Grenouilleau, *Les Traites négrières, Essai d'histoire globale* (Paris: NRF Gallimard, 2004). Emancipation in 1794 was an *ex post facto* nominal application of the rights of man. Napoleon had no difficulty in reintroducing it. It was abolished only during the 1848 Revolution, by a decree of Victor Schoelcher, a philanthropist who happened to be in charge as undersecretary of State at the Ministry of the Marine. By that time, however, plantation owners had liberated many slaves, understanding the prevailing sentiment against the institution. On the other hand, human rights did not fit well into the English political and cultural system of the eighteenth century. Liberty was cherished as a tradition confirmed in common law which in principle could have been limited by statute. The situation was different in the United States, which developed a fundamental rights-based political culture. However, given the compromises in the Constitution, the rights argument was of limited use.

92. Elizabeth Heyrick (1769–1831) published *Immediate not Gradual Abolition* in 1824. After strong resistance the Anti-Slavery Society accepted her position only in 1830.

93. Richard Dagger, "Rights," in *Political Innovation and Conceptual Change*, ed. Terence Ball, James Farr, and Russell L. Hanson (Cambridge: Cambridge University Press, 1989), 292–308, 301.

5. Freedom to Express What?

1. Paul Horwitz, "Free Speech as Risk Analysis: Heuristics, Biases, and Institutions in the First Amendment," *Temple Law Review* 76, no. 1 (Spring 2003): 1–68, 6, referring to Thomas Emerson; James Kuklinski, Ellen Riggle, Victor Ottati, Norbert Schwarz, and Robert S. Wyer, "The Cognitive and Affective Bases of Political Tolerance Judgments," *American Journal of Political Science* 35, no. 1 (January 1991): 1–27, 22.

2. *Paris Adult Theatre I v. Slaton*, 413 U.S. 49, 67 (1973).

3. Georg Wilhelm Friedrich Hegel, *Hegel's Philosophy of Right*, trans. Thomas Malcolm Knox (Oxford: Clarendon Press, 1942), 315 [emphasis added]. But even Hegel admits that speech is not only about truth. By permitting speech, one gets *psychological satisfaction* that contributes to public order: "Once he [everyone] has had his say and so his share of responsibility, his subjectivity has been satisfied and he puts up with a lot. In France freedom of speech has turned out far less dangerous than enforced silence, because with the latter the fear is that men bottle up their objections to a thing, whereas argument gives them an outlet and a measure of satisfaction, and this is in addition a means whereby the thing can be pushed ahead more easily" (317, Addition).

4. See *Abrams v. United States*, 250 U.S. 616, 630 (1919). For the modern formulation, see *Gertz v. Robert Welch, Inc.*, 418 U.S. 323 (1974) declaring that "(h)owever pernicious an opinion may seem, we depend for its correction not on the conscience" of legislators, judges, juries, or voters "but on the competition of other ideas" (339–340).

5. Laurence H. Tribe, *American Constitutional Law* (Mineola, N.Y.: Foundation Press, 1988), 837 [emphasis added]. See also Jefferson, "First Inaugural Address" (4 March, 1801): "error of opinion may be tolerated where reason is left free to combat it." <www.yale.edu/lawweb/avalon/presiden/inaug/jefinau1.htm> (29 Apr. 2009).

6. John Stuart Mill, *On Liberty* (London: Penguin Books, 1985), 69, 72.

7. Stephen Holmes, *The Matador's Cape* (Cambridge: Cambridge University Press, 2007), 218.

8. For American jurisprudence the need to protect speech originates in the belief that this way truth will prevail, but the protection is not related to the production of truth. "The Framers undoubtedly believed it. As a general matter it is true. But the Constitution does not make the dominance of truth a necessary condition of freedom of speech." *American Booksellers Association, Inc. v. Hudnut*, 771 F.2d 323, 330 (7th Cir. 1985), affirmed 475 U.S. 1001 (1986) (ordinance that criminalizes pornography defined as subordinating women found to be point of view discrimination, notwithstanding negative emotional and other impacts of pornography).

Owen Fiss claims, however, that "personal development lies at the heart of *On Liberty*," while the founding fathers of the American Constitution were concerned with the proper functioning of governance. Owen Fiss, "A Freedom Both Personal and Political," in John Stuart Mill, *On Liberty*, ed. David Bromwich and George

Kateb with essays by Jean Bethke Elshtain (New Haven: Yale University Press, 2003), 183.

9. *Schenck v. United States*, 249 U.S. 47, 52 (1919). The concept of militant democracy that is concerned with emotional politics would restrict speech that is directed primarily to stir political emotions. Karl Loewenstein, "Militant Democracy and Fundamental Rights I," *American Political Science Review* 31, no. 3 (June 1937): 417–432.

10. "Stupidity" does not rule out rationality; vice versa rational beings produce a fair number of stupid statements. What matters for "rational discourse" is, first, that no one has a claim to determine unilaterally what is stupid, second, that people are capable of finding out in a comparative way what is less stupid, and third, that humans are capable of correcting their mistakes reasonably often.

11. As recently as 2009, violent demonstrations of Indian believers against a reprint of an English article disrespectful of religion resulted in the arrest of the editor and publisher of the Kolkata-based English daily *The Statesman*. They were charged under section 295A of the Indian Penal Code, which forbids "deliberate and malicious acts intended to outrage religious feelings." Jerome Taylor, "Editor arrested for 'outraging Muslims.' Protests against Indian newspaper over article reprinted from Independent," <http://www.independent.co.uk/news/world/asia/editor-arrested-for-outraging-muslims-1607256.html> (12 Febr. 2009).

12. In the American context see *R.A.V. v. City of St. Paul, Minn.*, 505 U.S. 377 (1992) (city ordinance criminalizing the display of alarming racist symbols, including cross-burning found unconstitutional for being content discriminatory or overbroad, irrespective of the negative impact on the target population); *American Booksellers Association, Inc. v. Hudnut*, 771 F.2d 323 (7th Cir. 1985). However, "true threat" does not receive constitutional protection.

13. See Antoine de Baecque, Wolfgang Schmale, and Michel Vovelle, eds., *L'an 1 des droits de l'homme* (Paris: Presses du CRNS, 1988), 240, 243, 262.

14. Samuel Warren and Louis Brandeis, "The Right to Privacy," *Harvard Law Review* 4, no. 5 (December 1890): 193–220, 198 [emphasis added].

15. Judge Posner, in *Miller v. Civil City of South Bend*, 904 F.2d 1081, 1089 (7th Cir. 1990), reversed, *Barnes v. Glen Theatre, Inc.*, 501 U.S. 560 (1991).

16. There is something poetically surrealistic in the psychological assumptions of free speech theories that refer to psychological needs. Lee C. Bollinger celebrates the First Amendment as a mechanism of generating a spirit of tolerance. Lee C. Bollinger, *The Tolerant Society: Freedom of Speech and Extremist Speech in America* (New York: Oxford University Press, 1986). In Shiffrin's self-realization theory, the dissent enabled by the First Amendment helps resistance to totalitarianism through giving more chance to reasoned deliberation and nonconformity. Steven H. Shiffrin, *The First Amendment, Democracy, and Romance* (Cambridge, Mass.: Harvard University Press, 1990), 5–8. It seems that dissent as self-realization may be a genuine human aspiration, but it does not fit easily into conformity, which is a fundamental psychological drive. For a current review of the Asch-Milgram conformity tradition see Thomas Blass, ed., *Obedience to*

Authority: Current Perspectives on the Milgram Paradigm (Mahwah, N.J.: Lawrence Erlbaum Associates, 2000). For Cass Sunstein speech is protected in order (among other reasons) to counter conformism. Without such extensive protection for dissent, the socially and psychologically "natural" conformist patterns would prevail. Cass R. Sunstein, *Why Societies Need Dissent* (Cambridge, Mass.: Harvard University Press, 2003), 2.

17. The duality of speech justification reflects the dual (intellectual and emotional) nature of human communication; the personal development concern is also reflected in the contemporary protection of freedom of expression. On Mill's dual theory, see Martha Craven Nussbaum, *Hiding from Humanity: Disgust, Shame, and the Law* (Princeton: Princeton University Press, 2004), 329–330.

18. Freedom of belief, which centrally implies a belief about one's own identity, and speech are very intimately related. In fact, from the practical perspective of law they are inseparable.

Mill tells us that human liberty "comprises, first, the inward domain of consciousness, demanding liberty of conscience in the most comprehensive sense, liberty of thought and feeling, absolute freedom of opinion and sentiment on all subjects, practical or speculative, scientific, moral, or theological." To express opinions, is "almost of as much importance as the liberty of thought," "resting in great part on the same reasons," and "practically inseparable from it." Mill, *On Liberty, 71.*

19. Marci A. Hamilton, "Art Speech," *Vanderbilt Law Review* 49, no. 1 (January 1996): 72–122, 79–96, justifies the protection of art that conveys emotions that cannot be expressed in alternative forms in political discourse terms. Art enables imagination, and imagination is critical for political opposition.

20. Mill, *On Liberty*, 116 [emphasis added].

21. Justice Harlan put the point as follows: "Of course it is disagreeable to see a group, to which one has been required to contribute, decide to spend its money for purposes the contributor opposes. But the Constitution does not protect against the mere play of personal emotions." *Lathrop v. Donahue*, 367 U.S. 820, 857 (1961) (Justice Harlan, concurring).

22. *Cohen v. California*, 403 U.S. 15 (1971), 26.

23. Case of *Oberschlick v. Austria*, ECtHR Application no. 11662/85, judgment of 23 May 1991.

24. *Miller v. California*, 413 U.S. 15, 24 (1973).

25. "First Amendment jurisprudence must contend with the unmistakable truth that people are not rational, and that the individual can in fact be 'irrational, a captive of emotion rather than reflection, capable of being 'swept away by hysterical, emotional appeals.'" Horwitz, "Free Speech," 6.

26. *Nat'l Endowment for the Arts v. Finley*, 524 U.S. 569, 606 (1998).

27. *Virginia v. Black et al.* 538 U.S. 343 (2003) (cross-burning case) arguably finds intent of intimidation on the basis of excessive fear generated by the cross-burning. Justice Thomas, dissenting, emphasized experiences of lasting fear generated by the display of Ku Klux Klan symbols.

28. Kuklinski, Riggle, Ottati, Schwarz, and Wyer, "The Cognitive and Affective Bases," 5 (evaluation of abstract rights changes once the rights are exercised by groups which elicit strong reactions).

29. Anthony Giddens, *Modernity and Self-Identity: Self and Society in the Late Modern Age* (Stanford: Stanford University Press, 1991), 198.

30. *R. v. Zundel*, 2 S.C.R. 73 (1992), para. 53. The Zundel Court refers to the 1966 Report of the Special Committee on Hate Propaganda in Canada that was accepted as an authoritative summary in *R. v. Keegstra*, 3 S.C.R. 697, 747 (1990), which reads in the opening paragraph of its preface (referring to the Report of the Special Committee on Hate Propaganda in Canada, 1966, 8):

> In the 18th and 19th centuries, there was a widespread belief that man was a rational creature, and that if his mind was trained and liberated from superstition by education, he would always distinguish truth from falsehood, good from evil.
>
> We cannot share this faith today in such a simple form. While holding that over the long run, the human mind is repelled by blatant falsehood and seeks the good, it is too often true, in the short run, that emotion displaces reason and individuals perversely reject the demonstrations of truth put before them and forsake the good they know. The successes of modern advertising, the triumphs of impudent propaganda such as Hitler's, have qualified sharply our belief in the rationality of man.

31. Yoav Hammer, "Expressions Which Preclude Rational Processing: The Case for Regulating Non-informational Advertisements," *Whittier Law Review* 27, no. 4 (Winter 2005): 435–493, 437.

32. Jack M. Balkin, "Some Realism about Pluralism: Legal Realist Approaches to the First Amendment," *Duke Law Journal* 1990, no. 3 (June 1990): 375–430, 409.

33. Ronald K. L. Collins and David M. Skover, *The Death of Discourse* (Boulder, Colo.: Westview Press, 1996), 16–17.

34. Chief Justice Rehnquist, dissenting in *Virginia State Board of Pharmacy v. Virginia Citizens Consumer Council*, 425 U.S. 748, 787 (1976) argued:

> I had understood this view to relate to public decisionmaking as to political, social, and other public issues, rather than the decision of a particular individual as to whether to purchase one or another kind of shampoo. It is undoubtedly arguable that many people in the country regard the choice of shampoo as just as important as who may be elected to . . . political office, but that does not automatically bring information about competing shampoos within the protection of the First Amendment.

In reality, rational advertisements are less successful than emotional influences and are sometimes counterproductive. See Sarah C. Haan, "The 'Persuasion Route' of the Law: Advertising and Legal Persuasion," Columbia Law Review 100, no. 5 (June 2000): 1281–1326, 1281; Ellen C. Garbarino and Julie A. Edell, "Cognitive Effort, Affect, and Choice," Journal of Consumer Research 24, no. 2 (September 1997): 147–158, 153–156.

35. For a Habermasian sphere in public communication see the position of the Hungarian Constitutional Court, Decision 30/1992 (V. 26) AB.

36. Richard A. Posner, "Free Speech in an Economic Perspective," *Suffolk University Law Review* 20, no. 1 (Spring 1986): 1–54, 7.

Fear-based concerns about the emotional consequences of speech are, however, present in jurisdictions coming out of authoritarian regimes, and even classic common law had provisions against scare-mongering. Anti-scare-mongering laws remain, however, highly suspect from a free speech perspective, given that a requirement of certainty in information, especially when it comes to uncertain events, is censorial and invites abuse. For the expression of such concerns, see *R. v. Zundel*, 2 S.C.R. 73 (1992), para. 224 and Decision of the Hungarian Constitutional Court, Decision 18/2004 (V. 25.) AB. <http://www.mkab.hu/content/en/en3/18_2004.pdf> (29 Apr. 2009).

37. The Declaration of 1789 sets limits to free speech in the form of abuse of the right, but the then prevailing, extremely broad concept of libel included all sorts of "abuse" of speech. "Libelle" included criticism of deputies for their voting. *AP*, IX 271 (January 1790).

38. Cf. Pierre Bourdieu, *Language and Symbolic Power*, trans. Gino Raymond and Matthew Adamson (Cambridge, Mass.: Harvard University Press, 1991), 105–106. See generally, Alexander Tsesis, *Destructive Messages: How Hate Speech Paves the Way for Harmful Social Movements* (New York: New York University Press, 2002).

39. Other kinds of social institutions that regulate speech and communication also generate resistance to arguments. Religion is one of these obstacles to communication. Rules of court procedure single out specific admissible communications. Even science is based on disregard of noncanonical communication. It is claimed that the exclusionary rules are for the advancement of rational discourse.

40. In fact, Enlightenment authors did not contrast sentiments and reason the way this is understood in contemporary literature that emphasizes the one-sidedness of the Project of Reason. See Chapter 3.

41. Mill, *On Liberty*, 7, 5.

42. Religions continue to play a role in the control of certain emotions by defining what should result in disgust: for example, homosexuality. As such, religion remains a major social organizer of emotions and emotion display against free speech.

43. *Gertz v. Robert Welch, Inc.*, 418 U.S. 323, 339 (1974).

44. Posner, "Free Speech," 7.

45. See Joseph Raz, *Practical Reasons and Norms* (Princeton: Princeton University Press, 1975).

46. This problem cannot be solved in standard market transactions, because the conditions of efficient transaction are hardly satisfied. Cf. Michael Rushton, "Economic Analysis of Freedom of Expression," *Georgia State University Law Review* 21, no. 3 (Spring 2005): 693–719, 697; Ronald H. Coase, "Advertising and Free Speech," *Journal of Legal Studies* 6, no. 1 (January 1977): 1–34, 2.

47. Although the press seems to have an interest in access to news and communication, this often conflicts with financial interests of the press (owners) related to advertisement, sponsors, or other political and business interests.

48. It is interesting to note that in Great Britain, following some continental countries, the "apology of terrorism" (i.e., its exoneration) became a crime, while in the United States, where the terrorist damage and feeling of threat are probably greater, First Amendment rights were not affected after 9/11 outside privacy (wiretapping).

49. Heidi Kitrosser, "Containing Unprotected Speech," *Florida Law Review* 57, no. 4 (September 2005): 843–906, 884.

50. This is certainly a somewhat problematic interpretation of the Supreme Court's jurisprudence, given its interest in communicative impact, even if this is seldom decisive. See *R.A.V. v. City of St. Paul*, 505 U.S. 377 (1992) and *Virginia v. Black*, 548 U.S. 343 (2003).

51. Even in the speech area, there is intervention in the name of time, place, and manner, and through the definition of what is protected speech and what qualifies as "act." Workplace harassment (speech in a private context) is simply categorically excluded from First Amendment protection.

52. Of course, what we read at the level of constitutions is quite misleading; consider press laws and the whole area of broadcasting.

53. My personal experience is that American lawyers and other observers of American society are somewhat reluctant to admit that the sphere of protected speech is subject to social reinterpretation. However, seditious libel was an actual possibility until 1964; group libel was found constitutional in 1952, in *Beauharnais v. Illinois*, 343 U.S. 250 (1952), a case that was never overruled; abolitionist speech was criminalized in the nineteenth century; communist advocacy was found a crime in *United States v. Dennis*, 183 F.2d 201, 212 (2d Cir. 1950), affirmed 341 U.S. 494 (1951); there was a conviction for blasphemy in 1959; there are many colleges with problematic speech codes, etc.

54. Richard A. Posner, *Frontiers of Legal Theory* (Cambridge, Mass.: Harvard University Press, 2001), 68; Richard A. Posner, *Economic Analysis of Law* (New York: Aspen, 2003), 695; see further Posner, "Free Speech." Richard Posner refers to the Learned Hand formula which proposes that the courts must "ask whether the gravity of the 'evil,' discounted by its improbability, justifies such invasion of free speech as is necessary to avoid danger." *United States v. Dennis*, 183 F.2d 201, 212 (2d Cir. 1950), affirmed 341 U.S. 494 (1951).

55. See, e.g., the Swedish law that criminalizes agitation against a group by making a statement that threatens or expresses contempt for an ethnic or other group with reference to their race, sexual orientation, etc. (Chapter 16, Section 8 of the Criminal Code). See the *Prosecutor General v. Ake Ingemar Teodor Green* case, decided by the Supreme Court of Sweden, 29 November 2005, B 1050–05. [Pastor Green was convicted for a sermon in which he attributed the spread of AIDS to the "abnormality" of homosexuality.]

56. Geoffrey R. Stone, *Perilous Times: Free Speech in Wartime from the Sedition Act of 1798 to the War on Terrorism* (New York: W. W. Norton, 2004), 5. See further Leonard M. Niehoff, "Free Speech in Wartime Conference," *Rutgers Law Journal* 36, no. 3 (Spring 2005): 821–951, 889.

57. Of course, lack of public presence of a viewpoint makes its reinforcement more difficult, but, except under totalitarian control, there is enough reinforcement of sectarianism in private groups, and therefore the isolation of opinions does not work.

58. It is not by accident that surveys indicate a relatively low public rating of speech in many countries, including the United States. "While most Americans support censorship, some clearly distinguish between restrictions on overseas and domestic news, and they are much more comfortable with the former than the latter. By better than five-to-one, those who believe that news from Afghanistan is being censored favor those restrictions." See Public Views of Terrorism Coverage: Terror Coverage Boost News Media's Images, Pew Research Center for the People & the Press, Washington, D.C., 28 November 2001, available at <http://people-press.org/reports/display.php3?PageID=10> (29 Apr. 2009).

59. 75 BverfGE 369 (1987). [Bavarian Prime Minister represented in political cartoon as copulating pig].

60. *Miller v. California*, 413 U.S. 15, 24 (1973).

61. *R. v. Zundel*, 2 S.C.R. 73 (1992), section 53.

62. See, e.g., Catharine A. MacKinnon, *Feminism Unmodified: Discourses on Life and Law* (Cambridge, Mass.: Harvard University Press, 1987); Andrea Dworkin, *Pornography: Men Possessing Women* (London: Women's Press, 1981); Catharine A. MacKinnon, *Only Words* (Cambridge, Mass.: Harvard University Press, 1993); and Catharine A. MacKinnon and Andrea Dworkin, eds., *In Harm's Way: The Pornography Civil Rights Hearings* (Cambridge, Mass.: Harvard University Press, 1997).

63. *American Booksellers Association, Inc. v. Hudnut*, 771 F.2d 323 (7th Cir. 1985), 329. The Court agreed that such materials may influence the formation of attitudes, but ruled that the ordinance violated the First Amendment because it contained content-based discrimination.

64. *Woods v. Graphic Communications*, 925 F.2d 1195, 1201–1202 (9th Cir. 1991).

65. In a number of jurisdictions around the world, in line with the International Convention on the Elimination of All Forms of Racial Discrimination, racist speech (advocacy of racial supremacy/inferiority) has been criminalized. Arguably, this speech restriction has more to do with equality-related concerns than with the psychological consequences of the speech: when it comes to specific individual injuries, the laws of many countries are more reluctant to impose restrictions on speech.

66. Hate speech refers to a set of different motives, emotions, content, and effects of speech in the different legal cultures. In continental legal systems all sorts of racist statements and racial slurs are considered hate speech—to the extent the term is used in the literature. The Canadian definition is "communication that willfully promotes hatred against any identifiable minority." Hate speech is deemed "non-speech" in Europe, partly in reference to international treaty law that requires the criminalization of the dissemination of racial superiority or hatred; see International Convention on the Elimination of All Forms of Racial Discrimination (1966), Article 4. [The U.S. is not party to the Convention.]

For a typical European (ECtHR) position see, e.g., *Gündüz v. Turkey*, ECtHR Application no. 35071/97, judgment of 4 December 2003, para. 21, 40; for contempt in Sweden see the Green Case.

Bringing into contempt was a common crime in many states of the United States in the nineteen-fifties. An Illinois statute declared it unlawful to distribute any publication that "portrays depravity, criminality, unchastity, or lack of virtue of a class of citizens, of any race, color, creed or religion, which [publication] exposes to *contempt, derision, obloquy* or which is productive of breach of peace or riots." [emphasis added] In *Beauharnais v. Illinois*, 343 U. S. 250 (1952) the statute was held constitutional, as such libelous utterances were held not to be an essential part of any exposition of ideas. Justice Frankfurter writing for the Court referred to historical experiences of race riots and the role of propaganda in such riots where malicious defamation of racial groups "by means calculated to have a powerful emotional impact on those to whom it was presented" did play a prominent role. The *Beauharnais* position reflects an assumption about rational discourse, limiting the protection of speech to this sphere, and finding for this reason against the protection of emotion-influencing propaganda. In the last fifty years speech issues have been decided on a different line of principles.

67. In the nineteenth century continental hate propaganda restrictions were related to social classes and not race, and were understood as protection against breach of peace. In the multi-ethnic Austro-Hungarian Monarchy nationalistic agitation was criminalized as breach of peace.

Where the expression of hatred and contempt concerns a nonfundamental personality trait, it is difficult to apply the antiracism paradigm.

68. Charles R. Lawrence III, "If He Hollers Let Him Go: Regulating Racist Speech on Campus," *Duke Law Journal* 1990, no. 3 (June 1990): 431–483, 461.

69. Cf. Jack McDevitt, Jennifer Balboni, Luis Garcia, and Joann Gu, "Consequences for Victims: A Comparison of Bias- and Non-Bias-Motivated Assaults," *American Behavioral Scientist* 45, no. 4 (December 2001): 697–713; Arnold Barnes and Paul H. Ephross, "The Impact of Hate Violence on Victims: Emotional and Behavioral Responses to Attacks," *Social Work* 39, no. 3 (May 1994): 247–251; Laura Beth Nielsen, *License to Harass, Law, Hierarchy, and Offensive Public Speech* (Princeton: Princeton University Press, 2004).

For a recent summary of contemporary approaches to hate in social psychology see Robert J. Sternberg, ed., *The Psychology of Hate* (Washington, D.C.: American Psychological Association, 2005). Hate involves negation of intimacy, passion, and commitment. Negation of intimacy means dehumanization by classifying other people as having lesser value. It would follow that the way to fight hate is to restrict "the propaganda that leads people to internalize stories about their targets, which in turn promote negation of intimacy, passion and commitment." Robert J. Sternberg, "Enough of hate!" *Monitor on Psychology* 34, no. 9 (October 2003). <http://www.apa.org/monitor/oct03/pc.html> (29 Apr. 2009).

One psychological problem with such policy, among others, is that people often experience hate not as hate, but as self-righteous feelings of anger or aversion; vice versa, there are instances of justified anger which are hard to distinguish from hate but which turn out to be vital for social life.

70. Cf. e.g. Jack Levin and Jack McDevitt, *Hate Crimes: The Rising Tide of Bigotry and Bloodshed* (New York: Plenum Press, 1993). For a critical view on bias crimes see James B. Jacobs and Kimberly Potter, *Hate Crimes: Criminal Law & Identity Politics* (New York: Oxford University Press, 1998).

71. *R. v. Zundel*, 2 S.C.R. 73 (1992), para. 220. Race-related and other sensitivities continue to receive recognition to the detriment of free speech in many countries, though in a somewhat inconsequential way. Holocaust denial is criminalized in many continental systems, which is sometimes partly justified by the need to protect Jewish identity that contains elements of Holocaust victimization. See *Holocaust Denial Case*, 90 BverfGE 241 (1994): "It is part of their [the Jews] personal self-perception to be understood as part of a group of people who stand out by virtue of their fate and in relation to whom there is a special moral responsibility on the part of all others, and this is part of their dignity." Reprinted and translated in Donald P. Kommers, *The Constitutional Jurisprudence of the Federal Republic of Germany* (Durham, N.C.: Duke University Press, 1997), 386.

In Germany in 2005, in order to avoid the embarrassment and disorder of a neo-Nazi protest march, the Bundestag hastily adopted (by a large majority) a law that prohibited demonstrations at locations to which specific sentiments are attached, namely at places of particular sensitivity to victims of Nazism.

72. "But in the world of debate about public affairs, many things done with motives that are less than admirable are protected by the First Amendment. In *Garrison v. Louisiana*, 379 U.S. 64 (1964), we held that even when a speaker or writer is motivated by hatred or ill will his expression was protected by the First Amendment:

> 'Debate on public issues will not be uninhibited if the speaker must run the risk that it will be proved in court that he spoke out of hatred; even if he did speak out of hatred, utterances honestly believed contribute to the free interchange of ideas and the ascertainment of truth.' Id., at 73. *Hustler v. Falwell*, 485 U.S. 46, 54 (1988)"

For the classic psychological mechanism that seems to prevail in the legal imagination, notwithstanding, or exactly because of, its simplifications, see Gordon W. Allport, The Nature of Prejudice (Reading, Mass.: Addison-Wesley, 1979), 57.

73. Sara Ahmed, "Affective Economies," *Social Text* 22, no. 2 (Summer 2004): 117–139, 118.

74. *Chaplinsky v. New Hampshire*, 315 U.S. 568, 572 (1942).

75. See *R.A.V. v. St. Paul*, 505 U.S. 377, 382 (1992). [City of St. Paul's ordinance provides that "Whoever places on public or private property a symbol, object, appellation, characterization, or graffiti, including, but not limited to, a burning cross or Nazi swastika, commits disorderly conduct and shall be guilty of a misdemeanor." Criminalization of expression violates First Amendment, under the technical concerns of content discrimination, overbreadth, and vagueness.]

76. The Supreme Court exceptionally recognizes aggregate consequences in the context of bias crime as the "societal harm" which is responsible for ". . . inciting community unrest" where it is perpetrated. *Wisconsin v. Mitchell*, 508 U.S. 476, 489 (1993).

77. The model of such legislation is the French Press Act of 1881, still in force with amendments. Article 161 of the Ukraine penal code that provides for imprisonment for up to two years over "humiliation of national honor and dignity" is a typical modern example of insult laws.

For a discussion of flag burning see *supra*.

78. Verbal attacks are likely to trigger some of the symptoms of victimization in the sense of "being wronged," including affective responses of fear and anxiety (about personal vulnerability) and may have cognitive impacts as to the justness of the world.

79. Mill, *On Liberty*, 144.

80. Will Kymlicka, *Multicultural Citizenship: A Liberal Theory of Minority Rights* (Oxford: Clarendon Press, 1995).

81. In the sense Nussbaum uses the concept. See Nussbaum, *Hiding from Humanity*, 19–70.

82. *New York Times v. Sullivan*, 376 U.S. 254 (1964), 295; *Lingens v. Austria*, ECtHR Application no. 9815/82, judgment of 8 July 1986, para. 24.

83. See the "equality" argument in *New York Times*, referring to *Barr v. Matteo*, 360 U.S. 564 (1959). See further the German *Gegenschlag* [counter-strike] theory in the Schmid-Spiegel Case 12 BVerfGE 113, in Kommers, *The Constitutional Jurisprudence of the Federal Republic of Germany*, 372 [politician responds to defamatory statements with comparably outrageous statements in election campaign].

84. See *Lingens v. Austria*, ECtHR Application no. 9815/82, judgment of 8 July 1986, para. 41; *Oberschlick v. Austria*, ECtHR Application no. 11662/85, judgment of 23 May 1991, para. 57.

85. Mill, *On Liberty*, 151.

86. Ibid., 151–152. It is remarkable that Mill relates the feeling of disgust that exists beyond religion as one that is related to uncleanness (contamination anxiety).

87. On September 30, 2005, a Danish paper published 12 cartoons, a collection suggesting that there is a relationship between Islam and terrorism as well as oppression of women. Some of these depicted the Prophet, whose representation is prohibited by most tenets of Islam. On January 30, 2006, right after the electoral victory of Hamas, violent demonstrations began in Gaza and elsewhere in the Islamic world. See, e.g., András Sajó, ed., *Censorial Sensitivities: Free Speech and Religion in a Fundamentalist World* (Utrecht: Eleven International Publishing, 2007).

88. *Otto-Preminger-Institut v. Austria*, ECtHR Application no. 13470/87, judgment of 20 September 1994, para. 26.

89. Robert C. Solomon, *The Passions: Emotions and the Meaning of Life* (Garden City, N.Y.: Anchor Press, 1976), 185–186.

6. The Containment of Passion

1. *Conseil Constitutionnel*, 94–352 DC of January 18, 1995. The recognition relates the right to freedom of expression. Demonstrations have been an integrative part of French politics in the last 150 years; many of them ended in violence.

2. Historically the term "assembly" referred in English and (to a lesser extent) in French law to the operation of deliberative bodies, though mass demonstration was not unknown: "Unlawfull assembly is where people assemble themselves together to doe some unlawfull thing against the peace." John Rastell, ed., *Les Termes de la Ley: or, Certaine Difficult and Obscure Words and Termes of the Common Lawes of this Realme Expounded* (London: Beale & R. Hearne, 1641), 187.

3. Dieter Groh, "Collective Behavior from the 17th to the 20th Century: Change of Phenomena, Change of Perception, or No Change at All? Some Preliminary Reflections," in *Changing Conceptions of Crowd, Mind, and Behavior*, ed. Carl F. Graumann and Serge Moscovici (New York: Springer-Verlag, 1985), 143–162, 148; Eric J. Hobsbawm, *Primitive Rebels; Studies in Archaic Forms of Social Movement in the 19th and 20th Centuries* (Manchester: Manchester University Press, 1971).

4. Albert O. Hirschman, *The Passions and the Interests* (Princeton: Princeton University Press, 1977), 92.

5. In line with the rights-generating effect of personal experience, the personal observers of the massacres felt it necessary to establish the *Manchester Guardian*, a radical newspaper that was the predecessor of the contemporary *Guardian*, in order to "zealously enforce the principles of civil and religious Liberty." The gathering to push for electoral reform was intended to remain peaceful, and little mob behavior was observed (though it was assumed by the authorities to be forthcoming). <http://www.gmgplc.co.uk/ScottTrust/History/tabid/193/Default.aspx> (23 Apr. 2009).

The Peterloo massacre was followed by restrictions on assemblies, not so much from concerns about a crowd turning into an unruly mob, but because of fears of radical conspiracy (see also the Cato Street Conspiracy, an attempt to murder cabinet members in 1820).

6. W. Ivor Jennings, "The Right of Assembly in England," *New York University Law Review* 9 (1931–1932): 217, quoted after Bogdan Iancu, "Balancing Emotionalism: Contemporary Implications of the Impact of Street Demonstrations on Third-Party Interests," in *Free to Protest: Constituent Power and Street Demonstration*, ed. András Sajó (Utrecht: Eleven International Publishing, 2009), 17–40, 17.

7. Helen Fenwick and Gavin Phillipson, "Public Protest, the Human Rights Act, and Judicial Responses to Political Expression," *Public Law* (Winter 2000): 627–648.

8. Art. XVI: "That the people have a right to assemble together, to consult for their common good, to instruct their representatives, and to apply to the legislature for redress of grievances, by address, petition, or remonstrance." However, most other state constitutions were silent on the matter.

9. James Madison, *Federalist Papers*, No. 55 (New York: Penguin, Mentor, 1961), 342. Note that Madison is not writing of large crowds in public places, and still fears "the confusion and intemperance of the multitude."

10. The liberal *Acte additionnel aux constitutions de l'Empire du 22 avril 1815* that Benjamin Constant drafted at Napoleon's request after the Emperor's return was adopted by five million votes in a plebiscite. It not only disregards the right to assembly, but limits the right to petition to individual petition. In Europe the more assembly-friendly solution of the 1791 French Constitution was taken up in its heir, the 1831 Belgian Constitution, and it found its way into such revolutionary constitutional documents as the German *Paulskirchenverfassung* of 1849 (Art. 161).

11. Aurélien Lignereux, "1800–1859. Comment naissent les rébellions," *Revue d'histoire du XIXe siècle* 35 (2007): 2007–2035, La Restauration revisitée—Les formes de la protestation—Une histoire de l'Etat <http://rh19.revues.org/document2162.html> (23 Apr. 2009).

See further William M. Reddy, "Skeins, Scales, Discounts, Steam, and Other Objects of Crowd Justice in Early French Textile Mills," *Comparative Studies in Society and History* 21, no. 2 (April 1979): 204–213. For the importance of police resources and related patterns of behavior and an overview of the changes in police violence in Germany, see Thomas Lindenberger, "From the Chopped-off Hand to the Twisted Foot: Citizenship and Police Violence in 20th-Century Germany," in *Citizenship and National Identity in Twentieth Century Germany*, ed. Geoff Eley and Jan Palmowski (Stanford: Stanford University Press, 2008), 108–128.

12. The distinction is emphasized in Serge Moscovici, "The Discovery of the Masses," in *Changing Conceptions of Crowd Mind and Behavior*, ed. Graumann and Moscovici, 5–26, 22, referring to Tarde and Freud.

13. For the relevance of Freud for neuroscience see, for example, Robert L. Solso, *Mind and Brain Sciences in the 21st Century* (Cambridge, Mass.: MIT Press, 1997); and John E. Gedo, "The Enduring Scientific Contributions of Sigmund Freud," *Perspectives in Biology and Medicine* 45, no. 2 (Spring 2002): 200–211.

14. Writing in the later part of the eighteenth century John Millar of Glasgow (1735–1801) stressed that in the conditions of urban industrial development, laborers who are in "constant intercourse, are enabled, with great rapidity, to communicate all their sentiments and passions." Millar's Manuscript quoted in Groh, "Collective Behavior," 149; for France see Lignereux, "Restauration."

15. See Moscovici, "Discovery," 8.; Serge Moscovici, *The Age of the Crowd: A Historical Treatise on Mass Psychology*, trans. J. C. Whitehouse (Cambridge: Cambridge University Press, 1985).

Following Margaret Mead, American social psychology and sociology turned against the suggestibility thesis providing the grounds for the rationality of masses (movements) approach. In the 1980s it was Serge Moscovici who reintroduced the issue of the crowd to social psychology and sociology as a genuine problem.

16. See, e.g., the French liberal position in the first half of the nineteenth century. François Guizot, *Des moyens de gouvernement et d'opposition dans l'état actuel de la France*, introduction by Claude Lefort (Paris: Belin, 1988), 251; see further Lignereux, "Restauration."

17. See Moscovici, *Age*, 25–26. One possible reason for the manageability and acceptability of the assemblies was that participants were more integrated into the national society, having a sense of national citizenship which in turn had to be respected by the authorities. Once the demonstrators are not passionate criminals and brutes but fellow citizens, it is more difficult to treat them as objects. For the transformation during the Third French Republic, see Eugene Weber, *Peasants into Frenchmen: The Modernization of Rural France, 1870–1914* (Stanford: Stanford University Press, 1976).

18. Groh, "Collective Behavior." Crowd psychology was an easy political target given the problematic political prejudices of its founder, Gustave Le Bon.

19. Beyond the works of Moscovici cited above, see Christian Borch, "The Exclusion of the Crowd: The Destiny of a Sociological Figure of the Irrational," *European Journal of Social Theory* 9, no. 1 (February 2006): 83–102. For a rehabilitation of Tarde see Gilles Deleuze, *Difference and Repetition*, trans. Paul Patton (London: Athlone Press, 1994).

20. Joseph Alois Schumpeter, *Capitalism, Socialism, and Democracy* (London: Allen and Unwin, 1976), 256. Quoted in Moscovici, *Age*, 68.

21. Before the Nazi takeover, Nazi Party gatherings were much less peaceful and orderly, often inciting to violence. The rational demonstration model is rich in excessive optimism.

22. "Treating everyone harshly may lead previously disparate groups to unite in common hostility to the police. In other words, policing all crowds and all members of a crowd as if they were dangerous may sometimes become a self-fulfilling prophecy." Stephen Reicher and Clifford Stott, "Crowd Action as Intergroup Process: Introducing the Police Perspective," *European Journal of Social Psychology* 28, no. 4 (July–August 1998): 509–529, 523.

23. See, for example, Léon Duguit, *Traité de droit constitutionnel. Les libertés publiques*, Volume V (Paris: Fontemoing-Boccard, 1925), 339. Duguit used this argument to explain the absence of the right to assembly from the Declaration, claiming that this was implied in freedom of communication.

24. See, for example, *Éva Molnár v. Hungary*, ECtHR Application no. 10346/05, judgment of 7 October 2008, para. 37.

25. Case *Eugen Schmidberger, Internationale Transporte und Planzüge v. Republik Österreich*, European Court of Justice C-112/00, 12 June 2003. The issue was whether "the fact that the authorities of a Member State did not ban a demonstration with primarily environmental aims which resulted in the complete closure of a major transit route, such as the Brenner motorway, for almost 30 hours without interruption amounts to an unjustified restriction of the free movement of goods which is a fundamental principle laid down by Articles 30 and 34 of the Treaty [of the European Union]."

26. *Schmidberger*, para. 92.

27. The ambiguity is clearly demonstrated in a Spanish case. Batasuna, a Basque party, was banned in 2003 for its links to terrorist separatists. The illegal party called for demonstrations, which were banned, but these bans were often overturned by the regional Supreme Court. In 2005 the regional Supreme Court upheld the ban, accepting

the police argument that referred to past violence. The dissent claimed that the ban on a party does not take away individual members' right to demonstrate.

28. *Ezelin v. France*, ECtHR Application no. 11800/85, judgment of 26 April 1991, para. 53.

29. *Sürek v Turkey (No. 1)*, ECtHR Application no. 26682/95, judgment of 8 July 1999, para. 62. The reference was made in the context of letters, not demonstrations.

30. The Supreme Court of India upheld on March 13, 2002, a 1994 ban on holding religious observances at Ayodhya, where a Hindu mob destroyed a temple, resulting in ongoing violence in several states. For the Orange parades see Michael Hamilton and Dominique Bryan, "Deepening Democracy? Dispute System Design and the Mediation of Contested Parades in Northern Ireland," *Ohio State Journal on Dispute Resolution* 22, no. 1 (2006): 133–187.

31. Bernard Stirn, *Les libertés en question* (Clefs Politics) (Paris: Montchrestien, 2006), § 37 (no page). The German Constitutional Court had no difficulty upholding the banning of an assembly where David Irwin, the Holocaust-denying British historian, was scheduled to give a speech. It was argued that the speech to be given (whose content was unknown) would violate the law, as it would deny the Holocaust. BVerfGE 90, 241 (1994).

32. Robert Musil, *The Man without Qualities*, trans. Eithne Wilkis and Ernst Kaiser (London: Picador, 1988), 352.

33. Nan D. Hunter, "Identity, Speech, and Equality," in *Sex Wars: Sexual Dissent and Political Culture*, ed. Lisa Duggan and Nan D. Hunter (New York: Routledge, 1995), 123–141, 140.

34. Cf. Michael Hamilton, "We, the People: Freedom of Assembly, the Rights of Others, and Inclusive Constitutionalism," in *Free to Protest*, ed. Sajó, 57.

35. Nevertheless, crimes of passion were culturally respectable in most nineteenth-century European countries.

36. "Spontaneous" demonstrations in many instances are organized. Organization may look absent simply because it is quite easy to coordinate when networked organizers employ text messaging and other techniques. The mass gathering at the fall of the Berlin Wall could have been spontaneous, but it presupposed that people were watching the same broadcasters. German constitutional law and the practice of the European Court of Human Rights provide protection to such gatherings, but only as reactions to exceptional events, which does not make sense if notification is given. The justification given for the requirement of notification (which in fact enables banning) is that notification makes possible police coordination. In France *réunions* (meetings that do not take place in public venues) were subject to notification under the original 1881 reunion law, but the notification requirement was abolished upon the request of the Catholic Church. Duguit, *Traité*, 348. The October 23, 1935, law-decree on demonstrations also grants exemption from advance notification for processions conforming to local usage.

37. In the case of some fundamentalist religions which are labeled cults or sects, the assumption is the opposite: these are suspect by definition, the fear being that the interaction of the believers enables self-destructive contagions.

38. "When we say that these are irrational what we really mean is that their 'constitution' and aims are dictated by memories of things past rather than by the perception of things present." Moscovici, "Discovery," 18.

39. Representation of the People Act 1867, 30 & 31 Vict. c. 102. The Act gave voting rights to the working class (males) by granting thoroughgoing household suffrage, and more proportionate representation by creating new boroughs. The Bill originated in an effort by Disraeli to redraw the electoral system in favor of the Tories. For Gladstone and the Liberals this was acceptable as in their view it did not put the majority into the hands of the working class, which was not expected to act as a single class. Gladstone expected that the reform would enable "an increase of attachment of the people to its laws, its institutions and its rulers." Henry C. Gray Matthew, *Gladstone, 1809–1874* (Oxford: Clarendon Press, 2001), 140. By an unintended interparty competition the Bill extended the franchise beyond the intent of the proposal.

40. The doctrine of militant democracy claims that not only must a constitutional democracy stand up against the politics of emotions when the radical forces have already gained ground and begun to exploit the democratic apparatus, but that it must also be ready and able to confine the politics of emotions.

41. Karl Loewenstein, "Militant Democracy and Fundamental Rights I," *American Political Science Review* 31, no. 3 (June 1937): 417–432, 417; Moscovici, *Age*, 89–90.

42. Moscovici, "Discovery," 15.

7. Shame

1. In more than 200 years the word "shame" occurred in only 78 decisions of the U.S. Supreme Court, mostly as quotes from scholarly literature regarding the operation of criminal punishment, or in emphatic criticism of other judges' position.

2. Erik Erikson, "Identity and the Life Cycle," *Psychological Issues* 1, no. 1, Monograph 1, (New York: International Universities Press, 1959), 42. See further Francis J. Broucek, *Shame and the Self* (New York: Guilford, 1991).

3. Gabriele Taylor, *Pride, Shame, and Guilt, Emotions of Self-Assessment* (Oxford: Clarendon Press, 1985), 83, 81.

"The basic experience connected with shame is that of being seen, inappropriately, by the wrong people, in the wrong condition." Bernard Williams, *Shame and Necessity* (Berkeley: University of California Press, 1993), 82. For the relation of exposure, shame, and the law of privacy, see Jeffrey Rosen, *The Unwanted Gaze: The Destruction of Privacy in America* (New York: Random House, 2000).

4. Silvan S. Tomkins, *Affect Imagery Consciousness: Volume 2: The Negative Affects* (New York: Springer, 1963), 123. The key sources of shame for him are being looked at and being strange.

5. Andrew Ortony, Gerald L. Clore, and Allan Collins, *The Cognitive Structure of Emotions* (Cambridge: Cambridge University Press, 1988). See further Jeff Elison, "Shame and Guilt: A Hundred Years of Apples and Oranges," *New Ideas in Psychology* 23, no. 1 (April 2005): 5–32.

On devaluation see Karen Caplovitz Barrett, "A Functionalist Perspective on the Development of Emotions," in *What Develops in Emotional Development?*, ed. Michael F. Mascolo and Sharon Griffin (New York: Plenum, 1998), 109–133.

6. Williams, *Shame and Necessity*, 89–90. Williams's approach avoids the difficulty that emerges from distinguishing guilt and shame on the basis of the nature of the norm transgressed.

7. Daniel M. T. Fessler, "Shame in Two Cultures: Implications for Evolutionary Approaches," *Journal of Cognition & Culture* 4, no. 2 (2004): 207–262, 207. However, Norbert Elias's classic work on European civilization shows the crucial social importance of shame in the formation of our increasingly individualistic Western civilization. Norbert Elias, *Power and Civility: The Civilizing Process*, trans. Edmund Jephcott (New York: Pantheon, 1982).

8. Dacher Keltner and Brenda N. Buswell, "Embarrassment: Its Distinct Form and Appeasement Functions," *Psychological Bulletin* 122, no. 3 (May 1997): 250–270, 252. Contrast with Nathan Harris, "Reassessing the Dimensionality of the Moral Emotions," *British Journal of Psychology* 94, no. 4 (November 2003): 457–473, 458.

In Turiel's view embarrassment is a feeling of shame in front of strangers, for transgression of social conventions. Elliot Turiel, *The Development of Social Knowledge: Morality and Convention* (Cambridge: Cambridge University Press, 1983). For others the feeling that emerges at the violation of social norms is shame, and the feeling at violation of moral norms is guilt.

The distinctions based on the elicitors of shame and guilt (social conventions for shame, moral norms for guilt) are hardly sustainable because the very distinction between moral norms and social conventions that alleges a difference between the underlying feelings is problematic. The social convention/moral norms distinction *may* be related to differences in cognitive processes; at least Kant and Kohlberg seem to have assumed such difference in the case of morally mature people.

9. Johnny R. J. Fontaine, Ype H. Poortinga, Bernadette Setiadi, and Suprapti S. Markam, "Cognitive Structure of Emotion Terms in Indonesia and the Netherlands," *Cognition and Emotion* 16, no. 1 (1 January 2002): 61–86.

Based on an fMRI study Hidehiko and colleagues find that embarrassment generates activities related to brain regions that have been implicated in the neural substrate of social cognition or Theory of Mind (ToM). Hidehiko Takahashia, Noriaki Yahatac, Michihiko Koedad, Tetsuya Matsudae, Kunihiko Asaib, and Yoshiro Okubo, "Brain Activation Associated with Evaluative Processes of Guilt and Embarrassment: An fMRI Study," *NeuroImage* 23, no. 3 (November 2004): 967–974.

10. Cf. June Price Tangney, Rowland S. Miller, Laura Flicker, and Deborah Hill Barlow, "Are Shame, Guilt, and Embarrassment Distinct Emotions?," *Journal of Personality and Social Psychology* 70, no. 6 (June 1996): 1256–1269. Tangney et al. claim that shame is the feeling of being immoral.

11. Mary K. Babcock and John Sabini, "On Differentiating Embarrassment from Shame," *European Journal of Social Psychology* 20, no. 2 (March–April 1990): 151–169.

12. Williams, *Shame and Necessity*, 88.

13. Susan Shott, "Emotion and Social Life: A Symbolic Interactionist Analysis," *American Journal of Sociology* 84, no. 6 (May 1979): 1317–1334; Millie R. Creighton, "Revisiting Shame and Guilt Cultures: A Forty-Year Pilgrimage," *Ethos* 18, no. 3 (September 1990): 279–307.

14. In the present discussion the shame family is singled out for analytical purposes, but the actual impact on law (institution-building) always presupposes the interaction of different emotions; shame interacts with fear, etc.

15. "While abortion among young, unmarried women is more accepted, many married women feel they have to justify their decision. Women are expected to feel sorrow, shame and guilt because of their sexual conduct for many reasons, but especially if the result is an unwanted pregnancy. It is easier to protect the law when there is recognition of the moral right to choose abortion. The legal battle has been won, but winning the moral battle is important in Norway now. I believe that until having an abortion is considered as acceptable morally as using contraception, women will not have gained their full reproductive rights." Mette Løkeland, "Abortion: The Legal Right Has Been Won, But Not the Moral Right," *Reproductive Health Matters* 12, no. 24, Supplement 1 (November 2004): 167–173 [Abstract].

16. Helen Block Lewis, *Shame and Guilt in Neurosis* (New York: International Universities Press, 1971), 197.

17. Thomas J. Scheff, "Shame and Conformity: The Deference Emotion System," *American Sociological Review* 53, no. 3 (June 1988): 395–406.

18. 98 Eng. Rep. 201 at 205 (1769) (recognizing perpetual common-law copyright), quoted in Samuel Warren and Louis Brandeis, "The Right to Privacy," *Harvard Law Review* 4, no. 5 (15 December 1890): 193–220, 198.

19. James Q. Whitman, "The Two Western Cultures of Privacy: Dignity versus Liberty," *Yale Law Journal* 113, no. 6 (April 2004): 1151–1222, 1153.

20. Justice Brandeis argued that the protection of one's *feelings* in the form of privacy is part of the constitutional project:

> The makers of our Constitution undertook to secure conditions favorable to the pursuit of happiness. They recognized the significance of man's spiritual nature, of his feelings and of his intellect. They knew that only a part of the pain, pleasure and satisfactions of life are to be found in material things. They sought to protect Americans in their beliefs, their thoughts, their emotions and their sensations. They conferred, as against the government, the right to be let alone—the most comprehensive of rights and the right most valued by civilized men. To protect, that right, every unjustifiable intrusion by the government upon the privacy of the individual, whatever the means employed, must be deemed a violation of the Fourth Amendment.

Olmstead v. U.S., 277 U.S. 438, 478 (1928) (evidence collected by governmental wiretapping is admissible in a court).

21. Judgment of June 16, 1858, Trib. Pr. Inst. de la Seine, 1858 D.P. III 62. (Fr.) Cf. Eric H. Reiter, "Personality and Patrimony: Comparative Perspectives on the Right to One's Image," *Tulane Law Review* 76, no. 3 (February 2002): 673–724, 673. See

further Jeanne M. Hauch, "Protecting Private Fact in France: The Warren & Brandeis Tort Is Alive and Well and Flourishing in Paris," *Tulane Law Review* 68, no. 5 (May 1994): 1219–1301, 1222–1223.

In Germany the photos of Bismarck lying on his deathbed are considered the origin of modern personality protection.

22. It is likely, as Jessica Bulman argues, that it was a "media-driven public sphere and the Victorian ideology of separate spheres" that bothered and influenced the authors, and a male concept "of domestic privacy and its attendant patriarchal ordering of the family also informed their article." Jessica Bulman, "Edith Wharton, Privacy and Publicity," *Yale Journal of Law and Feminism* 16, no. 1 (Spring 2004): 41–82, 45, 54.

23. Warren and Brandeis, "The Right to Privacy," 206; Henry James, *The Notebooks of Henry James*, ed. Francis Otto Matthiessen and Kenneth B. Murdock (New York: Oxford University Press, 1961), 82.

24. Bulman "Edith Wharton," 54.

25. Martha C. Nussbaum, *Hiding from Humanity* (Princeton: Princeton University Press, 2004), 297. The tension is present in leading U.S. privacy cases, beginning with *Griswold v. Connecticut*, 381 U.S. 479 (1965) and *Stanley v. Georgia*, 394 U.S. 557 (1969) to *Lawrence v. Texas*, 539 U.S. 558 (2003), where the immoral (disgusting or shameful) behavior occurred privately and police had to enter the premises. Such entry was always problematic, but it was found legitimate even where the act was held in the end constitutionally protected as in *Lawrence*.

26. Judgment of the Federal Constitutional Court of 15 December 1999, quoted after *Von Hannover v. Germany*, ECtHR Application no. 59320/00, judgment of 24 June 2004, para. 25. (Daughter of the Prince of Monaco trying to prevent the publication of her pictures taken at restaurant and other activities of private nature). For the ECtHR the photos served only the curiosity of a particular readership regarding the details of the applicant's private life while the protection of private life is needed for the development of personality (a development that seems to presuppose living without being shamed, at least without a legitimate reason). The difference between the two approaches indicates that the level of protection granted to intimacy remains a judicially contested cultural construction.

27. On the social history of emotions and norm generation and the concept of the rights of the weak see Chapter 4.

28. Jeremy Waldron, "Superseding Historical Injustice," *Ethics* 103, no. 1 (October 1992): 4–28, 6.

29. *Sturges v. Crowninshield*, 17 U.S. 122, 162 (1819).

30. *Pretoria City Council v. Walker*, (1998 (2) SA 363 (CC)) para. 1, 43–48.

31. Theunis Roux, "Legitimating Transformation: Political Resource Allocation in the South African Constitutional Court," *Democratization* 10, no. 4 (November 2003): 92–111, 101.

32. BVerfGE 90, 214 (1994).

33. Governmental forgiveness might suggest the need to forget. See Martha Minow, *Between Vengeance and Forgiveness* (Boston: Beacon Press, 1998), 17.

34. Desmond Mpilo Tutu, *No Future without Forgiveness* (New York: Image, 1999), 55.

35. Case CCT 17/96 *The Azanian Peoples Organization v. The President of the Republic of South Africa* para. 2, 50, 43.

36. Trevor Lubbe, "Victims, Perpetrators and Healers at the Truth & Reconciliation Commission: Being in the Same Boat" <http://human-nature.com/free-associations/lubbe.html> (16 Apr. 2009); Troy Urquhart, "Truth, Reconciliation, and the Restoration of the State: Coetzee's *Waiting for the Barbarians*," *Twentieth Century Literature* 52, no. 1 (Spring 2006): 1–21, 2.

I could not find convincing evidence in the literature on postwar German public sentiment regarding the shaming effects of the reeducation programs resulting in popular recognition of national and personal guilt. The majority understood (and felt in the light of their burning houses already) that the Hitler regime was a tragedy to be avoided at all costs. See in particular Norbert Frei, *Adenauer's Germany and the Nazi Past: The Politics of Amnesty and Integration*, trans. Joel Golb (New York: Columbia University Press, 2002).

37. Lubbe, "Victims, Perpetrators."

38. *Plessy v. Ferguson*, 163 U.S. 537 (1896).

The national shame argument was used after the Civil War, but it lost its power with time: "The validity of that State restriction upon the rights of conscience and the duty of life was affirmed, to the *shame and disgrace of America*, in the Supreme Court of the United States." These are the words of future president James Garfield, who had participated in the debates on the Fourteenth Amendment in 1866, in a legislative debate on the Civil Rights Bill. Cong. Globe, 42d Cong., 1st Sess. Part I (1871) 475, 476 [emphasis added].

In the Pretoria public utilities surcharge case in post-apartheid South Africa (*Pretoria v. Walker*), the members of the concerned taxpayers' association did not seem to have feelings of shame for a privileged past that they continued to benefit from, nor did the Court wish to remind them of this burden. For a rejection of shame for torture in post-colonial France, see Paul Aussaresses, *Sevices spéciaux. Algérie 1955–1957* (Paris: Perrin 2001).

39. Doc. 124, 88th Cong., 1st Sess. 2 (1963). Somewhat later, in 1987, World War II Japanese internees generated enough shame for compensation. See S. 1009., 100th Cong., 1st Session (1987).

40. *U.S. v. Stanley*, 483 U.S. 669, 703 (1987) quoting affirmatively Donaldson, "Constitutional Torts and Military Effectiveness: A Proposed Alternative to the *Feres* Doctrine," *Air Force Law Review* 23, no. 171 (1982–1983): 198–199. For the role of shame in privacy torts claims see *Housh v. Peth*, 165 Ohio St. 35, 133 N.E.2d 340, 341 (1956): "An actionable invasion of the right of privacy is the unwarranted appropriation or exploitation of one's personality, the publicizing of one's private affairs with which the public has no legitimate concern, or the wrongful *intrusion* into one's private activities in such a manner as to outrage or *cause* mental suffering, *shame or humiliation* to a person of ordinary sensibilities." [emphasis added] Quoted in *Zacchini v. Scripps-Howard Broadcasting Co.*, 433 U.S. 562, 574 (1977).

41. *Norwalk Core v. Norwalk Redevelopment Agency*, 395 F.2d 920, 931–932 (C.A.2 1968). Quoted in *Gratz v. Bollinger*, 539 U.S. 244, 301 (2003) (Justice Ginsburg, with whom Justice Souter joins, dissenting).

42. *Regents of University of California v. Bakke*, 438 U.S. 265, 402 (1978). The prevailing consideration in Justice Powell's rejection of any specific consideration of past injustice as ground for preferential treatment is one of (*otherwise*) sound judicial policy. He refused "the remedying of the effects of 'societal discrimination,' an amorphous concept of injury that may be ageless in its reach into the past," and only specific actual instances of present discrimination were held to be redressable. Id 307, 296–297.

43. "The primary purpose of the Civil Rights Act of 1964, however, as the Court recognizes, and as I would underscore, is the vindication of human dignity, and not mere economics. The Senate Commerce Committee made this quite clear: 'The primary purpose of . . . [the Civil Rights Act], then, is to solve this problem, the deprivation of personal dignity that surely accompanies denials of equal access to public establishments. Discrimination is not simply dollars and cents, hamburgers and movies; it is the humiliation, frustration, and embarrassment that a person must surely feel when he is told that he is unacceptable as a member.'" *Heart of Atlanta Motel, Inc. v. U. S.*, 379 U.S. 241, 291–292 (1964) (Justice Goldberg, concurring).

44. *City of Cleburne, Tex. v. Cleburne Living Center*, 473 U.S. 432, 464 (1985) (Justice Marshall, with whom Justice Brennan and Justice Blackmun join, concurring in the judgment in part and dissenting in part). "Surely one *has to feel sorry* for a person disabled by something he or she can't do anything about, but I'm not aware of any reason to suppose that elected officials are unusually unlikely to share that feeling." John Hart Ely, *Democracy and Distrust: A Theory of Judicial Review* (Cambridge: Harvard University Press, 1980), 150, quoted in *Cleburne*, 442, n. 10 [emphasis added].

45. *Romer v. Evans*, 517 U.S. 620, 635 (1996).

46. Justice Scalia in his dissenting opinion argued that "Coloradans are . . . entitled to be hostile toward homosexual conduct." Ibid., 644. Scalia relies on his earlier position in *Bowers*, where he found the criminalization of sodomy constitutional; *Bowers v. Hardwick*, 478 U.S. 186 (1986) [overruled in *Lawrence v. Texas*, 539 U.S. 558 (2003)]. For a classic summary of the legitimacy of emotional dictates in legislation, see Patrick Devlin, *The Enforcement of Morals* (London: Oxford University Press, 1965). Society's right to self-preservation necessitates that laws be made in response to the public's reactions to disgust. As William Ian Miller, *The Anatomy of Disgust* (Cambridge: Harvard University Press, 1977), 194, stated, disgust "marks out moral matters for which we can have no compromise."

47. Nussbaum, *Hiding from Humanity*, 171.

48. *Egan v. Canada (A.G.)*, (1995) 2 SCR 513, 518. The South African Constitutional Court followed the Canadian position; see *President of the Republic of South Africa v. Hugo* (1997) CCT 11/96. The position of the Canadian Supreme Court on the significance of reviewing past discrimination was expressed recently in an even stronger form in *Law v. Canada (Minister of Employment and Immigration)*, (1999) 1 SCR 497.

49. *Egan*, 520–521.

50. See *American Booksellers Association, Inc. v. Hudnut*, 771 F.2d 323 (7th Cir. 1985), 330, affirmed 475 U.S. 1001 (1986); *R.A.V. v. City of St. Paul, Minn.*, 505 U.S. 377 (1992).

51. Dov Cohen, "The American National Conservation about (Everything but) Shame," *Social Research* 70, no. 4 (Winter 2003): 1075–1108, 1096.

52. *Auschwitz bleibt uns anvertraut*; this is the title of the celebrated German writer's speech honoring the German Peace Prize in 1987.

53. See Karl Jaspers, *The Question of German Guilt*, trans. E. B. Ashton [pseud] (Westport, Conn.: Greenwood Press, 1978). It is quite possible that many Germans are fed up with the continued evaluation of German acts from the perspective of being non-Nazi. But it is clear that turning anti-Semitism into a taboo did and does work, notwithstanding the strength of neo-Nazi and other xenophobe extremist movements.

Increasingly, one can also observe shame- and outrage-induced developments in public international law that become part of domestic public law. Shame and compassion facilitate the public acceptance of government policies in matters of humanitarian intervention. Such shame emerges after nonintervention into genocide: the memory of genocide in Rwanda facilitates the claims for, and acceptance of, humanitarian intervention in Darfur.

54. In Poland the debate is about the responsibility of Poles for anti-Semitism that eventually led to popular participation in the Jedwabne (July, 1941) and Kielce (July, 1946) pogroms. See Jan Tomasz Gross, *Polish Society under German Occupation: The Generalgouvernement, 1939–1944* (Princeton: Princeton University Press, 1979); Jan Tomasz Gross, *Neighbors: The Destruction of the Jewish Community in Jedwabne, Poland* (Princeton: Princeton University Press, 2001); and Jan Tomasz Gross, *Fear: Anti-Semitism in Poland after Auschwitz: An Essay in Historical Interpretation* (New York: Random House, 2006).

There is a small war going on in countries with a colonial past about shaming and/or exempting the nation from it. This turns legislation into a symbolic act and interferes with history writing. For France see the Loi Toubon on the crimes of slavery, and the attempts to provide for the Armenian genocide the same criminal law status as the one that applies to the Holocaust and its denial.

55. Moreover, at least, since the beginning of the nineteen-eighties, French legislators have been ready to criminalize all sorts of racial slurs (although partly because of tensions with the immigrants), so at least assurances about the future have been given, although still without serious soul-searching.

56. Embarrassment was enough to bring down Philipp Jenninger, the Speaker of the Bundestag, a person otherwise known for philosemitism, when in a commemorative speech at the fiftieth anniversary of *Kristallnacht* (1988) he did not successfully distinguish between his views and the sentiments of Germans under Hitler that he reconstructed in the speech. He seemed to have been genuinely embarrassed for what he said once he realized the impression he made on the audience.

57. See *Lüth* case, BVerfGE 7, 198, 216 (1958). "A crucial interest exists . . . in assuring the world that the German people have abandoned [the] attitude [of persecution of the Jews] and condemn it not for political opportunism but because of an inner conversion."

58. A different, more pragmatic response to past mass injustices considers its lasting impacts on the victims, denying that undoing the injustice is shame-dictated (see the position of American constitutional law, below).

59. "Everybody is co-responsible for the way he is governed." Jaspers, *German Guilt*, 25. "Ein Volk haftet für seine Staatlichkeit." Karl Jaspers, *Die Schuldfrage: Ein Beitrag zur deutschen Frage* (Zurich: Artemis, 1946/1960), 100.

Note that Jaspers's whole argument is against collective guilt in favor of collective responsibility. For later debates see Jürgen Habermas, *Eine Art Schadensabwicklung. Kleine Politische Schriften*, Volume VI (Frankfurt am Main: Suhrkamp, 1987); Jürgen Habermas, "A Kind of Settling of Damages," [four essays], in Habermas, *The New Conservatism: Cultural Criticism and the Historians' Debate*, trans. Shierry Weber Nicholsen (Cambridge, Mass.: MIT Press, 1989), 207–248.

On the intimate relations of Habermas's constitutional patriotism and German responsibility see Jan-Werner Muller, "On the Origins of Constitutional Patriotism," *Contemporary Political Theory* 5, no. 3 (August 2006): 278–296. Muller argues that the criminalization of "impermissible lies" may exclude shaming.

A First Amendment liberal will have little sympathy with turning anti-Semitic rubbish into pulp by order of the government. A ban on Nazi commemorative meetings or the imprisonment of football hooligans for racist incitement may not be an adequate policy for breaking with the past. Shame dictates different, less authoritarian, behavior. Decent Europeans simply don't buy the Protocols of the Elders of Zion. Moreover, decent people boycott bookstores where such rubbish is available.

60. BVerfGE 90, 241 (Holocaust Denial Case, 1994), translated in Donald P. Kommers, *The Constitutional Jurisprudence of the Federal Republic of Germany* (Durham, N.C.: Duke University Press, 1997), 386. In the case the Constitutional Court quoted the German Supreme Court approvingly.

61. Muller, "Constitutional Patriotism," 294.

62. 1/1995. (II. 8.) AB decision.

63. See 1/1995. (II. 8.) AB decision, 22/1996. (VI. 25.) AB decision. When the Constitutional Court argued that compensation for past injustice is an *ex gratia* act, and not a constitutional duty, it denied legal continuity in terms of strict state responsibility. As a matter of fact, the Jews were murdered with the active complicity of the Hungarian authorities, while most of the other victims died in Russian camps as prisoners of war.

64. István Bibó, "The Jewish Question in Hungary after 1944" in Bibó, *Democracy, Revolution, Self-Determination: Selected Writings*, ed. Károly Nagy, trans. András Boros-Kazai (New York: Columbia University Press, 1991), 192–244.

65. Nenad Dimitrijevic, "Serbia after the Criminal Past: What Went Wrong and What Should Be Done," *International Journal of Transitional Justice* 2, no. 1 (March 2008): 5–22. András Sajó, "Affordable Shame," in *The Paradoxes of Unintended*

Consequences, ed. Lord Dahrendorf, Yehuda Elkana, and Aryeh Neier (Budapest: CEU Press, 2000), 163–191.

66. Peter Strelan, "Who Forgives Others, Themselves, and Situations? The Roles of Narcissism, Guilt, Self-Esteem, and Agreeableness," *Personality and Individual Differences* 42, no. 2 (January 2007): 259–269, 260. Strelan refers to Laura Yamhure Thompson, Charles Richard Snyder, Lesa Hoffman, Scott T. Michael, Heather N. Rasmussen, and Laura S. Billings, "Dispositional Forgiveness of Self, Others, and Situations," *Journal of Personality* 73, no. 2 (April 2005): 313–359.

The contemporary bad reputation of shame (see above) is partly related to the observation that people in depression are less likely to forgive themselves; hence guilt and shame are seen as perpetuating a miserable personal condition that is not conducive to pro-social behavior. But it does not follow that shame per se caused the depression: the negative effects of shame are related to people with depression.

67. Avishai Margalit formulated the above criteria of the decent society. Avishai Margalit, *The Decent Society* (Cambridge, Mass.: Harvard University Press, 1996), 133.

68. Patricia Greenspan, *Emotions and Reason: An Inquiry into Emotional Justification* (London: Routledge & Kegan Paul, 1988); Taylor, *Pride, Shame, and Guilt*, 91.

69. Jeffrie G. Murphy, "Shame Creeps Through Guilt and Feels Like Retribution," *Law and Philosophy* 18 (4 July 1999): 327–344, 342, referring to Herbert Morris, "We are attached to the source of the command and thus disobedience becomes like self-betrayal. With this there is an inevitable loss of self-esteem. . . . We experience a form of fragmentation; there is a breakdown in our sense of wholeness." Herbert Morris, "Reflections on Feeling Guilty," *Philosophical Studies* 40, no. 2 (September 1981): 187–193, 192, 193. See further Herbert Morris, "Nonmoral Guilt," in *Responsibility, Character, and the Emotions*, ed. Ferdinand Schoeman (Cambridge: Cambridge University Press, 1987).

70. Quoted in Murphy, "Shame," 341.

71. Habermas, *The New Conservatism*, 233. "The suffering of the victims imposed a debt of 'intersubjective liability' on successive generations." Muller, "Constitutional Patriotism," 292.

72. On constitutional strategies in the context of another moral emotion with negative action tendencies, see Laura E. Little, "Envy and Jealousy: A Study of Separation of Powers and Judicial Review," *Hastings Law Journal* 52, no. 1 (November 2000): 47–121.

73. John Berger, *Ways of Seeing* (London: Penguin Books, 1972), 46–47.

Once again, shaming can be a tool of oppression. Moreover, highly respected emotions may result in despicable acts or hypocrisy and action dictated by honest and noble feelings may contribute to structural oppression. On the ambiguity of compassion see Patrick West, *Conspicuous Compassion: Why Sometimes It Really Is Cruel to Be Kind* (Civitas: Institute for the Study of Civil Society, 2004).

74. Nussbaum, *Hiding from Humanity*, 15. Nussbaum claims that, contrary to shame, guilt may have a legitimate place in the social control system of a liberal society. Her rather peculiar concept of guilt is based on the child's recognition that

"her aggressive wishes have harmed . . . another person who does not deserve to be harmed" (207).

75. Lewis, *Shame and Guilt*, was probably the most vocal accuser, turning shame into the culprit that causes developmental disorders. But even the criticism of narcissism behind shame is to some extent misplaced, even for psychoanalysts. "Since the self is, in general, cathected with narcissistic libido, the term 'narcissistic self' may with some justification be looked upon as a tautology." Heinz Kohut, *The Analysis of the Self* (Madison, Conn.: International Universities Press, 1971), 26.

76. *Shame and Its Sisters: A Silvan Tomkins Reader*, ed. Eve Kosofsky Sedgwick and Adam Frank (Durham: Duke University Press, 1995), 173; Thomas M Scheff and S. Retzinger. *Emotions and Violence* (Lexington: Lexington Books, 1991.); Virginia Held, "Terrorism and War," *The Journal of Ethics* 8, no. 11 (March 2004): 59–75, 75.

77. Stanley I. Benn, "Privacy, Freedom, and Respect for Persons," in *Nomos XIII, Privacy*, ed. J. Ronald Pennock and John W. Chapman (New York: Atherton Press, 1971), (drawing on Jean-Paul Sartre's philosophy to discuss the role of surveillance in limiting the individual's freedom).

78. See Strelan, "Who Forgives Others"; James Gilligan, "Shame, Guilt, and Violence," *Social Research*, 70, no. 4 (Winter 2003): 1149–1180.

79. Eliza Ahmed, "Shame Management: Regulating Bullying," in *Shame Management through Reintegration*, ed. Eliza Ahmed, Nathan Harris, John Braithwaite, and Valerie Braithwaite (Cambridge: Cambridge University Press, 2001), 211–314. "Shame may be expressed in attempts to reconstruct or improve oneself"; Williams, *Shame and Necessity*, 90.

80. Alfred Allan, Maria M. Allan, Debra Kaminev, and Dan J. Stein, "Exploration of the Association between Apology and Forgiveness amongst Victims of Human Rights Violations," *Behavioral Sciences & the Law* 24, no. 1 (January/February 2006): 87–102, 99.

81. Helen Lynd, *On Shame and the Search for Identity* (New York: Plenum, 1958), 66.

82. Erving Goffman, *Interaction Ritual: Essays on Face-to-Face Behavior* (New York: Anchor Doubleday, 1967).

83. Amitai Etzioni, *The Monochrome Society* (Princeton: Princeton University Press, 2001).

84. Williams, *Shame and Necessity*, 77–78.

85. See in particular Taylor, *Pride, Shame, and Guilt.*

86. John Kekes, "Shame and Moral Progress," in *Midwest Studies in Philosophy*, Volume 13, *Ethical Theory: Character and Virtue*, ed. Peter A. French et al. (Notre Dame: University of Notre Dame Press, 1988), 282–296. As to the actual social processes of shame, Kekes subscribes to the condemnation of shame as undermining self-confidence.

87. Williams, *Shame and Necessity*, is very critical of the lack of social, cultural, and psychological realism of strict autonomy theories denying shame.

88. Cheshire Calhoun, "An Apology for Moral Shame," *Journal of Political Philosophy* 12, no. 2 (June 2004): 127–146, 129.

89. Williams, *Shame and Necessity*, 100.

90. Ruth Benedict, *The Chrysanthemum and the Sword: Patterns of Japanese Culture* (Boston: Houghton Mifflin, 1946). See further Hildred Geertz, *The Javanese Family: A Study of Kinship and Socialization* (New York: Free Press of Glencoe, 1961).

91. Scheff and Retzinger, "Shame, Anger."

Perhaps shame is so important in the Japanese culture that it precludes admission of wrongdoing and shame-dictated apologies for the atrocities the Japanese committed in World War II.

92. Cohen, "American National Conversation," 1098.

93. See the references above, describing the destructive nature of shame.

94. The fight for animal rights is a good example of the use of shame and strategies to avoid it. See [No author listed], "Animal Research Is a Source of Human Compassion, Not Shame," *The Lancet* (Editorial) 364, no. 9437 (4 September 2004): 815–816.

INDEX